NATIONAL BUREAU OF ECONOMIC RESEARCH

Studies in Business Cycles

No. 5

What Happens
During Business Cycles

A PROGRESS REPORT

Relation of the Directors to the Work and Publications

of the

National Bureau of Economic Research

1. The object of the National Bureau of Economic Research is to ascertain and to present to the public important economic facts and their interpretation in a scientific and impartial manner. The Board of Directors is charged with the responsibility of ensuring that the work of the National Bureau is carried on in strict conformity with this object.

2. To this end the Board of Directors shall appoint one or more Directors of Research.

3. The Director or Directors of Research shall submit to the members of the Board, or to its Executive Committee, for their formal adoption, all specific proposals concerning researches to be instituted.

4. No report shall be published until the Director or Directors of Research shall have submitted to the Board a summary drawing attention to the character of the data and their utilization in the report, the nature and treatment of the problems involved, the main conclusions and such other information as in their opinion would serve to determine the suitability of the report for publication in accordance with the principles of the Bureau.

5. A copy of any manuscript proposed for publication shall also be submitted to each member of the Board. For each manuscript to be so submitted a special committee shall be appointed by the President, or at his designation by the Executive Director, consisting of three Directors selected as nearly as may be one from each general division of the Board. The names of the special manuscript committee shall be stated to each Director when the summary and report described in paragraph (4) are sent to him. It shall be the duty of each member of the committee to read the manuscript. If each member of the special committee signifies his approval within thirty days, the manuscript may be published. If each member of the special committee has not signified his approval within thirty days of the transmittal of the report and manuscript, the Director of Research shall then notify each member of the Board, requesting approval or disapproval of publication, and thirty additional days shall be granted for this purpose. The manuscript shall then not be published unless at least a majority of the entire Board and a two-thirds majority of those members of the Board who shall have voted on the proposal within the time fixed for the receipt of votes on the publication proposed shall have approved.

6. No manuscript may be published, though approved by each member of the special committee, until forty-five days have elapsed from the transmittal of the summary and report. The interval is allowed for the receipt of any memorandum of dissent or reservation, together with a brief statement of his reasons, that any member may wish to express; and such memorandum of dissent or reservation shall be published with the manuscript if he so desires. Publication does not, however, imply that each member of the Board has read the manuscript, or that either members of the Board in general, or of the special committee, have passed upon its validity in every detail.

7. A copy of this resolution shall, unless otherwise determined by the Board, be printed in each copy of every National Bureau book.

(Resolution adopted October 25, 1926 and revised February 6, 1933 and February 24, 1941)

Studies in Business Cycles

What Happens During Business Cycles

A Progress Report

❧

WESLEY C. MITCHELL

National Bureau of Economic Research, Inc.

Introduction

Shortly before his death Wesley Mitchell put in my care the completed parts of the "progress report" he was preparing on his long and elaborate investigation of "what happens during business cycles". This book is substantially the document he left behind. I have felt free to make numerous changes of detail, but I have not interfered with the design, nor attempted to complete the narrative. The work of a major scientist, even if not half done, deserves a life of its own, unencumbered by the hand or voice of another. So it is especially when, as in the present case, the fragment has well defined contours, balance, and direction. But for the guidance of students who may take up the book for the first time, I shall put down a few remarks about Mitchell's objectives and what he accomplished.

I

Business cycles are not merely fluctuations in aggregate economic activity. The critical feature that distinguishes them from the commercial convulsions of earlier centuries or from the seasonal and other short-term variations of our own age is that the fluctuations are widely diffused over the economy—its industry, its commercial dealings, and its tangles of finance. The economy of the western world is a system of closely interrelated parts. He who would understand business cycles must master the workings of an economic system organized largely in a network of free enterprises searching for profit. The problem of how business cycles come about is therefore inseparable from the problem of how a capitalist economy functions.

This conception governs Mitchell's posthumous book, as it does his earlier writings. Mitchell was not content to focus analysis on the fluctuations of one or two great variables, such as production or employment. His concern was with *business* cycles and he therefore sought to interpret the system of business as a whole—the formation of firms and their disappearance, prices as well as output, the employment of labor and other resources, the flow of incomes to and from the public, costs and profits, savings and investments, the merchandising of securities as well as commodities, the money supply, its turnover, and the fiscal operations of government. Not only that, but he sought to penetrate the facade of business aggregates and trace the detailed processes—psychological, institutional, and technological—by which they are fashioned and linked together.

Thus Mitchell took as his scientific province a terrain as far-flung and intricate as Walras' and Marshall's. But he explored more fully than his predecessors the obstacles to the mutual adjustment of economic quantities in a disturbed environment. "Time . . . is the centre of the chief difficulty of almost every economic problem." [1] Pursuing this Marshallian theme through uncharted jungles of statistics, Mitchell detected systematic differences in the rates of movement of economic variables, and arrived at an early stage of his scientific work at the conception that our economic system of interdependent parts generates a cyclical path instead of moving toward an equilibrium position. This fateful twist aside, Mitchell's economic outlook was thoroughly Marshallian. Had he lived to finish this book, he would have inscribed on its title page Marshall's motto: "The many in the one, the one in the many."

The hypothesis that each stage of the business situation tends to develop out of the preceding stage and to grow into the next in a cyclical pattern poses two major questions: Does economic life actually proceed in recurrent fluctuations having similar characteristics? If so, by what processes are continuous and repetitive movements of this character brought about? In a search for definite and dependable answers, Mitchell examined "facts on a wholesale scale", as had Darwin before him in a related field, and Lyell before Darwin. "My success as a man of science", wrote Darwin, "has been deter-

[1] Alfred Marshall, Preface to the first edition of his *Principles*.

mined . . . by complex and diversified mental qualities and conditions. Of these, the most important have been—the love of
science—unbounded patience in long reflecting over any subject—industry in observing and collecting facts—and a fair
share of invention as well as of common sense."[2] These, too,
were the sources of Mitchell's scientific strength. In his quarto
on *Business Cycles*, published in 1913, he anchored a theory of
fluctuations to an array of empirical observations unprece-
dentedly full for its time. But Mitchell was not content with
this achievement. World War I had ushered in a new era of
economic statistics, able theorists were elaborating new hypotheses, and statistical analysts were rapidly fashioning new
devices for disentangling economic movements. Eager to exploit the new materials for research, Mitchell launched in 1922
a fresh investigation of business cycles.

II

The science of economic fluctuations is only beginning to pass
into an inductive stage. Even today the descriptions of business cycles by economists often resemble the descriptions of
plant life by writers of antiquity, who commonly relied on
"casual observations, no experiments and much speculative
thinking".[3] If later botanists often "could not identify the
plants by the descriptions", so it has also been in economics.
As long as investigators worked by themselves, they could not
very well "collect the masses of raw data pertinent to the study
of cyclical behavior, segregate the cyclical components from
movements of other sorts, and assemble the findings to form a
realistic model of business cycles by which explanations could
be judged".[4] In recent decades the organization of scientific

---

[2] Charles Darwin, "Autobiography", in *Life and Letters*, edited by Francis
Darwin (D. Appleton & Co., 1888), Vol. I, pp. 68, 85-6.

[3] William Crocker, "Botany of the Future", *Science*, Oct. 28, 1938, pp. 387,
388.

[4] Mitchell, *infra*, p. 4. All other page references, unless otherwise indicated.
are to the text.

institutes has greatly enlarged the possibilities of empirical research in economics. Mitchell made the most of the opportunity afforded by the resources of the National Bureau. Taking his own and others' explanations of business cycles as "guides to research, not objects of research" (p. 5), he delved deeply into the facts of cyclical behavior and the relationships among them. The wish to contribute to economic policy was strong in Mitchell. Stronger still was his conviction that intelligent control of business cycles depends upon sound theoretical understanding, which requires tolerably full and accurate knowledge of what the business cycles of experience have been like.

Business Cycles: The Problem and Its Setting, the first major instalment of Mitchell's investigation, was published in 1927. The second appeared in 1946 under the title *Measuring Business Cycles*. In the meantime numerous studies of special aspects of cyclical fluctuations were prepared by the Bureau's staff, and a small group was steadily engaged in analyzing the cyclical behavior of economic processes.[5] It was Mitchell's hope to integrate the findings of his collaborators with his own and other investigators' results; that is, to develop a model of business cycles from carefully screened observations, to use it in explaining how the cycles of experience are typically propagated, and then press on to account for the outstanding differences among them.[6] But he would have fallen short of the goal even if he had lived to complete the present book. Many of the needed materials—especially for foreign countries —were not in shape for use, and the subject of business-cycle differences required systematic investigations yet to be undertaken. As it stands, Mitchell's report barely covers the first three of the seven parts he had planned. Part I sets out his aims, methods, and materials. Part II deals with the great variety of cyclical movements characteristic of individual economic ac-

[5] See the list of publications on business cycles at the end of this volume.

[6] For a fuller account, see "Wesley Mitchell and the National Bureau", in the Bureau's *Twenty-Ninth Annual Report*.

tivities. Part III, not fully completed, shows how the cyclical movements of different parts of the American economy fit together into business cycles, and paves the way for analyzing the processes of expansion, recession, contraction, and revival, to which the last four parts were to be devoted.

Thus the book is a 'progress report', both in the sense in which Mitchell intended the phrase and in the poignant sense forced by his death. Yet no existing publication elucidates so fully or so authoritatively what happens during business cycles as Mitchell's fragment. The accent of the book is on character-istic behavior, formalized in the concept of a 'typical cycle'. "The only normal condition" of business, as Mitchell once ex-pressed it, "is a state of change";[1] but some states of change are 'normal' and others 'abnormal', and Mitchell's 'typical cycle' is designed to take account of such differences. Hence, this concept is similar in some respects to the classicists' 'normal'. The role of each is to segregate the effects of complex causes: both are devices of abstraction: both are tools for analyzing new, concrete situations. Mitchell was keenly concerned about the wide variations among the business cycles of experience and eager to press investigations of them. But he deemed it essential, as a first step, to lay bare the typical characteristics of the alternating waves of prosperity and depression that have swept the economic world in modern times. In this emphasis he conformed to the usual practice of business-cycle theorists. He broke with tradition, however, by extracting what is 'typi-cal' or 'aberrant' from mass observations, and thus substituting fact and measure, as well as may be, for the impressionistic judgments that have ruled business-cycle literature.

III

Mitchell begins his survey of what happens during business cycles by illustrating the varieties of behavior characteristic of economic activities in the United States. Some of the figures

---

[1] *Business Cycles: The Problem and Its Setting*, p. 376.

in his introductory chart merely confirm common knowledge.
For example, commodity prices generally rise and fall with the
tides in production; business failures increase during contractions of aggregate economic activity and diminish during expansions; the output of durables fluctuates more widely than
the output of perishables; and prices are more stable at retail
than at wholesale. It is less generally known, however, that
crop production moves rather independently of business cycles,
or that production typically fluctuates over a much wider
range than prices, that the liabilities of business failures usually
turn down months before economic recovery becomes general
and turn up months before recession, that both durables and
perishables experience their most vigorous decline well before
the end of contraction, and that retail prices characteristically
move later as well as less than wholesale prices.

Students who will take the trouble to ponder these facts are
not likely to leave Mitchell's chart quickly. They will notice
that orders for investment goods tend to lead the tides in
aggregate activity, that private construction is more closely related to business cycles than public construction, that call
money rates or even commercial paper rates greatly overstate
the fluctuations in the rates of interest at which bank customers
ordinarily borrow, that interest rates in New York tend to
move before and more widely than in the interior, that the
number of business failures lags behind the liabilities, that bond
prices tend to lead stock prices which themselves lead the
turns in aggregate activity, that bank deposits appear to be
comparatively steady during depressions, that imports conform closely to business cycles while exports do not, that
grocery sales fail to show the regular response to business
cycles characteristic of retail trade at large, etc. And if the
reader looks beyond the large processes that have dominated
theoretical literature, he will see how peculiar the cyclical behavior of smaller sectors of activity can be. For example, cattle
slaughter tends to move with the tides in aggregate activity
while hog slaughter moves inversely; the dollar volume of
residential construction contracts fluctuates less, not more, than

the physical volume; cotton stocks held at mills run parallel
with mill production, while stocks in public storage move inversely.

Thus business cycles are complex phenomena—far more so
than has been commonly supposed. The sales of a large firm
may be dominated by the tides in aggregate activity; the fortunes of a small firm are rather at the mercy of personal factors
and conditions peculiar to the trade or locality. Some activities,
like local transit or net gold movements between the United
States and Great Britain, are apparently free from cyclical
fluctuations. Others, notably farming, undergo cyclical movements, but they have little or no relation in time to business
cycles. And these irregular responses, passed over lightly by
theoretical writers, accord with reason:

> We cannot expect any activity to respond regularly to business cycles
> unless it is subject to man's control within the periods occupied by
> cyclical phases, and unless this control is swayed, consciously or not,
> by short-period economic considerations. The domination of harvests
> by weather, the 'migratory property' of petroleum underground, the
> mixed motives of governments in undertaking construction work, the
> long-range planning that weighs with many men in a position to set
> 'administered prices', the time-consuming negotiations that prevent
> prompt adjustments of certain other prices and many wage rates, the
> existence of long-term contracts, the years required to complete some
> large undertakings—these are concrete examples of the multifarious
> obstacles that interfere with prompt and regular response to the
> cyclical tides (p. 95).

The processes that fail to bear the imprint of business cycles
are nevertheless a minority. Almost nine-tenths of Mitchell's
basic sample of approximately 800 time series fluctuate in sym-
pathy with the tides in aggregate activity, but the movements
of this imposing majority are far from uniform. Between the
cyclical recalcitrants like farming and the cyclical regulars like
factory employment, there is a continuous gradation. Coal and
iron production conform more closely to the tides in aggregate
activity than the production of textiles or gasoline. The prices
of industrial commodities do not conform as well as their production, while the opposite relation rules in farming. Employment conforms better than wage rates, bank loans than invest-

ments, open-market interest rates than customer rates, stock prices than bond prices, etc. Some conforming processes move early in the cyclical procession; for example, orders for investment goods. Others, like interest rates, are laggards.

Of course, most processes respond to the tides in aggregate activity by rising during expansions and declining during contractions, though they may do so with a lead or lag. But business cycles also generate countercyclical movements:

Brisk business increases the domestic demand for textile goods and so diminishes the exports of raw cotton; it increases the sale of fresh milk and so restricts the production of butter; it increases the volume of coin and paper money held by the public and stimulates borrowing from the banks, thereby enlarging demand liabilities and tending to impair reserve ratios; it leads department stores to carry larger stocks of merchandise and lowers the piles of iron ore at blast furnaces; it activates share transactions on stock exchanges and discourages transactions in bonds. The declines in this list, and many others, are as characteristic a feature of business cycles as the advances (p. 66).

However, the processes that run counter to business cycles do so, by and large, with less regularity than those that respond positively. An expansion of money incomes stimulates a general increase in buying, and this influence may obscure the concomitant impulse to shift demand away from inferior articles to goods of higher quality. As it turns out, purchases of staples such as pork, flour, coffee, and potatoes frequently decline during expansion, but their inverted response is less regular than the positive response of more costly articles.

In general, influences that tend to repress an activity in expansion encounter more opposition than influences favoring an increase, and when repressing influences win out, their victories are less regular from cycle to cycle than the victories won by influences that push forward. *Mutatis mutandis*, the like holds true in contraction (p. 96).

Large as are the variations in the cyclical timing of economic processes, the differences in amplitude of fluctuation are more impressive still. In high grade bond yields, for example, the cyclical wanderings are confined to a narrow range; the total rise and fall is typically only about 10 percent of their average value during a business cycle. The amplitude of the overall index of wholesale prices, excluding war episodes, is nearly twice as large; the amplitude of factory employment four or five times as large, of private construction contracts over ten times and of machine tool orders over twenty times as large. On the other hand, stocks of industrial equipment are remarkably steady, expanding usually during contractions as well as expansions of business cycles. The proportions among economic quantities keep changing so systematically over a business cycle that the

very essence of the phenomenon is omitted unless the chart of business cycles contains numerous lines that indicate the wide differences among the rates at which, and also some of the differences in the times at which, various elements in the economy expand and contract. For, unless these divergencies in cyclical behavior are pictured by fit symbols, we have no suggestion of the basic business-cycle problem: how an economic system of interrelated parts develops internal stresses during expansions, stresses that bring on recessions, and how the uneven contractions of its varied parts pave the way for revivals (p. 295).

IV

So much for the varieties of cyclical behavior that come to the surface once the lid is lifted from aggregate activity. What sort of whole do the parts make up? When the individual pieces are put together it appears that every month some activities reach cyclical peaks and others decline to their troughs; so that expansion and contraction run side by side all the time. But the peaks tend to come in bunches and likewise the troughs. Hence, when troughs gain on the peaks, expansions grow more numerous and in time dominate the economy. Their supremacy is short lived, however, and gradually gives way to the encroachments of contraction. The business cycle of experience is the alternating succession of these sustained majorities—first of individual expansions, next of contractions, then of expansions once again, and so on.

Business cycles consist not only of roughly synchronous expansions in many activities, followed by roughly synchronous contractions in a slightly smaller number; they consist also of numerous contractions while expansion is dominant, and numerous expansions while contraction is dominant (p. 79).

Characteristic Direction of Twenty-six 'Comprehensive' Series during a Business Cycle[a]

Series	Expansion				Contraction				No. of Business Cycles Covered	% of Conforming Movements during Span of Stages in Which Series Is Said to	
	Trough to first third	First third to middle third	Middle third to last third	Last third to peak	Peak to first third	First third to middle third	Middle third to last third	Last third to trough		Rise	Fall
Bonds sold, N. Y. Stock Exchange	+	−	−	−	−	−	+	+	14	86	79
R.R. bond prices	+	+	−	−	−	+	+	+	19	65	74
Business failures, liabilities, *inv.*	+	+	+	−	−	−	+	+	14	86	100
Common stock prices	+	+	+	−	−	−	+	+	16	94	82
Shares sold, N. Y. Stock Exchange	+	+	+	−	−	−	+	+	16	94	88
Corporate security issues	+	+	+	−	−	−	−	+	8	100	75
Construction contracts, value	+	+	+	−	−	−	−	+	7	86	75
Deposits activity	+	+	+	−	−	−	−	+	16	94	88
Bank clearings or debits, N.Y.C.	+	+	+	−	−	−	−	+	18	100	89
Incorporations, no.	+	+	+	+	−	−	−	+	19	84	80
Bank clearings or debits, outside N.Y.C.	+	+	+	+	−	−	−	+	14	100	79
Bank clearings or debits, total	+	+	+	+	−	−	−	+	14	100	93
Imports, value	+	+	+	+	−	−	−	−	16	94	75
Industrial production, total	+	+	+	+	−	−	−	−	5	100	100
Fuel & electricity production	+	+	+	+	−	−	−	−	5	100	100
Pig iron production	+	+	+	+	−	−	−	−	16	100	100
R.R. freight ton miles	+	+	+	+	−	−	−	−	9	100	89
Factory employment	+	+	+	+	−	−	−	−	6	100	100
Factory payrolls	+	+	+	+	−	−	−	−	5	100	100
Income payments, total	+	+	+	+	−	−	−	−	4	100	50
Corporate profits	+	+	+	+	−	−	−	−	4	100	100
Business failures, no., *inv.*	+	+	+	+	−	−	−	−	16	75	88
Department store sales, deflated	+	+	+	+	−	−	−	−	4	100	75
Wholesale trade sales, value	+	+	+	+	−	−	−	−	3	100	100
Wholesale commodity prices	+	+	+	+	+	−	−	−	11	82	91
R.R. bond yields	−	−	+	+	+	−	−	−	19	74	65

ᵃ Derived from Table 31, Sec. A. A plus denotes rise, a minus denotes fall. The two series on failures are inverted here. Bond prices are treated as the inverted replica of bond yields; see Table 31, note e, concerning their sign in the second segment of contraction.

According as the expansions or contractions of individual activities dominate, the aggregate activity of the economy surges forward or recedes. And when economic crosscurrents are at or near their maximum, the direction of aggregate activity is reversed: it begins to rise if it has been falling, or to fall if it has been rising.

The turmoil that goes on within the cycles in aggregate activity has a systematic core. A highly simplified picture of the system is afforded by the accompanying table, which condenses Mitchell's analysis of "comprehensive series" in Chapter 10. The table shows directions of movement during a typical business cycle—here divided into eight segments, four each for expansion and contraction. Of course, each segment includes several months, and the table is therefore insensitive to minor differences in timing, such as the short lag in income payments. Further, it hides many crosscurrents that would appear in less comprehensive series, and omits certain business factors of which we should take account—especially wage rates, inventories, banking, and governmental finance. But with all its faults, the table gives an effective glimpse of the typical round of developments that constitute a business cycle.[8]

Let us then take our stand at the bottom of a depression and watch events as they unfold. Production characteristically rises in the first segment of expansion; so does employment and money income; and so do commodity prices, imports, domestic trade, security transactions. Indeed, every series moves upward except bond yields and bankruptcies. In the second stage the broad advance continues, though it is checked at one point— the bond market where trading begins to decline. Bond prices join bond sales in the next stage; in other words, long-term interest rates—which fell during the first half of expansion— begin to rise. In the final stretch of expansion, declines become fairly general in the financial sector. Share trading and stock

[8] This and the three following paragraphs are adapted from the National Bureau's *Thirtieth Annual Report.*

prices move downward; the liabilities of business failures, which hitherto have been receding, move up again; security issues and construction contracts drop; the turnover of bank deposits slackens; and bank debits in New York City, though not as yet in the interior, become smaller.

These adverse developments soon engulf the economic system as a whole, and the next stage of the business cycle is the first stage of contraction. Production, employment, commodity prices, personal incomes, business profits—indeed, practically every process represented in the table declines. Of course, the liabilities of business failures continue to rise, which merely attests the sweep of depression. Long-term interest rates also maintain their rise. But in the next stage the downward drift of bond prices ceases; that is, the rise in long-term interest rates is arrested. By the middle of contraction, bond sales join the upward movement of bond prices. More important still, the liabilities of business failures begin declining, which signifies that the liquidation of distressed business firms has passed its worst phase. These favorable developments are reinforced in the following stage. Share trading and prices revive; business incorporations, security issues, and construction contracts move upward; money begins to turn over more rapidly; even total money payments expand. Before long the expansion spreads to production, employment, prices, money incomes, and domestic trade. But this is already the initial stage of general expansion—the point at which our hurried trip around the business cycle started.

Of course, this recital delineates characteristic movements during business cycles, not invariant sequences. That the description fits imperfectly individual business cycles is apparent from the conformity percentages in the table. Yet these percentages also suggest that the deviations from type are not so numerous as to destroy the value of a generalized sketch. And if this much is accepted, an important conclusion immediately follows, notwithstanding the omissions of the table; namely, that the check to the dominant movement of business activity, whether it be expansion or contraction, is typically felt especially early in financial processes and activities preparatory to investment expenditure.

The contraction phase of business cycles is not, however, the precise counterpart of expansion. This is clear from the table and becomes clearer still when numerical values are attached to its signs and intervals. The arrays of individual turning points at business-cycle troughs "are more dispersed and skewed toward leads" than are the arrays at peaks. Expansions of aggregate activity average longer than contractions. They are also more vigorous, so that the trough from which a given expansion starts is ordinarily above the level from which the preceding expansion started. In the first segment of expansion the rate of improvement "is more rapid than at any other stage of the cycle". A "sharp and general retardation" of the advance occurs in the next segment. In the third, while "reacceleration is the rule", the advance "does not regain the speed" it had at the beginning of expansion. In the final stage of expansion "the business tide . . . becomes fuller of eddies". Contractions follow a different pattern. "The fall accelerates somewhat in the second segment of contraction, whereas the rise is much retarded in the second segment of expansion." The next stage "brings a moderate retardation" of the decline, whereas it "brought a moderate reacceleration" of the advance. The closing stages of expansion and contraction are similar "in that the rate of change becomes slower; but this retardation is much more marked at the end of contraction than at the end of expansion".[9]

Thus the notions often suggested by the picturesque phrasing beloved of writers upon 'booms and busts'—that prosperity grows at a dizzier pace the longer it lasts, and that slumps gather momentum as they proceed—are wrong if our measures are right. Scarcely less misleading are the implications of the mathematical constructions often used to represent business cycles. A set of straight lines sloping upward to represent expansion, connected at a sharp peak with downward sloping straight lines to represent contraction, misrepresents the facts. . . . Sine curves are not less objectionable. . . . What our observations suggest is that the shapes of business cycles are phenomena *sui generis* (p. 300).

---

[9] See pp. 75, 299-305.

V

These, then, are some of the broad results that emerge from Mitchell's examination of the cyclical process of the American economy. The full range of the book, its suggestions for further research, and its exemplary scientific care await the reader. Economists anxious to wield a simple formula of the causes of business cycles or the means of controlling them will not find Mitchell's fragment to their liking. Those willing to take conclusions on faith may chafe at its patient elaboration of evidence. But men who seek so earnestly to understand how our economic organization works that they insist on judging evidence for themselves are more likely to lament that too much detail has been suppressed. Scholars will respect Mitchell's pronouncement that his report on findings, after many years of research, is "ill proportioned, tentative, and subject to change as the investigation proceeds" (p.5).

This book is not easy and everyone will save time by a careful reading of Part I which, besides outlining aims and methods, provides the modicum of technical vocabulary required for comprehending what follows. Economic theorists are likely to find especially suggestive Chapter 7, which sets out the facts and inquires into the causes of the changing proportions among economic quantities in the course of a business cycle; also Part III, which centers on the consensus of fluctuations in leading sectors of the economy. Chapter 8 is a useful reminder to all that, despite their persistent traits, business cycles are changing phenomena; and that just as each new member of a group has traits of his own, which cannot be inferred from knowledge of the 'average man', so each business situation must be judged in the light of its own circumstances as well as according to historical patterns. The bulk of this chapter is devoted to technical problems in the decomposition of time series, and only specialists will want to study it fully. Readers pressed for time might move lightly through Chapters 5 and 6 also, except for the closing sections which will repay careful reading.

The modern theory of employment, which for a time pushed aside both value and business-cycle theory, is now slowly being fitted into older economic knowledge. The younger economists are rediscovering that cost-price relations play a significant role in shaping the national income and its movements, that the 'consumption function' itself moves cyclically, that investment is not an autonomous variable, that price inflation does not wait for full employment, and that both investment and consumption are heterogeneous aggregates that cannot be understood without separate analysis of their parts. If our harassed generation can win the opportunity to pursue the arts of peace, the fruit and example of Mitchell's work will have their quiet but decisive part over the years in bringing the theory of fluctuations into ever closer contact with the ebb and flow of experience.

Arthur F. Burns

August 1950

Acknowledgments

My task as editor has been greatly lightened by Millard Hastay, who helped me verify factual details and took charge of the preparation of the appendices. Geoffrey H. Moore also put his knowledge at my disposal. Both Moore and Hastay had worked very closely with Wesley Mitchell and he records in the text his indebtedness to them on special points. It is only proper to add here that Geoffrey Moore participated over a long period in the planning and execution of the statistical compilations of this book, and that Millard Hastay's participation was especially extensive in the closing stages of Mitchell's work. A committee of the Board of Directors, consisting of Gottfried Haberler, C. Reinold Noyes, and George Soule, read the manuscript with critical care. So also did Moses Abramovitz, Daniel Creamer, and Ruth Mack of the research staff. Of the many others who have made a contribution to this book, either by serving at one time or another as Mitchell's assistants or aiding me at the editing stage, I wish to mention particularly Martha Anderson, Cicely Applebaum, Florence Cohen, Dorothy Cook, Sally Edwards, Harry Eisenpress, Frances Goldberg, H. Irving Forman, Simon Kuznets, Karl Laubenstein, Sophie Sakowitz, Regina S. Sands, Julius Shiskin, Johanna Stern, and the late Denis Volkenau.

A. F. B.

CONTENTS

Part II

Varieties of Cyclical Behavior

Part III

The Consensus of Cyclical Behavior

List of Tables

List of Charts

Part I

AIMS, METHODS, AND MATERIALS

CHAPTER 1

The Task Essayed by the National Bureau

Business cycles had been studied with increasing thoroughness for many years before the National Bureau entered the field. The basic observation that commercial crises recur at somewhat regular intervals was made at least as early as 1833. Historians had demonstrated that these crises have common features as well as innumerable differences of detail. The growth of statistical recording had provided fairly precise knowledge of changes in an expanding range of economic activities. In these time series several types of movements had been identified, and rough methods devised for segregating them. The original problem of explaining commercial crises had been reformulated to embrace the full cycle of changes in which a crisis is merely the most dramatic phase. But, despite these advances, theorists who sought to explain business cycles were insufficiently informed about the phenomena with which they were dealing, and had to reason for the most part from untested assumptions. The complexity of economic organization suggested to ingenious minds an embarrassing array of plausible hypotheses. No one could determine which among these jostling competitors was least inadequate, or whether any combination of them would account for what happens.

The study of business cycles lingered in the speculative stage, not because economists were averse to 'inductive verification', but because this type of testing was so hard to apply to a consensus among differing fluctuations in the many activities of a modern economy. Of the activities to be considered, relatively few were statistically recorded before 1900. What time series were available required laborious analysis before

3

they could be utilized. Economists were accustomed to work single handed, and no individual was able to collect the masses of raw data pertinent to the study of cyclical behavior, segregate the cyclical components from movements of other sorts, and assemble the findings to form a realistic model of business cycles by which explanations could be judged. A few investigators did what they could in this direction, but their best was inadequate.[1]

In its second year the National Bureau decided to devote part of its resources to this pressing task. We had a staff of several investigators with complementary skills, we could employ compilers and computers, we hoped to keep at the job long enough to learn how to do it. A group with these advantages should at least be able to perform more of the necessary spade work than any individual. Realizing full well that we could achieve no more than an approximation to the knowledge needed, we thought that anything we might learn concerning what happens during a business cycle should be useful to all who were trying to find out why nations practicing private enterprise fail so lamentably to make full use of their resources all of the time.

Yet we did not organize our program as a series of efforts to test current explanations of business cycles.[2] Our interest cen-

[1] As one of those who had tried to observe cyclical movements systematically, I can appreciate the prudence of men who relied upon common impressions, vague as they were. My own effort (*Business Cycles*, University of California Press, 1913) now seems to me sadly deficient on the factual side, and therefore of uncertain value theoretically.

[2] At least two projects of this sort have been started, but neither was completed. In 1926 Warren M. Persons began a "series of papers" in which he planned "to examine critically the theories of business fluctuations". An investigator so addicted to quantitative work presumably had statistical testing in mind. Unfortunately, Persons did not carry out his plan. Only the first paper appeared, and that was confined to the classification of 'theories'. ("Theories of Business Fluctuations", *Quarterly Journal of Economics*, XLI, Nov. 1926, pp. 94–128).

Ten years later the Economic Intelligence Service of the League of Nations undertook an extended inquiry "into the causes of the recurrence of periods of economic depression". With the aid of leading specialists from several countries, Gottfried Haberler analyzed "existing theories of the business

tered in the phenomena that should be explained. If our studies brought to light facts not previously known, or set dimly apprehended relations in clearer perspective, fresh explanations might be called for. A new theoretical structure founded on more exact and extensive knowledge would doubtless incorporate some familiar hypotheses; but we could not tell in advance what the ground plan of the new building would be. To us, the existing explanations were guides to research, not objects of research, and all the more useful because they pointed in so many directions.

That our undertaking grew as we worked on it will surprise no one familiar with empirical studies. After years of continuous effort, we have just reached a stage at which we venture to report some of our findings regarding the broad characteristics of business cycles. Even now what we can say is ill proportioned, tentative, and subject to change as the investigation proceeds.

---

cycle" and derived from them "a synthetic account of the nature and possible causes of economic fluctuations". Haberler's *Prosperity and Depression: A Theoretical Analysis of Cyclical Movements* (Geneva, 1st edition, 1937) was an excellent beginning; but "the next stage in this investigation—the application, as far as possible, of quantitative tests to the various causal hypotheses" was a much more formidable undertaking. Jan Tinbergen's two monographs, *Statistical Testing of Business-Cycle Theories: A Method and Its Application to Investment Activity* and *Business Cycles in the United States of America, 1919–1932* (both Geneva, 1939), apply multiple correlation analysis to test several hypotheses concerning the interrelations among cyclical fluctuations in different activities. The work is notable for its blend of statistical skill with theoretical finesse, and the cautiously stated conclusions are highly suggestive. But Tinbergen could cover only a few hypotheses concerning a few activities during a few cycles. Further, he relied upon annual data, which are sadly deficient for his purpose.

CHAPTER 2

Our Basic Concept

Many writers on business cycles have dispensed with a formal definition. Assuming that they and their readers understood the term, they have plunged promptly into the subject matter. We cannot imitate this pleasant directness. For those who set out to observe certain phenomena must have at least a preliminary notion of what to look for. As they find and examine specimens, they may revise their first concept, but without some guiding idea they can hardly begin to observe.

The first step in our program, accordingly, was to develop a working definition of business cycles. To that end we studied theoretical writings to see what their authors believed to be the salient phenomena. Then we examined the descriptions of cyclical fluctuations in historical sources, the efforts of statisticians to isolate the cyclical component in time series, and 'indexes of business activity'. Our findings were published in 1927 under the title *Business Cycles: The Problem and Its Setting.* The book culminated in a definition of the kind we needed. Experience in using it as a guide to observation led to several emendations. In its present—still tentative—form, our working concept is as follows:

Business cycles are a type of fluctuation found in the aggregate economic activity of nations that organize their work mainly in business enterprises: a cycle consists of expansions occurring at about the same time in many economic activities, followed by similarly general recessions, contractions, and revivals which merge into the expansion phase of the next cycle; this sequence of changes is recurrent but not periodic; in duration business cycles vary from more than one year to ten or twelve years; they are not divisible into shorter cycles of similar character with amplitudes approximating their own.[1]

---

[1] A. F. Burns and W. C. Mitchell, *Measuring Business Cycles* (National Bureau, 1946), p. 3.

This definition stated our preliminary notion about the cultures in which business cycles appear, and described what we thought to be the common features by which they can be recognized and distinguished from movements of other types. Whether the definition would serve its purpose could be determined only by using it as a guide to observation. Do cyclical fluctuations of the alleged duration occur in most economic activities? If so, is there substantial agreement in their timing? What leads and lags appear? If a dominant pattern emerges, what activities share in it and what follow different courses? Do cyclical expansions and contractions run a continuous round, or is one cycle sometimes separated from its successor by an interval during which the tide neither ebbs nor flows? Do business cycles occur in all nations where private enterprise prevails, and only there? How far back can they be traced in history? What relations subsist among the cycles in different nations?

To answer all these questions with assurance would require wider ranging studies than we have been able to make. Our detailed observations have been confined to four nations—the United States, Great Britain, France, and pre-Nazi Germany. Relatively few of the time series we have found run back of 1900; many begin at the close of World War I, and some exceedingly valuable records are still shorter. Concerning the economic fluctuations of precapitalistic times in our four nations, in other nations practicing private enterprise, and in nations where private enterprise has been superseded by other forms of economic organization, our evidence is vague. Even within our four-nation, recent-time limits we have used only parts of the available data; but we have gone far enough to test the definition as a tool of research.

Since time series constitute the most definite records of economic fluctuations, we began collecting them while we were experimenting with our analytic technique. That the collection should and could cover a wide variety of activities had been shown by the work of our predecessors. Whenever possible we gathered monthly data, supposing from the first, and

later proving by comparisons of test series in monthly and
annual form, that annual entries often misrepresent cyclical
movements in ways one cannot predict. However, annual
totals are proper records of crop fluctuations, and we fall back
upon them in other instances when monthly or quarterly
figures cannot be had. We dared not economize by relying
solely upon index numbers and broad aggregates to represent
the movements of prices, production, employment, and the
like; for these broad summaries conceal highly significant
differences in the cyclical behavior of their components. To
represent important types of activity, such as producing durable goods or disbursing wages, we sought groups of series;
by so doing we gained a better chance of reaching valid conclusions than if we depended upon a single witness. Further,
since business cycles are a highly variable species of phenomena, we wished to observe as many as possible. To meet that
requirement, we usually included the full time span covered by
each series. Though our collection has come to include well
over a thousand series, we have gathered only a part of the
evidence that can be and should be exploited.

CHAPTER 3

Our Methods of Measuring Cyclical Behavior

How to prepare these raw materials for use was the next problem. Again we built upon preceding work. But the methods of time-series analysis devised by others were not perfectly suited to our needs, so that we had to make numerous adaptations and some innovations. The basic features of our technique were sketched at the end of *Business Cycles: The Problem and Its Setting.* Its development was supervised by Simon Kuznets for a time; then by Arthur F. Burns, who introduced many improvements and subjected the evolving scheme to numerous tests. Its latest form is set forth at length in *Measuring Business Cycles*, published in 1946. To make what follows intelligible, I must describe briefly parts of the procedure. Readers who wish a fuller account should consult our formidable monograph.

I Specific Cycles

Determining whether a series undergoes seasonal variations, measuring and removing such as appear are the first operations. Next, the seasonally-adjusted data are charted and examined to see whether 'specific cycles' are present. This is our name for wave movements in a time series corresponding in duration to our working concept of business cycles; that is, waves lasting from over one year to ten or twelve years when measured from crest to crest or trough to trough. Such cycles appear plainly in a large majority of the series we have analyzed, but not in all. Examples of the exceptional cases are 'sticky' prices that remain unchanged for long stretches, then suddenly jump to a different level; net gold movements between the United States and the United Kingdom, which fluctuate so choppily

9

that cycles can hardly be seen; and transit rides in New York City, which shrink appreciably only under the pressure of exceedingly hard times. Presumably a statistician who resorted to smoothing devices or fitted trend lines to the series we classify as noncyclical could show wavelike movements in most of them. Even without such practices we find that more than 95 percent of some 830 monthly or quarterly series from the United States undergo specific cycles.

We identify the specific cycles in a series by the dates of their troughs and peaks. Usually we take the cycles as units that begin and end with a trough. But approximately an eighth of our American series move inversely to the cyclical tides; for example, bankruptcies, idle freight cars, numerous inventories, and bank reserve ratios. In such series, we treat the specific cycles as units beginning and ending with peaks.

II RELATION OF SPECIFIC TO BUSINESS CYCLES

One clause in our basic definition can be restated in this form: business cycles are due to the predominance of agreement in timing among specific cycles. If that is true, the peaks of positive and the troughs of inverted specific cycles in a representative collection of time series must occur in clusters, and so also must the troughs of positive and the peaks of inverted specific cycles. Thus our concept of business cycles can be subjected to one crucial test as soon as the specific-cycle turning dates in a diversified sample of time series have been determined.

III REFERENCE DATES

In designing this test we started with the contributions of financial journalists, business annalists, and statisticians who have identified successive business cycles in our four countries. Their dates and even their lists of cycles differ; nevertheless, they give rough indications of the periods within which clusters of specific-cycle peaks are likely to occur, and of other periods in which clusters of troughs may be expected. Arranging our findings to see whether they confirm earlier conclusions, to resolve a few conflicts of opinion, and to make sure that notable clusters have not been overlooked is a laborious task, and one that cannot be regarded as finished until all the evidence has been carefully weighed. When we find a definite cluster of specific-cycle turning dates, we accept it as marking the culmination of a business-cycle expansion or contraction, and seek to determine the month within the clustering zone when economic activity reached its largest or smallest volume. These months constitute a tentative set of 'reference dates', which purport to show the troughs and peaks of successive business cycles within a country during the period we can cover statistically.

Table 1 presents the monthly and annual reference dates for the United States since 1854 that underlie the cyclical measures exhibited in later chapters. The word 'tentative' in the title of the table is to be taken seriously. These dates were developed at a time when our collection of series, our methods of analysis, and our knowledge concerning the cyclical behavior of different activities were poorer than they have since become. A systematic review of the dates, begun in 1940, was interrupted by the war. When we are able to resume it, we shall presumably make numerous minor and perhaps a few major changes, especially in the earlier decades for which statistical records are scanty. Meanwhile we work with the approximations in hand. Chapter 4 of *Measuring Business Cycles* demonstrates that they agree well with the findings of earlier investigators, and the sequel will show that they yield significant results when used as the time scale for analyzing the movements of several hundred series.

It would be far easier to base a chronology of business cycles upon the cyclical turning dates in some single aggregate such as national income or employment, and these dates would have a more definite meaning than can be attached to culminations of cyclical expansions and contractions in 'general business activity'. But we could find no series from any of the four nations we were studying that summarizes the cyclical fluctuations of its economy in a way we could trust over the

Table 1

TENTATIVE REFERENCE DATES OF BUSINESS CYCLES IN THE
UNITED STATES[a]

BY MONTHS

Initial Trough	Peak	Terminal Trough	Expansion (mos.)	Contraction (mos.)	Total (mos.)
December 1854 — June	1857 — December 1858	30	18	48
December 1858 — October	1860 — June 1861	22	8	30
June 1861 — April	1865 — December 1867	46	32	78
December 1867 — June	1869 — December 1870	18	18	36
December 1870 — October	1873 — March 1879	34	65	99
March 1879 — March	1882 — May 1885	36	38	74
May 1885 — March	1887 — April 1888	22	13	35
April 1888 — July	1890 — May 1891	27	10	37
May 1891 — January	1893 — June 1894	20	17	37
June 1894 — December	1895 — June 1897	18	18	36
June 1897 — June	1899 — December 1900	24	18	42
December 1900 — September	1902 — August 1904	21	23	44
August 1904 — May	1907 — June 1908	33	13	46
June 1908 — January	1910 — January 1912	19	24	43
January 1912 — January	1913 — December 1914	12	23	35
December 1914 — August	1918 — April 1919	44	8	52
April 1919 — January	1920 — September 1921	9	20	29
September 1921 — May	1923 — July 1924	20	14	34
July 1924 — October	1926 — December 1927	27	14	41
December 1927 — June	1929 — March 1933	18	45	63
March 1933 — May	1937 — May 1938	50	12	62

BY CALENDAR YEARS

Trough	Peak	Trough	Peak	Trough	Peak
1855	1856	1888	1890	1914	1918
1858	1860	1891	1892	1919	1920
1861	1864	1894	1895	1921	1923
1867	1869	1896	1899	1924	1926
1870	1873	1900	1903	1927	1929
1878	1882	1904	1907	1932	1937
1885	1887	1908	1910	1938	
		1911	1913		

[a] The reference dates since 1919 have recently been revised as follows: July instead of September 1921, November instead of December 1927, June instead of May 1938.

periods we wished to cover. While the concept of general business activity is fuzzy, it has the advantage of adaptability to differences in the composition of national economies and to changes in composition that occur within each of them from decade to decade. About the several senses in which the term can be taken and their statistical counterparts, more will be said in Part III, The Consensus of Cyclical Behavior.

IV REFERENCE-CYCLE BASES AND RELATIVES

A chronology of our sort is tested in the process of use. We break every series from a country into 'reference-cycle segments' on the basis of the reference dates in order to observe its behavior during successive business cycles. But before we can compare our observations upon different series we must put into similar form the data expressed in tons, cubic feet, gallons, dozens, dollars, hours, percentages, passenger miles, or other units. That we do by turning the seasonally-adjusted data for each reference cycle into percentages of their average value. This average value we call a 'cycle base'; percentages of it are 'cycle relatives'. For example, the figures of a series during the latest peacetime business cycle covered by Table 1 are percentages of the average monthly value of its seasonally-adjusted data for the 62 months from March 1933 to May 1938. This base in New York City bank debits is $15.3 billion; in trading on the New York Stock Exchange it is 37.8 million shares; in call money rates, 0.908 percent.

V TREATMENT OF SECULAR MOVEMENTS

The conversion of data into cycle relatives renders comparable the early and late cycles in the same series, however different the levels on which they run. That is, it eliminates in stepwise fashion 'intercycle' trends. But it does not eliminate 'intracycle' trends. When output is growing rapidly, our cycle relatives have an upward tilt reflecting whatever secular change occurs within the limits of each cycle. In a declining industry the cycle relatives tilt downward. Thus we do not separate cyclical from secular movements in the usual fashion by fitting trend lines and treating wavelike deviations from them as cyclical fluctuations.

The inclusion of intracycle trends in cycle relatives helps to reveal and to explain what happens during business cycles. Rapidly growing industries affect business cycles otherwise than do industries barely holding their own or shrinking. The role played by railroad purchasing and financing in American

business cycles changed notably when the great era of construction came to a close. To understand the country's fortunes
after 1910, we should take account of the spectacular rise in
motor car production. As in these familiar instances, so in many
others a radical elimination of all changes persisting over
periods longer than business cycles would erase differentiating
factors of great practical and theoretical significance.

Of course, we could add to our knowledge by making two
sets of cycle relatives for each time series, one as free as possible
from trend factors, the other including intracycle trends. But
double analyses would be so expensive as to reduce greatly the
number of series we could cover. For reasons that will appear
presently, restricting the economic scope of the investigation
would seriously detract from its value.

VI REFERENCE-CYCLE PATTERNS

Next we prepare 'cyclical patterns' from the cycle relatives.
For that purpose we divide each reference cycle into nine
stages. Stage I includes three months centered on the initial
trough, stage V three months centered on the peak, and stage
IX three months centered on the terminal trough. The phase
of expansion between stages I and V is divided into thirds,
which constitute stages II, III, and IV. The contraction phase
is similarly divided into stages VI, VII, and VIII. Patterns of
successive cycles overlap, in that stage I of a cycle includes the
same months as stage IX of its predecessor, and its stage IX
includes the same months as stage I of its successor. Then we
compute an average of the cycle relatives of all months covered
by each stage, thereby reducing the influence of erratic movements on the patterns. By observing how a series behaves as it
passes through the nine stages of successive reference cycles,
we obtain a sufficiently detailed picture of its response to, and
a basis for judging its reaction upon, individual business cycles.
Finally, to determine what behavior is 'characteristic' of the
series—a venturesome step to be discussed presently—we average the measures of individual cycles and record their average
deviation.

VII Average Rates of Rise or Fall per Month

In deriving the cyclical patterns we disregard for the moment differences in the duration of business cycles. To us one such cycle in one country is a unit of experience to be assembled with other units in an array, from which we hope to learn the features characteristic of the species. But the relation of our units to calendar time is one of the features we wish to analyze. A simple transformation of the cyclical patterns serves this purpose. Starting with the average standings of the cycle relatives as shown by the cyclical pattern, we determine the differences between the standings in successive stages, divide each difference by the corresponding number of months between the midpoints of the stages, and so get the average rates of change per month from stage to stage. As the sequel will show, we rely heavily upon these measures of the changing pace at which expansions and contractions run their course in different series.

VIII Indexes of Conformity

When charted, our average reference-cycle patterns show vividly how different series conform to business cycles, but we need explicit measures of this trait. For that purpose, we find by how much a series rises (or falls) from the trough to the peak of each reference-cycle expansion, and by how much it falls (or rises) from the peak to the trough of each contraction. The *amplitudes* of these responses are measured in reference-cycle relatives; that is, percentages of reference-cycle bases. The *regularity* of the responses from cycle to cycle is measured by an 'index of conformity'. Thus a rise from stage I to stage V is marked +100, a fall is marked −100, and no change, 0. The algebraic sum of these marks divided by their number yields an index of conformity to reference expansions. It ranges from +100 (indicating positive conformity in every expansion), through 0 (indicating no change in any expansion, or an equal number of positive and inverted responses), to −100 (indicating inverse movement in every expansion). The index of conformity to reference contractions is made in the same way except that the signs are reversed, for a fall in stages V–IX now constitutes positive conformity and a rise constitutes inverted conformity.

Some series with intracycle trends sloping steeply upward continue to rise throughout reference contractions, yielding indexes of $+100$ in expansion and -100 in contraction. But if the rise in contractions is uniformly slower than the rise in the preceding and following expansions, the series plainly conforms after a fashion to business cycles. Rapidly falling trends sometimes have the opposite effect. Even moderate trends may produce lapses from conformity to mild reference contractions when tilted upward, and lapses in mild expansions when tilted downward. To measure the regularity of these relations, we compare the rate of change in a series during each contraction with its rate of change during the preceding and also during the subsequent expansion, recording what we find in a third index—that is, an index of 'conformity to business cycles'. Here $+100$ signifies a rise in every expansion and a fall in contraction, or a rise in expansion and no change in contraction, or no change in expansion and a fall in contraction, or a rise in both phases but at a slower pace in contraction, or a fall in both phases but at a faster pace in contraction. Opposite behavior of any of these types yields an index of conformity to business cycles of -100.

Thus, for every series we compute three indexes of conformity, one for reference expansion, a second for reference contraction, and a third comparing the movements in the two phases. But while these indexes are useful in all instances, and adequate for series that follow the standard timing scheme closely or depart from it in a random fashion, they do not present clearly the behavior of series that usually lead or lag behind the cyclical procession. For these numerous and highly interesting series we make a second set of conformity indexes based upon whatever group of reference stages represents their typical cyclical timing. When a series shows no regular timing relation to business cycles, we content ourselves with the first

Table 2

SPECIMEN INDEXES OF CONFORMITY

Series[a]	No. of Reference Cycles Covered	Stages Covered by		Timing Characteristics	Stages Used in Making Index of Conformity to		Index of Conformity to		
		Expansion	Contraction		Reference expansion	Reference contraction	Reference expansion	Reference contraction	Business cycles
1 Index of industrial production	5	I–V	V–IX	Positive, no lead or lag	I–V	V–IX	+100	+100	+100
2 Bank clearings, N.Y. City	18	VIII–IV	IV–VIII	Positive, lead at both turns	VIII–IV	IV–VIII	+100	+78	+88
3 Commercial paper rates, N.Y. City	20	II–VI	VI–II	Positive, lag at both turns	II–VI	VI–II	+80	+71	+95
4 Contracts, commercial buildings, value	5	VIII–V	V–VIII	Positive, lead at trough	VIII–V	V–VIII	+100	+60	+100
5 Yields of high grade corp. & munic. bonds	10	III–VII	VII–III	Neutral	III–VII	VII–III	+40	+40	+68
6 Plans for new buildings, Manhattan, N.Y.	15	VII–III	III–VII	Neutral	VII–III	III–VII	+73	+62	+87
7 Gum rosin stocks	5	VI–IX	I–VI	Inverted, lag at peak	I–VI	VI–IX	−67	−67	−82
8 Visible supply of wheat	16	...	...	Irregular	I–V	V–IX	0	−12	−10

[a] See Appendix B for sources of data.

17

set of indexes on the standard basis of expansion in stages I–V and contraction in V–IX.

The examples of our indexes in Table 2 illustrate the varieties of cyclical timing and degrees of conformity. The Federal Reserve Board's index of industrial production is treated on a I–V basis because it conforms closely to the cyclical tides in every instance. The visible supply of wheat, which undergoes highly irregular fluctuations from one business cycle to the next, is treated in the same way. Bank clearings and commercial paper rates in New York City respond positively to business cycles, but the first usually leads and the second usually lags at reference troughs and peaks. Bond yields usually turn up in midexpansion and turn down in midcontraction, while building plans in Manhattan usually turn up in midcontraction and down in midexpansion. We call both of these opposite types of timing 'neutral'. Obviously, the expansion stages on which the indexes are based require close attention.

The numerical values of our conformity indexes differ from ordinary percentages. The indexes show, not the percentage of business cycles covered by a series in which its movements conform to the cyclical tides, but the percentage of conforming minus contrary movements. A lapse in any cycle will make our index lower than the corresponding percentage as usually computed, and the fewer the cycles covered by a series the larger will be the difference caused by a single lapse. For example, if a series spans 3 reference cycles, conforms positively to 2 and inversely to the third, the percentage of positive conformity is 67; but our index is +33. If we ignore instances of no change, an index of +50 means positive conformity in 3 cycles out of 4, an index of −60 means inverse conformity in 4 out of 5, +80 means positive conformity in 9 out of 10, and +90 in 19 out of 20.

IX OUR USE OF AVERAGES

A complete history of business cycles would describe not only the characteristics common to all members of the species but also the characteristics that make each cycle unique. A complete theory would explain not only how business cycles come about but also how each cycle comes to differ from the others. Our observations upon individual time series should provide data for pursuing both of these ideals. They should cover arrays of cycles as wide as the data allow. In each array, they should record both the typical features of cyclical behavior and the cycle-by-cycle idiosyncrasies.

The usual method of observing statistical arrays is to describe their 'central tendency' by an average of some sort, and their variability by some measure of dispersion. We wished to adapt this standard procedure to the study of cyclical behavior. But for that step we had no precedents. On the contrary, some earlier investigators had reached conclusions that, if valid, would impose narrow restrictions upon averaging of the sort we planned, or bar it altogether. Before we could proceed, we had to examine these views.

Chapter 10 of *Measuring Business Cycles* tests several variants of the hypothesis that cyclical behavior is subject to secular or discontinuous changes. If the alleged secular changes are large, they may dominate our measures of individual cycles and vitiate the averages—a risk to which our findings seem especially exposed, for, though we exclude intercycle, we retain intracycle trends. Will not reference-cycle relatives containing a progressively changing element of trend show different types of response to the early and to the late cycles in our arrays? Then what meaning can we attach to averages including all the cycles? On the other hand, if cyclical behavior changes discontinuously in the course of a nation's development, averaging may be permissible, but only within the limits of each historical phase. A third group of hypotheses is examined in Chapter 11—several forms of the view that cyclical behavior undergoes cyclical changes. If there are 'cycles of cycles', the relatively short waves in which our interest centers should be classified according to the positions they occupy in a longer sequence, and any averaging done should be confined to waves in a similar position. Thus, our desire to work with the widest arrays of cycles covered by statistical records is open to at least three sets of forcibly presented objections.

In general, our tests of the hypotheses so baldly summarized here yielded negative results. We found no convincing evidence that secular, discontinuous, or cyclical changes in cyclical behavior were so marked and pervasive as to debar us in principle from treating the cycles covered by a series as a single array. However, the tests show some instances, and detailed work with our full sample of series adds others, in which division of reference cycles into groups is necessary.[1] To cite examples: the output of beehive coke changed its behavior drastically when byproduct furnaces became the chief producers; the establishment of the Federal Reserve System was followed by significant changes in the behavior of numerous series on banking and interest rates; long waves in indexes of prices lead us at times to segregate the cycles occurring during the phases of progressive increases and progressive declines in reference-cycle bases. Thus, when occasion requires, we take account of secular, discontinuous, and cyclical changes in the behavior we are trying to measure. But such instances are not numerous. Usually we make a single set of averages including all the reference cycles covered by a series.

No tests are necessary to prove that the behavior of virtually every series is subject to a fourth set of changes—the irregular movements that are so troublesome to all time-series analysts. The standard device for mitigating their disturbing effects upon cyclical measures of individual series is averaging of some sort. Our use of nine 'stages', usually covering three months or more, in making reference-cycle patterns affords some protection; for even three-month averages are freer from erratic perturbations than monthly data. We take a further and more effective step when we average the stage-by-stage measures of several cycles. In such averages, whatever features are peculiar to single cycles tend to offset one another, while whatever features are common to most cycles tend to stand out more clearly. Desire to protect our measures as much as we can

[1] See Chart 1 below, Figures 8, 13–14, 32, and 35.

against random movements is one of our strongest reasons for observing as many cycles as the data allow. We have more confidence in the representative value of averages derived from long than from short series, and more confidence when we can treat long series as wholes than when we are forced to break them into segments. As a rule, the more cycles we can cover the better.

But this rule does not apply when the movements in a few cycles are exceptionally violent. For example, indexes of commodity prices behave sedately most of the time, but they ran wild during and immediately after the Civil War and World War I. Our averages would give a distorted picture of the way in which these prices typically react to business cycles if the war episodes were not excluded.[2] They are excluded also from the averages of most series representing the dollar values of goods produced or exchanged. More rarely, we exclude cycles dominated by wartime demands or great labor disputes from averages of series expressed in physical units.

After finishing the analysis of a series we cannot tell precisely what mixture of movements our averages and average deviations represent. Probably all of these measures include a residue of irregular movements, which often seems disturbingly large. They may include also many vestiges of secular or discontinuous changes or of long cycles. They are warped further by whatever errors we committed in identifying business cycles and dating their peaks and troughs. Often more disturbing still are doubts about the trustworthiness or adequacy of the original data and of our adjustments for seasonal variations. Certainly the majority of series cover periods so brief that averaging has a poor chance of performing the wonders we ask of it.

All that can be expected from the simple and rough methods we apply to imperfect records are tolerable approximations. Refining and elaborating our statistical technique might lessen doubts, but we have not thought the gains would offset the limitations a more time-consuming treatment would impose

[2] See Chart 1, Figure 17.

upon the scope of the investigation. There is another and we believe a more effective way of determining the economic significance of our statistical findings.

X   Tests of Consilience

What one series tells us about the cyclical behavior of some activity can often be checked by what other series tell. By examining several fallible witnesses, noting the points of agreement and conflict in their testimony, we can usually get a well buttressed story of the salient points. The opportunities for testing of this sort are wider than one not well acquainted with statistical records may suppose.

Many of the factors that concern a student of business cycles are nowadays recorded by two or more agencies. Certain activities have several branches so closely allied that conclusions concerning the cyclical characteristics of each can be checked by comparisons with the others. When an industry flourishes in several countries, international comparisons are helpful. The same factor may be reported in physical units for one purpose, in monetary units for others, and the two recordings may be supplemented by price quotations. Of the making of index numbers there is no end; seldom if ever do two indexes of commodity prices, security prices, cost of living, production, retail sales, employment, payrolls, business activity, or what not, agree precisely; but the divergencies may tell as much as the agreements, provided the compilers have given adequate descriptions of their data and methods. Often an index can be compared also with several of its own components. Nor is the testing of series by one another confined to comparing records of the same or of closely related factors; it can often be extended to comparisons of factors one expects to differ in specifiable ways. As the last clause implies, designing these tests involves more than the mechanical assembling of measures derived from several sources. What practical experience and theoretical analysis have taught about the interrelations among economic activities guides us in selecting series to be compared and in interpreting the similarities and differences of their behavior.

Early in the investigation we found that we could best determine the cyclical characteristics of agricultural production by focusing attention upon traits common to the records of several crops in the same country, and the records of the same crop in several countries. As our experience grew, we relied increasingly upon such tests of consilience. Many of the doubts we harbored when trying to extract meanings from individual series were dissipated when we examined groups. Desire for this type of evidence led us to collect many more time series than we originally thought necessary. The detailed conclusions presented in later chapters rest for the most part on studies of group behavior, while the broader conclusions rest on the consilience among the group studies when interpreted in the light of what we know about the relations of one activity to another, and of each activity to the economy as a whole.

XI Our Sample of Time Series

To match our working definition of business cycles, our statistical observations should extend over all economic activities, whether organized in business enterprises or not. Ideally, the time series used should cover many cycles in strictly comparable fashion. In practice we are forced to work with records that are far from complete and uniform. Even now in the United States satisfactory data cannot be had upon numerous matters of importance, and the supply dwindles rapidly as we delve into the past or go abroad. Yet on some heads the record is so voluminous that we have not been able to collect and analyze all the series in form for use, not to speak of those which might be compiled from original sources.

Table 3 indicates how far we had carried our analysis of American data by months or quarters when the basic compilations for this report were drawn up. In addition, we then had some 160 annual series from the United States as well as some 300 British, French, and German series upon which I could draw at need. While I was studying the American sample of monthly or quarterly series, our computing unit was seeking to remedy its most glaring deficiencies. So far, we have added

Table 3

BASIC SAMPLE OF 794 MONTHLY OR QUARTERLY SERIES
FOR THE UNITED STATES USED IN LATER TABLES

Group	Total No. of Series	Classified by Number of Reference Cycles Covered by Averages				
		Under 4	4–5	6–10	11–15	16–21
Retail & wholesale trade	27	14	10	3	..	..
Foreign commerce	20	..	..	11	1	8
Orders from manufacturers	18	6	4	4	1	3
Contracts & permits for construction	58	1	43	13	..	1
Inventories	62	15	35	7	1	4
Production	188	34	101	39	6	8
Transportation & communication	31	..	13	11	6	1
Employment & hours of work	46	2	40	4	..	..
Wage rates & average earnings	15	..	15	..	..	..
Payrolls & total incomes	30	..	29	1	..	..
Prices of commodities	147	..	61	20	57	9
Banking & money	69	..	10	52	6	1
Interest rates & bond yields	23	..	10	8	2	3
Stock exchange transactions & prices	10	..	2	2	2	4
Security issues & savings	15	..	10	4	1	..
Business profits	5	..	4	..	1	..
Business failures	11	3	..	2	4	2
Bank clearings & debits	8	..	3	1	2	2
Indexes of business activity	11	..	1	2	3	5
Summary [a]						
Flow of commodities, services, or incomes	478	72	272	94	14	26
Prices of commodities or services	168	..	80	20	59	9
Financial activities or prices	135	3	37	68	16	11
General business activity	13	..	2	2	4	5
All series	794	75	391	184	93	51
% of all series	100.0	9.4	49.2	23.2	11.7	6.4

[a] Based on a more detailed classification than is provided above.

more than 30 monthly and more than 90 annual series, of which use is made in the text, though they have been incorporated into few of the tables.

The grouping of series in Table 3 is an adaptation of the familiar headings under which statistical data are compiled for practical uses. It serves some of our needs, but has to be supplemented by other arrangements based upon analytic criteria. For example, in studying investment, we assemble series selected from the groups 'security issues and savings', 'interest rates and bond yields', 'stock exchange transactions and prices', 'orders from manufacturers', 'contracts and permits for construction', 'inventories', 'production', 'employment and hours of work', 'prices of commodities', and 'banking and money'.

The number of series in the 19 groups of the table reflects partly the unevenness of our progress in different segments of the field and partly the relative abundance of suitable data. To give examples of both factors: we have exploited the series on construction rather fully, but have confined our work on security prices to a few indexes, neglecting so far the readily available quotations of individual stocks and bonds; foreign commerce has long been recorded in considerable detail, while data on the far larger volume of domestic trade are relatively recent and unsystematic. The gravest inadequacies of the sample appear in personal incomes other than factory wages, and the profits or losses of business enterprises. Despite the special attention given to these groups in the supplementary work mentioned above, the evidence remains sketchy and largely in annual form.

Another disturbing feature of our sample is that in only 41 percent of our series are more than 5 reference cycles covered by the averages. Can we trust measures based on so few cycles? To find out, we experimented with 7 series representing widely different activities during the 15 reference cycles of 1879–1933. Each series was broken into 3 segments of 5 cycles. The results presented at length in Chapter 12 of *Measuring Business Cycles* show differences among the 3 group averages of each series; but these differences are notably smaller than the differences among the individual cycles within each group. Further, the differences among the averages of groups belonging to the same series are significantly smaller than the differences among the averages of groups belonging to different series. These experiments are reassuring as far as the broad features of cyclical behavior are concerned; but they warn us against taking seriously small differences among our averages. For example, it would be naive to trust the decimals of our reference-cycle patterns: only when the amplitudes of these patterns are small are the first integers likely to be good approximations; when the amplitudes are large only the tens, or even hundreds are significant. What merits attention is the ranges within which the measures of different activities fall—not the exact figures.

If averages are broadly similar whether based upon the 5 reference cycles of 1879–97, 1897–1914, or 1914–33, as these tests indicate, we seem warranted in comparing measures of series covering unlike periods, provided always that we have taken the precautions described in an earlier section against marked changes in the cyclical movements we average. We should be delighted to maintain strict uniformity of time coverage if we could do so by lengthening short series; but to attain it by shortening long ones would be to sacrifice more than we should gain. However, in detailed comparisons of cyclical behavior, we often make special averages of the longer series to match the periods covered by shorter ones; for the briefer the time span of comparisons, the more are our averages influenced by the idiosyncrasies of individual cycles. Now and then the reader will find us cutting down 5-cycle series to match a 4-cycle group, or performing some equally repugnant amputation. He will find also that the shorter the statistical records of an economic activity, the more series we seek to use and the more heavily we lean upon tests of consilience.

Descriptions of methods and raw materials acquire livelier meaning when one examines the results they help to produce. To that task we now turn. But, while pressing onward, we shall have to recur ever and again to methodological problems concerning the adequacy of our data, the logical implications of our technique, and the economic significance of our measures.

Part II

VARIETIES OF CYCLICAL BEHAVIOR

CHAPTER 4

A Sample of Reference-Cycle Patterns

'Observing business cycles' is a figurative expression. What
we actually see are tables of figures or charts that purport to
show in standardized symbols one among several species of
changes found in time series, which are themselves bleak numerical records of certain mass activities. These series give
many glimpses of our cycles, but none of them gives a well
rounded view. The changes on which we focus attention never
occur by themselves in the way our symbols suggest. Our
measures are averages covering groups of cycles; rarely if ever
do they fit snugly any one cycle. Like other scientific concepts,
ours is a man-made entity, created by pulling apart items of
experience that can be observed directly; then putting like
parts together into a new whole that cannot be seen by the eye
or touched by the fingers. Such synthetic products of the mind
have often turned out to be useless or worse, in that they led
to logical contradictions, conflicts with factual evidence, or
futile practices. Most of the useful ones have to be recon-
structed from time to time in the light of fresh discoveries they
have helped men to achieve.

One standard procedure for trying to test or improve such a
concept is to repeat with greater care and thoroughness the
process by which it was produced. In this recapitulation, the
investigator first defines the concept as best he can, considers
the elements of experience he should separate from their original matrix, devises analytic methods for that purpose, applies
them to appropriate materials, and finally assembles his findings to see whether they form a whole corresponding to the
idea with which he started. If they do, he judges the concept as
he defined it to be valid, at least for the time being. If not, he

may learn how the definition should be amended; or he may conclude that the whole concept should be abandoned as one more illusion from which men should free themselves.

Part I has presented our working definition of business cycles, outlined our methods of segregating cyclical fluctuations plus intracycle trends from movements of other types, and indicated the kinds of time series we have analyzed. In the results of this analysis, we have a stockpile of prefabricated parts designed to be assembled into a business cycle complying with the specifications laid down in advance. These parts are our average reference-cycle patterns, average rates of change per month from one reference stage to the next, and measures of conformity to business cycles.[1]

Before starting the job of final assembly, we should inspect these parts critically. One aim is to discover defects. Though the parts have been made by uniform methods, the materials used differ widely in kind, quality, and abundance. Because of such differences, some parts are oversized and some too small, while others are of such doubtful precision that we must use them with caution, if at all. A not less important aim of the inspection is to increase our own skills as assemblers. It would be a rash and wasteful effort to start selecting parts from our stockpile and trying to fit one to another before we had gained familiarity with their many shapes, sizes, and other peculiarities. Further, the knowledge we acquire of the parts by studying them individually will contribute directly to our ultimate aim by enabling us to make some subassemblies that should be delivered as units to the final assembly line.

Part II is devoted to this job of inspection. It begins with a sample of reference-cycle patterns selected to illustrate the diversities of business-cycle behavior found among the economic activities represented by the time series of our sample. Reference-cycle patterns afford the easiest and best introduction to the varieties of cyclical behavior. Readers are advised

---

[1] Little use is made here of the specific-cycle measures described in *Measuring Business Cycles*. They were not available in comparable form when this report was prepared.

to study the sample patterns in Chart 1 thoughtfully, comparing not only the two or more patterns in each figure but also the patterns in different figures, considering the nature of the activities represented, and thinking of reasons why these activities differ from or resemble one another in cyclical behavior. That exercise should prove interesting, and whet the appetite for the analytic chapters to follow.

All of the 'figures' in the chart have been derived by uniform methods. They are drawn on the same scale of time and the same scale of amplitude, so that the differences are due wholly to the data. Horizontal lines (TT) at the top and the bottom of each figure show the average durations of the reference cycles represented by the patterns. Since the varying groups of cycles covered by our series differ in average duration, these lines are not of uniform length, but the differences among them are not very large.[2] Amplitudes are to be read from the vertical scales on the left. Here 100 represents the cycle bases (that is, the average value of a series during each cycle covered), in percentages of which the average standings are expressed. The average standing of a series at each of the nine stages into which reference cycles are divided is plotted at the center of the stage as indicated by the time scale. One percent on the amplitude scale equals one month on the time scale, so that a slope of 45 degrees represents change at the rate of 1 percent monthly. A vertical line is drawn at the central point of each stage to represent the average deviation of standings in individual cycles from their mean. Like the average standings themselves, the average deviations from them are expressed in percentages of the cycle bases.

Our practice of plotting average standings at the midpoints of cycle stages and connecting them by straight lines tends to give the patterns an angularity that may at times be specious. A test of this effect is reported in *Measuring Business Cycles*, pages 347–9. We made special patterns of pig iron production covering 15 specific and 15 reference cycles by using 19 'stages' per cycle instead of 9. The resulting patterns are somewhat

[2] T stands for reference trough, and P for reference peak.

Chart 1
Average Reference-Cycle Patterns of a Sample of American Series

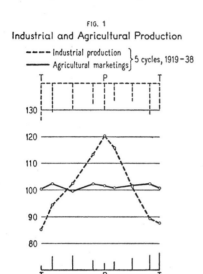

FIG. 1
Industrial and Agricultural Production

---- Industrial production
——— Agricultural marketings } 5 cycles, 1919–38

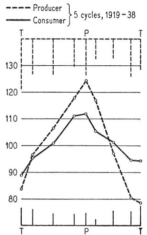

FIG. 2
Production of Producer and Consumer Goods

---- Producer
——— Consumer } 5 cycles, 1919–38

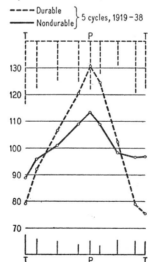

FIG. 3
Production of Durable and Nondurable Goods

---- Durable
——— Nondurable } 5 cycles, 1919–38

See Table 42 for data on which chart is based and Appendix B for sources.

32

Chart 1 (cont.)

FIG. 4
Automobile Production

--- Trucks
— Passenger cars } 6 cycles, 1914–38

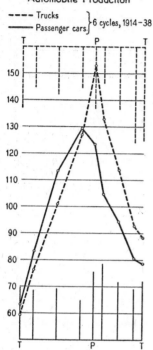

FIG. 5
Animal Slaughter

--- Cattle (8 cycles, 1908–1938)
— Hogs (16 cycles, 1879–1938)

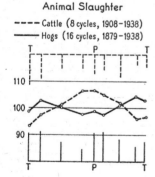

FIG. 6
Butter and Ice Cream Production

--- Butter
— Ice cream } 5 cycles, 1919–38

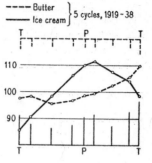

FIG. 7
Textile Manufacturing Activity

--- Cotton consumption
— Rayon deliveries } 3 cycles, 1924–38

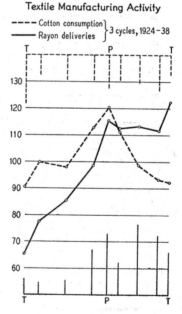

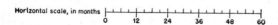

Horizontal scale, in months
0   12   24   36   48   60

Chart 1 (cont.)

FIG. 8
Beehive Coke Production

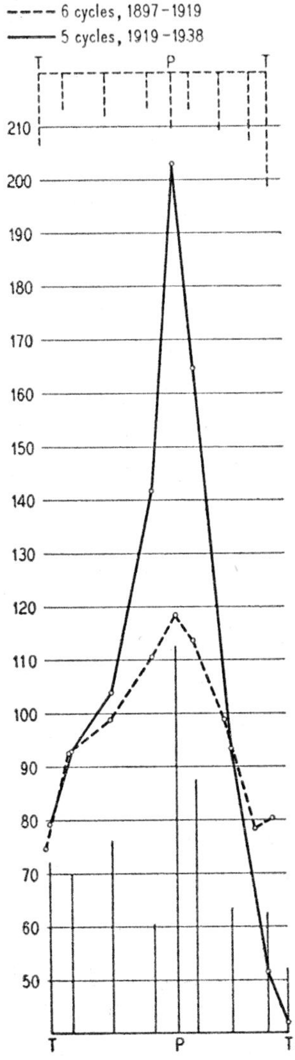

---- 6 cycles, 1897-1919
—— 5 cycles, 1919-1938

FIG. 9
Construction Contracts and
Building Permits, Value

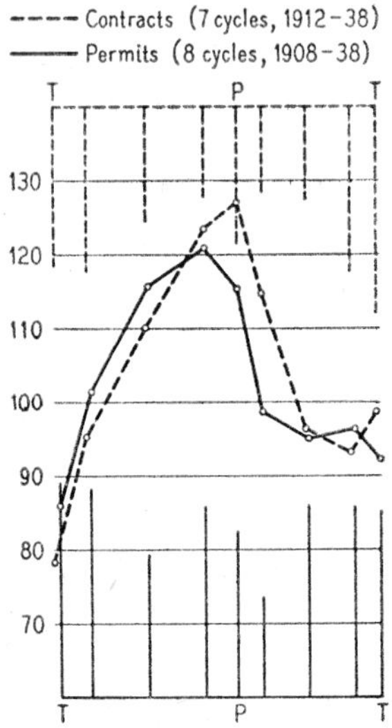

---- Contracts (7 cycles, 1912-38)
—— Permits (8 cycles, 1908-38)

FIG. 10
Private and Public
Construction Contracts, Value

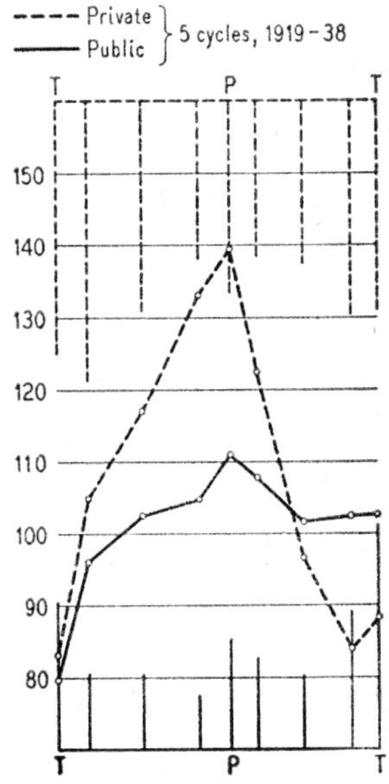

---- Private ⎤
—— Public ⎦ 5 cycles, 1919-38

Chart 1 (cont.)

FIG. 11
Nonresidential Building
Contracts, Value

- - - - Public buildings, etc.
· · · · · · · · Commercial buildings ⎫ 5 cycles,
———— Industrial buildings ⎭ 1919-38

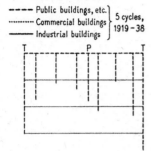

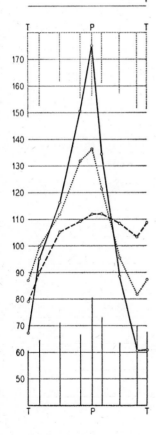

FIG. 12
Residential Building Contracts

- - - - Value
———— Floor space ⎫ 5 cycles, 1919-38

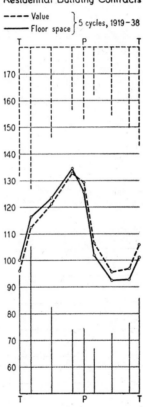

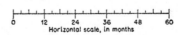

Horizontal scale, in months

35

Chart 1 (cont.)

FIG. 13
Railroad Traffic, 1867–1904

---- Freight ton miles ⎫
—— Gross earnings   ⎬ 9 cycles, 1867–1904
⎭

FIG. 14
Railroad Traffic, 1904–1938

---- Freight ton miles (9 cycles, 1904–38)
·········· Passenger miles (5 cycles, 1919–38)
—— Gross earnings (7 cycles, 1904–14, 1921–38)

FIG. 15
Factory Employment, Hours, and Payrolls

---- Employment ⎫
·········· Hours   ⎬ 4 cycles, 1921–38
—— Payrolls   ⎭

FIG. 16
Factory Employment: Four Industries

---- Food products ⎫
·········· Textiles   ⎪
·········· Iron and steel ⎬ 5 cycles, 1919–38
—— Machinery   ⎭

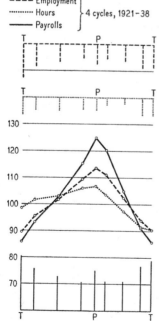

Chart 1 (cont.)

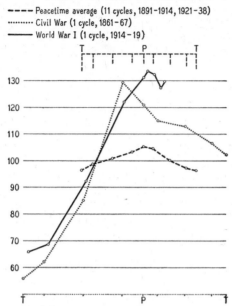

FIG. 17
Wholesale Price Indexes in Peace and War

- - - - Peacetime average (11 cycles, 1891-1914, 1921-38)
·········· Civil War (1 cycle, 1861-67)
———— World War I (1 cycle, 1914-19)

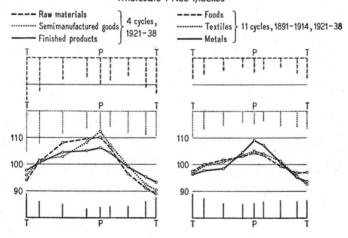

FIG. 18
Wholesale Price Indexes

- - - - Raw materials ⎫ 4 cycles,
·········· Semimanufactured goods ⎬ 1921-38
———— Finished products ⎭

- - - - Foods ⎫
·········· Textiles ⎬ 11 cycles, 1891-1914, 1921-38
———— Metals ⎭

Horizontal scale, in months

0   12   24   36   48   60

Chart 1 (cont.)

FIG. 19
Wholesale and Retail Prices, Foods

- - - - Wholesale ⎫
———— Retail ⎬ 4 cycles, 1921–38

FIG. 20
Farm and Retail Price Indexes, Foods

- - - - Farm ⎫
———— Retail ⎬ 4 cycles, 1921–38

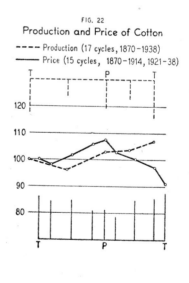

FIG. 21
Production and Price of Pig Iron

- - - - Production (16 cycles, 1879–1938)
———— Price (14 cycles, 1879–1914, 1921–38)

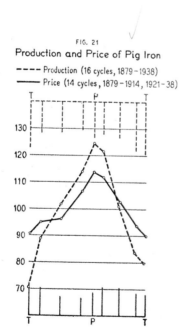

FIG. 22
Production and Price of Cotton

- - - - Production (17 cycles, 1870–1938)
———— Price (15 cycles, 1870–1914, 1921–38)

Chart 1 (cont.)

FIG. 23
Production and Price of Wheat
---- Production (18 cycles, 1867–1938)
—— Price (16 cycles, 1867–1914, 1921–38)

FIG. 24
Production and Price of Corn
---- Production (18 cycles, 1867–1938)
—— Price (16 cycles, 1867–1914, 1921–38)

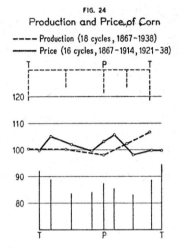

FIG. 25
Production and Price of Potatoes
---- Production (13 cycles, 1891–1938)
—— Price (11 cycles, 1891–1914, 1921–38)

FIG. 26
Production and Price of Hogs
---- Production (16 cycles, 1879–1938)
—— Price (14 cycles, 1879–1914, 1921–38)

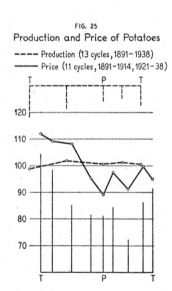

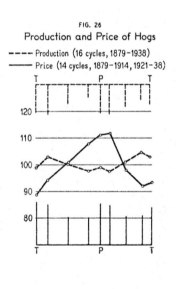

Horizontal scale, in months

0   12   24   36   48   60

Chart 1 (cont.)

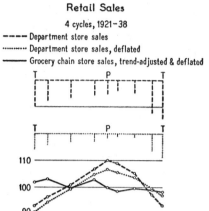

FIG. 27
Retail Sales

4 cycles, 1921–38
- - - - Department store sales
·········· Department store sales, deflated
———— Grocery chain store sales, trend-adjusted & deflated

FIG. 28
Flow of Consumers' Perishables and Durables

- - - - Butter consumption
·········· Newsprint paper consumption ⎫ 5 cycles, 1919–38
———— Vacuum cleaner shipments ⎭

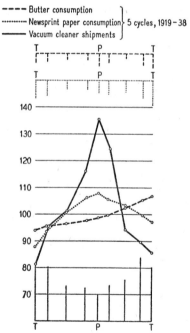

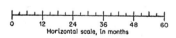

O   12   24   36   48   60
Horizontal scale, in months

40

Chart 1 (cont.)

FIG. 29
New Orders for Durable Goods

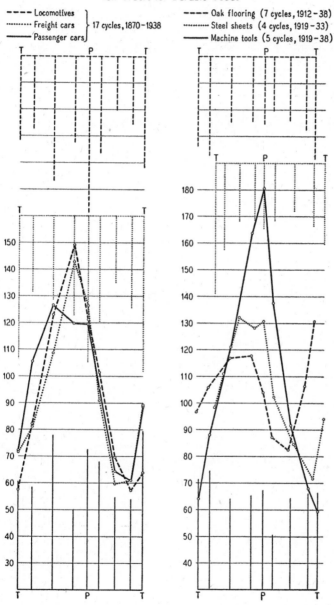

- - - Locomotives ⎫
········· Freight cars ⎬ 17 cycles, 1870–1938
——— Passenger cars ⎭

- - - Oak flooring (7 cycles, 1912–38)
·········· Steel sheets (4 cycles, 1919–33)
——— Machine tools (5 cycles, 1919–38)

Chart 1 (cont.)

FIG. 30
Foreign Trade

- - - - Exports ⎫
———— Imports ⎭ 16 cycles, 1867–1914, 1921–38

FIG. 31
Consumption and Stocks of Raw Cotton

- - - - Stocks in public storage ⎫
·············· Stocks at mills ⎬ 6 cycles, 1914–38
———— Consumption by mills ⎭

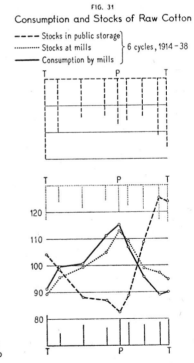

Horizontal scale, in months

42

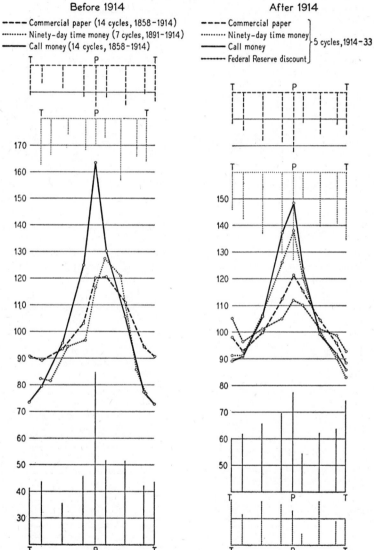

Chart 1 (cont.)

FIG. 32
Short-Term Interest Rates, New York City

Before 1914	After 1914
---- Commercial paper (14 cycles, 1858-1914)	---- Commercial paper
·········· Ninety-day time money (7 cycles, 1891-1914)	·········· Ninety-day time money
—— Call money (14 cycles, 1858-1914)	—— Call money
	-·-·- Federal Reserve discount

5 cycles, 1914-33

Chart 1 (cont.)

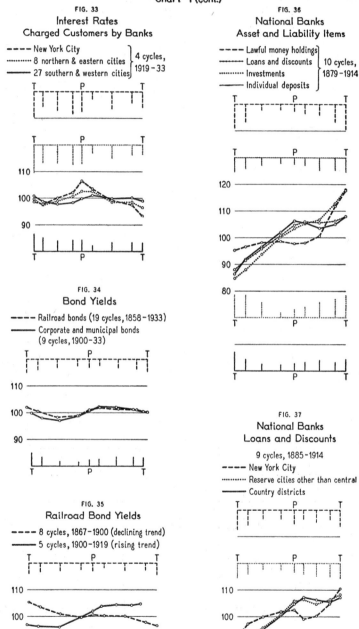

FIG. 33
Interest Rates
Charged Customers by Banks

---- New York City
.... 8 northern & eastern cities
——— 27 southern & western cities

} 4 cycles,
1919–33

FIG. 34
Bond Yields

---- Railroad bonds (19 cycles, 1858–1933)
——— Corporate and municipal bonds
(9 cycles, 1900–33)

FIG. 35
Railroad Bond Yields

---- 8 cycles, 1867–1900 (declining trend)
——— 5 cycles, 1900–1919 (rising trend)

FIG. 36
National Banks
Asset and Liability Items

---- Lawful money holdings
.... Loans and discounts
.... Investments
——— Individual deposits

} 10 cycles,
1879–1914

FIG. 37
National Banks
Loans and Discounts

9 cycles, 1885–1914
---- New York City
.... Reserve cities other than central
——— Country districts

44

Chart 1 (cont.)

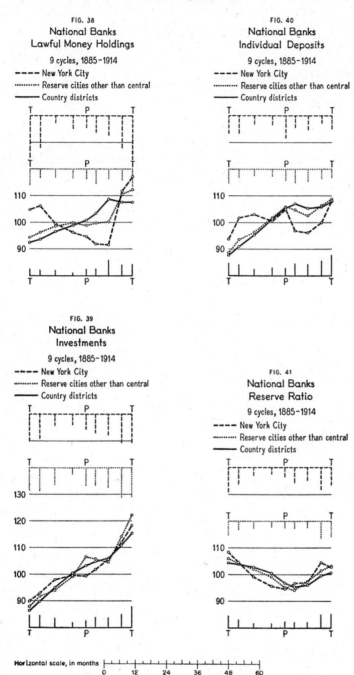

FIG. 38
National Banks
Lawful Money Holdings

9 cycles, 1885–1914
---- New York City
········· Reserve cities other than central
——— Country districts

FIG. 40
National Banks
Individual Deposits

9 cycles, 1885–1914
---- New York City
·········· Reserve cities other than central
——— Country districts

FIG. 39
National Banks
Investments

9 cycles, 1885–1914
---- New York City
·········· Reserve cities other than central
——— Country districts

FIG. 41
National Banks
Reserve Ratio

9 cycles, 1885–1914
---- New York City
·········· Reserve cities other than central
——— Country districts

Horizontal scale, in months

0   12   24   36   48   60

45

Chart 1 (cont.)

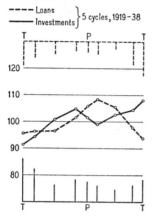

FIG. 42
Federal Reserve Member Banks
Loans and Investments

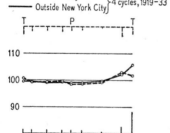

FIG. 43
Federal Reserve Member Banks
Reserve Ratio

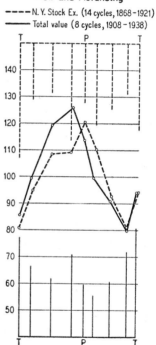

FIG. 44
Corporate Security Issues
New and Refunding

Horizontal scale, in months

0   12   24   36   48   60

Chart 1 (cont.)

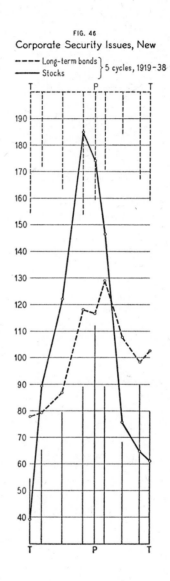

FIG. 45
Corporate Security Issues

---- New
———— Refunding } 5 cycles, 1919 – 38

FIG. 46
Corporate Security Issues, New

---- Long-term bonds
———— Stocks } 5 cycles, 1919 – 38

Chart 1 (cont.)

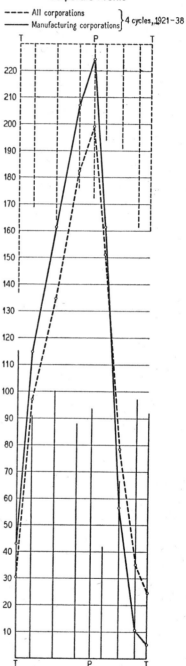

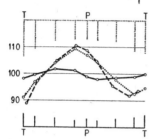

FIG. 47
Indexes of Security Prices

- - - - 'All' common stocks (15 cycles, 1879–1933)
.... Railroad stocks ⎫
————— Railroad bonds ⎬ 19 cycles, 1858–1933

FIG. 49
Corporate Profits

- - - - All corporations ⎫
————— Manufacturing corporations ⎬ 4 cycles, 1921–38

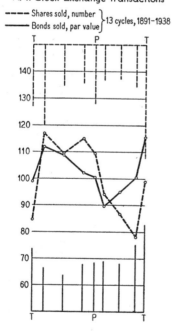

FIG. 48
N. Y. Stock Exchange Transactions

- - - - Shares sold, number ⎫
————— Bonds sold, par value ⎬ 13 cycles, 1891–1938

0   12   24   36   48   60
Horizontal scale, in months

48

Chart 1 (concl.)

FIG. 50
Corporate Profits and Losses

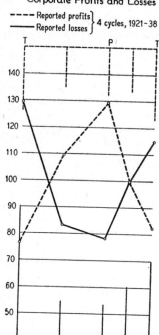

FIG. 51
Business Failures

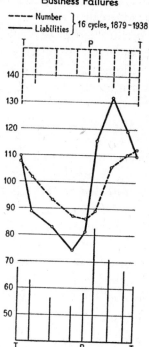

FIG. 52
Farm Income

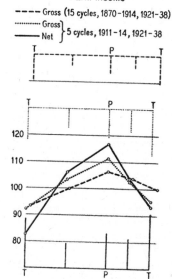

less regular than their standard counterparts, but one can hardly call them less angular. This single experiment is not conclusive, but in view of its result we cannot be sure that exaggerated angularity is a common fault in our patterns.

Figures 20, 50, and 52 are drawn from annual data such as we must use now and then to supplement the quarterly and monthly series in our regular sample. In them, we use 5-stage instead of 9-stage patterns, but call the stages I, III, V, VII, and IX. Even so, standings in stage III must often be interpolated between the standings in I and V, and standings in VII between V and IX. However, the annual reference dates of Table 1 show that 17 of the 21 expansions between 1855 and 1937 and 6 of the following contractions last two years or more, so that the average standings at III and VII rest in part upon independently reported values.[3]

In subsequent chapters the chief reference-cycle measures are discussed one by one, and an effort is made not only to exhibit but also to explain the varieties they present. What kinds of activities conform to business activities with a high degree of regularity and what do not? To what are these differences due? Why do certain of the regular conformers have positive, others neutral, and still others inverted patterns? In what sectors of the economy do we find leads and in what do we find lags at business-cycle peaks and troughs? How can these varieties of timing be accounted for? Most striking of all are the differences in the average amplitudes of the reference-cycle patterns. Why do some series have amplitudes approximating zero, while others rise and then fall by twice their average value? Finally, why do the cycle-by-cycle deviations from the average patterns differ so widely, and what have they to tell about the representative value of the patterns we wish to use? Such are the leading questions asked, and partly answered.

---

[3] On the chart, the character of the activities represented is indicated by very brief captions. Fuller titles are given in Appendix A, together with the numerical values plotted, average reference-cycle amplitudes, and indexes of conformity.

CHAPTER 5

Varieties of Cyclical Timing

I Our Measures of Cyclical Timing

According to our definition, the basic feature of business cycles is substantial agreement among many economic activities in the timing of their expansions and of their contractions. Yet less than half of the average patterns of the series in our sample characteristically reach their lowest points at reference troughs and their highest points at reference peaks. Our efforts to observe and to understand what happens during business cycles begin with the differences found in this fundamental trait.

First a word about how cyclical timing is determined. We plot the patterns traced by a series during successive reference cycles one above another, so that likenesses and differences can readily be seen. Seldom do the troughs of these patterns invariably fall in the same stage; not much oftener do the peaks. But usually there is a substantial preponderance of troughs in some one stage, likewise of peaks, and this preponderance fixes our tentative judgment concerning the timing characteristic of the series, which is then tested by comparisons with other arrangements of the data. "When a decision is finally reached, we usually feel reasonably certain that we have made that division into 'expansion' and 'contraction' which best represents the behavior of the series during successive reference cycles." When the behavior differs so erratically from one cycle to the next that there is serious doubt whether the series is correlated at all with business cycles, we classify the timing as 'irregular'.[1] A few series with rapidly rising trends and moderate cyclical movements do not decline in contractions; then we look for the stages during which the rise is usually accelerated and those

[1] For further details and illustrations, see *Measuring Business Cycles*, pp. 185–9.

Table 4

DISTRIBUTION OF 794 MONTHLY OR QUARTERLY SERIES ACCORDING TO THEIR CHARACTERISTIC CYCLICAL TIMING [a]

Reference-Cycle Stages Characteristic of		Type of Timing	Timing at Reference-Cycle		No. of Series	% of Sample [b]
Expansion	Contraction		Troughs	Peaks		
(1)	(2)	(3)	(4)	(5)	(6)	(7)
V–VIII	VIII–V	Inverted	−1	0	7	0.9
V–IX	I–V	"	0	0	38	4.8
V–II	II–V	"	+1	0	3	0.4
VI–IX	I–VI	"	0	+1	5	0.6
VI–II	II–VI	"	+1	+1	3	0.4
VI–III	III–VI	"	+2	+1	2.5	0.3
VII–II	II–VII	"	+1	+2	4	0.5
VII–III	III–VII	Neutral	−2 or +2	−2 or +2	6.5	0.8
VII–IV	IV–VII	Positive	−2	−1	25	3.1
VIII–III	III–VIII	"	−1	−2	4.5	0.6
VIII–IV	IV–VIII	"	−1	−1	46.5	5.9
VIII–V	V–VIII	"	−1	0	69.5	8.8
I–IV	IV–IX	"	0	−1	17	2.1
I–V	V–IX	"	0	0	345	43.5
I–VI	VI–IX	"	0	+1	60.5	7.6
II–V	V–II	"	+1	0	11	1.4
II–VI	VI–II	"	+1	+1	14	1.8
II–VII	VII–II	"	+1	+2	6	0.8
III–VI	VI–III	"	+2	+1	8	1.0
III–VII	VII–III	Neutral	+2 or −2	+2 or −2	18.5	2.3
III–VIII	VIII–III	Inverted	−1	−2	0	0.0
IV–VII	VII–IV	"	−2	−1	6	0.8
IV–VIII	VIII–IV	"	−1	−1	5	0.6
IV–IX	I–IV	"	0	−1	4	0.5
Irregular	Irregular	Irregular	Irregular	Irregular	84.5	10.6
					794	100.0

[a] In inverted series the troughs are matched with reference peaks, and the peaks with reference troughs. In columns (4) and (5) of the first half of the table the 'minus' symbol represents a lead, 0 a coincidence, and 'plus' a lag. Numerals following one of the symbols indicate the number of reference-cycle stages by which a series leads or lags. Fractions occur in column (6) of the first half and columns (2)–(6) of the later half of the table because a few series fit two varieties of timing equally well and are credited half to each.

[b] Failure of detail to total 100 percent is due to rounding.

during which it is usually retarded—a remark that applies to declines in the even fewer series with rapidly falling trends. All of which means that 'characteristic' cyclical timing is an average representing the central tendency of the array of reference-cycle patterns from which it is drawn. Though not derived by numerical computation, it is brother to the average standings that determine the patterns of Chart 1.

Table 4 (concl.)

(1)	SUMMARY BY TYPES OF TIMING				TOTAL	
	Posi-tive	Neutral, Exp. III–VII	Neutral, Exp. VII–III	In-verted	No. of Series	% of Sample
	(2)	(3)	(4)	(5)	(6)	(7)
No. of series	607	18.5	6.5	77.5	709.5	...
% of sample	76.5	2.3	0.8	9.8	...	89.4
	No. of series	No. of series	No. of series	No. of series		
BEHAVIOR AT TROUGHS						
2-stage leads	25	...	6.5ᵉ	6	37.5	4.7
1-stage leads	120.5	...	...	12	132.5	16.7
Coincidences	422.5	...	...	47	469.5	59.1
1-stage lags	31	...	...	10	41	5.2
2-stage lags	8	18.5ᵉ	...	2.5	29	3.7
All leads	145.5	...	6.5ᵉ	18	170	21.4
Coincidences	422.5	...	...	47	469.5	59.1
All lags	39	18.5ᵉ	...	12.5	70	8.8
BEHAVIOR AT PEAKS						
2-stage leads	4.5	...	6.5ᵉ	0	11	1.4
1-stage leads	88.5	...	...	15	103.5	13.0
Coincidences	425.5	...	...	48	473.5	59.6
1-stage lags	82.5	...	...	10.5	93	11.7
2-stage lags	6	18.5ᵉ	...	4	28.5	3.6
All leads	93	...	6.5ᵉ	15	114.5	14.4
Coincidences	425.5	...	...	48	473.5	59.6
All lags	88.5	18.5ᵉ	...	14.5	121.5	15.3

ᵉ May with equal propriety be entered as lead or as lag.

Our decisions regarding the cyclical timing of all the series in the sample used here are summarized by Table 4 and Chart 2. Columns (1) and (2) of the table show the varieties of timing recognized by our standard analysis. Since we think of business-cycle expansions and contractions as cumulative movements usually lasting more than a year, we seldom admit that a series shares in the business-cycle consensus unless it rises for at least 3 consecutive stages, or falls for at least 3. Rigidly applied, this criterion bars from consideration all timing schemes other than 3 stages of expansion to 5 stages of contraction, 4 stages to each phase, or 5 stages of expansion to 3 of contraction. Since a series can begin to rise in any of the 8 stages and continue the movement for 3, 4, or 5 stages, there are 24 standard varieties of

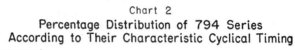

Chart 2

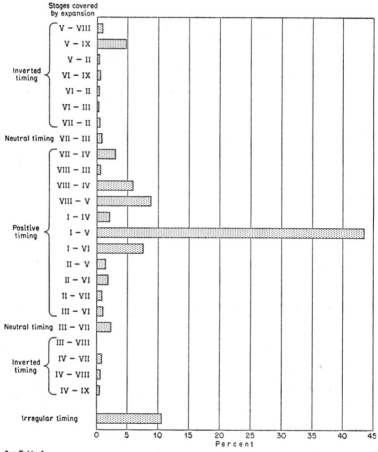

Percentage Distribution of 794 Series
According to Their Characteristic Cyclical Timing

See Table 4.

characteristic timing.[2] Irregular timing constitutes a 25th vari-

[2] We speak here of 8 instead of 9 'stages', because stage IX of one cycle is stage I of its successor. A series that expands in stages IX–IV is more conveniently described as rising in I–IV.

In two series of the present sample we have divided the 8 stages into 6 for expansion and 2 for contraction. One is Babson's, the other Partington's, estimate of railroad gross earnings in 1870–1908. Both rise characteristically from stage VIII of one cycle to stage VI of its successor. In Table 4 these series are entered under expansion stages VIII–V.

ety. All the varieties possible under this scheme are represented in our sample, except expansion in stages III–VIII. Some series conform about equally well to two varieties; they are credited half to one, half to the other. The timing schemes of the table are arranged to place the commonest variety (expansion in stages I–V) near the middle, so that the rough symmetry of the array may stand out clearly in the chart.

In column (3) of the table the 25 standard varieties of timing are classified under 4, or better 5, types. If a series moves in the same direction as general business in more than half of the reference-cycle stages, the timing is called 'positive'. If this proportion is less than half, the timing is 'inverted'. When the expansion in a series covers two stages of business-cycle expansion and two of contraction, the timing is 'neutral'. But this type should be divided, for it embraces two diametrically opposite schemes: expansion in stages III–VII and expansion in VII–III. The final type, 'irregular' timing, means that the expansion stages in a series differ erratically from cycle to cycle.

Columns (4) and (5) show the leads, coincidences, or lags implied by each variety of timing, and the length of the lead or lag in reference-cycle stages. Of course the peaks of positive series are compared with reference-cycle peaks, and troughs with reference troughs, while the peaks of inverted series are compared with reference-cycle troughs, and their troughs with reference peaks. Which way of matching is more significant in dealing with neutral series depends upon economic interpretations. For example, one may say that the rise of certain bond yields in stages III–VII means that the long-term interest rates implicit in these series lag two stages at revival; one may equally well say that the decline in these rates in VII–III leads revival by two stages. Hence the peculiar entries opposite both groups of neutral series in columns (4) and (5). Irregular series lead, coincide with, or lag behind reference-cycle turns in erratic fashion; they have no 'characteristic' timing.

At present we are not concerned with the marked preponderance of one variety of timing over all its rivals—that dramatic feature of Chart 2 will be duly exploited in Part III. Instead we concentrate upon the fact that more than half of the series in our sample, 56.5 percent to be exact, do *not* characteristically rise from our reference dates for business-cycle troughs to our reference dates for business-cycle peaks, and then fall to the next trough dates. How account for the 11 percent that show irregular timing and the 10 percent of inversions? Why do some series rise from the middle of business-cycle expansions to the middle of contractions and then fall to the middle of the following expansions, or behave in the opposite fashion? Among positive and inverted series, why do some lead and others lag at troughs and peaks?

In good part, the answers to these questions must be sought by analyzing the economic interrelations among the cyclical movements typical of different activities. Though we are not yet ready for systematic work of that sort, it is not premature to inquire what kinds of activities have irregular, inverted, and neutral timing, or what kinds lead and what kinds lag at revivals and recessions. Nor is it premature to draw some conclusions that information of this simple sort suggests.

II Irregular Timing

Of the 85 series in our sample classified as irregular in cyclical timing, 41 represent the output, prices, inventories, exports, imports, or sales of farm products or foods. If we included annual data in the present sample, most of the series on harvests, acreage planted, and yields per acre would be added to this timing type. Here we meet for the first time a peculiarity of farming that will reappear time and again in later chapters. Fortunately an explanation can be given at once that will be recalled frequently.

The chief reason why the basic industry of growing crops does not expand and contract in unison with mining, manufacturing, trading, transportation, and finance is that farmers cannot control the short-time fluctuations in their output. To a limited extent they can shift their acreage from one crop to another, and alter the intensity of cultivation. But the factor that dominates year-to-year changes in the harvests is that intricate complex called weather. Plant diseases and insect pests also exert an appreciable influence. "The best laid schemes o' mice and men gang aft a-gley" was written by a farmer of the eighteenth century; his successors remain almost as much at the mercy of nature's freaks as was Robert Burns.

Though no one practically familiar with crop raising is likely to hold that farmers can adjust their output neatly to the rhythm of business, distinguished theorists from W. Stanley Jevons to Henry L. Moore have held that the rhythm of business is dominated by the crops. Moore formulated this view in the following 'law':

The weather conditions represented by the rainfall in the central part of the United States, and probably in other continental areas, pass through cycles of approximately thirty-three years and eight years in duration, causing like cycles in the yield per acre of the crops; these cycles of crops constitute the natural, material current which drags upon its surface the lagging, rhythmically changing values and prices with which the economist is more immediately concerned.[3]

That our observations do not obey this 'law' appears from the reference dates. According to them, the duration of business cycles in the United States between 1854 and 1938 ranged from 17 to 101 months, and averaged 48 months. Nor can one get a neat series of eight-year cycles by adding the durations of consecutive cycles in our list. For that matter, we cannot confirm the eight-year cycle in crops or in yields per acre. Our analysis of specific cycles in the official index of crop production gives an average duration of about 49 months, while for yields per acre we get means of 35 months for wheat, 39 for oats, 37 for corn, 38 for potatoes, and 32 for cotton. Our British, French, and German series on crops behave much like the American series, aside from differences in trend. Even when the average duration of the specific cycles in an agricultural series agrees closely with the corresponding average of business cycles, the two sets of cycles seldom if ever approxi-

[3] *Economic Cycles: Their Law and Cause* (Macmillan, 1914), p. 149. Cf. Moore's later book, *Generating Economic Cycles* (Macmillan, 1923), in which "the eight-year generating cycle" is traced to an astronomical cause.

mate one-to-one correspondence. In no other great industry
for which we have records are the cyclical fluctuations so
irregularly related to business cycles as in crop husbandry. And
the farmer's inability to control his output leads to many irregularities in the cyclical timing of agricultural shipments, processing, prices, inventories, exports, imports, and domestic sales.

These statements do not imply that crop husbandry is a
negligible factor in business cycles. On the contrary, no one
can understand the cycles of actual experience unless he takes
account of the changing fortunes of farmers as consumers and
borrowers, the changing prices of the great staples they sell to
merchants and manufacturers, food costs in family budgets,
or the farmer's share in foreign trade. There will be frequent
occasion to dwell on such matters even in this preliminary
discussion of the typical features of business cycles. If we were
dealing with individual cycles, agricultural factors would play
a still more prominent role; now and then they would appear
to dominate the cyclical tides for a while.[4] What our findings
mean is merely that these patent influences upon the economic
state of the nation sometimes tend to enhance and perhaps as
often tend to restrain expansions; sometimes to mitigate and.
sometimes to aggravate contractions. Whether times are good
or bad, we never know what nature will do to next year's
crops.[5]

Numerous factors besides dependence on the weather may
prevent activities from rising and falling with the cyclical tides.
Private construction rises when the prospects of profits improve and declines when these prospects fade, but 8 of our
series on public construction work have irregular timing, because governments do not build for profit to themselves. Just
why they time the letting of contracts for public buildings,
roads, bridges, sewers, waterworks, docks, dams, and power
houses as they do is a question that has many answers—pressing

[4] Interesting examples occurred in 1878 and 1891.

[5] Geoffrey H. Moore's forthcoming monograph, "Harvest Cycles", deals
thoroughly with fluctuations in agricultural output and their relation to
business cycles.

needs for more schoolrooms, sanitary requirements, desire to provide work in hard times, local pride, political jobbery, and so on. It would be hard indeed to determine the motives animating the men jointly responsible for the decisions. What matters for present purposes is that half of our series on public construction show no regular relation in time to business cycles, while most of the others usually, though not always, rise in cyclical expansions and fall in cyclical contractions.[6]

A third group of irregular series, 12 in number, is made up of 'sticky' prices, clerical wage rates and earnings, railway rates, and street-car fares. The commodity prices in the list relate to one grade of men's shoes, anthracite coal in New York, asphalt, sulphuric acid, haymowers, and passenger automobiles. Those in position to 'administer' the prices of their products often seek to avoid frequent changes. They do not regularly charge all that the traffic would bear in brisk times, and they do not regularly offer cuts when demand falls off. Presumably street-car companies and in less measure railways, even when left to themselves, prefer constant to variable rates under ordinary circumstances, though they may make drastic changes under pressure of rapidly rising costs or rapidly falling traffic. Public supervision, with its time-consuming hearings and quasi-judicial decisions, is likely to interfere still further with the prompt adjustment of rates to the cyclical tides. Collective bargaining has a similar effect upon changes in wage rates, especially when it is elaborate and results in formal contracts running for a year or longer.[7]

Over the remaining 24 irregular series I shall pass lightly, mainly for lack of knowledge. Eleven represent inventories of building materials, raw silk, or cattle-hide leather. Petroleum production from the old Appalachian field was highly irregular because intermixed surface holdings and American

[6] Arthur F. Burns has in hand a monograph upon cyclical movements in construction that will deal more adequately with this problem—and many others. The completion of this monograph has been delayed by other pressing tasks.

[7] See Daniel Creamer, "Behavior of Wage Rates during Business Cycles" (National Bureau, *Occasional Paper 34*).

law concerning ownership of minerals under ground forced drillers to pump oil as fast as they could, with little regard to market demand, in order to prevent wells on neighboring plots from draining the whole pool. Even in recent years, stocks of crude petroleum and of gasoline at refineries have fluctuated irregularly. Three of our 14 series on security issues, and one of our 11 series on bond yields, belong here. So also do new postal savings deposits, imports of lead, the production of knit underwear, and 2 series whose regularity of timing we cannot judge because they cover a single cycle. The last in the list is one of the most important—the monetary gold stock of the United States since 1879. That the basic element in our monetary system rose and fell with slight regard to the nation's business meant that whatever 'elasticity' the circulating medium attained came from some form of credit currency.

Writers who form their concepts or 'models' of business cycles without careful study of actual processes are prone to overlook the sectors of the economy that do not regularly expand and contract in unison. It might be argued that irregular series have no share in the cyclical tides and that omitting them from consideration is a proper simplification of the theorist's task. One who wishes to deal with actual cycles cannot accept such a view. Surely the behavior of the activities that expand and contract in unison would be other than it is if farming followed the timing of steel, if all inventories were either positive or inverted, if the prices of no commodities or services were 'sticky', and if governments used all their construction projects as a balance wheel to moderate fluctuations in employment. Successive business cycles would differ less from one another than they do if these cyclical recalcitrants could be brought into line. We could draw a more elegant sketch of what typically happens during a cycle if we dropped the 11 percent of irregular series from our sample. But in so doing we would be distorting the facts, and discarding many of the materials needed to account for the cyclical behavior of the series we kept.

III Inverted Timing

Whether a series that keeps step with business cycles has a positive or an inverted pattern depends upon the form in which it is recorded. For example, trade unions sometimes report the number or percentages of their members out of work; the Bureau of Labor Statistics reports the number of men employed. Railroads record both the number of surplus freight cars (an inverted series), and freight car shortages (which move positively). Our 14 ratios of bank reserves are all inverted; they would become positive if the ratios showed demand liabilities divided by reserves instead of reserves divided by liabilities. Price series can be inverted by computing how many commodity units are sold for a dollar, production series by computing time per unit of product instead of product per unit of time.

However, the form in which economic records are kept is seldom arbitrary. The purpose for which the figures are to be used and ease of compilation are controlling considerations. A factory manager wants to know how many articles he can produce in a day or week; a consumer wants to know how many of his dollars he must spend for the goods he needs; a banker wants to know whether his reserves are adequate to protect the liabilities he will assume by increasing loans or investments; the nation is interested in both employment and unemployment, but finds it easier to count men at work, while a trade union needs to know how many members are drawing unemployment benefits from its treasury.

Our practice is to accept time series in their original form, trusting that the familiar figures will be more readily understood. On the few occasions when a change in form helps to clarify a special point, we reverse signs, or play other tricks, though never without due warning. What really matters is that we think about the economic meaning of the data. If we realize just what a given series represents, we should be able to draw the same conclusion from the figures whether they are stated in a form that involves a positive or an inverted relation to business cycles.

Seventy-seven series in our sample are inverted and a 78th may equally well be treated as expanding in stages VI–III, which means inversion under our rules, or as expanding in VII–III, which means neutral timing. In some instances the reasons for inversion are obvious; in others they are readily found; but there remain numerous puzzles.

In the obvious group belong the records of unfavorable business developments—our 7 series on commercial failures, and the railway series on idle freight cars. Unemployment percentages would belong here, but we have shifted them to percentages of union members employed.

A second group includes various records of a less desirable alternative that is chosen more frequently in bad times than in good. Certain production series seem to illustrate such choices. Beef is generally preferred to mutton or pork, but it is more expensive. Hence cattle slaughter has positive timing, while sheep and hog slaughter are inverted.[8] Perhaps a hard-times shift of demand toward cheap vegetable foods explains the inverted timing of the wholesale prices of wheat, wheat flour, potatoes, and bananas—which are often the cheapest of fruits on a poundage basis. Presumably the inverted timing of the imports of coffee is due to its relatively low cost. A similar shift from a more to a less desirable alternative dominated the cyclical changes in national bank circulation before 1914. The conditions under which notes could be issued left a narrower margin of profit than could be had from the extension of credit in the form of deposits. Hence national banks reduced their note issues in brisk times, and increased them again when they could find no more profitable way of using funds.

Another situation that produces numerous inversions arises

[8] Probably in no case do the factors mentioned in the text account fully for the cyclical timing of a series. A complete analysis of hog slaughter, for example, would deal with prospects at the time sows are bred, the period of gestation, the ratio between the prices of hogs and corn, and the changing efficiency of a pig in converting corn into pork as its age increases. More thorough treatment may be expected in our monographs.

when the supply of some good is not reduced by cyclical contraction as much as demand falls off. For example, when domestic demand for cotton expands, we use a larger fraction of our output at home; when contraction comes, production usually contines to rise, we use less cotton at home, and sell more abroad.[9] Again, the flow of milk seems to be the steadiest production process of which we have a record. Most of the current supply is sold to families, and the remainder turned into a wide variety of products, among which butter bulks larger than all the rest. When contraction forces painful economies upon many consumers, sales of fresh milk grow more slowly or shrink a little. Then the volume of milk used in factory production rises; so do the production and market receipts of butter. The price falls sharply at retail as well as wholesale, and the consumption of butter rises faster than it had risen during expansion. But consumption runs smaller than production, and cold-storage holdings of butter therefore rise. On somewhat similar lines we can account, at least in part, for the inverted inventories of tallow, oats, cotton, cottonseed, and cottonseed oil.

[9] Here as elsewhere I am dealing, not with what happens in every cycle, but with what happens as a rule. Between 1867 and 1938, the American cotton crop increased in 10 and declined in 8 expansions; it increased in 12 and declined in 6 contractions. Even domestic consumption does not respond to the cyclical tides with perfect regularity. In the period covered by our analysis (1914–38), it rose in the mild contraction of 1926–27 and fell a trifle in the succeeding expansion; that is, there were 2 countermovements in the 12 phases for which we have evidence. American exports of cotton are influenced by business conditions abroad as well as at home, and, while cyclical fluctuations in different countries influence one another, they often move in opposite directions for a while. Other factors influencing cotton exports from the United States are the changing supplies from competing areas, and the changing policies of foreign governments concerning imports. Yet, in the 18 American cycles of 1867–1938, cotton exports fell in 12 expansions and rose in 13 contractions. However, the larger exports in contraction offset only partly the joint effects of bigger crops and smaller domestic consumption; for the visible supply of cotton rose in 12 and fell in 5 of the 17 contractions between 1870 and 1938, while it fell in 12 and rose in 5 of the 17 expansions.

Similar elaborations might be made of what is said briefly about the cyclical timing characteristic of other series.

Perhaps the same principle can be stretched to cover in-verted inventories at large. Almost all industries require the carrying of stocks at each stage of the process from producing raw materials to distributing finished products to final con-sumers. To keep these stocks adjusted to the current volume of business is extremely difficult. Especially when efficient operation requires the placing of firm orders some months before goods are needed, or when a considerable volume of goods must be kept 'in process' for weeks or months, there is grave danger that any slackening of sales will cause some stocks of materials and products to pile up rapidly in the hands of reluctant holders. Although aggregate inventories appear to keep step with business except for a lag at cyclical turns, in many industries technological necessity or commercial organi-zation puts certain enterprises 'on the spot'. They must assume the risk that a slackening of sales will cause their stocks to ac-cumulate, and in such cases the statistics register inverted in-ventory cycles. Clearly the dangers become especially great when a sudden recession occurs in business activity.[10]

Banking provides other cases of inversion. The volume of coin and paper money has not been regularly adjusted to cyclical changes in the dollar volume of transactions. In ex-pansion the public absorbed a larger fraction of the circulating money and left a smaller fraction in the banks; in contraction the reduction of wage disbursements and till money held by retail stores reversed this flow and let 'idle' money pile up in the banks. Hence the 'lawful money holdings' of all national banks before 1914 had an inverted pattern. More emphatically inverted were the patterns of money holdings of the national banks in New York and the class of 'central reserve cities' (New York, Chicago, and St. Louis). In other 'reserve cities'

---

[10] Little has been known about this important feature of production and trade, but Moses Abramovitz has prepared a monograph upon cyclical changes in manufacturers' stocks, which should be followed in due course by similarly thorough analyses of stocks held by other agencies. See his *Inventories and Business Cycles, with Special Reference to Manufacturers' Inventories* (National Bureau, 1950).

and 'country districts', banks were able to adjust their money holdings to current requirements by drawing needed currency from or shipping surplus currency to their correspondents in the financial centers.

In turn the cyclical changes in the distribution of lawful money between banks and the public contributed to the inversion of bank reserve ratios. But here another factor comes into play. Banks make their profits primarily by lending or 'investing'. They can lend more and find more attractive investments in expansion than in contraction. Deposits keep fairly close step with loans plus investments, and hence have positive timing. Of course these positive movements produce inverted movements in reserve ratios, unless the reserves rise faster than deposits in expansion and fall faster in contraction. That they did not do under the National Banking System, and that they have not done under the Federal Reserve System. So all our American reserve ratios are inverted.

There remain 9 or 10 cases of inversion that must be explained in other ways. The short series on mileage of federal-aid roads under construction has a declining trend in 1924–38; it falls in each expansion, but in contraction the decline had been checked or reversed spasmodically by efforts to provide work for the unemployed. The mildly inverted movements in the average revenue received by railroads for hauling a ton of freight one mile are tentatively ascribed by Thor Hultgren to cyclical changes in the composition of traffic and the lagged timing of rate decisions by the Interstate Commerce Commission.[11] The remaining cases are either complicated or obscure, or both, and I pass them by in silence.

All the preceding suggestions regarding the reasons for cyclical inversions require further study, and I shall be surprised if some of them are not amended or replaced in due time. But, even in their present imperfect form, I hope these suggestions suffice to show that business cycles themselves generate

[11] See Hultgren's *American Transportation in Prosperity and Depression* (National Bureau, 1948), Chapter 9 and the section on "Changes in the Composition of Traffic" in Chapter 1.

numerous movements counter to the tides of expansion and
contraction. Brisk business increases the domestic demand for
textile goods and so diminishes the exports of raw cotton; it
increases the sale of fresh milk and so restricts the production of
butter; it increases the volume of coin and paper money held
by the public and stimulates borrowing from the banks,
thereby enlarging demand liabilities and tending to impair
reserve ratios; it leads department stores to carry larger stocks
of merchandise and lowers the piles of iron ore at blast furnaces; it activates share transactions on stock exchanges and
discourages transactions in bonds. The declines in this list, and
many others, are as characteristic a feature of business cycles as
the advances. We could reverse the signs of measures showing
the cyclical response of business failures and idle freight cars
with a clear conscience. But to reverse the signs of hog slaughter and coffee imports would distort the facts; in expansion the
nation does not have more beef and more pork, more coffee
and more milk; instead it has more beef and less pork, more
milk and less coffee. Just as a realistic picture of what happens
during business cycles should include the considerable list of
activities having no regular relation in time to the cyclical tides,
so it should include the activities that contract when the
majority expand and expand when the majority contract.

IV NEUTRAL TIMING

The perfect poise maintained by 25 of our series between a
positive and an inverted response to business cycles presents
especially subtle problems with which we cannot deal effec-
tively until we are ready to follow the stage-by-stage interactions among various industrial, commercial, and financial
processes. For the present, I shall merely indicate the character
of the series that rise from the middle of business-cycle expansions to the middle of contractions, then fall from the middle
of contractions to the middle of expansions, and the character
of the series that behave in the opposite fashion.

Among the 18½ series that rise in III–VII, bond yields are

most numerous.[12] Four series on the ratio of national bank
loans to individual and to net deposits belong here; so also do
the total cash and the gold reserves of Federal Reserve Banks
(not the reserve ratios). The number of commercial failures
is clearly inverted; but the number of banks suspended is neutral, if we may believe the three brief time series available.
There remain two inventories (newsprint at publishers and
oak flooring), a wage rate (average hourly earnings in northern
cotton mills), and the price of iron ore.

The 6½ series that rise from the middle of contraction to the
middle of expansion include three on bank investments, the
individual deposits of national banks in New York City, plans
filed for new buildings in Manhattan, new orders for oak flooring (which move oppositely to inventories), and one of the
two ways in which the timing of Macaulay's railroad bond
prices can be treated. Even this brief list, like its longer predecessor, is varied enough to suggest that neutral timing may
arise from quite different situations, among which chance
happenings should be included.

V Positive Timing

I have thought it necessary to discuss at some length the types
of timing that are likely to receive little attention. Together
they constitute less than 24 percent of our sample. Whether this
proportion is representative of the American economy, I have
no satisfactory basis for judging; but I can say that we have
neither excluded any series because its timing is peculiar, nor
hunted for odd cases.

In effect, I have been trying to answer the question: Why
do not certain series rise and fall with the cyclical tides of expansion and contraction? Here there may be suspected a tacit

---

[12] The awkward half-number in this group comes from Macaulay's series
on the yields of American railroad bonds, 1858–1933. Its timing fits equally
well into the (positive) III–VI and the (neutral) III–VII group. When this
series of yields is converted into a series of bond prices, the timing fits
equally well the (inverted) VI–III and the (neutral) VII–III group. Hence
it provides also the half-number in the second type of neutral timing.

assumption that positive timing is 'normal', and only the deviations from it need be accounted for. On the contrary, positive
timing is just as much a puzzle as the four other types. From
our viewpoint, the central problem of business-cycle theory
is to learn why a large majority of economic series rise and
then fall in unison. The heavy preponderance of positive series
in our sample is statistical evidence that this problem is presented to us by 'real life'—not by fancy. We cannot expect to
solve it in an introductory chapter.

VI LEADS AND LAGS

Yet Table 4 and Chart 2 raise another timing problem that
should be stated here. According to our decisions about the
cyclical timing characteristic of each series in our collection,
three-tenths of our positive and four-tenths of our inverted
series lead or lag by one or two stages at business-cycle troughs,
and almost as many at peaks. All the neutral series also may be
thought of as leading or lagging by two stages at both turns.
These are rough measures at best, expressed in an overlong unit
(a reference-cycle stage) that varies from one business cycle
to the next. More precise measures in months can be made by
matching the dates of comparable specific- and reference-cycle
turns. But in many series the number of comparable turns is
small, or the arrays of monthly leads and lags are excessively
scattered. Later I shall use what monthly figures seem to be
significant, though they may not give so systematic a view of
leads and lags as the coarser measures implicit in judgments
about the reference-cycle stages during which a series characteristically rises.

The summary of these rough measures in Table 5 can be
made to tell much about the round of developments within the
economy that transform expansions into contractions and contractions into expansions—so far as our sample covers and
mirrors what typically happens. But the table must be scanned
with a mind alert to its omissions and tacit implications no less
than its explicit entries. A few general observations may
heighten the reader's curiosity about what the table shows, and
his impatience to follow the clues it offers.

1) Only the 30 percent of our series that characteristically lead or lag at reference-cycle troughs or peaks, or both, are allowed to appear; those that coincide at the turns or have irregular timing are conspicuous by their absence. Focusing attention upon the vanguard and the rear guard of the cyclical procession is necessary; we get clearer impressions by keeping them apart for a while; but before we are done we must put them back in their proper places in front of or behind the mass of the marchers, and intermingled with the considerable number of stragglers.

2) The table distinguishes between one-stage and two-stage leads and lags—clearly a matter of moment. No three- or four-stage leads or lags are entered because a series that begins to fall in I–II or II–III, or begins to rise in V–VI or VI–VII, gets classed as inverted; with coincident timing at the turn if the change starts in I–II or V–VI, with a lag if it starts in II–III or VI–VII. But from the viewpoint of business-cycle theory, some of these inverted movements are the longest of leads; that is, they represent the beginning of readjustments within the economy that culminate many months later in general recessions or revivals. To repeat what has already been said, careful thought about the activity represented by a series, and its relations to the rest of the economy, is needed to grasp the meaning of its cyclical timing.

3) This last remark applies emphatically to the neutral series. In Table 5 I have entered those which rise in VII–III as leading by two stages at both turns, and those which rise in III–VII as lagging equally far behind the procession. As suggested above, that is a formal arrangement and might be reversed. Both of these timing groups must later be considered series by series, and more discriminating judgments formed concerning their roles in the business-cycle complex.

4) The descriptions of series in the table are exceedingly general, but I hope they suggest the character of the business factors that lead or lag. That should suffice for the present. No attempt is made to explain why the series behave as they do, but anyone who goes over the entries thoughtfully will find his mind seething with rationalizations, and with conjectures

Table 5

ECONOMIC CHARACTER OF SERIES THAT LEAD OR LAG
AT REFERENCE-CYCLE TROUGHS AND PEAKS[a]

TROUGHS

Leads	*Lags*
TWO-STAGE LEADS	TWO-STAGE LAGS
Neutral Series $(6\frac{1}{2})$[b]	Neutral Series $(18\frac{1}{2})$[b]
1 new orders	6 bank reserves (not ratios) and
1 construction contracts	ratios of loans to deposits
4 bank investments and deposits	$5\frac{1}{2}$ bond yields
$\frac{1}{2}$ bond prices	3 bank suspensions
	4 scattering
Positive Series (25)	Positive Series (8)
13 bank holdings of lawful money,	$5\frac{1}{2}$ interest rates or bond yields
loans, investments, interbank or	1 locomotive shipments
individual deposits	$1\frac{1}{2}$ scattering
12 investment (mainly early stages):	
security issues, orders, contracts,	
production of building materials	
Inverted Series (6)	Inverted Series $(2\frac{1}{2})$
3 ratios of loans to deposits, and	Orders for rails, bond prices, im-
reserve ratios	ports of coffee
3 liabilities of commercial failures	
ONE-STAGE LEADS	ONE-STAGE LAGS
Positive Series $(120\frac{1}{2})$	Positive Series (31)
$52\frac{1}{2}$ investment (mainly early stages):	4 bank holdings of lawful money,
security issues, orders, contracts,	and ratios of loans to deposits
production of building materials	$5\frac{1}{2}$ interest rates or bond yields
and other durables	$15\frac{1}{2}$ commodity prices
10 bank loans, interbank or indi-	1 vessels under construction
vidual deposits	5 scattering
10 bank clearings or indexes of busi-	
ness activity	
7 stock exchange transactions or	
prices	
7 commodity prices	
$11\frac{1}{2}$ production of semidurables	
4 inventories	
$18\frac{1}{2}$ scattering	
Inverted Series (12)	Inverted Series (10)
7 bank note circulation and reserve	3 bank reserve ratios and lawful
ratios	money holdings
2 liabilities and number of failures	1 bond sales
3 scattering	1 exports of raw cotton
	3 inventories
	2 prices, wheat and wheat flour

Total number of leads: 170   *Total number of lags:* 70

[a] The fractions occur because a few series fit equally well two of our standard varieties of timing.

Table 5 (concl.)

PEAKS

Leads	*Lags*

TWO-STAGE LEADS

Neutral Series (6½)[b]
    Same as two-stage, neutral, leads
    at troughs

TWO-STAGE LAGS

Neutral Series (18½)[b]
    Same as two-stage, neutral, lags at
    troughs

Positive Series (4½)
  2 stock exchange transactions and
    prices
  1 orders for steel sheets
  1 consumption of tobacco
  ½ prices, brick

Positive Series (6)
  4 bank loans and ratios of loans
    to deposits
  1 vessels under construction
  1 payrolls, bakeries

No Inverted Series

Inverted Series (4)
  1 bank holdings of lawful money
  1 bond sales
  2 prices, wheat and wheat flour

ONE-STAGE LEADS

Positive Series (88½)
  25 are same as 25 two-stage, posi-
    tive, leads at troughs
  32 investment (mainly early stages):
    orders, contracts, security issues,
    production of building materials
    and other durables
  6 stock exchange transactions or
    prices
  4 bank clearings or indexes of busi-
    ness activity
  7½ prices of commodities
  14 scattering

ONE-STAGE LAGS

Positive Series (82½)
  8 are same as 8 two-stage, positive,
    lags at troughs
  9 investment (mainly late stages):
    production and employment in
    durable goods industries, con-
    struction in process, contracts,
    security issues
  9 hourly wages, weekly earnings,
    payrolls
  4 bank loans and investments
  17½ consumer goods: production,
    employment, trade
  22 prices of commodities
  3½ interest rates, short-term
  9½ scattering

Inverted Series (15)
  5 bank note circulation, ratios of
    loans to deposits, reserve ratios
  2 bond yields
  1 prices, newsprint paper
  3 inventories
  4 liabilities or number of failures

Inverted Series (10½)
  5 bank holdings of lawful money,
    ratios of loans to deposits, re-
    serve ratios
  1 orders for rails
  1 prices, bananas
  2 inventories
  1 imports, coffee
  ½ bond prices

Total number of leads: 114½

Total number of lags: 121½

[b] See Table 4, note *c.*

regarding the effects produced by the recorded movements.

Especially noteworthy are the readjustments in banking conditions that occur in contraction, and the opposite movements in expansion. In good part they are inverted movements entered as lags at peaks and also at troughs. In contraction these movements pave the way for and directly contribute toward the revival in financial activities, many of which antedate cyclical turns in the processes of producing and distributing commodities and personal incomes. In expansions the early banking changes are precursors of recessions. No one should be disturbed by the fact that a given banking item sometimes appears in the column for leads and also in the opposite column for lags. Often the explanation is that one entry refers to banks in the financial centers, the other to banks in 'country districts'. Sometimes the explanation is of a technical sort: a two-stage lead of an inverted series at reference troughs means that it reached a peak in stage VII, and a two-stage lag of a neutral series at reference troughs implies exactly the same thing.

Closely associated with banking leads at troughs is the early upturn in preparations for investing capital—issuing corporate securities, placing orders for durable goods, entering into contracts for construction work, and the like. Such actions do not mean an immediate increase in employment and production, though the statistical record indicates that the output of some building materials responds promptly. In general, these preliminaries to the actual investment of capital lead also at recession, though seemingly by shorter intervals.

Other early signs of change are the decline after stage VII in the number of bank suspensions and the liabilities (not the number) of commercial failures; likewise their rise after stages III or IV. Stock market transactions and prices follow suit a little later, rising before the trough in general business activity is reached and falling before the peak; so also do bank clearings in New York City and in less measure outside clearings. The latter leads, however, are not so numerous at peaks as at troughs.

Among lags at troughs, the most notable are bond yields and

interest rates. More than twice as many commodity prices lag as lead, whereas a substantial minority of our series on production lead and only two lag, both representing the execution of plans for investment entered into much earlier. Another interesting group of lags relates to banking—the amounts of 'lawful money' held by national banks, ratios of loans to deposits and of reserves to demand liabilities.

Lags at peaks are much more numerous than at troughs. Interest rates, bond yields, bank loans and their ratios to deposits, lawful money holdings, reserve ratios, and commodity prices reappear—the list of prices increased by half. They are joined by series representing the execution of plans for investing, wage rates, weekly earnings, payroll disbursements, and numerous series on the production and distribution of consumer goods. Rising trends combined with moderate cyclical movements are responsible for many of these lags.

Doubtless the reader has noticed that the leads reported in Table 4 and classified roughly in Table 5 outnumber the lags by over two to one at reference-cycle troughs, whereas at peaks the lags are slightly more numerous than leads. If we omitted the neutral series, which may be called 'ambivalent', the contrast between the two turns as pictured by our measures of characteristic timing would be yet more striking. To what is the contrast due?

Probably in part—I think small part—to errors in our choices of reference dates. As explained in Chapter 4 of *Measuring Business Cycles*, these dates were determined by studying arrays of the specific-cycle troughs and peaks in numerous series, making due allowances for what we knew about their conformity to business cycles, their relative scopes, their secular trends, their timing propensities, and other traits. As a rule, these arrays are less compact at troughs than at peaks. Hence it is usually more difficult to date the ebb of contraction than the crest of expansion. Since our present chronology was drawn up, we have had occasion to reexamine our reference dates since World War I, and now believe that two trough dates should be put earlier, one by a single month, the other by two months, while a third trough date should be set a month later.[13] No change in peak dates seems necessary. The relative scarcity of data for earlier years makes equally intensive work impossible before 1919, but a careful consideration of all the series we now have in the light of our fuller knowledge of cyclical behavior will doubtless lead to further revisions. Whatever alterations are finally made will certainly affect the *monthly* leads, coincidences, and lags ascertained by comparing specific-cycle with reference-cycle troughs. What effect they will have upon the measures of characteristic cyclical timing is harder to gauge. One month is a minor fraction of most reference-cycle stages, and reference-date shifts of that length will probaby cause few alterations in the stages already chosen to represent the expansions characteristic of a series. It would take a heavy preponderance of backward shifts of at least two or three months to make the lags at the troughs equal the leads in number.[14]

A second factor in causing leads to outnumber lags at the troughs is our concept that, ideally, the reference dates should mark the 'culminations' of expansions and contractions in 'general business activity'. That is, a peak should show the last month before this rather nebulous congeries enters a sustained contraction, and a trough should mark the last month before a sustained expansion starts. When the expansion culminates in a flat top, or in two approximately equal peaks separated by a brief interval, we choose, not the central month in this time of hesitation, but the final month. The same rule with the proper reversals of terms applies to contractions. Obviously, this rule tends to place our turning dates in months that are more often

[13] See note to Table 1.

[14] Subsequent studies by G. H. Moore indicate that revisions of reference dates prior to 1919 will shift more of the troughs back than forward, will shift more of the troughs than the peaks, and will shift about as many peaks one way as the other. However, such revisions will not eliminate the difference in the distribution of timing observations at peaks and troughs. See Moore's "Statistical Indicators of Cyclical Revivals and Recessions" (National Bureau, *Occasional Paper 31*).

preceded than followed by specific-cycle turns, and tends also to make leads average longer than lags.

Both tendencies are clearly revealed by our measures of characteristic cyclical timing at troughs. If we omit the ambivalent neutral series, the leads outnumber lags by about three to one; the two-stage leads number 31, the two-stage lags 10.5. But at peaks these tendencies are virtually counteracted by other influences. Positive and inverted leads number 108, while lags number 103; two-stage leads number 4½, two-stage lags number 10. Now this difference between troughs and peaks is not due to the rule that we shall date 'culminations', for that rule is applied to both turns. It is due mainly to a difference between peaks and troughs in the average character of the arrays of specific-cycle turning dates to which the rule is applied. At the peak these arrays on the average are relatively compact and symmetrical; at the trough the arrays are more dispersed and skewed toward leads. The differences between the arrays mean that what happens at revivals is not a replica in reverse of what happens at recessions. The economic conditions that encourage men to expand operations at the culmination of contraction are not direct opposites of conditions that force men to contract operations at the culmination of expansion. Other measures will confirm and amplify what the varieties of cyclical timing suggest.

VII Summary, Doubts, and the Next Step

A pause to reflect upon what we have done so far will make clearer what we have next to do. To begin once more at the beginning: we assumed on the basis of sketchy evidence that business cycles consist of "expansions occurring at about the same time in many economic activities, followed by similarly general recessions, contractions, and revivals". Our first tasks were obviously to determine whether this basic assumption is valid, and, if so, to replace the vague phrases 'about the same time' and 'many economic activities' by more definite statements. Toward these ends we collected as large and varied a sample of time series as our means allowed, identified the specific cycles in these series by the dates of their troughs and peaks, and from the clusters found in specific-cycle turns derived reference dates purporting to show when business-cycle expansions and contractions culminated. By applying this chronology to the series of our sample we could find out what activities have risen in business-cycle expansions and fallen in contractions. As in measuring other behavior traits, we wanted to ascertain what cyclical timing is 'characteristic' of each series. By studying the timing of a series in successive reference cycles, we formed judgments concerning the group of consecutive stages over which the cyclical movement was upward and the stages over which the cyclical movement was downward, or, when no sustained decline occurred, the stages over which the rise was accelerated and the stages over which the rise was retarded.

It is these judgments that we have just been summarizing, then reviewing in some detail. The findings reveal, not uniformity of cyclical timing, but as wide a diversity as our analysis allows. All of our 25 varieties of timing except one are represented by at least two series in the present sample, and any day some new series may pop into the 'empty box' (expansion in stages III–VIII, contraction in VIII–III).

Numerous as the varieties of cyclical timing are, they form a rather orderly array, as Chart 2 shows. Very much the commonest kind coincides neatly with business cycles—expansion in stages I–V, contraction in V–IX. Nearly 44 percent of all series in our sample belong in this group. That is still a minority. But many other series rise characteristically in one or more of the stages dominated by business-cycle expansion, and fall characteristically in the stages dominated by contraction. If we count all the series that move in successive stages with the cyclical tides, we get substantial majorities of our sample. During the 4 stages of expansion, 74, 77, 78, and 69 percent of all series characteristically rise; during the 4 stages of contraction, 68, 77, 76, and 63 percent characteristically fall. The phrases 'many economic activities' and 'about the same time' in our basic definition are made less vague by these percentages. But the word 'characteristically' now requires clarification, which will be offered in the next chapter.

Even the figures just given considerably understate the extent to which business cycles dominate the American economy. For when we examine the series that lead or lag at the troughs and peaks of business cycles, the neutral series that move half of the time with and half of the time counter to the general tides, and the series that move inversely in all or a majority of stages, we can often ascribe their characteristic timing to the impact of business cycles upon the economic activities represented. To account for the timing of any series we have to know something, the more the better, about the conditions under which the activity it records is conducted. The incompleteness of the preceding explanations is due partly to my ignorance, and partly to the desirability of postponing complicated analyses. Pending the appearance of evidence to the contrary, I shall assume that every variety of *characteristic* timing means that the cyclical movements of the activities represented are dominated by business-cycle expansions and contractions. On this hypothesis, 89 percent of our series should be thought of as typically swayed by the cyclical tides throughout reference cycles. Only in the 11 percent of irregular series do cyclical influences fail to dominate the short-run movements.

Objection may well be raised to this blunt statement. It suggests argument in a circle. First we define business cycles as a congeries of roughly synchronous expansions in many activities followed by similarly general contractions; then we attribute the cyclical movements in a large majority of individual series to the cyclical tides, which are merely a summation of movements in individual series.

At best, the phrases I have used are elliptical; but I think this is also the worst that can be said against them. When the analysis is written out in full it becomes a long chain of commonplace observations upon familiar experiences. Department stores sell more goods in expansion because income payments to individuals have increased. Less butter is produced because families buy more milk as their incomes rise; the flow of milk cannot be increased as rapidly as consumption grows, so less milk is turned into butter. Essentially similar reasoning can be extended to all sectors of the economy. Every enterprise finds its customers among other enterprises, or among individuals who are receiving wages, rent, interest, dividends, or profits. If we accept the statement that a national economy is a system of interrelated parts, we must accept the corollary that every part is influenced by changes in other parts. Expansion in activity X tends to produce expansions in certain activities but contractions in others; in some directions the effects are vigorous, in others slight; some effects are felt immediately, even anticipated, while others are spread over considerable periods or long delayed; the influences exerted by X are nullified in some sectors by opposing factors, in other sectors they are unopposed or even reinforced by special conditions; whatever effects the expansion in X produces will presently react upon X itself, these reactions will differ in the ways suggested, and the new changes thus produced in X will set going a new wave of repercussions upon other activities. X stands for any activity; the reasoning is general. But in thinking about business cycles, we should not invoke a *ceteris paribus* clause. Never do the cyclical fluctuations spread through the economy without being reinforced and also opposed by noncyclical factors, some of which can be identified and accounted for. To follow the complicated interactions in detail exceeds the power of economic analysis; however, given adequate statistical records, we can ascertain the general outcome by empirical observation.

That is what we have done by assembling our measures of characteristic cyclical timing. It is not surprising to find that the bulk of the activities represented by our sample of time series fluctuate in unison. Nor is it surprising to find that many of the positive series lead or lag at business-cycle troughs and peaks, or that some series have neutral timing, or that others characteristically move counter to the general tides, or that an appreciable number reveal no regular relation in time to business cycles. Indeed, these differences of characteristic timing make it easier to grasp the way in which business cycles propagate (I do not say cause) themselves. But that is a later part of the complicated story.

Meanwhile we should note that the interpretation here put upon neutral and inverted timing, as well as on the leads and lags of positive series, suggests a revision of our basic definition. If our sample is representative, business cycles consist not only of roughly synchronous expansions in many activities, followed by roughly synchronous contractions in a slightly smaller number; they consist also of numerous contractions while expansion is dominant, and numerous expansions while contraction is dominant. This amendment might have proved confusing had we thought of adopting it at the outset of our study; later it will prove clarifying.

The next step concerns the representative value of the timing measures themselves. As explained in Chapter 3, our indexes of conformity measure the regularity with which series rise between the first and last of the stages thought to be characteristic of their expansions, and the regularity of their behavior during the stages when we think they characteristically decline. The best way to appraise our judgments of characteristic timing is to examine these conformity indexes.

CHAPTER 6

Degrees of Conformity to Business Cycles

I Numerical Values of the Conformity Indexes

Table 6 and Chart 3 offer evidence concerning the trustworthiness of the measures of 'characteristic' cyclical timing described in Chapter 5.

We shall save time by recalling what was said in Chapter 3 about conformity indexes before trying to interpret the table and chart. (1) In making the indexes of conformity, a series is first divided into stages characteristic of its own expansions and contractions. (2) Its index of conformity to reference expansions shows the consistency of movement from cycle to cycle during the stages matched with reference expansions. (3) Similarly, the contraction index shows the consistency of movement during the stages matched with reference contractions. (4) While the two phase indexes relate to consistency only in direction of change, the business-cycle index shows the consistency of *differences* in response to expansion and to contraction. Like the phase indexes, it is limited to direction of movement when the directions in the two phases differ; it compares *rates* of change when the direction is the same. (5) These indexes are percentages of conforming movements not offset by nonconformities. Ordinary percentages of conforming movements would run on a higher level. If a 10-cycle series rises in its characteristic expansion stages in 9 cycles and falls in 1 cycle, our expansion index is $(900 - 100) \div 10 = 80$; the percentage of conforming movements is 90. If we disregard zero entries, indexes of 50 are equivalent to conformity percentages of 75, indexes of 33 to percentages of 67, and indexes of 0 to percentages of 50. (6) When the number of cycles covered by a series is small, our indexes can assume only a few values separated by wide intervals. With 4 cycles, for example, the pos-

Table 6

Two Summaries of the Numerical Values of Conformity Indexes of 794 Monthly or Quarterly Series

RANGE, DECILES, AND QUARTILES OF ARRAYS OF INDEXES, TAKEN WITHOUT REGARD TO SIGN				PERCENTAGE DISTRIBUTION OF BUSINESS-CYCLE INDEXES BY SIGN AND NUMERICAL VALUE			
Extreme & Partition Values	Indexes of Conformity to			Numerical Value of Indexes	Indexes with		
	Ref. exp.	Ref. contr.	Bus. cycles		Plus sign	Minus sign	Either sign
(1)	(2)	(3)	(4)	(5)	(6)	(7)	(8)
Highest	100	100	100	100	35.0	1.6	36.7
9th decile	100	100	100	90–99	2.1	0.3	2.4
8th decile	100	100	100	80–89	7.3	1.5	8.8
7th decile	100	100	100	70–79	10.8	1.1	12.0
6th decile	100	69	88	60–69	6.2	1.9	8.1
Median	67	60	78	50–59	7.4	1.8	9.2
4th decile	60	50	69	40–49	3.9	1.1	5.0
3rd decile	50	40	57	30–39	4.0	1.4	5.4
2nd decile	33	25	43	20–29	2.1	2.1	4.3
1st decile	20	17	24	10–19	3.0	1.5	4.5
Lowest	0	0	0	1–9	0.8	0.8	1.5
				0	...	...	2.1
Upper quartile	100	100	100	50–100	68.9	8.2	77.1
Lower quartile	45	33	50	0–49	13.9[a]	6.9[a]	22.9[b]
Range	100	100	100	Total[c]	82.7[a]	15.1[a]	100.0[b]

[a] Excludes zeros.

[b] Includes zeros.

[c] Failure of detail to total precisely in every instance is due to rounding.

sible values of the phase indexes are plus or minus 100, 75, 50, 25, and 0. The business-cycle index, however, rests on 7 comparisons and may take these numerical values: 100, 86, 71, 57, 43, 29, 14, 0. When a series covers 20 cycles the possible numerical values of the phase indexes are 100, 95, 90, 85 ... 0, and those of the business-cycle index are 100, 97, 95, 92, 90 ... 0.[1]

Table 6 shows that the conformity indexes of our sample run the full gamut from 100 to 0. Of the 794 series, 149 have indexes of +100, +100, +100; that is, they invariably conform positively to successive reference expansions, contractions, and full cycles. Four series have indexes of −100, −100, −100. As it happens, no series has indexes of 0, 0, 0; the nearest approach is −20, 0, 0, or 0, −20, 0.

Conformity to expansion is decidedly more regular than

[1] For fuller explanations see *Measuring Business Cycles*, pp. 176–97.

Chart 3
Percentage Distribution of 794 Series According to the Numerical Value of Their Indexes of Conformity to Business Cycles

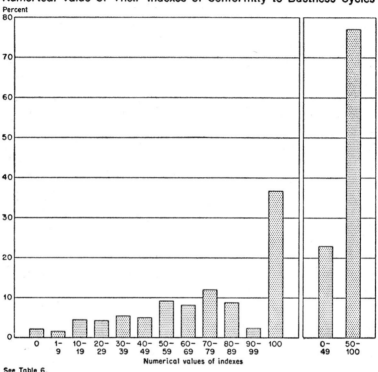

See Table 6.

conformity to contraction—a result of the prevalence of rising secular trends and of positive timing in our sample. Of course, rising trends reenforce cyclical expansions in positive series and tend to weaken their cyclical contractions.

Business-cycle indexes with plus signs outnumber those with minus signs by more than 5 to 1. This distinction is not equivalent to that between positive and inverted timing, primarily because series with irregular timing may have either plus or minus indexes. As it happens, 34 irregulars are in the plus and 40 in the minus list, while 11 have indexes of zero. Otherwise stated, about 1 in 20 of the series with plus, and 1 in 3 of the series with minus indexes are irregular conformers. Since irregularity in timing usually means a low conformity index, this distribution of the irregular series tends to depress the average of negative conformity indexes below the positive average. The mean business-cycle index for all negative series is −52, that for all positive series +76. If we exclude irregular series from both lists, these averages become −66 and +79. Even after this adjustment half of the original difference remains to be explained, a problem to which we shall return in Section IV.

The peculiar distribution of the business-cycle indexes is best seen in the chart. These indexes include fewer values of ±100 than the indexes for expansion, which, as already noted, are raised by the prevalence of positive timing and rising trends. But all the deciles in column (4) of Table 6 except one are equal to or higher than their opposite numbers in column (2). Almost 37 percent of our series conform to every business cycle they cover, and more than half of this list conform also to every expansion and every contraction. Forty-eight percent conform to full business cycles 9 or more times out of 10; 68 percent 4 or more times out of 5; 77 percent 3 or more times out of 4; and 88 percent 2 or more times out of 3.[2]

II THE PROBLEM OF BIAS IN THE INDEXES

Could they be taken at face value these findings would justify considerable confidence in the representativeness of our judgments concerning cyclical timing. But an offhand acceptance of the indexes is not warranted. They have hidden defects and merits.

1) The series that conform to business cycles less than 2 times out of 3 form 12½ percent of our sample. Nearly two-

[2] The small number of business-cycle indexes in the '90–99' column of the chart is due to the unfortunate preponderance of short series in our sample. To attain a business-cycle index in the 90's, a series must cover at least 6 cycles, must have only one lapse from perfect conformity, and that lapse must be confined to identity of direction and rate of change in one of the 11 comparisons between a contraction and the preceding or following expansion. Then the index will be $1000 \div 11 = 91$. Barring the infrequent zero entries, we need at least 11 cycles to get into the 90's (21 comparisons; 20 with plus signs, 1 with minus, or 1 plus to 20 minus; then we get $1900 \div 21 = 90$). Only 41 percent of our 794 series cover 6 or more business cycles; 18 percent cover 11 or more.

thirds of this poorly conforming group are classified as having irregular timing. A judgment that a series has irregular timing is confirmed by a *low* index. Only 6 percent of our positive, none of our neutral, and 6 percent of our inverted series conform less frequently than 2 times out of 3. Of course these observations tend to strengthen confidence.

2) On the other hand, the brevity of many series raises doubts about the significance of any decisions regarding the regularity of responses to business cycles. Granted the tendency of a series to conform, it is more likely to have a perfect record for 3 or 4 cycles than it is to continue conforming perfectly throughout a run twice or thrice as long. So, also, a record of nonconformity in a few consecutive cycles may well be spoiled if the number is doubled or tripled. Our 291 series with business-cycle indexes of ± 100, and our 17 series with business-cycle indexes of 0, both include proportionately more series covering fewer than 5 cycles and proportionately fewer series covering 10 or more cycles than does the rest of the sample. Table 7 presents the relevant figures and percentages.

If all the series in our sample could be extended backward or forward to include more cycles, and new short series were not added, it is virtually certain that the distribution of the business-cycle indexes in Chart 3 would be altered considerably. None of the 291 indexes of ± 100 could be raised; but any of them could and many of them would be lowered. The 17 indexes of 0 could not be lowered, but they could and some would be raised. All these changed indexes would fall into the intermediate group. Of course the present intermediate indexes ranging from ± 3 to ± 95 might be either raised or lowered. However, the average value of the whole sample of indexes would probably be reduced if their signs continued to be disregarded, since the average absolute value of the conformity indexes of 'irregular' series would fall as the series lengthened. The percentages of horizontal sums in Table 7 indicate what sort of effects the 'aging' of our sample would tend to produce.

In short, however sound our judgments concerning the

Table 7

SERIES WITH BUSINESS-CYCLE CONFORMITY INDEXES OF ±100, 0,
AND INTERMEDIATE VALUES CLASSIFIED BY THE NUMBER
OF BUSINESS CYCLES THEY COVER

| NO. OF CYCLES COVERED | NO. OF SERIES HAVING INDEXES OF CONFORMITY OF | | | ALL SERIES IN SAMPLE |
	±100	Intermediate values	Zero	
1– 4	119	90	8	217
5– 9	141	244	8	393
10–21	31	152	1	184
1–21	291	486	17	794

Percentages of vertical sums [a]

1– 4	40.9	18.5	47.1	27.3
5– 9	48.5	50.2	47.1	49.5
10–21	10.7	31.3	5.9	23.2
1–21	100.0	100.0	100.0	100.0

Percentages of horizontal sums [a]

1– 4	54.8	41.5	3.7	100.0
5– 9	35.9	62.1	2.0	100.0
10–21	16.8	82.6	0.5	100.0
1–21	36.6	61.2	2.1	100.0

[a] Failure of detail to total 100% is due to rounding.

timing characteristic of our series in their present form may be, these judgments do exaggerate the prevalence of perfect conformity to business cycles and may exaggerate the prevalence of zero conformity. So would judgments based upon any other sample whose compilers were more concerned to include a wide range of economic activities than to exclude recent additions to statistical records because of their brevity.

How serious this bias is we can estimate after a fashion by comparing the business-cycle indexes of the 184 series covering 10 or more cycles with the indexes of the whole sample. Chart 4, which shows the distribution of the long-series indexes, has a much lower spike at ±100 than Chart 3; also a squattier column at 0. On the other hand, 7 of the 10 intermediate columns are higher in Chart 4 than their counterparts in Chart 3. Especially marked are the increases at 90–99, 80–89, and 40–49. The median is 78 in the full sample, 68 in the sample of long series; the arithmetic means are respectively 71 and 64. Ignoring possible zero entries once more, we find that conformity prevails in 3 business cycles out of 4, or oftener, in 70 percent of the long series as contrasted with 77 percent of the full sample.[3]

3) But the relatively low conformity of the long series is due partly to a second bias, arising from defective economic coverage. This sample includes no series on retail or wholesale trade, employment, hours of work, earnings per employee, or payrolls. It gives scanty representation to production, construction work, inventories, or the issuing of securities. These two sets of groups form no less than 56 percent of our full sample and only 14 percent of the sample of long series. On the other hand, the long series give much greater weight than the full sample to prices of commodities, banking under the National Banking Act, indexes of business activity, bank clearings, bankruptcies, and imports. These groups furnish 71 per-

[3] Detailed comparisons can be made more readily from the following figures than from the chart.

DISTRIBUTION OF ALL SERIES AND OF SERIES COVERING 10 OR MORE CYCLES
ACCORDING TO INDEXES OF CONFORMITY TO BUSINESS CYCLES,
TAKEN WITHOUT REGARD TO SIGN

BUSINESS-CYCLE INDEX	LONG SERIES (% OF 184)	ALL SERIES (% OF 794)	BUSINESS-CYCLE INDEX	LONG SERIES (% OF 184)	ALL SERIES (% OF 794)
100	16.8	36.7	40–49	10.3	5.0
90–99	7.6	2.4	30–39	3.8	5.4
80–89	13.0	8.8	20–29	7.6	4.3
70–79	11.4	12.0	10–19	4.3	4.5
60–69	9.8	8.1	1– 9	3.8	1.5
50–59	10.9	9.2	0	0.5	2.1
50–100	69.6	77.1	0–49	30.4	22.9

A simpler summary is afforded by the following arithmetic means of the business-cycle indexes of conformity:

	NO. OF SERIES	MEAN INDEX	SERIES WITH INDEXES ABOVE 0 AND LESS THAN 100	
			Number	Mean Index
Full sample	794	71.1	486	56.3
Series covering 10 or more business cycles	184	64.2	152	57.3
Series covering less than 10 business cycles	610	73.2	334	55.8

It will be noted that the exclusion of series with indexes of 0 and 100 lifts the mean index of the long series from decidedly the lowest to slightly the highest rank.

Chart 4
Percentage Distribution of 184 Series
Covering 10 or More Cycles According to the
Numerical Value of Their Indexes of Conformity to Business Cycles

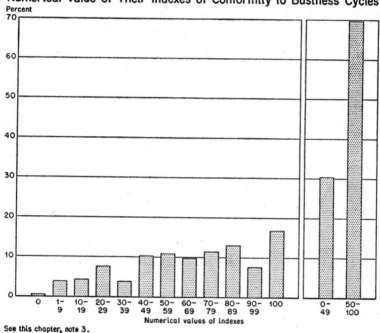

See this chapter, note 3.

cent of the long series and only 31 percent of the full sample. Though I have pointed out serious deficiencies in the economic coverage of the full sample,[4] the deficiencies in the long-series sample are more glaring. The great advances of the last generation in collecting economic statistics have been largely in processes that conform closely to business cycles—industrial production, building, employment, merchandising, and the distribution of money income, especially wages. In our sample at least, the conformity indexes of the groups not represented at all, or seriously underrepresented by the long series, average

[4] See Ch. 3, Sec. XI.

higher than the indexes of the groups that are overrepresented.[5]

Still other factors may influence the relative conformity of our samples. (4) For reasons given in the next section, index numbers and national aggregates tend to conform more closely to business cycles than do their component series on the aver-

[5] The influence exerted by differences in economic coverage upon indexes of conformity to business cycles may be illustrated by comparing the group most overrepresented in the sample of long series (commodity prices) with the group most underrepresented (production). In this comparison, differences in the number of cycles should be neutralized so far as possible. Also, series on farm products and foods should be segregated because their prices conform better to business cycles than their output, instead of less well, which is the rule among other commodities. These steps are taken in the accompanying table, and a fourth sample of price and production series is added to the three derived by dividing the full sample into long and short series. This additional sample, prepared by Geoffrey H. Moore, includes 60 commodities for which we have comparable data on prices and quantities covering in each instance identical cycles, which average 4.7 in number. The mean number of cycles covered by the full sample is 8.2 in prices and 5.6 in production; the corresponding means for the sample of long series are 12.0 and 14.1 and for the sample of short series, 5.0 and 4.7. Here, as elsewhere in this volume, certain series that reflect production indirectly, such as shipments or consumption of materials, are classified as production series.

MEAN CONFORMITY TO BUSINESS CYCLES AND THE WEIGHTING OF PRICES
AND PRODUCTION OF AGRICULTURAL AND NONAGRICULTURAL
COMMODITIES IN FOUR SAMPLES OF SERIES

		PRICES			PRODUCTION		
	ALL SERIES	Agri-cultural	Nonagri-cultural	Both	Agri-cultural	Nonagri-cultural	Both
Number of series							
Full sample	794	51	96	147	47	141	188
Long series	184	21	47	68	9	9	18
Short series	610	30	49	79	38	132	170
Matched pairs	120	18	42	60	18	42	60
Percent of number							
Full sample	100.0	6.4	12.1	18.5	5.9	17.8	23.7
Long series	100.0	11.4	25.5	37.0	4.9	4.9	9.8
Short series	100.0	4.9	8.0	13.0	6.2	21.6	27.9
Matched pairs	100.0	15.0	35.0	50.0	15.0	35.0	50.0
Mean conformity index							
Full sample	71.1	51.6	64.2	59.8	41.8	84.2	73.6
Long series	64.2	46.2	60.0	55.8	27.4	64.9	46.2
Short series	73.2	55.5	68.2	63.4	45.2	85.5	76.5
Matched pairs	66.1	52.7	71.7	66.0	36.3	79.0	66.2

When we compare the conformity of agricultural with nonagricultural series within any sample, we find the agricultural index lower in both prices

age. The long-series sample seems to have a higher ratio of such broadly inclusive series than the full sample; it is hard to be precise because inclusiveness is difficult to measure in a uniform fashion from one of our samples to another. (5) In the next chapter we shall see that the business cycles between the two world wars seem to have been more 'violent' on the average than their predecessors. The larger the amplitude of cyclical fluctuations, the more generally they stamp their pattern upon the many sectors of a national economy; that is, the more prevalent conformity tends to become. This suggestion may contain a partial explanation of the relatively high indexes of our short series.

Of these several factors, the first is most fundamental. Irregular cyclical timing is a genuine behavior trait of certain activities. As said in the preceding chapter, our sample of time series would seriously misrepresent the workings of the American economy if it did not include numerous and important series of this sort, and their low conformity indexes confirm the soundness of our judgments that the timing is irregular. Whether the 11 percent of irregular series included is too large or too small a proportion we cannot say with assurance.

---

and production. When we compare prices in any sample with production, we find that prices conform better than production in agriculture; the reverse is true in other industries. Hence, a large representation of agricultural series tends to lower the mean conformity index of a sample, and this tendency is stronger when the agricultural series are for quantities produced than for prices.

The long series have the lowest mean conformity index of the four samples, not merely because they cover more cycles than the others, but also because they include no more series on nonagricultural than on agricultural production, and many more series on prices than on production. It is the only sample in which all the production series taken together have a lower mean index than all the price series.

The sample of matched series has the next lowest index primarily because of its relatively large number of agricultural series.

Finally, we may note that differences among the samples in respect of conformity are smaller in prices than in production, whether we compare agricultural or nonagricultural commodities, or the two groups combined.

Though these observations refer specifically to the results of a single investigation, they have some interest in that they illustrate the importance of knowing the economic coverage of historical data, and the behavior characteristic of different activities.

The low conformity indexes that should concern us are confined to series we classify as having positive, neutral, or inverted timing. If we exclude all irregulars, the mean conformity index of the full sample is 77, that of the long series 70, and of the short series 79. These indexes are equivalent to conformity percentages of 88, 85, and 90. Another way of summarizing the results is to say that, if zero entries are neglected, conformity to 3 business cycles out of 4, or oftener, occurs among our regulars in 85 percent of the series in the full sample, 77 percent of the long, and 87 percent of the short series.

In choosing among the results, we prefer the lowest—that for the long series. True, we have found evidence that the economic coverage of this sample is defective in a fashion that tends toward low conformity. But this consideration is counterbalanced in part at least by what seems to be a large proportion of comprehensive series with relatively high indexes. Regular conformity in 3 or more cycles out of 4 may not be significant when the number of cycles covered by a series is small, but we think it is significant when the number exceeds 9. And that level of conformity is equaled or surpassed by more than three-quarters of our positive, neutral, and inverted series covering from 10 to 21 cycles. On the other hand, we think our short series exaggerate the prevalence of conformity, and so also does the full sample in slightly less degree.

These conclusions indicate merely the measure of confidence we may repose in indexes of conformity made by our methods from samples that include both comprehensive series and series of narrow coverage. As will be shown in the next section, we could obtain much higher average indexes if we included only broad index numbers and aggregates, somewhat higher averages if we weighted our present series by some acceptable criterion of 'importance', and we should obtain much lower averages if we used only series of limited coverage. But the effort to appraise the general economic significance of our measures belongs in Part III on 'The Consensus of Cyclical Behavior'.

III What Activities Conform Well and What Ill

Table 8 and its three 'summaries' need only a word of explanation. Signs are disregarded except in the last summary, because we have found reason to believe that inverted and neutral timing are dominated by business cycles in much the same manner as is the timing we call 'positive'. But when we classify the series by timing types, the signs are not always what the type indicates, which suggests that we strike a second set of averages in which the signs are respected. The contrast between the average indexes of the full sample computed in these two ways is instructive.

Of the 29 groups listed in Table 8, only 3 have average indexes of business-cycle conformity less than 50, which is equivalent to regularity of timing 3 times out of 4. If the reader will turn back to the discussion of irregular timing, he will find explanations of these low indexes. We expect irregular inventories to rank low in conformity, and they rank lowest.[6] Public construction work is not undertaken for profit. The production of foodstuffs is dominated by the weather.

Only 3 more groups have averages below 60, that is, a conforming frequency of less than 4 out of 5. They represent the prices of farm products and foods, which, as we have learned, conform somewhat better than output; the prices of semidurable commodities, such as textiles and leather; and that highly volatile process, the issuing of corporate stocks, notes, and bonds.

At the opposite end of the array, in the business-cycle column, 5 groups have average frequencies of conformity exceeding 19 out of 20, and 7 more groups have frequencies exceeding 9 out of 10. In only one group does every series conform perfectly to every expansion, every contraction, and

[6] The mechanical classification of inventories in the table is awkward, and should be replaced in time by an economic classification. It may be noted, however, that numerous commodities whose output is not subject to close business control in the short run are included in 'inverted inventories', though finished staples held by manufacturers also bulk large in this category.

Table 8

GROUPS OF SERIES RANKED ACCORDING TO THEIR INDEXES OF CONFORMITY TO BUSINESS CYCLES[a]

AVERAGES COMPUTED WITHOUT REGARD TO SIGN

	Group	No. of Series	Indexes of Conformity to Reference exp.	Reference contr.	Business cycles
1	Inventories, irregular timing	18	35	31	24
2	Construction contracts, public	16	54	28	32
3	Production, foodstuffs	47	44	43	42
4	Prices, farm products & foods	51	41	42	52
5	Prices, semidurables	18	35	46	52
6	Security issues, corporate	14	75	48	55
7	Prices, perishables other than foods	22	50	61	63
8	Inventories, inverted timing	24	53	57	64
9	Prices, durables	45	48	68	65
10	Bond yields & other long-term interest rates	12	39	42	66
11	Inventories, positive timing	18	64	68	69
12	Payrolls, perishable goods industries	8	70	71	76
13	Interest rates, short-term	11	38	71	77
14	Employment, semidurable goods industries	13	85	69	77
15	Employment, perishable goods industries	8	62	85	78
16	Payrolls, semidurable goods industries	13	85	75	78
17	Production, semidurables	29	80	64	79
18	Production, durables	57	76	75	82
19	Retail sales	10	88	49	82
20	Production, perishables other than foods	29	92	57	83
21	Bank clearings or debits	8	100	49	83
22	New orders from manufacturers	17	68	85	86
23	Construction contracts, private	26	80	81	87
24	Wholesale sales	15	77	72	87
25	Earnings per week, month, or year	10	85	55	94
26	Employment, durable goods industries	9	87	96	98
27	Indexes of business activity	11	99	97	99
28	Payrolls, durable goods industries	6	93	100	100
29	Hours of work per week	9	100	100	100

Summaries

All series on

	Prices of commodities	147	44	56	60
	Construction contracts or permits	58	74	60	71
	Production	188	74	65	74
	Payrolls & other income payments	30	84	78	84
	Employment	37	81	83	87

All series on

	Prices of commodities or services	168	47	55	61
	Financial activities	135	72	52	73
	Flow of commodities, services, or income	478	73	65	74
	General business activity	13	99	87	98

All series in sample		794	68	61	71

[a] The 29 groups include 574 series. Omitted are groups consisting of only a very few series, large groups of such miscellaneous character that an average would have little meaning, and groups consisting of broad indexes that overlap subdivisions. The first set of summaries includes series of the last type. The second set of summaries includes all series in the sample (see Table 3).

Table 8 (concl.)

AVERAGES COMPUTED WITH REGARD TO SIGN

Summaries	No. of Series	Indexes of Conformity to		
		Reference exp.	Reference contr.	Business cycles
All series with				
Irregular timing	85[b]	+14	−9	0
Inverted timing	77[c]	−48	−55	−68
Neutral timing	24	+74	+45	+75
Positive timing	608[d]	+73	+62	+78
All series in sample	794	+55	+43	+55

[b] Includes one series analyzed in part as positive.

[c] Includes one series analyzed also as neutral.

[d] Includes two odd cases: rail orders (see note 7) and one series analyzed also as neutral.

every full cycle. That group is composed of 9 series on hours of labor per week, covering only 4 cycles. The next group in rank, payrolls in durable goods industries, consists of six 5-cycle series. In the long run, the indexes of business activity, all except two of which already cover 10 or more cycles, presumably will take the lead. Only 2 of the 11 fall short of perfect records—Carl Snyder's 'index of deposits activity' (VIII–IV: +88, +75, +94), and the Axe-Houghton 'index of trade and industrial activity' unadjusted for trend (I–V: +100, +88, +100).

The summaries indicate that, despite the low record of farming, production conforms more faithfully than prices, employment and payrolls more faithfully than production. When we put together all series that represent the producing and distributing of goods—including such services as transportation and merchandising—average conformity is higher than in the best corresponding aggregate we can make for commodity prices, wage rates, and freight rates.

The final summary, average indexes of timing groups, which be it noted again are computed with regard to signs, meets expectations. Zero conformity to business cycles on the average among irregular series; negative and relatively modest conformity among inverted series, which swim against the cyclical tides most or all of the time; decidedly higher conformity among the two varieties of neutral series, both of which swim half of the time with and half against the cyclical tides; finally,

the highest indexes among positive series, which swim with
the tides except when they are leading or lagging—these results
seem so natural that the explanation to be offered in a moment
may strike the reader as superfluous.

Of course all these averages would be a little or considerably
higher if they were made like the others in Table 8. The largest
increase would appear in the irregular group, but disregard of
signs would raise its mean business-cycle index only to 23.
Even the positive group would be affected, for of its 608 series[7]
4 have low negative indexes of conformity to business cycles
—a paradoxical but not a nonsensical result, since a variety of
considerations sways our timing decisions in marginal instances.[8]

Of the two averages for the whole sample of 794 series, we
rate the one made without regard to signs as far more significant. Even the smaller of the business-cycle indexes, $+55$, is
equivalent to 77 percent of positive conformities. But if we
think that characteristic inversions are cyclical in origin, that
the same is true of neutral timing, and that irregular series can
be taken at whatever values their indexes assume, we must
accept the higher index, 71, as a better expression of the average
regularity with which our sample responds to business cycles.
This figure, however, is slightly swollen by ignoring signs of
'irregular' series and by permitting a few minus indexes of
'positive' series to count as if they were plus. These difficulties
can be removed by casting an average in still another way;
that is, by striking an algebraic mean of all conformity indexes
in our sample after the signs of series classified as 'inverted'
have been reversed. On this basis the average business-cycle

[7] Table 4 gives 607 series in the positive group; but we have analyzed one
series, orders of rails, on a positive basis although its characteristic expansion
stages, VI–III, are inverted according to our rules.

[8] For example, the index of farm prices of crops is treated as a positive
series, but its business-cycle conformity index is -11. The index is based
on the period 1910–14, 1921–38, the war cycles being omitted. If the cycles during 1914–21 had been included, the conformity index would mount to $+29$.
And even this value fails to indicate that the lapses from conformity occur
predominantly during mild cyclical phases.

index comes out 69, which means a conforming percentage of 84.[9] These figures are the best estimates we can now frame of the average regularity with which the series in our sample have responded to business cycles.

IV Factors Influencing Degree of Conformity

Of the factors influencing conformity to business cycles, logically the most basic and perhaps practically the most important cropped up in our examination of irregular timing. We cannot expect any activity to respond regularly to business cycles unless it is subject to man's control within the periods occupied by cyclical phases, and unless this control is swayed, consciously or not, by short-period economic considerations. The domination of harvests by weather, the 'migratory property' of petroleum underground, the mixed motives of governments in undertaking construction work, the long-range planning that weighs with many men in a position to set 'administered prices', the time-consuming negotiations that prevent prompt adjustments of certain other prices and many wage rates, the existence of long-term contracts, the years required to complete some large undertakings—these are concrete examples of the multifarious obstacles that interfere with prompt and regular response to the cyclical tides. My negatively stated proposition about the basic importance of short-period control on business lines is a blatant matter of course that thrusts itself upon one's attention in a realistic inquiry, but has not been given its due place in economic theorizing.

Another factor affecting conformity cropped up first near the beginning of the chapter when we observed the values of conformity indexes with plus and minus signs. Even after we had excluded all series with irregular timing from both groups, we found mean business-cycle indexes of +79 and −66. The same factor cropped up again when I spoke surreptitiously of "relatively modest conformity among inverted series, which swim against the cyclical tides most or all of the time", and of

[9] The average expansion index is 64 and the average contraction index is 53; the corresponding conformity percentages are 82 and 77.

high conformity among positive series "which swim with the tides". If inverted and neutral timing are due no less than positive timing to the impact of business cycles upon certain activities, why should the countermovements be less regular than movements with the cyclical tides?

An answer is suggested by conflicts among the numerous cyclical influences that impinge upon every segment of an economy in which business enterprise prevails. To take a large-scale example: a cyclical expansion in employment brings higher family incomes and so encourages larger expenditures; but expansion brings also higher prices, which tend to restrict purchases. Both of these conflicting influences affect the demand for most consumer goods. The outcome is usually a rise in purchases. We noted, however, in Chapter 5, Section III that expansion has another effect: it tends to shift demand toward goods of higher quality and away from cheap staples. This influence appears to decide the issue against an increase in the purchases of such staples as pork, flour, coffee, and potatoes. But in none of these instances is the inversion so regular as the positive conformity of the more costly articles toward which demand shifts. Somewhat similar reasoning applies to the contrast between the relatively low inverted conformity of note issues of national banks and the higher positive conformity of their deposits; also to the contrast between the inverted conformity of bond sales on the New York Stock Exchange and the higher positive conformity of stock sales. In general, influences that tend to repress an activity in expansion encounter more opposition than influences favoring an increase, and when repressing influences win out, their victories are less regular from cycle to cycle than the victories won by influences that push upward. *Mutatis mutandis*, the like holds true in contraction.

A third factor affecting the conformity of time series is the volume and variety of the activities they severally represent. Inclusive indexes and national aggregates tend to conform more closely to business cycles than do their components. By way of illustration, Table 9 contrasts the average conformity

Table 9

AVERAGE CONFORMITY OF GROUPS OF SERIES COMPARED WITH
CONFORMITY OF INCLUSIVE INDEXES OR AGGREGATES

GROUPS	No. of Series	Mean Index of Conformity[a] to		
		Reference exp.	Reference contr.	Business cycles
Prices of commodities	147	44	56	60
Construction contracts[b]	58	74	60	71
Production	188	74	65	74
Payrolls[c]	30	84	78	84
Employment	37	81	83	87

INCLUSIVE SERIES[d]	Index of Conformity to		
	Reference exp.	Reference contr.	Business cycles
Index of wholesale prices, 'all' commodities	+64	+82	+100
Construction contracts, total, value	+71	+50	+86
Index of industrial production	+100	+100	+100
Index of factory payrolls	+100	+100	+100
Index of factory employment	+100	+100	+100

[a] The group indexes are computed without regard to sign.
[b] Includes building permits.
[c] Includes a series on total income payments.
[d] For sources of data, see Appendix B.

indexes of the 5 broad groups in the first summary of Table 8 with the corresponding indexes of the most inclusive series in each group. Of course the rule is not invariable, especially when the group includes both positive and inverted series, and the average group index is computed without regard to sign. The rule may fail also because of differences between an even-weighted average of series and the formal or implicit weighting of the comprehensive index or aggregate. But the prevalence of the rule is deducible from the logic of time series analysis such as we practice. Cyclical and irregular movements are inter-twined in our data. While a few of the movements classified as irregular, such as those produced by major wars, influence the whole economy, most of them are virtually peculiar to certain areas, markets, industries, enterprises, or individuals. Our method of segregating cyclical behavior from these hap-hazard changes relies upon averaging. The wider the variety of activities included in a series, the more mutual offsetting will occur among irregular movements of less than economy-wide incidence.

This point is of more than technical interest. First, it sets a limit upon our observations of cyclical behavior. As we press deeper and deeper into the detail of economic activities in an effort to grasp economic problems as they confront the man on the street, our view of cyclical movements is obscured by a thicker and thicker cloud of random happenings. The United States Steel Corporation is so huge and makes such a variety of products that its record of unfilled orders conforms perfectly to business cycles. We should not expect that to be true of the unfilled orders of a small concern building one type of machine tools. Still less could we expect the sales of a corner grocery or the income of an individual carpenter to obey faithfully the cyclical tides.

Further, the conditions that obstruct observation of cyclical fluctuations in records of small units explain why businessmen have been slow to grasp the importance of business cycles. In looking back over his own experience, or that of his associates and competitors, the average man rightly concludes that personal factors and conditions peculiar to his industry or locality have had more to do with success and failure than the general tides of expansion and contraction. One who has acquired self-assurance from minding his own business with profit often generalizes his personal experience, and concludes wrongly that recurrent cycles are at worst a figment of the academic imagination and at best a minor factor in practice. Doubtless, this skeptical attitude is becoming less common. The secular trend toward closer integration of the economy is laggingly followed by a secular trend toward a fuller realization of our dependence upon one another's fortunes. About this trend twines a cyclical curve of popular interest in business cycles that falls during expansions and rises during contractions. Yet there is still almost as much need of broadcasting what is known about business cycles as there is of lifting that knowledge to a scientific level. A factor that affects the fortunes of millions in much the same way, though almost always in secondary degree, has far greater significance to the nation than any one of the numberless factors that seem, and are, of decisive importance to individuals taken one at a time.

A fourth factor influencing conformity is the amplitude of the cyclical movements characteristic of different series. The larger this amplitude, the higher tend to be the indexes of conformity. Conversely, the more closely a series conforms to business cycles, the larger tends to be the amplitude of its reference-cycle pattern. These complex relations are explored in the next chapter, which will borrow from and add to what we have learned about cyclical timing.

CHAPTER 7

Varieties of Reference-Cycle Amplitude

I RANGE AND DISTRIBUTION OF AMPLITUDES

Reference-cycle amplitudes are tied closely to our judgments about cyclical timing and the indexes of conformity. Having decided in what stages the reference-cycle pattern of a series typically reaches its trough and peak, we compute three amplitude measures from the average standings of the series in its typical peak and trough stages: (1) for the phase matched with reference expansion, (2) for the phase matched with reference contraction, and (3) for the two phases combined.[1] The last measure is the arithmetic sum of the phase movements when one is a rise and the other a fall. It is the difference between the phase movements when both are advances or both are declines; for, when a series either rises or falls during both expansions and contractions, the influence of business cycles upon its behavior is limited to accelerating the movement in one of the phases and retarding it in the other. A plus sign prefixed to the expansion or to the full-cycle amplitude indicates positive and a minus sign indicates inverted conformity; but a minus sign prefixed to the contraction amplitude indicates positive and a plus sign inverted conformity.

Table 10 and Chart 5, which summarize the amplitude measures, correspond to Table 6 and Chart 3, which summarize the indexes of conformity. While the numerical value of conformity indexes cannot fall below 0 or rise above 100, amplitudes have a lower but not an upper limit. How radically the two measures differ in their distribution is most readily seen by comparing the two charts. Over a third of the conformity indexes are concentrated at the extreme upper limit of their possible range; the heaviest concentration of amplitudes occurs near to the lower limit. More than two-thirds of the amplitudes

[1] In general, $(3) = (1) - (2)$, all signs regarded.

100

fall in the range 0–49, and another fifth in 50–99. Yet the 13 percent of the amplitudes of 100 or more run to such high values that the arithmetic mean stands well above the median of the array, whereas the mean of the conformity indexes is lower than the median.

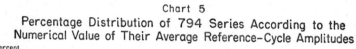

Chart 5

Percentage Distribution of 794 Series According to the Numerical Value of Their Average Reference-Cycle Amplitudes

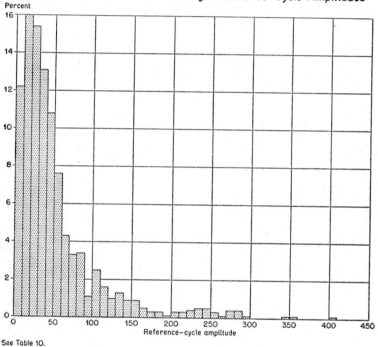

See Table 10.

II THE PROBLEM OF BIAS

The number of cycles covered by a series has no such technical influence upon its amplitude as upon the numerical value of its conformity index. But the fact that so many of our series are confined to the years between the two world wars, or a part of that unsettled period, raises the question whether this small sample of cycles presents unusually violent or unusually mild fluctuations. We can answer with confidence that it presents both. For example, the contraction of 1926–27 was exceptionally mild, that of 1929–33 exceptionally severe; the expansion of 1921–23 was much more vigorous than that of 1927–29. All in all, the average amplitudes of the 5 reference cycles in 1919–38, and of the 4 in 1921–38, seem to exceed those of the

Table 10

SUMMARIES OF AVERAGE REFERENCE-CYCLE AMPLITUDES OF 794 MONTHLY OR QUARTERLY SERIES[a]

RANGE, DECILES, AND QUARTILES OF ARRAYS

	Average Reference-Cycle Amplitude			
	Expansion (signs regarded)	Contraction (signs regarded)	Full cycle Signs regarded	Full cycle Signs disregarded
Lowest (in contraction, highest)	−122.9	+126.1	−249.0	0.2
1st decile	−4.7	+8.6	−10.8	8.2
2nd "	+3.5	−0.3	+6.7	15.1
3rd "	+7.8	−5.6	+16.0	21.2
4th "	+11.7	−9.9	+22.9	27.4
Median	+16.7	−14.2	+30.4	34.3
6th decile	+22.0	−18.7	+39.2	42.4
7th "	+27.1	−24.0	+49.6	53.5
8th "	+35.1	−33.0	+67.6	71.2
9th "	+53.6	−54.7	+106.8	111.2
Highest (in contraction, lowest)	+187.6	−219.0	+400.3	400.3
Lower quartile	+5.4	−2.9	+11.8	17.6
Upper quartile	+30.2	−27.7	+54.7	59.7
Range: Lowest to highest	310.5	345.1	649.3	400.1
Central four-fifths	58.3	63.3	117.6	103.0
Central three-fifths	31.6	32.7	60.9	56.1
Central two-fifths	19.3	18.4	33.6	32.3
Central fifth	10.3	8.8	16.3	15.0
Interquartile	24.8	24.8	42.9	42.1

PERCENTAGE DISTRIBUTION OF AVERAGE FULL-CYCLE AMPLITUDES, SIGNS DISREGARDED

Amplitude	%	Amplitude	%	Amplitude	%	Amplitude	%
0– 9.9	12.2	100–109.9	2.5	200–209.9	0.3	300–309.9	...
10–19.9	16.0	110–119.9	1.6	210–219.9	0.3	310–319.9	...
20–29.9	15.4	120–129.9	1.0	220–229.9	0.4	320–329.9	...
30–39.9	13.1	130–139.9	1.3	230–239.9	0.5	330–339.9	...
40–49.9	10.8	140–149.9	0.9	240–249.9	0.5	340–349.9	0.1
50–59.9	7.6	150–159.9	0.9	250–259.9	0.3	350–359.9	0.1
60–69.9	4.3	160–169.9	0.5	260–269.9	0.1	360–369.9	...
70–79.9	3.3	170–179.9	0.3	270–279.9	0.4	370–379.9	...
80–89.9	3.4	180–189.9	0.3	280–289.9	0.4	380–389.9	...
90–99.9	1.1	190–199.9	0.1	290–299.9	0.1	390–399.9	...
						400–409.9	0.1
0–99.9	87.2	100–199.9	9.3	200–299.9	3.1	300–409.9	0.4

[a] 'Signs disregarded' means that the sign is dropped *after* the average reference-cycle amplitude of a series is computed.

Table 10 (concl.)

MEANS AND MEDIANS OF AVERAGE FULL-CYCLE AMPLITUDES

	Median	Arithmetic mean
668 series with positive amplitudes	+36.8	+53.9
126 series with negative amplitudes	−17.2	−33.7
794 series without regard to sign	34.3	50.7
794 series with regard to sign	+30.4	+40.0

PERCENTAGE DISTRIBUTIONS OF FULL-CYCLE AMPLITUDE AND CONFORMITY COMPARED

Amplitude	%	%	Conformity index
0– 39.9	56.7	3.6	0– 9
40– 79.9	25.9	4.5	10– 19
80–119.9	8.7	4.3	20– 29
120–159.9	4.0	5.4	30– 39
160–199.9	1.1	5.0	40– 49
200–239.9	1.4	9.2	50– 59
240–279.9	1.3	8.1	60– 69
280–319.9	0.5	12.0	70– 79
320–359.9	0.3	8.8	80– 89
360–400.3	0.1	39.1	90–100
Total	100.0	100.0	Total

earlier cycles covered by our data.[2] If so, most of the amplitude averages of our present sample are higher than they would be

[2] Our most definite evidence for this opinion comes from the relatively long series in our collection. Millard Hastay has selected 30 series covering 15 to 21 business cycles, plus 11 covering 10 to 14, and compared their average amplitudes in 1919–38 with those in earlier periods. Averages were taken both before and after extreme movements had been excluded—mainly the war and first postwar cycles in price and value series. Three-quarters of the comparisons showed a higher mean amplitude in 1919–38 than before 1919. The 10 exceptions to this rule were 3 open market interest rates, bank clearings in New York, outside clearings after 'deflation', Snyder's clearings index of business (also deflated), bonds (but not shares) traded on the New York Stock Exchange, Evans' record of business incorporations, liabilities (but not the number) of business failures, and the Bureau of Labor Statistics index of the prices of metals and metal products.

Hastay's sample includes 11 series that can be taken as indicators of 'general business activity', 3 that represent investment decisions, 3 that reflect industrial output or employment, 2 on foreign commerce, 9 on commodity prices, 9 on the money and security markets in New York, 2 on corporate earnings, and 2 on failures. Production is most inadequately represented; the single series on construction relates to Manhattan; there are no series on retail trade, personal incomes, inventories, or banking. Yet, pending a more thorough investigation, we incline to accept the conclusion toward which this sample, and much nonstatistical evidence, points.

if all our series could be carried back to 1900, or 1880, or 1850. By the same token, the averages are lower than they would be if we discarded all data earlier than 1919. Thus the measures in Table 10 and Chart 5 seem to be biased, but whether the bias is in an upward or downward direction depends upon the range of experience one wishes to cover. If one wants a long-range average, our measures are probably too high; if one wants to summarize the conditions with which the current generation has had to contend, our measures are probably too low. How grave either bias is cannot be determined with assurance from data now available.[3]

III Amplitudes in Various Sectors of the Economy

Table 11 is similar in form to Table 8. In discussing measures of timing and conformity, I argued that indexes of a given value are as indicative of the impact of business cycles upon an activity when the timing is neutral or inverted as when the timing is positive. But I also had occasion to point out that some inversions—butter production, for example—make expansions less buoyant and contractions less drastic. When we think about the range and variety of activities swayed by business cycles, the first consideration must be stressed; when we think about the cyclical fluctuations of the whole economy, the second consideration becomes the more important. So we proceed as before, presenting amplitude measures with and without regard to sign, knowing that we shall have use for both sets.

[3] Perhaps the least hazardous guess at the order of magnitude of the bias can be made by averaging the amplitudes of Hastay's 11 indicators of 'general business activity'. Measures which cover from 10 to 21 cycles yield averages of +22, −17, +39, while the averages of the cycles before 1919 come out +21, −12, +33, and the averages for 1919-38 are +24, −28, +52. (The successive entries show respectively the amplitude during stages matched with reference expansion, contraction, and full reference cycles.) Thus our standard average reference-cycle amplitude is 6 points higher than that for the earlier and 13 points lower than that for the recent group of cycles. It should be noted that the differences are wider in contraction (mainly because of the 'Great Depression') than in expansion. On the problem of secular change in amplitudes, see however *Measuring Business Cycles*, Ch. 10, especially pp. 406–12.

Minus amplitude signs do not always mean inversion, or plus signs positive timing. Of the 608 positive series[4] in our sample, 2 have average reference-cycle amplitudes of —0.2 and —0.6; of the 77 inverted series, 1 has an amplitude of +0.2; of the neutral series, 22 have plus and 2 minus amplitudes; finally, of the 85 irregular series, 39 are scattered through the array of plus and 46 through the array of minus amplitudes. Of course, only in groups where irregular series are relatively numerous, or where there is a mixture of inverted and positive series, are there appreciable differences between the average amplitudes computed with and without regard to sign.

Most basic of all the facts brought out by the table is the wide range of the amplitudes presented by different segments of our economy. When amplitudes are measured in percentages of the average standing of a series during a reference cycle, contracts for construction work let by private parties rise and fall in the course of a business cycle 13 times as much as bond yields and long-term interest rates. The five highest ranking groups represent aspects of investing; but so also do the interest rates yielded by bonds, which rank lowest. How can an economic system function when its interrelated parts have such widely different 'coefficients of expansion'? And how can we account for these differences?

The coefficient of rank correlation between the reference-cycle amplitudes and the business-cycle conformity indexes of Table 11 is only +.33. It is clear that conformity influences the average amplitudes; but it is equally clear that various other factors must be taken into account.

IV FACTORS THAT INFLUENCE AMPLITUDES

A RELATIONS BETWEEN SPECIFIC- AND REFERENCE-CYCLE AMPLITUDES

We may start with the formal proposition that the reference-cycle amplitudes of a series are determined jointly by its specific-cycle amplitudes, reference-cycle timing, and degree of conformity.

[4] See Ch. 6, p. 94, note 7.

Table 11

GROUPS OF SERIES RANKED ACCORDING TO THEIR AVERAGE REFERENCE-CYCLE AMPLITUDES [a]

		AVERAGE REFERENCE-CYCLE			RANK, SIGNS DISREGARDED	
		Amplitude		Con-		
GROUP	NO. OF SERIES	Signs re-garded	Signs disre-garded	formity, Signs Dis-regarded	Am-pli-tude	Con-form-ity [e]
(1)	(2)	(3)	(4)	(5)	(6)	(7)
Bond yields & other long-term interest rates	12	+3.6	12.8	66	1	10
Production, foodstuffs	47	+8.3	15.3	42	2	3
Employment, perishable goods industries	8	+18.2	18.2	78	3	15
Hours of work per week	9	+20.4	20.4	100	4	28.5
Earnings per week, month, or year	10	+23.0	23.0	94	5	25
Prices, semidurables	18	+24.1	24.1	52	6	5
Prices, farm products & foods	51	+20.3	24.9	52	7	4
Prices, durables	45	+26.0	26.3	65	8	9
Employment, semidurable goods industries	13	+27.2	27.2	77	9	14
Retail sales	10	+27.6	27.8	82	10	19
Prices, perishables other than foods	22	+27.6	29.5	63	11	7
Payrolls, perishable goods industries	8	+31.2	31.2	76	12	12
Inventories, irregular timing	18	−23.6	33.6	24	13	1
Construction contracts, public	16	+42.5	42.5	32	14	2
Inventories, positive timing	18	+44.3	44.3	69	15	11
Bank clearings or debits	8	+45.8	45.8	83	16	21
Indexes of business activity	11	+46.3	46.3	99	17	27
Production, semidurables	29	+47.5	47.6	79	18	17
Wholesale sales	15	+48.1	48.1	87	19	24
Interest rates, short-term	11	+49.1	49.1	77	20	13
Production, perishables other than foods	29	+51.2	51.4	83	21	20
Payrolls, semidurable goods industries	13	+55.7	55.7	78	22	16
Employment, durable goods industries	9	+62.8	62.8	98	23	26
Inventories, inverted timing	24	−68.2	68.2	64	24	8
Payrolls, durable goods industries	6	+95.0	95.0	100	25	28.5
Production, durables	57	+99.6	100.8	82	26	18
Security issues, corporate	14	+122.8	124.9	55	27	6
New orders from manufacturers	17	+147.6	147.6	86	28	22
Construction contracts, private	26	+166.0	166.0	87	29	23
Summaries						
All series on						
Prices of commodities	147	+23.8	25.7	60	1	1
Employment	37	+35.3	35.3	87	2	5
Payrolls & other income payments	30	+57.6	57.6	84	3	4
Production	188	+55.5	57.7	74	4	3
Construction contracts or permits	58	+106.1	106.1	71	5	2

Table 11 (concl.)

GROUP (1)	NO. OF SERIES (2)	AVERAGE REFERENCE-CYCLE Amplitude Signs regarded (3)	Amplitude Signs disregarded (4)	Conformity, Signs Disregarded (5)	RANK, SIGNS DISREGARDED Amplitude (6)	Conformity[e] (7)
Summaries						
All series on						
Prices of commodities or services	168	+22.4	24.4	61	1	1
Financial activities	135	+27.3	46.6	73	2	2
General business activity	13	+46.9	46.9	98	3	4
Flow of commodities, services, or income	478	+49.5	61.1	74	4	3
All series in sample	794	+40.0	50.7	71	..	..

	NO.	AVERAGE REFERENCE-CYCLE Amplitude (*Signs regarded*)	Conformity	RANK[f] IN Amplitude	Conformity
All series with					
Irregular timing	85[b]	+1.9	0	1	1
Neutral timing	24	+30.6	+75	2	3
Inverted timing	77[c]	−44.3	−68	3	2
Positive timing	608[d]	+56.3	+78	4	4
All series in sample	794	+40.0	+55	..	..

[a] See Table 8, note *a*.

[b] Includes one series analyzed in part as positive.

[c] Includes one series analyzed also as neutral.

[d] Includes two odd cases: rail orders (see Ch. 6, note 7) and one series analyzed also as neutral.

[e] Based on column (5), computed to an additional place.

[f] These ranks, like those above, are based on averages in the two preceding columns; but the signs of the averages are disregarded in the present ranking, whereas the signs of the individual series are disregarded in the averages on which the ranks of the 29 groups and of the first two summaries are based.

Most of our series are subject to fluctuations corresponding to business cycles in duration. We locate the peaks and troughs of these movements, convert the seasonally-adjusted data during each specific cycle into percentages of their average value, and strike 3-month averages of these percentages centered on the peak and trough dates, from which we compute the rise from trough to peak and the fall from peak to trough, or, in cases of inversion, the fall and the rise. Granted our methods, these measures represent the full amplitude of the cyclical movements peculiar to each series analyzed. It can be exceeded by the corresponding reference-cycle amplitude only when some bit of freakish behavior interferes, of which more in a moment.

How closely the reference-cycle amplitude of a series approaches the upper limit set by its specific-cycle amplitude depends upon the relationship over time between the two sets of cycles. If the specific-cycle peaks and troughs invariably coincide with our reference dates for business-cycle peaks and troughs, or if the specific cycles are inverted so that their peaks coincide with reference troughs and the troughs with reference peaks, the two amplitudes are equal. This condition is occasionally satisfied by monthly or quarterly, and more often by annual, series during one or more cycles; but I do not recall any monthly series covering several cycles that shows throughout perfect coincidence of its specific- and reference-cycle turns.

The timing varieties that tend to preserve specific-cycle amplitudes most fully are expansion in stages I–V or V–IX. All the other varieties listed in Table 4 put the specific-cycle peaks, or troughs, or both into reference stages that usually cover more than three months, which of course tends to lower peaks or raise troughs, or do both.

Whatever the timing type, any irregularity in the relations between the movements peculiar to a series and the general tides of business tends to widen the gap between the two amplitudes. For, in the specific-cycle analysis, all of the cyclical peaks of a series are added together and averaged, whereas irregular reference-cycle timing scatters these specific-cycle peaks among different reference stages, none of which has as high a total standing as the sum of specific-cycle peaks. So also, irregular timing makes the average reference-cycle trough higher than that of specific cycles. When the irregularity is extreme it may reduce a high specific-cycle amplitude to a very low reference-cycle amplitude. For example, contracts for building bridges underwent 5 specific cycles in 1919–38;

their average amplitude was $+119$, -120, $+239$; but the conformity was only $+20$, -20, -33, and this irregular timing reduced the average reference-cycle amplitude to $+12$, $+1$, $+11$.

Specific cycles cannot have zero amplitudes, for they are conceived to consist of alternating advances and declines. Though a few series have no specific cycles, there may be small differences between their average movements during reference expansions and contractions, which means low reference-cycle amplitudes. These cases are not exceptions to the rule that reference-cycle are lower than specific-cycle amplitudes;[5] for the absence of specific cycles is not equivalent to

[5] The exceptional conditions under which reference-cycle exceed specific-cycle amplitudes are of two sorts.

In fixing specific-cycle turns we sometimes disregard isolated high or low points because they seem erratic rather than cyclical in character. If a disregarded high point happens to be in the reference-cycle stage that characteristically brings the culmination of expansions in the series, or a disregarded low point happens to be in the culminating stage of its contractions, the reference-cycle amplitude of this cycle may exceed its specific-cycle mate. If the series has highly regular cyclical timing, so that in other cycles the reference-cycle approximates the specific-cycle amplitude, the one cycle affected by the erratic high or low point may dominate the average of all cycles. Such a combination of contingencies is unlikely, and I cannot supply an example.

Not infrequently one specific cycle occurs within the period occupied by two business cycles, or one business cycle spans two specific cycles. When one specific cycle matches two business cycles, the tendency of specific-cycle to exceed reference-cycle amplitudes is reenforced; it may be weakened in the opposite case of two specific cycles within one business cycle. The one exceptional cycle may dominate the average relation between the two amplitudes, provided that regularity of timing makes the reference-cycle amplitudes of the other cycles nearly equal to their specific-cycle counterparts. Production of automobile trucks in 1914–38 affords an illustration. This series had two specific cycles during World War I; their mean amplitude was 120; that of the corresponding reference cycle was 158. The next 5 specific cycles were in one-to-one correspondence with reference cycles and exceeded them only a little in amplitude, so that the war episode decided the issue. The average amplitude of the 7 specific cycles is $+92$, -62, $+154$, that of the 6 reference cycles is $+94$, -65, $+159$. Another illustration, mentioned in *Measuring Business Cycles*, p. 175, is the inverted series showing stocks of slab zinc held in warehouses, which had 5 specific cycles in 1921–38, 2 of which matched one business cycle.

the presence of ghostly specific cycles without amplitudes. Finally, reference-cycle amplitudes can fall to zero. Several series come close to that limit and one reaches it in contraction.[6]

B RELATIONS BETWEEN SPECIFIC AND BUSINESS CYCLES

While helpful in organizing ideas, the preceding statements are patently incomplete, for we must ask: On what do specific cycles depend?

We conceive these cycles to be movements in specific activities corresponding in character and order of duration to business cycles. Conversely, we conceive business cycles to be congeries of specific cycles. There is nothing novel in this way of thinking; it comes from applying to our problem the familiar idea that, in a system of private enterprise, all economic activities are interdependent. The intricacies of the crisscrossing relationships among the elements of such an economy have been schematically indicated by the systems of simultaneous equations devised by Leon Walras and his successors. Fundamentally the same conception runs through Alfred Marshall's more concrete description of the interactions of demand, supply, and value in the operations of producing and distributing the national income. If we must recognize 'the one in many' and 'the many in the one' when dwelling upon problems of equilibrium, so must we recognize them when thinking about economic fluctuations.

How the concepts of specific and business cycles are re-

[6] Some commodity prices, transportation charges, and official discount rates of central banks have been kept unchanged for years at a time. We have examples of such behavior during one or more reference cycles, but not during all the reference cycles covered by a series. Also a series might rise (or fall) by the same percentage of its base in both phases of every cycle, or on the average, which would give identical amplitudes in expansion and contraction but a zero reference-cycle amplitude. Again I can cite no example. Or the changes during successive reference expansions might neatly cancel one another, and so might the changes during successive contractions, which would produce amplitudes of 0, 0, 0. One of our short series achieves this feat in contraction—hourly earnings in northern cotton mills. The lowest expansion amplitude in our sample is −0.05 (wholesale price of sulphuric acid); the lowest reference-cycle amplitudes are +0.2 and −0.2, of which the former appears in one and the latter in three series.

lated is best indicated by recalling the way in which they evolved in the course of men's thinking about economic troubles. The notion of business cycles in hazy forms goes back more than a century to 'commercial crises', which were slumps occurring at about the same time in the markets for many commodities. Our predecessors had no difficulty in grasping both the particular and the general features of these episodes. As recurrences brought fuller opportunities for observation and analysis, the concept of crises broadened into that of cycles, and clearer distinctions were drawn between what happened in the economy as a whole and what happened in its component parts. The present effort to increase knowledge of cyclical movements takes over these familiar ideas. But it defines them somewhat more precisely, and tests their objective validity more systematically.

For the latter purpose, we have collected a diversified sample of time series, and examined each specimen to see whether it is subject to movements corresponding in character and duration to those postulated by our definition of business cycles. Finding 'specific cycles' (the name alone is new) in a great majority of series, we examined their relations to one another in time.[7] Covariation appeared to be the rule. To verify or disprove this impression, we tabulated the trough and the peak dates of specific cycles in the most representative samples of series that we could arrange in successive periods. These dates appeared mainly in clusters and the clusters usually came during periods in which nonstatistical observers had sensed reversals in the direction of business movements. By analyzing the clusters of specific-cycle turning dates in the light of what we were learning about the relations of individual activities to the national economy, we could tell the years, the quarters, and approximately the months when general expansions and contractions in business activity had culminated. These inferences of the general from the particular could be checked and often improved by supposing them to be correct. That is, we imposed the business-cycle chronology derived from specific-

[7] See *Measuring Business Cycles*, p. 66 ff.

cycle turns upon the individual series, and shifted the business-cycle dates first chosen if they misrepresented the consensus of specific-cycle turns. The broad outcome of these operations to date has been presented in the two preceding chapters. Eight-ninths of our sample of monthly and quarterly series from the United States seem to have a definite timing relation to business-cycle expansions and contractions—a behavior pattern to which they adhere on the average with a regularity exceeding three cases out of four.

The prevalence of wavelike forms among the reference-cycle patterns of Chart 1 and their infinite differences of detail illustrate these findings graphically. Both the similarities and the differences are explicable on the assumption that economic activities are functionally related to one another in the numberless direct and indirect ways suggested in fancy by the equations of Walras and the analyses of Marshall. For explanations of the behavior of one series, an investigator turns as a matter of course to the behavior of other series that he believes on independent grounds to be functionally related to the first.[8] That is the course followed in Chapter 5 where departures from the dominant variety of timing are discussed. Probably few readers had methodological misgivings then.

In no case, however, can the cyclical behavior of an activity be explained wholly by what other activities do to it. Each activity has characteristics of its own that affect its behavior and the influence it exercises upon other components of the economy. For example, the inverted pattern of butter production in factories was traced in Chapter 5, not only to the positive patterns of income receipts and milk purchases by consumers, but also to the conditions that prevent dairymen from adjusting their supply promptly to fluctuations in demand. Cows are not precisely like any other equipment for producing goods in which businessmen invest; but the possession of

---

[8] The prevailing similarity of reference-cycle patterns may suggest 'nonsense correlations' without number to the incautious. On purely statistical evidence one can explain the movements of any series that conforms perfectly to business cycles by that of any other perfect conformer.

idiosyncrasies is not an idiosyncrasy, on the contrary it is a characteristic common to all goods.

To generalize: the specific cycles of every economic activity are joint products of factors peculiar to the activity itself, and of movements in other activities that impinge upon it in numerous ways and with varying force. Among these impinging activities, if our observations are representative, a majority expand and contract in unison. Thus the specific cycles of each activity are partially shaped by those congeries of specific cycles in other activities which we call business cycles. If the specific cycles of a series are formed in this fashion, so also are its reference cycles; for they are merely specific cycles transferred to a new time schedule, which has itself been derived from the consensus of specific-cycle turning dates in supposedly representative samples of series.

In trying to account for the wide variety of reference-cycle amplitudes, then, we might take up one series after another, considering in each case the conditions under which the activity represented is conducted, the other activities by which it is most influenced, and their behavior as factors shaping the behavior of the activity on which we are focusing attention for the time being. That is the procedure to follow whenever one is concerned with the cyclical amplitudes of particular series; but it is ill adapted to a systematic survey because of its mountainous detail. For the present, we can get on faster by asking, not why steel production has large reference-cycle amplitudes and department store sales much smaller ones, but by asking what factors tend to produce large and what tend to produce small fluctuations.

Even this modest inquiry will be rather long. To keep the crisscrossing influences that must be considered from getting hopelessly tangled, I shall deal first with the factors that influence the amplitudes of consumers' purchases, then turn to producers' purchases, the employment of resources, and the broad behavior of prices and production in different sectors of the economy and the system at large.

C CYCLICAL FLUCTUATIONS IN CONSUMERS' PURCHASES

Though an individual has virtually no control over the business conditions that affect his money income, he has a considerable measure of freedom in deciding how to use whatever money he receives, and the larger his income after taxes the fuller this freedom becomes. Studies of family budgets in many lands since Ernst Engel formulated his 'law of consumption' in 1857 have demonstrated that the allocation of family income among different lines of expenditure changes notably as income increases. Our measures show corresponding differences in the cyclical behavior characteristic of aggregate expenditure for different types of goods. The factors chiefly responsible for differences in reference-cycle timing and amplitude seem to be the nature of the wants to be met and the characteristics of the goods bought.

The first factor recalls the time-honored but rather fuzzy distinction between necessities, conveniences, and luxuries—fuzzy in that it changes with living standards, and differs at any given time with the past income and the personal tastes of consumers. Every day everyone requires a minimum of food, clothing, and housing. In a country as well to do as the United States, no one is knowingly allowed to starve, to go naked, or to perish from exposure; public relief and private charity prevent aggregate consumption from falling so low in hard times as it would if there were not a large-scale sharing of goods by the more fortunate. However, the demand for food declines very rapidly in intensity as consumption increases. As suggested above, people do not eat much more in the United States during expansions than during contractions, though the kinds of food they buy shift appreciably. The demand for clothing, and still more the demand for additional housing, is subject to larger cyclical fluctuations than the demand for food, partly because the appetite for additional supplies of these goods does not fall so fast after biological needs have been met.

Demand for comforts and luxuries hardly appears until the

means of subsistence have been obtained; thereafter it extends to an ever wider variety of goods. Of course, dainty viands, choice beverages, large wardrobes, and roomy dwellings are themselves luxuries. The purchasing of such goods may fall very low when consumers feel poor, and rise very rapidly when they feel rich. Because the United States comes nearest to being a land of abundance, the buying of staple foods has low cyclical amplitudes; for the same reason purchases of luxuries have high cyclical amplitudes; between these rather vague boundaries fall the amplitudes of outlays upon the growing variety of conveniences that make American standards of living what they are in successive decades.

The characteristic of goods that seems to have most influence upon cyclical amplitudes is durability—a somewhat ambiguous term. A unit of electricity can be used only once, and it must be used, if at all, the minute it is generated. An egg can be eaten only once, but it can be kept in cold storage for months and still be salable. Some types of clothing have for most consumers a useful life limited by their physical properties; other types are discarded by the well-to-do when the fashion changes. A machine may have years of efficient service left in it, but be junked because a more efficient model has been put on the market.

The subtle mixtures of physical and economic considerations illustrated by these examples have to be drastically simplified in statistical classifications. There the prevailing distinction seems to be between perishables that can be used only once or for a short while, however long they may have been preserved; semidurables that are typically used, say, for six months to three years; and durables that are typically used for more than three years. All foods are treated as perishables—canned goods on the same basis as fresh fruit. Fuels and electricity are perishable—coke used in making steel, as well as gasoline for 'joy rides'. So too 'chemicals' and paper are put here, despite the repeated use of some industrial chemicals, and the indefinitely long life of many books and building papers. Semidurables comprise mainly articles of clothing, leather, and rubber goods; multiple but not indefinitely numerous uses are inferred from the physical character of the materials. Durables are in practice ores, which are really used only once, metals, metallic products, construction materials, buildings, and other man-made structures from roads to dams. As Table 11 shows, this classification brings out highly significant differences in the cyclical behavior of production and employment; but its crudity also hides certain differences.

For present purposes, the point of chief importance is that durability confers ability to control the timing of purchases for replacement. When a perishable is used, it must be replaced before another use can be enjoyed. We have already noticed that the practical effects of this truism depend upon whether the good is a necessity or not. If a single-use good is felt by its users to be as vital as coffee is to millions of Americans, perishability maintains a rather steady flow of purchases, which in this instance increase in contraction. An operatic performance is no less perishable than coffee; but to few Americans is grand opera a necessity; most people can adjust their indulgences to the state of their pocketbooks with less sacrifice than they feel in postponing the purchase of a new automobile. Thus, to understand many of the differences in cyclical amplitudes, we must cross our first classification upon the second.

Semidurables in the necessary class typically have amplitudes larger than basic perishables because consumers have more leeway in determining when to buy. But this leeway has time limits narrower than most business cycles. Shirts will not come back wearable after more than so many trips to the laundry. Shoes cannot be reheeled and resoled indefinitely. The specific cycles in our series on the production of textiles, shoes, and automobile tires conform rather closely to most business cycles, but when a contraction lasts more than 18 or 24 months, the output of these articles is apt to rise, which suggests that mass buying expands somewhat despite the continued shrinking of family incomes. If we could secure production records of fine attire, we might find continuous decreases even in long contractions.

Durables have limits of useful life so elastic that consumers are seldom forced to buy when very reluctant to do so. The recent war gave the whole nation a demonstration of how long motor cars can be kept running. Contracts for residential buildings, it is true, typically rise before contractions are over, but not because the old buildings have been used up like shirts and shoes. Durability cushions the shocks of cyclical fluctuations in that the longer goods last, the more leeway people have in deciding when to buy new units. Rather paradoxically, this cushioning of the shocks upon consumers induces a type of behavior that makes cyclical fluctuations more violent.

Of other factors that influence consumer purchasing, at least three should be mentioned. First is the ability to carry stocks of goods adequate to meet needs for considerable periods, which increases control over the timing of purchases. The close connection of this factor with differences in durability is obvious. Nations at war can restrict drastically the output of consumer durables for several years at a stretch without undermining civilian morale. So, too, a prosperous people entering a cyclical contraction with relatively well stocked wardrobes can restrict their purchases of wearing apparel for months without grave discomfort. Perishables present a different case. Many a farm family keeps in its cellar a winter's supply of potatoes, canned vegetables and fruits, smoked and pickled meats, and it may have also a shed filled with firewood. The age-old arts of preserving perishables have been enormously improved and extended by applications of scientific discoveries. But broader trends have tended to reduce the carrying of food and fuel stocks by families. An increasing percentage of people live in cities where few families have the space and equipment required for storing appreciable stocks. That task has been handed over to commercial enterprises, and will be discussed in connection with business inventories.

The second factor is the availability of 'consumer credit'. By emancipating people from the restrictions that current income or assets place upon their purchases, credit increases control over the timing of demand. Being based upon expecta-

tions of future ability to pay, credit gives imagination tinged
with emotional coloring a larger role in determining action.
But the freedom to buy conferred by the granting of credit is
followed by a restriction: part of future income is committed
to repayment and less is left to spend on the wants that will
crop up in days to come. How much influence this factor has
upon cyclical amplitudes we cannot say with assurance, for the
availability of credit is merely a condition that gives other
factors fuller sway over consumers' choices. Yet we can observe its effects here and there, because consumers resort to
credit in financing certain kinds of goods with especial freedom.

We may set aside the large volume of 'charge account'
credit that is used by shoppers merely as a convenience. For
our purposes, it matters little whether goods are paid for at
the time of purchase, at the end of the week, or on the first of
next month. But when charge accounts are allowed to run for
months at a time, and become a means of tiding needy families
over serious emergencies, they must be counted among the
influences that sustain the demand for basic consumer goods
during contraction, and so mitigate somewhat the hardships it
imposes. About these credit arrangements between retail stores
and their customers we have little information, but collections
doubtless become slower in hard times, and perhaps the un-
paid balances mount despite the decline in sales.

Much more is known about sales of goods on instalment and
the granting of short-term loans to consumers. The first type
of transaction is largely confined to purchases of durable
goods that can be 'repossessed' by the lender in case of default.
A large proportion of short-term loans serves the same purpose
as instalment sales, but a part is negotiated to meet emergencies
of divers sorts. What chiefly concerns us about transactions
of both types is that they enable consumers to increase their
purchases of durables as soon as their *prospects* improve after a
cyclical contraction and many months before they have saved
enough money to pay in cash. Such transactions continue to
increase as long as the prospects of more and more people keep

improving, or until reluctance to assume further debts over-balances desires for further goods. Meeting the payments on purchases made during expansion contributes toward the drastic reduction in the buying of durables during contraction.

While it seems plain that instalment credit tends to heighten the amplitude of cyclical fluctuations, the relative importance of this factor has been much debated. Holthausen, Merriam, and Nugent have estimated that the total instalment credit granted by retailers of goods (including automobiles) and cash lending institutions exceeded 5 billion dollars in 1929, fell to 2 billion in 1932, and rose again to more than 5 billion in 1937. These are imposing sums, but in no year did they reach 11 percent of the annual incomes of consumers receiving $5,000 or less. More important is the fact that every year consumers were paying instalments on earlier contracts. That is, the change in purchasing power effected by instalment credit consisted, not of the volume of credit granted, but of that sum minus repayments. This 'net credit change' varied between an excess of repayments of 711 million dollars in 1932 and an excess of new credits of 773 million in 1936. In only one year did these balances reach 2 percent of consumer incomes up to $5,000. Similar results have been reached by Blanche Bernstein, who used a quite different source.[9] The Study of Consumer Purchases in 1935–36, a Works Progress Administration project that covered some 60,000 nonrelief families in all parts of the country, made it possible to determine the net change in purchasing power arising from all forms of consumer credit. Dr. Bernstein summed up her findings as follows:

For the nonrelief population as a whole, the gross addition to purchasing power [in 1935–36] . . . from the use of consumer credit . . . came to less than 3 percent of the total income received, and after subtraction for repayments the net addition to income was less than 2 percent, or approximately $805,000,000. The entire class of families with

[9] See Holthausen, Merriam, and Nugent, *The Volume of Consumer Instalment Credit, 1929–38* (National Bureau, 1940), especially pp. 99, 101; Bernstein, *The Pattern of Consumer Debt, 1935–36* (National Bureau, 1940), especially p. 10; Gottfried Haberler, *Consumer Instalment Credit and Economic Fluctuations* (National Bureau, 1942).

incomes under $500, however, added a net 10 percent to their immediate purchasing power through the use of consumer credit, and families with incomes of $500–2,000 added from 2 to 5 percent. On the other hand, for families receiving more than $2,000 consumer credit was relatively insignificant as a source of funds for additional spending.

A third factor that bears on the satisfaction of consumer wants, and which is probably more important than the highly fluctuating item of consumer credit, is the relatively stable provision for certain consumer needs supplied through government. Public schools, highways, public health offices, police and fire protection, not to mention the multiform services performed by departments of the federal government, make a substantial contribution to the American standard of living. Though the production of these goods is authorized indirectly by consumers as voters, and the costs are met from taxes they consent to have levied, the whole process of deciding what services to render and how to pay for them differs so radically from the business model that these operations are commonly disregarded in cyclical studies. While we have not yet investigated governmental activities systematically, we know that they conform less closely to the cyclical tides on the whole than do private activities organized in business enterprises, except when a great war expands governmental operations to a scale that dominates the economy. Yet even in peacetime, the governmental sector has become so considerable that lack of detailed data concerning its fluctuations is a serious deficiency in our sample.

D CYCLICAL FLUCTUATIONS IN PRODUCERS' PURCHASES

The common statement that the demands of business enterprises for goods depend directly or indirectly upon what consumers buy is substantially valid, though it requires the qualification that producers and distributors spend much energy in trying to influence consumer choices, and the reminder that how much consumers can buy depends primarily upon how much business enterprises pay out in wages, salaries, interest, rent, and dividends, plus what Simon Kuznets calls 'entrepreneurial

withdrawals' from the incomes of small concerns operated by
their owners.

Since retailers pass on consumers' demands to preceding
links in chains of supply, the differences we have noted in the
cyclical amplitudes of demand for various types of goods tend
to be maintained in the dealings of business enterprises with
one another. But the conditions under which enterprises of
different sorts operate modify the timing and amplitudes of
fluctuations in considerable degree.

One of the leading factors responsible for these alterations
is the size of the inventories carried by business enterprises in
relation to their sales. We have noted that the possession of
stocks of goods gives consumers fuller control over the timing
of purchases, and so tends to increase the amplitude of cyclical
fluctuations in the quantities bought. The like is true of business houses. Dealers in fresh vegetables, fish, meats, milk,
bakery goods, newspapers, and other ultraperishables try to
buy every day what they think they can sell. That is, they
pass along to wholesale houses, bakers, publishers, or other
suppliers whatever changes occur in their daily sales. Dealers
in perishables that deteriorate less rapidly, in semidurables, and
in durables carry stocks varying from a few days' sales to the
sales of several months—in some trades, a year or more. Carrying stocks becomes a competitive necessity where it is physi-
cally and financially feasible; for customers can satisfy their
tastes best in a shop that offers a considerable assortment of
qualities, sizes, styles, and prices. The successful retailer learns
from experience approximately how large a stock in proportion to sales it is profitable to carry. The prevailing stock-sales
ratios, or 'turnover rates', differ not only from one branch of
trade to another, but also within a given branch from one shop
to another according to the class of customers catered to.

Now the larger a retailer's stock in proportion to daily sales,
the less is he forced to buy his merchandise on a hand-to-mouth
basis, and so to pass on unmodified the variations in consumer
demand. Much work can be saved, and better terms can be had
by ordering the bulk of his requirements in rather large lots

and at considerable intervals, with the expectation of placing 'fill-in' orders if sales exceed estimates. This clustering of orders tends to produce wider fluctuations, both seasonal and cyclical, in the purchases of goods by retailers than in their sales to consumers. Furthermore, good times tempt the retail merchant to 'speculate in inventories'. Even the man who consciously resists this dangerous practice, and not all merchants do resist all the time, may think it safe to base his expectation of future sales on changes occurring in current sales.

Say, for example, that experience has taught some merchant to maintain a monthly stock-sales ratio of 3:1, and that he places his bulk orders at monthly intervals. Say also that monthly sales have gone up 5 percent, and that the larger volume seems likely to be maintained. To obey his rule of thumb, the retailer must increase his purchases more than his sales have risen; for his inventory has been depleted by the 5 percent increase in sales, and he must not only make up this deficiency but also raise his inventory from 3×100 to 3×105; that is, his increase in purchases must be 20 percent. If the merchant takes a chance that sales will continue to increase 5 percent a month, similar reasoning will lead him to increase monthly purchases about 35 percent. If, on the contrary, sales decline, purchases will be reduced more than sales have fallen off, and the more pessimistic are expectations regarding the volume of future sales, the more will the reduction in purchases exceed the reduction in sales.

Not only is the amplitude of purchases likely to be larger than that of sales, but the cyclical timing may be different. An unexpected decline in the *rate* at which sales rise in late expansion may leave our merchant with awkwardly large stocks, and lead him to reduce his purchases before sales turn downward. Seemingly more common is an upturn of purchasing by merchants in late contraction, while their sales are still shrinking, though more slowly than before, to replenish inventories that have fallen below standard.

Needless to say, my numerical example is fanciful. But it suggests how the carrying of stocks tends to amplify the modest fluctuations characteristic of much consumer purchasing as orders are passed back by retailers who carry appreciable stocks instead of buying hand to mouth. The higher the stock-sales ratio, the greater the amplification. In Table 11 the mean reference-cycle amplitude of our 10 series on retail sales is 28 points, of our 15 series on wholesale sales 48 points. Unfortunately, the available series of sales at wholesale do not match at all well the series of retail sales. Neither the comparison of the group averages nor any comparison of individual series in our sample affords a convincing test of the reasoning.

A further increase in amplitudes is probable when the wholesaler who carries stocks buys consumer goods from the manufacturer. Our 17 series on new orders have average reference-cycle amplitudes of 148. But all of these orders call for durable goods, whereas our wholesale series relate mainly to sales of perishables and semidurables, and again no satisfactory comparisons can be arranged between individual series in the two groups.

In turn, manufacturers who carry stocks of the materials they use may group their purchases in large lots, and pass on demands that fluctuate even more violently than the orders they receive. But the opposite may often be true. For when merchants place large orders, they seldom wish the goods delivered all in one shipment. Our series on the physical volume of merchandise received by department stores has reference-cycle amplitudes only a trifle larger than those of the series on the physical volume of department store sales ($+16$, -13, $+29$ as compared with $+16$, -10, $+26$). The task of supplying consumers can be carried on most efficiently by maintaining as steady a flow of goods as technological and economic conditions allow from the producers of raw materials to factories, thence to distributors, and finally to individual purchasers. For the steadier this flow, the better can production be organized, the more fully can industrial equipment be utilized, and the smaller will be the capital investment per unit of output.

Our best bit of evidence about what actually happens comes

from Ruth P. Mack, who has managed to assemble fairly comparable data upon successive links in the shoe-leather-hide chain of supply. Table 12 presents certain of her findings concerning the physical and the dollar volume of sales and output. The reference-cycle amplitudes increase modestly from retail to wholesale sales of shoes, increase again from wholesaling to manufacturing, and increase a third time (now more sharply) from making up shoes to tanning leather. At the raw material stage, however, the succession of increases is reversed in the physical volume records, and—in spite of the high cyclical variability of hide prices—in two of the three dollar comparisons. 'Movement of hides into sight' is dominated by the inspected slaughter of cattle, although the power of increased demand to attract hides from country areas and abroad imparts some additional flexibility to their supply. The reference-cycle amplitudes of federally inspected slaughter in 1908–38 averaged +13, −10, +23, well inside the range of Dr. Mack's briefer averages for the movement of hides. In this country, of course, cattle are slaughtered primarily for beef, and the cyclical behavior of the series is characteristic of the food group. Hides are a not very consequential byproduct, of which the price fluctuates much more than the output. If all leather were produced domestically and made from some synthetic substance turned out for that one use in readily controllable volume, the production of the raw material would probably have cyclical amplitudes equaling or exceeding those of leather, while its price would fluctuate less than the price of hides and probably less than its output.

One feature of the table may arouse misgivings: the fluctuations of employment in shoe factories are much smaller than the fluctuations in pairs produced, and a minor fraction of the fluctuations in payrolls. 'Employment' means here the number of names on payrolls, not manhours of work performed. A shrinkage in the buying of shoes is met only in part by reducing the number of employees; for the rest, it is met by sharing what work is to be had in smaller lots among those who remain on the factory rolls. In the shoe industry, wages are paid mainly

Table 12

Average Reference-Cycle Amplitudes at Successive Links in the Shoe-Leather-Hide Chain of Supply

				AVERAGE REFERENCE-CYCLE AMPLITUDE					
		2 Cycles, 1927–38			3 Cycles, 1924–38			4 Cycles, 1921–38	
SERIES[a]	EXPANSION STAGES	Expansion	Contraction	Full cycle	Expansion	Contraction	Full cycle	Expansion	Contraction	Full cycle
Physical Volume										
1 Pairs of shoes sold at retail	I–V	+17.2	−13.6	+30.8	...	...	...	...	...	...
2 Index of wholesale sales of shoes, deflated	VIII–V	+10.0	−25.4	+35.4	+9.6	−18.0	+27.6	+11.4	−18.2	+29.6
3 Total shoe production	VIII–V	+20.6	−19.6	+40.2	+16.7	−12.0	+28.7	...	...	...
4 Index of factory employment, boots & shoes	I–V	+11.5	−11.4	+22.9	+9.5	−9.1	+18.6	+10.8	−10.9	+21.7
5 Cattle hide & kip leather production	VIII–V	+19.3	−31.7	+51.0	+12.9	−23.6	+36.5	+18.6	−22.6	+41.2
6 Cattle hides, total movement into sight	VIII–V	+4.4	−23.4	+27.8	+3.4	−14.8	+18.2	+13.8	−17.8	+31.6
Value										
7 Retail sales of shoes	I–V	+26.4	−37.6	+64.0	...	...	...	...	...	...
8 Index of wholesale sales of shoes	I–V	+15.8	−49.6	+65.4	+14.6	−32.8	+47.4	+13.0	−30.3	+43.3
9 Value of total shoe production at factories	I–V	+31.4	−46.4	+77.8	+25.4	−29.0	+54.4	+23.7[b]	−27.7	+51.4[b]
10 Index of factory payrolls, boots & shoes	I–V	+29.4	−43.2	+72.6	+22.8	−31.4	+54.2	+21.8	−29.2	+51.0
11 Value of cattle hide & kip leather production	I–V	+34.2	−77.1	+111.3	+23.3	−41.5	+64.8	+23.8	−40.6	+64.4
12 Value of cattle hides moving into sight	VIII–IV	+11.2	−74.4	+85.6	+11.2	−32.0	+43.2	+30.0	−40.6	+70.6

[a] See Appendix B for sources of data.
[b] Initial expansion covers only stages II–V.

on a piecework basis, and changes in total payrolls are a better indicator of fluctuations in the amount of work done than is the number of people to whom some wages are paid. The table indicates that the cyclical amplitudes of payrolls differ little from those of value produced.

We should note also that the increase of cyclical amplitudes as we pass from retailing shoes to tanning leather is accompanied by a shift toward earlier timing. On the average of the few cycles covered, the shoe industry has somehow managed toward the end of contraction to begin increasing the whole-sale distribution of shoes, their manufacture, and the production of the basic material one stage earlier than consumers have begun increasing their purchases. That such differences are economically feasible is suggested by what was said above about changes in the sales and in the purchases of merchants in branches of trade where the monthly stock-sales ratio is moderately high. Nor is the failure of the employment series to rise as soon as the output of shoes suspicious in the light of what was said in the preceding paragraph. Finally, the failure of all except one of the dollar series to rise in stage VIII–IX may mean merely that commodity prices and wage rates lag behind production at revival.[10]

Of course we cannot assume that the shoe-leather-hide chain represents accurately what happens in other industries producing semidurable consumer goods, not to speak of perishables on the one side or durables on the other. Not until what Dr. Mack has done with much difficulty and various reservations for one industry during a brief period can be supplemented by numerous similar researches shall we have a clear view of the relations between consumer purchasing and cyclical fluctuations in antecedent links of the chains that run back to the production of raw materials, and that disburse much of the income wherewith consumers buy. Meanwhile we seem warranted in proceeding on the assumption that cy-

---

[10] For a much more thorough analysis and a demonstration of 'subcycles' in this group of series, see the forthcoming monograph, "Consumption and Business Cycles, A Case Study: Shoes", by Ruth P. Mack.

clical amplitudes tend to grow larger, and that cyclical turns tend to occur earlier (at least at troughs) as we pass from retailing to wholesaling, to manufacturing, and sometimes as we go on to the production of raw materials. On the one hand, these tendencies are deducible from what we know about the influences exerted by the carrying of inventories upon the relations between the sales and the purchases of business enterprises. On the other hand, such rough comparisons as we can make among the series of our sample indicate that the tendencies in question commonly manifest themselves in practice. Indeed, I think that our statistical evidence for the groups of Table 11 exaggerates the increase in amplitudes, because the data available for the earlier industrial stages more often than not represent processes that are highly sensitive to business cycles for reasons besides their remoteness from retail distribution to consumers.

The preceding analysis applies most definitely to industrial chains in which a finished product can be traced link by link from specialty shops or 'departments' through factories that turn out one type of goods, to a chief raw material for which the product in question provides the main market. The transmission of cyclical impulses becomes much more complicated when several materials are combined on a somewhat similar scale in a single product, and when a single material or other good is put to many uses. The latter condition and its consequences for cyclical behavior are illustrated by fuel, electric current, transportation, communications, paper, and lubricating oil, which are bought by virtually all business enterprises and, except for lubricating oil, by all or by most families. Purchases and output of these goods, after due allowance is made for differences in intracycle trends, fluctuate cyclically much as do indexes of business activity. Yet even among them we can trace the amplification of amplitudes characteristic of the passage from retailing to manufacturing, whenever it is possible to distinguish roughly between consumer and producer goods. Compare, for example, the reference-cycle amplitudes of the following pairs of goods related in origin and mode of production but used primarily by families in one case, by business enterprises in the other—a brief list eked out by two index numbers.

PRIMARILY CONSUMER GOODS	AV. REFERENCE-CYCLE AMPLITUDE		PRIMARILY PRODUCER GOODS
Anthracite coal production	+17.5	+56.0	Bituminous coal production
Gasoline production	+27.7	+41.5	Lubricants production
R.R. passenger miles	+29.6	+52.9	R.R. freight ton miles
Newsprint paper consumption	+31.1	+55.2	Wrapping paper production
Passenger automobiles, production	+104.8	+158.5	Automobile trucks, production
Index of production, consumer goods (Fed. Res. Bank of N.Y.)	+33.9	+68.6	Index of production, producer goods (Fed. Res. Bank of N.Y.)

E CYCLICAL FLUCTUATIONS IN EMPLOYMENT OF RESOURCES

The next problem is whether amplification of amplitudes continues as we pass on to demands for the 'factors of production', which we may group under their time-honored captions, land, labor, and capital.

1 Land

In one sense, farm land approaches the ideal of full employment more closely than any other resource. When times are hard, most producers can cut their losses by letting their facilities for production stand idle part of the time. A farmer may do the like if he depends upon hired labor to put in his crops, or is subject to other heavy costs that vary directly with the scale on which he operates. But even the large-scale farmer usually thinks it better to grow a crop, if he can, than to let his land lie fallow, while the typical American farmer can get a return for his own labor and that of his children only by working his land. Indeed, if the financial outlook is unpromising when crops are put in, the farmer is tempted to *increase* the acreage he plants in an effort to offset the drop in prices. For the little an individual can add to the year's supply will not have any appreciable influence upon the selling price per unit; but each unit an individual can add to his sales at any price above out-of-pocket expenditures will make an appreciable, perhaps a crucial, addition to family income. In practice, the total area used as crop land, meadow, and pasture varies little, year by year.

About cyclical variations in land purchases we have little direct evidence and not much to say. The demand for farm lands, and their prices, fluctuates with current expectations concerning the profits of agriculture, and concerning the future of land prices themselves. It is affected by the cyclical tides, and reacts upon them. Indeed, few factors have played so spectacular a role as land speculation in the history of American business. But land booms and depressions have suffered a secular decline in relative importance as other industries have come to surpass farming in number of workers and contribution to gross national product. Within most of the period covered by our investigation, the demand for farm lands, like farm output, seems to have had only a loose connection with business cycles. In studies of differences among individual cycles, this topic retains importance down to the present moment; but in a preliminary effort to ascertain what typically happens in the course of these cycles we seem justified in classifying it as an irregular element of secondary consequence concerning which we have no satisfactory statistical record.

About the market for mineral and timber lands our information is even more vague. Here we may assume a somewhat closer and more regular relation to business cycles, apart from the discoveries of new ore deposits and oil fields—an important exception in some cases. Concerning the amplitude of fluctuations we have no systematic evidence.

We are somewhat better off in dealing with land wanted primarily for its location. Every construction project requires a site, and the parcels used, whether previously owned or newly acquired, must fluctuate with the volume of construction. Hence to this type of demand for land we may attribute the large cyclical amplitudes characteristic of our series on construction, of which the most comprehensive is the F. W. Dodge Corporation's record of value of total contracts, first in 27, later in 36 and 37 states. Our analysis covers the 7 reference cycles of 1912–38, is based on expansion stages VIII–IV, and yields conformity indexes of $+71$, $+50$, $+86$. The mean amplitude is $+43$, -30, $+74$. More direct, though more restricted, evidence is afforded by annual records running back to the 1830's of the 'number of acres subdivided' in Chicago, and the net increase of building lots in the Detroit and Pittsburgh 'areas'. The reference-cycle timing, conformity, and amplitudes of these three series are as follows:

			INDEX OF CONFORMITY TO			AV. REFERENCE-CYCLE AMPLITUDE		
PERIOD COVERED	NO. OF REF. CY-CLES	EX-PAN-SION STAGES	Ex-pan-sion	Con-trac-tion	Busi-ness cycles	Ex-pan-sion	Con-trac-tion	Full cycle
Chicago	1834–1932	25	I–V	+56	+36	+47	+48	−42	+90
Detroit area	1834–1924	23	I–V	+65	+30	+38	+75	−44	+119
Pittsburgh area	1834–1932	25	I–V	+16	+4	+12	+14	−9	+23

Why the conformity and reference-cycle amplitude should be so much lower in the big steel center than in the other two cities I do not know. The Chicago and Detroit amplitudes are large for annual data, and confirm the inference from the Dodge record of contracts. Despite the mysterious warning from Pittsburgh, I think the demand for land as building sites must conform tolerably well on the average to business cycles, and must undergo the large reference-cycle fluctuations characteristic of durable goods.

2 Labor

Mankind's hope of some day attaining a genuine 'economy of abundance' rests on the possibility of making the goods it wants with ever less labor. But under the conditions imposed by pecuniary organization, the chief agents to whom society entrusts the utilization of its labor, its science, and other resources must give precedence to making money over making goods. Only as far as it enhances profit, is technological efficiency valued in the world of business. Production itself must stop if making goods threatens heavier losses than remaining idle will impose. There is little of the personal or the arbitrary about decisions to reduce output, and with it employment. For business managers are not free agents. They are under obligation to protect as best they can the property entrusted to them, and in times of poor markets must choose the course that promises to keep losses light and to maintain solvency. The basic difficulty lies in our economic organization, or rather in our inability to keep this organization in good working order all the time. Industrial 'know how' will not bring a satisfactory life to a nation until that nation gains also the economic 'know how' to use its resources at tolerably full capacity year in and year out. If anyone thinks the United States has the practical economic knowledge it needs, the cyclical patterns of Chart 1 should disabuse him.

Of course the worst sufferers in seasons when it does not pay to make goods are those who live by selling labor. While labor is an ultraperishable, laborers are durables—durables in need of constant upkeep. The nation has—for present purposes, we may say the nation is—a huge inventory of producer durables in various stages of maturing and decaying. As with other durables, the changes in the total stock are slight within brief periods. Indeed, the rate of increase in the potential supply of labor is not reduced by a cyclical contraction; and the current market supply may be augmented, for when the chief bread-winner of a family is looking for work in vain, he may be joined in the search by young people and women who in better times would go to school or keep house.[11]

Since labor is an ultraperishable, no inventory can be piled up by an employer for future use. At most, the employer can arrange for a flow of services varying with his requirements by entering into contracts with individuals or trade unions and by trying in less formal ways to hold his working force together even when he cannot offer regular work. Consequently, within

11 The logic of pecuniary organization implies that wage earners should consume less than they receive in good times so that they may save enough to tide over periods of slack employment. As far as that rule is practiced, it tends to keep down the reference-cycle amplitudes of demand for staple consumer goods. Though many families cannot and others will not save in good times, these amplitudes remain modest because families that have exhausted their savings and their credit can turn to relatives, private charity, or public relief for at least the bare essentials of livelihood.

the relatively short periods of cyclical phases, employment is dominated by the volume of production. For example, we find that in the 5 business cycles of 1919–38 records of factory employment compiled by the Bureau of Labor Statistics have mean amplitudes of +12 in flour mills, +31 in cotton mills, and +63 in steel mills—differences that correspond roughly to those in the output of the perishable, semidurable, and durable commodities in question.

However, the bond between production and employment is not rigid. Even within business cycles, we can often observe a rising trend in manhour output and its effects upon the number of employees. Immediately, this increasing efficiency must be credited mainly to employers, though fundamentally it is a cultural product of which alert businessmen make use as they do of other resources. The most active agent in developing the industrial 'know how' responsible for the great achievements and the dazzling or horrible promises of our day has been scientific research. But to utilize this fastest growing of resources requires command over capital, business organization, and commercial skills such as few scientists possess. So the task of applying discoveries to daily work falls to businessmen. They perform it by employing scientifically trained experts to plan the technical features of production processes, and also with increasing frequency by investing in scientific research itself, usually of an applied type. When manhour efficiency increases, employment rises less than output in cyclical expansions, and falls more rapidly than output in contractions. Such differences are shown by our measures, as will presently appear.

Around the generally rising trend of manhour efficiency are twined two sets of cyclical fluctuations, one positively, the other inversely, related to production. The positive cyclical movements arise from the fact that modern plants attain their highest technological efficiency when operated steadily at the capacity for which they are designed. An irregular flow of work, substandard in volume, causes expensive stoppages, and makes it harder to integrate smoothly the numerous processes that contribute to the final product. Hence unit costs tend to rise in contraction, and to fall at least during the earlier stages of expansion—a result to which other factors to be noted later also contribute, often in larger degree. In the later stages of expansion, however, the volume of work sometimes exceeds the optimum, and unit costs turn upward. It may be necessary to use substandard equipment; similarly, a shortage of well trained workers may lead to the hiring of less desirable recruits. Under such conditions, the maintenance of shop discipline becomes difficult—the penalty of discharge is less dreaded when new jobs are easy to get. These conditions are reversed in contraction, and the efficiency of personnel tends to increase again, while the reduced flow of work is tending to raise unit costs.[12]

The preceding considerations help to clarify the reference-cycle movements of our comprehensive series on employment, payrolls, and closely associated factors, which are assembled in Table 13. To secure such uniformity as is possible, longer series are cut to the time coverage of the shortest—the 4 reference cycles of 1921–38. Several features of the table merit comment.

Fluctuations in employment as reported by the Bureau of Labor Statistics are usually slighter than the corresponding fluctuations in production.[13] As noted in the discussion of Dr. Mack's shoe-leather-hide sequence, 'employment' means the number of names on payrolls, and takes no account of hours worked per week. Unfortunately, data on the length of the working week, compiled by the National Industrial Conference Board, are not classified in the same fashion as the BLS data on employment, so that we cannot readily estimate total hours of work per month in individual industries. But we may

[12] For one industry, railroads, these relations have been studied with care. See Thor Hultgren, *op. cit.*, especially Ch. 7 and 9.

[13] The exceptions seem to be confined to food processing industries. They may be due to differences of coverage in the employment and production data, or to differences between the relative labor requirements of the industrial processes combined in an employment index and the formal weights assigned to the corresponding products in an index of production, or to technological factors of which I am unaware.

Table 13

REFERENCE-CYCLE TIMING, CONFORMITY, AND AMPLITUDE OF 'COMPREHENSIVE' SERIES ON EMPLOYMENT AND RELATED FACTORS IN FOUR BUSINESS CYCLES, 1921–1938

Series	Expansion Stages	Conformity to Business Cycles	Av. Reference-Cycle Amplitude		
			Expansion	Contraction	Full cycle
1 Employment, all mfg. (BLS index)	I–V	+100	+24	−23	+48
2 Av. hours worked per week, mfg. wage earners (NICB)	I–V	+100	+8	−16	+25
3 Manhours per week, estimated from 2 preceding series	I–V	+100	+33	−40	+73
4 Industrial production, manufactures (FRB index)	I–V	+100	+41	−35	+76
5 Composite wages (FRB N.Y. index)	I–VI	+71	+10	−5	+15
6 Av. hourly earnings, 25 mfg. industries (NICB)	I–VI	+71	+14	−5	+19
7 Av. weekly earnings, representative factories, N.Y. State	I–VI	+100	+12	−10	+22
8 Factory payrolls, total (BLS index)	I–V	+100	+39	−39	+78
9 Production of consumer goods (FRB N.Y. index)	VIII–IV	+100	+14	−17	+31
10 Cost of living (BLS index)	I–VI	+71	+3	−8	+11

BLS: Bureau of Labor Statistics
FRB: Federal Reserve Board
FRB N.Y.: Federal Reserve Bank of New York
NICB: National Industrial Conference Board

For fuller identification of sources, see Appendix B.

hazard a rough estimate for all manufactures by multiplying together the mean reference-cycle relatives of the BLS index of total factory employment and the NICB index of hours worked. In the interwar period the secular decline in the length of the working week proceeded apace, while the trend in the number of factory employees was nearly horizontal. Hence their product rises in expansion decidedly less than it falls in contraction. The opposite is true of the FRB index of manufacturing production. Though the average of the 4 cycles covered is heavily influenced by the 'Great Depression', the production index rises 41 points in expansion and falls 35 points in contraction. The difference between the expansion rise of 41 points in output and 33 points in manhours, together with the difference between the contraction decline of 35 points in output and 40 points in manhours, is a rough measure of the increasing technical efficiency with which factory labor was used. That the total cyclical amplitudes of manhours and output round off to nearly the same figure is a statistical accident—not a proof that our manhour estimate is precise or that the cyclical amplitude of output per manhour is slight.[14] The above-mentioned fluctuations in efficiency will be treated later, when we enter upon the stage-by-stage analysis of a typical cycle.

Wage rates are of crucial importance to the employer because, in conjunction with manhour efficiency, they bear directly upon unit costs of production. Their interest to the worker is obvious; indeed, it sometimes seems that trade-union officials and members, likewise government officials, over-stress the importance of rates and give insufficient attention to the reaction of high prices for labor upon employment and upon the prices of consumer staples. As is well known, American wages have had a rising secular trend, at least since the resumption of specie payments in 1879—a trend that has become steeper with the progress of organized labor. To measure this broad secular movement is exceedingly difficult, and the best series we have found are none too trustworthy. Formally, at least, the FRB N.Y. index of composite wages is our 'purest' measure of changes in the monthly prices paid for supposedly

[14] For fuller evidence and analysis of changes in output per manhour, see Solomon Fabricant, *Employment in Manufacturing, 1899–1939: An Analysis of Its Relation to the Volume of Production* (National Bureau, 1942). The leading results for all industries are summarized on pp. 16–22; individual industries are treated in Ch. 4. Fabricant's data are mostly in annual form and come chiefly from other sources than do the monthly series of our sample.

That similar, though usually less striking, increases of manhour output have occurred in other sectors of the economy is shown by other National Bureau studies of employment and productivity. See especially, Harold Barger and H. H. Landsberg, *American Agriculture, 1899–1939* (1942); Barger and S. H. Schurr, *The Mining Industries, 1899–1939* (1944); and J. M. Gould, *Output and Productivity in the Electric and Gas Utilities, 1899–1942* (1946). Similar investigations are in progress relating to the service industries. For some partial results, see the Bureau's *Occasional Papers*, No. 24, 29, and 33. A summary of these related studies to date is provided by George J. Stigler, *Trends in Output and Employment* (National Bureau, 1947).

comparable units of work. Average hourly earnings in 25 manufacturing industries approximate wage rates, but must be influenced also in some degree by changes in the composition of the working forces. However, the two series behave much alike and show what other information leads one to expect: the rising secular trend has been attained not so much by great gains in expansion, as by stubborn resistance to rate reductions in contraction. The advances in expansion have been moderate, though more than three times as fast as the rise in living costs during the brief period covered by Table 13, if we may trust our indexes. Of the moderate gains in expansion, only half on the average is lost in the succeeding contractions, so that the gains in the next expansion typically start from a higher level than in the preceding cycle.[15]

Average weekly earnings per employee should have larger cyclical amplitudes than hourly earnings, or wage rates proper, because they are influenced by number of hours worked. Our table shows such a difference, but it is smaller than is to be expected. There seems no reason why changes in the composition of working forces should affect this series more than they affect average hourly earnings. A more plausible explanation of the slightness of the difference in amplitude is that the industrial distribution of 'representative factories' in New York State gives greater weight to perishable and semidurable products than do the series on composite wages or hourly earnings.

Payrolls equal number of employees, times hours worked, times wages per hour; or number of employees times average weekly earnings. Since the factor series are positively correlated (except in stage V–VI, when wage rates, hourly earnings, and average weekly earnings rise a little), payrolls have relatively large cyclical amplitudes. They exceed the amplitudes of aggregate manhours per week, as they should because of the modest cyclical movements in wage rates, and exceed also the amplitudes of industrial production because a price factor enters into payrolls but not into physical output. Payrolls have more than twice the amplitude of consumer goods output according to the FRB N.Y. index. Of course the pro-

[15] See Creamer, *op. cit.*

duction index records changes in physical units. But it would have required cyclical fluctuations in the retail prices of consumer goods very much larger than those recorded by the Bureau of Labor Statistics in 1921–38 to prevent wage earners' purchases from keeping up with the rise of output in expansion —provided families did not alter radically their distribution of income between current expenditure and saving as conditions improved; provided also the cyclical amplitudes of aggregate payrolls matched the amplitudes of payrolls in manufacturing. Here we are getting merely our first glimpse of an intricate problem that is one of the foci of current debate among business-cycle theorists—a problem with which we must deal faithfully later on.

3 Capital

Our most realistic view of the demand for and supply of capital as the businessman thinks of it is afforded by the accounting analysis concerned with the uses and sources of funds. Concerning the magnitude of these funds in American corporations since 1916 much can be learned from the balance sheets and income statements compiled by the Treasury from annual income tax returns. However, frequent changes in tax laws, administrative rulings, and the classification of corporations impede the use of these data. Moreover, the official summaries are totals for groups large enough to conceal the conditions of individual enterprises. To ascertain differences hidden by this necessary practice, the National Bureau's Financial Research Program has compiled from state tax records and financial handbooks several samples of balance sheets and income statements for individual corporations. I shall borrow freely from the Bureau's *Studies in Business Financing*, identifying the books referred to by the names of the authors.[16]

16 The authors and titles of the reports most pertinent to this section are: Charles L. Merwin, *Financing Small Corporations in Five Manufacturing Industries, 1926–36* (1942); Albert R. Koch, *The Financing of Large Corporations, 1920–39* (1943); Walter A. Chudson, *The Pattern of Corporate Financial Structure: A Cross-Section View of Manufacturing, Mining, Trade, and Construction, 1937* (1945); Friedrich A. Lutz, *Corporate Cash Balances, 1914–43, Manufacturing and Trade* (1945); and Neil H. Jacoby and R. J. Saulnier, *Business Finance and Banking* (1947).

Financial Structure of Business Enterprises
Useful basing points for the coming analysis are provided by
Table 14, which summarizes Chudson's cross section of corporate balance sheets and income accounts as reported in 1937
to the Bureau of Internal Revenue by enterprises engaged in
61 branches of mining, manufacturing, construction work,
and trade. The table stresses the varieties of financial pattern;
but one who studies Chudson's charts finds that the distribution
of the 61 'minor industrial divisions' around the central tendencies of their arrays is such as to give the medians of Table 14
considerable significance.

Of chief interest for present purposes are the following
observations: (1) Three-quarters of total assets belong to the
stockholders on the average. This ratio varies within the moderate limits of 43 and 85 percent. (2) The heaviest investment is
usually in fixed capital assets; but here the range of variation
is very wide. Technological requirements are the chief de-
terminants of this ratio, which runs highest in public utilities
(not included in the table), and declines progressively as we
pass to mining, manufacturing, retailing, and wholesale trade.
(3) Working capital runs in Chudson's whole sample about as
high as fixed capital assets plus long-term investments. More
detailed figures show wide industrial differences in the percentage of current to total assets—trade 63 percent, manufacturing 39, electric light and power 6, telephone 6, railroads
4.[17] (4) Long-term debt is smaller than short-term on the
average. In 1937, sums due to commercial houses exceeded
sums due to banks. (5) In more than half of the groups covered,
annual sales exceeded total assets.

Fixed Capital
Outside the realm of finance, the bulk of an enterprise's 'fixed
capital' is usually invested in durable goods. The demand for
these 'producer durables' is subject to cyclical fluctuations
even more violent than those we have seen to be characteristic

[17] See Koch, *op. cit.*, p. 42.

Table 14

RANGE OF VARIATION OF BALANCE-SHEET RATIOS AMONG
MINOR INDUSTRIAL DIVISIONS, 1937[a]

	Range Low	High	Median	Index of Relative Variation[b]
PERCENTAGE OF TOTAL ASSETS				
Fixed capital assets	4.9	74.4	34.6	47.4
Other investments	5.3	25.6	12.6	72.2
Cash	1.4	13.0	6.2	35.5
Government securities	0.1	4.9	1.8	61.1
Receivables	5.5	37.9	13.7	58.4
Inventory	0.5	47.5	22.7	62.6
Notes payable	1.2	16.6	5.2	69.2
Accounts payable	4.4	29.4	7.6	43.4
Long-term debt	1.2	35.9	6.9	78.3
Capital stock	27.5	66.1	47.7	16.1
Surplus	6.1	51.7	25.2	32.1
Net worth	42.7	84.9	75.4	18.7
PERCENTAGE OF SALES				
Total assets	30.6	239.2	94.7	48.6
Fixed capital assets	3.8	186.3	30.6	84.6
Cash plus government securities	1.7	19.6	7.7	53.2
Receivables	4.9	28.0	12.7	59.8
Inventory	4.7	38.5	18.2	57.7
Notes payable	0.8	20.5	4.8	37.5
Accounts payable	2.5	23.4	7.7	59.7
Other liabilities	1.0	14.7	3.9	94.9
OTHER RATIOS				
Current assets to current liabilities	0.6	5.1	2.5	40.0
Invested capital to capital assets	1.1	10.8	2.2	45.5
Net income as percent of net worth	−7.7	14.5	5.8	70.5

[a] Adapted from Chudson, *op. cit.*, Table 2. Based upon 61 'minor industrial divisions' of the Bureau of Internal Revenue classification, which are grouped as follows: mining and quarrying (6), manufacturing (47), construction (2), shipbuilding (1), trade (5).

[b] Interquartile range expressed as a percentage of the median.

of consumer durables. Buyers have as wide a leeway in deciding when to make replacements in or additions to their stock; they have also keener incentives to purchase at certain stages of a business cycle than at others. It is not clear that the owner of an old passenger automobile feels a stronger desire for a new car after revival than he felt before; but it is clear that a trucking company with the poorest of its vehicles laid up during contraction has a stronger motive to get new trucks after all of its fleet come into use. Whatever differences appear between cyclical movements in the prices charged for producer and for consumer durables may be traceable to these underlying differences between the attitudes of the two sets of buyers. Anticipating correctly the cyclical swings in the requirements for industrial equipment, being financially ready to meet their cost, and placing orders betimes are matters of much moment in many industries, especially when the investment in durable goods is relatively heavy and the goods take months to produce.

As the stock of fixed capital increases, maintenance expenditures usually mount. But maintenance expenditures are not nearly so stable as are the stocks of fixed capital, nor so volatile as are orders or construction of new plant and equipment.[18] The current upkeep of physical structures, including repairs and replacements of minor parts, is usually treated as a current expense on a par with the cost of raw materials. In a few instances virtually no other charge is made. American railroads, for example, charge almost all of their outlays on maintaining 'way and structures' to 'operating costs'.[19] But not many physical properties can be kept efficient indefinitely by piecemeal repairs. No matter how faithfully maintenance work is done, the article, be it a huge building or a single machine, declines in value. If the enterprise is to remain in business, provision must be made for replacing old properties when they shall have fallen below the required standard of efficiency. Meanwhile the proprietors and creditors must know whether the enterprise is covering all its costs.[20]

---

[18] Ibid., p. 132, note 7, and Solomon Fabricant, Capital Consumption and Adjustment (National Bureau, 1938), Table 5.

[19] Cf. Fabricant, ibid., p. 44.

[20] Needless to say, I am skipping numberless problems of detail. For more adequate discussions of the distinction between maintenance and depreciation, and of the numerous ways in which durable properties depreciate, see George O. May's three chapters on depreciation in his Financial Accounting, A Distillation of Experience (Macmillan, 1943), and Fabricant, Capital Consumption and Adjustment.

To the latter end, the accountant accepts a (necessarily rough) estimate of the depreciation suffered during the year by the durable properties of an enterprise, and deducts this sum from current receipts when computing its profit or loss on the year's operations. Besides retaining from operations funds to offset depreciation, a successful enterprise usually retains part of its net earnings. These retained earnings may be used like depreciation reserves for whatever purpose the management thinks important—to increase any asset or diminish any liability. While depreciation reserves supposedly prevent the gradual decline in the value of an enterprise's fixed property from producing a decline in its net worth, the retention of earnings supposedly increases net worth. Within brief periods, the gross savings of business enterprises include both reserves to offset depreciation and undistributed profits; net savings include only the latter. But these internal sources of funds are not always sufficient to cover fixed capital requirements; in that event the enterprise may turn to other devices—chiefly borrowing or selling additional shares to stockholders, old or new.

The relative costs of acquiring and maintaining fixed property vary considerably, and so too does the importance of various sources of funds for financing the acquisition of fixed capital. Though the basic data leave much to be desired, a few broad conclusions can be drawn. (1) Maintenance charges exceed depreciation accruals several fold in American railroad practice, and to a less degree in some other utilities; but it appears that in most other nonfinancial types of business annual depreciation exceeds maintenance.[21] (2) In manufacturing, according to our sample of large corporation accounts covering the 19 years 1921–39, depreciation reserves (plus property revaluations) were much larger than the sum of undistributed earnings plus net funds obtained from security issues. Among trading companies, however, undistributed earnings exceed the sum of depreciation and new funds from the security

[21] See Fabricant, *ibid.*, pp. 44–8, and Table 29.

markets.[22] (3) According to the Kuznets-Fabricant estimates, of which more presently, nearly two-thirds of the capital 'formed' in the United States from 1921 to 1938 was required to offset the capital 'consumed' in those years. Presumably, in the economy as a whole, over a period of this length, depreciation charges roughly equal capital 'replacements'; whereas the increase in capital is provided mainly by retained profits and net increase of investments by stock and bond holders.

In cyclical behavior the several ways of financing durable properties differ widely. Unlike maintenance expenditures, depreciation charges are linked more closely to the book value of fixed physical assets at the beginning of successive years than to sales within years. Only in long contractions are the aggregate book values of the property held by all enterprises in an economy likely to decline. Thus the average fall in depreciation during reference-cycle contractions is relatively smaller than the average fall in maintenance. Of course, the absence of decline in a contraction tends to moderate the rise during the subsequent expansion. Fabricant's final summary of accounting measures of depreciation and of repairs and maintenance yields the following mean reference-cycle amplitudes in the four cycles of 1921–38:

	Expansion	Contraction	Full cycle
Depreciation (all business capital)	+8.2	−0.5	+8.7
Repairs & maintenance (public utilities only)	+12.6	−22.0	+34.6

These figures understate the differences in amplitude between depreciation and maintenance, because the maintenance figures

[22] The figures compiled from Koch's (*op. cit.*) samples (see his Tables 4, 12, 13, and 14), which seem to be broadly though not strictly comparable, are as follows:

	ANNUAL AVERAGE, $ MILLION, 1921–39	
	Manu-facturing	Trade
Depreciation & property revaluations	592	21
Undistributed earnings	177	35
New funds from issues & retirements of securities	128	9

are restricted to types of business well above average in cyclical stability.[23]

Retained proceeds have exceedingly large reference-cycle amplitudes, in contrast to depreciation charges. Profits themselves fluctuate violently. Dividends are usually kept more stable than profits. When dividends are subtracted from profits, the remainder is even more variable than the minuend. According to Kuznets' estimates, the net dissavings of American business corporations in 1930–38 exceeded their net savings in 1919–29, and we therefore cannot measure the enormous amplitude of their retained proceeds in our standard fashion.[24]

Concerning the issuing of securities we have monthly records that, with all their deficiencies, are convincing on one point: the amount of capital secured in this fashion is subject to very large cyclical swings. Among the 29 groups of series ranked in order of their average reference-cycle amplitudes in Table 11, corporate security issues are third from the top.

To sum up: retained profits have exceedingly large reference-cycle amplitudes, net sales of securities have large amplitudes, and depreciation accruals fluctuate little. Of these sources of funds, the one with the smallest amplitudes seems to be the most important for the purchasing of industrial equipment when we consider the whole economy and considerable periods. Not only does it yield larger funds; it gives business managements the fullest discretion as to when they shall buy, and thus allows very large amplitudes in the demand for equipment. There is no close connection between the time when depreciation accrues, and the time when depreciation reserves are expended for fresh equipment—indeed, the reserves may never be put to that use. But the possession of these reserves enables enterprises to increase their purchases of industrial equipment when managements think best, even though

[23] Professor Fabricant kindly extended his original estimates (*Capital Consumption and Adjustment*, Table 29) through 1938 for my benefit.

[24] See Simon Kuznets, *National Income and Its Composition, 1919–1938* (National Bureau, 1941), Table 39; and the comments on Table 15 below.

profits are nearing their lowest ebb, new security issues are inadvisable, and maintenance work is being deferred in many quarters. However, depreciation reserves cannot be used to obtain industrial equipment unless they have been kept in cash or assets readily convertible into cash. The next section will show how this condition is often met when times are hardest by certain developments in working capital.

Meanwhile we should note that investments in industrial equipment are not dominated by the *concomitant* volume of saving; they depend far more upon decisions by management as to the time when it is wise to use in this way certain funds retained from past operations. Also we should be clear regarding the strain we are putting upon the word 'saving' if we apply it to reserves for depreciation. Such a reserve does not represent an increase in the net worth of an enterprise. It is merely an estimate of the property used up in the conduct of business—property that has not yet been replaced, but the funds for replacing which are represented either in the increase of some asset or the decrease of some liability.

Working Capital

Among the components of working capital in the 61 branches of business represented in Table 14, much the largest as a rule is inventories. In his 1921–39 sample of large corporations, Koch shows that inventories constituted about 60 percent of the working capital in trading and about 50 percent in manufacturing companies. Abramovitz finds that manufacturing and trading concerns carry some three-quarters or four-fifths of all inventories, and that half of the remainder is held by farmers.[25]

In our sample of monthly and quarterly series for the United States we have direct evidence concerning the reference-cycle amplitudes of inventories. But these 62 series on stocks of commodities tell little about the volume of capital needed to carry

[25] See Koch, *op. cit.*, Chart 4; Abramovitz, *op. cit.*, Table 3, and context. Manufacturers' inventories are somewhat larger than traders' in this table—a conclusion not inconsistent with Koch's finding that inventories form a larger proportion of traders' than of manufacturers' working capital, which in turn is a larger proportion of traders' than of manufacturers' total assets.

inventories. First, all of our monthly series (except department store stocks) are expressed in physical units, and, as a factor in business, inventories vary with prices as well as quantities. Second, our series on stocks of commodities are badly split among the four types of cyclical timing we recognize: 18 of the 62 have positive timing, 2 neutral, 24 inverted, and 18 irregular. If we compute the reference-cycle amplitudes of the whole group without regard to sign, we get a mean rise and fall, or fall and rise of 50 points—nearly the same as the similarly computed average of all the 794 series in our sample (see Table 10). Of course a businessman would not compute the fluctuations in his inventory in this way. Instead, he would cast up the value of the stocks of all commodities he carries, and note the fluctuations in these totals. If, as often happens, some of his stocks have positive, others inverted, and still others irregular timing, there will be more or less offsetting among their cyclical movements.[26] So, when we work with sample balance sheets, we expect to find rather moderate amplitudes in inventories because of their mixed timing as well as because the data are usually reported only once a year. Koch's samples of 80 large manufacturing and of 26 large trading corporations give mean amplitudes for inventories in the 4 reference cycles of 1921–38 of +12, −3, +15 and +27, −1, +28, respectively. The nationwide estimates of inventories in current prices used in making Simon Kuznets' tables of gross national product have intermediate amplitudes in these cycles: namely, +11, −10, +21.

These modest amplitudes of total inventories accord with rational expectations. For the total business inventories of any given date are that portion of a nation's production which is

---

[26] If we respect signs in computing the mean reference-cycle amplitude of our 62 monthly series on stocks of commodities, the average comes out −19 points; for it happens that we have more inverted than positive series in our sample, and that the irregular series yield negative averages. The weighting of our samples of inventories is not representative. Perhaps the reason is that, in this field as in many others, men have recorded factors that cause them trouble (inverted inventories) more fully than factors that are easy to manage.

then passing through the hands of producers, fabricators, and distributors on its way to final consumers. The goods that make up the inventories of any reference-cycle stage will, in altered assortments, become the bulk of the gross product of that or some later stage, so that the reference-cycle amplitudes of total inventories do not differ drastically from the moderate amplitudes of gross product itself. This relation between total inventories and gross product explains also why positive prevails over inverted timing in all comprehensive series on inventories.

Perhaps the reader has noticed that I am implicitly measuring the amplitudes of inventories on a basis different from that which I stressed in considering the amplitudes of fixed capital. If I treated stocks of industrial equipment on the same basis as stocks of raw materials held by a factory or merchandise held by a retailer, I would get extremely low reference-cycle amplitudes, instead of the high amplitudes suggested by the preceding section. For the changes that occur during a reference cycle in the total fixed capital, or the aggregate industrial equipment, of an industry make small percentages of the whole capital or equipment that has accumulated over decades. But, on the average, these same changes make large percentages of the fixed capital or industrial equipment that is added to existing stocks during a business cycle. Both methods of treating amplitudes are valid; both are important, and in the sequel I shall employ both.[27]

Receivables have a median in Table 14 two-thirds that of inventory. Their amplitudes seem to be controlled by the amplitudes of sales; but their ratio to sales differs widely from one branch of business to another. It is not easy to rationalize all the long established differences in prevailing terms of sales, or

[27] In dealing with the cyclical aspects of employment, for example, it is not very pertinent to say that additions to the supply of industrial equipment rise and fall in the course of a business cycle less than 10 percent of the existing stock. Yet this method of measuring is appropriate when we deal with quantities that are turned over several times a year. Koch (*op. cit.*, p. 52) finds that in 1921–39 large manufacturing companies had average annual stock-sales ratios of about 1:3.9, and large trading companies of about 1:7.6.

in the proportions of receivables rediscounted with banks or sold to finance companies. According to our sample of large corporations, the collection period averages 41 days in manufacturing and 12 days in trade; but the range runs from 19 days in the motor car industry to 105 in machine building, and from 1 day in chain variety stores to 58 days in department stores.[28]

Cash holdings, the third item of working capital in average magnitude, behave in a fashion that is puzzling at first sight. In our sample of large corporations, cash increases in 3 out of 4 expansions; then increases further in all 4 contractions. The cyclical timing is irregular, and the mean amplitude is low (+9, +16, −7). But Friedrich A. Lutz has wrung an interesting story from these data by breaking the total holdings into two components—'transaction cash' and 'free cash'. Finding that the ratio of cash to payments was remarkably stable in 1922–29, when large corporations could lend any temporary surplus of funds on the active stock market, Lutz assumes that the average ratio shown by each corporation in his sample during this period measures its 'normal' requirements of 'transaction cash'. By applying this ratio to payments in each year from 1915–43, he determines when each company was embarrassed by a shortage of cash for transacting business, and when it had more cash than it needed. If we accept the two series into which Lutz thus decomposes the original record of year-end cash balances, and analyze them in our standard fashion, we find that transaction cash and free cash have precisely opposite cyclical timing (expansion in I–V and in V–IX), almost perfect positive and perfect inverted conformity, and substantial amplitudes.

What happens during expansion is that the need for transaction cash swells with the dollar volume of payments to be made. This increase presently brings into use any surplus balances enterprises had been holding, and then calls for additional cash, which may come from current sales or from borrowings. If the expansion is long and intense, a shortage of cash

[28] *Ibid.*, pp. 54, 55.

is likely to feature its closing stage. But during contraction, the shrinking physical volume of business and falling prices reduce the need for transaction cash; cash balances go on increasing, often faster than they had grown in expansion. This increase comes mainly from the 'liquidation' of receivables and inventories. The surplus balances piling up from the decreasing need for and increasing supply of cash are presumably used as far as feasible to pay off debts to banks and commercial houses, perhaps to maintain dividends, perhaps to buy marketable securities from which some income may be expected. But, after all such opportunities have been grasped, the corporations of our sample held their largest cash balances at cyclical troughs, and these balances enhanced the ability of business managements to increase their purchases of industrial equipment at this lowest stage of business cycles.[29]

[29] Our analyses of Lutz' estimates for large manufacturing companies (much the best of his samples) are summarized below. Our standard method of measuring reference-cycle amplitudes cannot be applied to series in which both plus and minus items are numerous, as they are in the estimates of 'free' cash. (Cf. *Measuring Business Cycles*, pp. 166, 167.) In such cases, we measure amplitudes as deviations from the cycle bases, expressed in whatever units are used—here millions of dollars. Our standard method can be applied to 3 of the series presented here, and the measurement in millions of dollars to all 5. The measures are averages of 4 reference cycles, 1921–38. For the annual data used, see Lutz, *op. cit.*, Appendix D-2, sample B. As far as they go, Lutz' other samples seem to yield similar results. What holds true of year-end cash balances and free cash is broadly true also of marketable securities and 'free liquid funds'—that is, the cash plus marketable securities not required for transactions.

SERIES & EXPANSION STAGES	REFER-ENCE-CYCLE BASE ($ mil.)	INDEX OF CONFORMITY TO			AV. REFERENCE-CYCLE AMPLITUDE					
		Ex-pan-sion	Con-trac-tion	Busi-ness cycles	In Millions of Dollars			In Reference-Cycle Relatives		
					Ex-pan-sion	Con-trac-tion	Full cycle	Ex-pan-sion	Con-trac-tion	Full cycle
Cash balances at year end (irreg.)	638	+50	−100	−43	+52	+111	−59	+9	+16	−7
Transaction cash (I-V)	530	+100	+50	+100	+197	−152	+349	+38	−27	+65
Free cash (V–IX)	103	−100	−100	−100	−157	+231	−388	...	...	...
Marketable securities, year end (I-V)	481	0	+100	+71	+84	−116	+200	+13	−20	+33
Free liquid funds (V–IX)	93	−100	−100	−100	−338	+336	−674	...	...	...

Failure of reference-cycle bases for 'transaction cash' and 'free cash' to add up to that for total cash is due to the fact that total cash was analyzed in its year-end version, whereas the components are estimated from a two-year moving average of total cash. Concerning the arithmetical relations of 'free cash' and 'free liquid funds', see Lutz, Ch. 4. It may also be noted that, according to Lutz' Preface, A. Kisselgoff developed the measures of 'free cash'.

In going concerns, most of the working capital is derived immediately from operations. The funds paid out for materials, merchandise, labor, and the like are supposedly recovered with a profit from sales. Most enterprises, however, supplement these internal sources by drawing upon outside funds. Almost all of them buy at least part of the goods they need on credit. Table 14 indicates that in 1937 accounts payable (supposedly to commercial houses) typically exceeded notes (supposedly owed to banks). However, the margin between the two forms of short-term debt is not wide, and the excess of payables may be a recent development. Our samples of corporation accounts indicate that, at least between the two world wars, short-term debt both to banks and to commercial houses declined in relation to total liabilities, but bank debt fell faster.[30] Mercantile enterprises use relatively more short-term credit than manufacturing enterprises. In both groups the volume rises and falls with the cyclical tides.[31]

Ultimate Sources of Funds

Enlightening as the preceding analysis may be, it is superficial in the sense of staying strictly within the limits of business enterprise. Proper as this limitation may be for the accountant's purposes, an economist must ask: Whence come the funds that business obtains from 'external sources'? For that matter, funds obtained from 'internal sources'—that is, from the operations of business enterprises—have not really been accounted for until we know whence come the funds wherewith outsiders buy what business has to sell. Thus accounting, like economic theory, raises the fundamental problem of interrelationships among the processes with which it deals. Each fresh encounter with this problem has its special lesson to teach, or may repeat an old lesson to our advantage.

To say that business enterprises get most of their funds, whether fixed or working capital, from internal sources is to recognize that their operations depend primarily upon dollar sales, which in turn depend primarily upon antecedent income

[30] Jacoby and Saulnier, *op. cit.*, pp. 91, 92.
[31] Koch, *op. cit.*, pp. 65–73.

disbursements by business enterprises to consumers, which in turn depend primarily upon antecedent purchases by consumers from business enterprises. To say that business enterprises get part of their funds from external sources is to recognize that this circular flow of funds from the realm of business to the realm of consumers and back to business is accompanied and complicated by eddies within the realm of business, and by whatever changes occur in the proportions of their current incomes consumers spend for consumer goods. The business eddies of moment here are connected with commercial credit, banking, and dealings in securities.

For the economy as a whole, including households as well as firms, the total credits received through 'accounts payable' are offset by the total credits extended through 'accounts receivable'. This equality does not appear in any of our samples, for they are compiled from the accounts of corporations, in which receivables usually exceed payables by substantial margins. As Koch explains, business enterprises are net trade creditors of consumers, corporations are net trade creditors of unincorporated enterprises, and large corporations are net trade creditors of small ones.[32] But though payables in the aggregate are offset by receivables, the institution of commercial credit has consequences of great moment for business cycles; it alters the cyclical timing of activities into which it enters on a large scale, and it creates a vast interlocking system of short-term debts, the paying of which has often presented a major problem at cyclical recessions.

Banks, however, make a net addition to the funds of an economy. The funds they provide consist in Anglo-Saxon countries chiefly of deposit credits, checks against which the lending banks must be ready to pay, for the most part on demand. The total volume of loans or investments a bank is able to make exceeds its capital, surplus, and undivided profits, and in this excess lies the net addition that banks make to the nation's funds. More than a century ago, American state governments began imposing limits upon the volume of credit banks might extend,

[32] *Ibid.*, p. 56.

usually by requiring them to hold reserves of lawful money equal to at least certain specified percentages of their demand liabilities. We shall have occasion to observe how alterations in these legal requirements concerning bank reserves have influenced business cycles in this country.

Meanwhile we may note that the above-mentioned 'decline in the commercial loan' between the two world wars has not meant a corresponding decline in the volume of credit supplied by banks to other business enterprises. For decades American banks have been investing an increasing part of their funds in the securities of corporations. When a bank buys a bond, the seller usually accepts a deposit credit, just as a borrower accepts a deposit credit when a bank discounts his note. The rules about minimum reserves apply to deposits originating in one way as in the other. By the end of the interwar years, member banks of the Federal Reserve System reported substantial investments in corporate securities and still larger investments in government securities.[33]

The contribution that banks make to business funds paves the way for a contribution by government. The minimum reserve provisions that are supposed to limit the volume of bank credit were designed to accompany monetary systems in which the volume of money was controlled by economic

[33] The following figures show how different have been the rates of growth in bank loans and investments since the 1880's.

REFERENCE CYCLE	REFERENCE-CYCLE BASE ($ MIL.)		INVESTMENTS AS % OF LOANS
	Loans	Investments, excl. U.S. securities	
All national banks			
Mar. 1879–May 1885	1,145	59	5.2
Jan. 1912–Dec. 1914	6,174	1,030	16.7
Reporting member banks			
Apr. 1919–Sept. 1921	12,450	1,909	15.3
Mar. 1933–May 1938	8,700	3,085	35.5

The greatest growth has been in the holdings of U. S. government securities. Total investments, including 'governments', of reporting member banks were 29.4 percent of loans in the 1919–21 cycle and 132.6 percent in the 1933–38 cycle.

forces other than the exigencies of public finance. Let the metallic standard be replaced by a standard of irredeemable paper money, and the economic safeguards against an indefinite increase of bank credit are radically altered and often swept aside. Our economic organization can adapt itself to the conditions created by huge issues of irredeemable paper money, but the business cycles that run their course under these conditions constitute a special variety of their species.

There remains as an outside source of funds the investing public made up of individuals, other business enterprises, and at times governments. Our definite information about this source concerns chiefly the organized markets for securities, to which noncorporate enterprises and small corporations have virtually no access. How large manufacturing corporations use the securities markets is illustrated by Koch's tables.[34] Every year from 1921 to 1939 they sold their own securities in amounts that varied between $1,256 million in 1929 and $46 million in 1933. Also in every year they retired securities in amounts varying between $680 million in 1929 and $76 million in 1938. Sales exceeded retirements by $576 million in 1929; retirements exceeded sales by $164 million in 1935. On the average, sales were $341 million, retirements $213 million, new funds obtained $128 million. Only in 1921 did new funds from security sales exceed total funds retained from operations; on the average, retentions exceeded net funds drawn from outside investors by more than 7 to 1. But even in the depressed decade 1930–39, when assertions that the United States had reached 'economic maturity' became common, our 'large' manufacturing corporations were obtaining an average of $43 million a year net from the investing public toward their fixed capital expenditures of $736 million.

Where the investing public gets its funds is the next question. For an answer we had best turn to the overall view of economic operations in the United States provided by Simon Kuznets' estimates of gross national product and national income.

[34] Koch, *op. cit.*, Tables 12–13.

Estimates of Capital Formation and of Saving

Table 15 presents these estimates in the form best adapted to present needs—that is, on a reference-cycle basis. Current rather than constant prices are used, for it is in current prices that businessmen confront their problems. As usual when treating price and value series, we exclude the first cycle after World War I, though that decision leaves only four cycles to average—a thin sample at best, and doubtfully representative of earlier experience. The thoughtful reader will be tempted to dwell upon various features of this table that do not concern us at the moment, for it would be hard to find elsewhere so instructive or, to the instructed, so fascinating an exhibit of how our economy works. Often in coming chapters we shall turn back to this table for basing points, but for the moment let us stick to capital formation and saving.

On the average of reference-cycle bases, 'capital goods' form less than 18 percent of gross national product, while more than 82 percent is devoted to meeting our wants as consumers (col. 3 of the table). Consequently, the cyclical fluctuations in output taken at current prices are larger in consumer than in capital goods. Rounded off to the nearest billion dollars, the mean amplitudes for consumer goods are +9, −7, +16; for capital goods, +6, −6, +12 (col. 8–10). But in relation to their own average volume, the cyclical fluctuations in the production of capital goods are four times as violent as those in consumer goods: +55, −49, +105 compared with +15, −10, +25 (col. 14–16). This sharp contrast suggests still a third way of measuring the amplitudes—reducing the cyclical rise and fall in the output of both consumer and capital goods to percentages of the cyclical rise and fall in the output of all goods (col. 11–13). On this basis, the amplitudes are +60, −52, +56 in consumer goods and +40, −48, +44 in capital goods. Though capital goods form less than 18 percent of gross national product, their output is subject to such violent alternations of good and ill fortune that this minor segment of the economy contributes 44 percent of the total cyclical fluctuations in output, and nearly half of the cyclical declines.

Table 15

REFERENCE-CYCLE BASES, TIMING, CONFORMITY, AND AMPLITUDE OF KUZNETS' ESTIMATES OF CAPITAL FORMATION, SAVINGS, AND RELATED MAGNITUDES, AT CURRENT PRICES, FOUR BUSINESS CYCLES, 1921–1938[a]

(1)	Average Reference-Cycle Base		Expansion Stages	Index of Conformity to			Millions of Dollars			Average Reference-Cycle Amplitude in % of Changes in GROSS PRODUCT			% of Reference-Cycle Bases		
	Millions of Dollars Per Year (2)	% of GROSS PRODUCT (3)	(4)	Ex-pansion (5)	Con-trac-tion (6)	Business cycles (7)	Ex-pansion (8)	Con-trac-tion (9)	Full cycle (10)	Ex-pansion (11)	Con-trac-tion (12)	Full cycle (13)	Ex-pansion (14)	Con-trac-tion (15)	Full cycle (16)
Gross National Product	77,057	100.0	I–V	+100	+50	+100	+15,140	−13,214	+28,354	+100.0	−100.0	+100.0	+21.2	−16.4	+37.6
Components of Product															
Consumer goods															
Perishable commodities	23,750	30.8	I–V	+100	+50	+71	+3,816	−2,828	+6,644	+25.2	−21.4	+23.4	+16.4	−11.4	+27.8
Semidurable commodities[b]	9,919	12.9	I–V	+100	+50	+100	+1,275	−1,555	+2,830	+8.4	−11.8	+10.0	+13.8	−15.1	+28.9
Durable commodities[b]	6,489	8.4	I–V	+100	+50	+100	+1,810	−1,748	+3,558	+12.0	−13.2	+12.5	+31.0	−27.0	+58.0
Services[c]	23,282	30.2	III–VII	+100	0	+43	+3,173	−1,758	+4,931	+21.0	−13.3	+17.4	+14.4	−6.4	+20.8
TOTAL	63,440	82.3	I–V	+100	+50	+57	+9,016	−6,862	+15,878	+59.6	−51.9	+56.0	+15.0	−9.9	+24.9
Gross capital formation															
Durable producer commodities[b]	5,061	6.6	I–V	+100	+100	+100	+2,078	−1,982	+4,060	+13.7	−15.0	+14.3	+46.0	−39.4	+85.4
Construction, residential	2,988	3.9	I–V	+50	0	+43	+658	−665	+1,323	+4.3	−5.0	+4.7	+33.9	−22.0	+55.9
Construction, other private	2,679	3.5	I–V	+100	0	+71	+631	−852	+1,483	+4.2	−6.4	+5.2	+30.6	−32.9	+63.5
Construction, public[b]	1,987	2.6	V–IX	+100	−50	−29	+148	−12	+160	+1.0	−0.1	+0.6	+7.7	+1.4	+6.3
Construction, total[b]	7,654	9.9	I–V	+50	0	+43	+1,438	−1,530	+2,968	+9.5	−11.6	+10.5	+24.0	−18.6	+42.6
Net change in inventories	556	0.7	I–V	+100	+100	+100	+3,063	−3,169	+6,232	+20.2	−24.0	+22.0			
Net change in international claims	344	0.4	V–IX	−100	−50	−43	−452	+328	−780	−3.0	+2.5	−2.8	−131.2[c]	+95.2[c]	−226.4[c]
TOTAL	13,617	17.7	I–V	+100	+100	+100	+6,124	−6,352	+12,476	+40.4	−48.1	+44.0	+55.4	−49.3	+104.7
Capital Consumption	8,772	11.4	I–V	+100	+50	+100	+1,036	−623	+1,659	+6.8	−4.7	+5.9	+12.0	−6.6	+18.6
Net Capital Formation	4,844	6.3	I–V	+100	+100	+100	+5,088	−5,729	+10,817	+33.6	−43.4	+38.1	...	...	...
National Income	68,284	88.6	I–V	+100	+50	+100	+14,104	−12,592	+26,696	+93.2	−95.3	+94.2	+22.5	−17.6	+40.1

[a] All series summarized in this table come from worksheets for Kuznets' *National Product since 1869* (National Bureau, 1946) or from worksheets for his *National Income and Its Composition* after revision to accord with published results in *National Product since 1869*. In most cases the figures used were carried to an additional place beyond those published.

[b] Derived from original data expressed in ten millions of dollars per year.

[c] Amplitude in millions of dollars per year expressed as a percentage of the average reference-cycle base for the four cycles of 1921–38.

Table 15 (concl.)

(1)	AVERAGE REFERENCE-CYCLE BASE		EXPAN-SION STAGES	INDEX OF CONFORMITY TO			AVERAGE REFERENCE-CYCLE AMPLITUDE IN — Millions of Dollars			AVERAGE REFERENCE-CYCLE AMPLITUDE IN — % of Changes in NATIONAL INCOME			% of Reference-Cycle Bases		
	Millions of Dollars Per Year (2)	% of NATIONAL INCOME (3)	(4)	Ex-pan-sion (5)	Con-trac-tion (6)	Busi-ness cycles (7)	Ex-pan-sion (8)	Con-trac-tion (9)	Full cycle (10)	Ex-pan-sion (11)	Con-trac-tion (12)	Full cycle (13)	Ex-pan-sion (14)	Con-trac-tion (15)	Full cycle (16)
National Income	68,284	100.0	I–V	+100	+50	+100	+14,104	−12,592	+26,696	+100.0	−100.0	+100.0	+22.5	−17.6	+40.1
Income of individuals															
Employees' compensation[a]	42,685	62.5	I–V	+100	+50	+100	+8,026	−5,822	+13,848	+56.9	−46.2	+51.9	+19.8	−13.0	+32.8
Entrepreneurial with-drawals	11,419	16.7	I–V	+100	0	+43	+957	−760	+1,717	+6.8	−6.0	+6.4	+8.7	−6.1	+14.8
Net rents	4,178	6.1	I–V	0	+50	−14	+133	−607	+740	+0.9	−4.8	+2.8	+5.7	−15.1	+20.8
Dividends	4,240	6.2	I–V	+100	+50	+100	+1,242	−1,112	+2,354	+8.8	−8.8	+8.8	+30.3	−23.7	+54.0
Interest[c]	4,766	7.0	III–V	+50	0	+43	+154	−1	+155	+1.1	f	+0.6	+3.2	+1.0	+2.2
TOTAL[e]	67,289	98.5	I–V	+100	+50	+100	+10,482	−8,245	+18,727	+74.3	−65.5	+70.1	+16.4	−11.6	+28.0
Total consumers' outlay	63,440	92.9	I–V	+100	+50	+57	+9,016	−6,862	+15,878	+63.9	−54.5	+59.5	+15.0	−9.9	+24.9
Savings															
Individual	3,849	5.6	I–V	+100	+50	+43	+1,468	−1,383	+2,851	+10.4	−11.0	+10.7	+40.1	−39.2	+79.3
Entrepreneurial	344	0.5	I–V	+50	+100	+100	+1,404	−1,495	+2,899	+10.0	−11.9	+10.9	…	…	…
Corporate	−315	−0.5	I–V	+100	+50	+71	+1,612	−1,963	+3,575	+11.4	−15.6	+13.4	…	…	…
Governmental[e]	967	1.4	III–V	+100	+50	+100	+819	−1,076	+1,895	+5.8	−8.5	+7.1	…	…	…
TOTAL	4,844	7.1	I–V	+100	+100	+100	+5,088	−5,729	+10,817	+36.1	−45.5	+40.5	…	…	…

[a] Includes 'other payments to employees', i.e., social security contributions of employers, pensions, etc. Our series 'wages and salaries' excluding such other payments is presented in note g.

[c] The sum of the preceding five items. Our series 'income payments' comprises this total plus entrepreneurial savings minus imputed rent; it is presented in note g.

[f] Less than 0.05 percent.

[g] Averages for the two series referred to in notes d and e and averages on a I–V basis for the three series with expansion stages III–V or III–VII are:

(1)	AVERAGE REFERENCE-CYCLE BASE		EXPAN-SION STAGES	INDEX OF CONFORMITY TO			AVERAGE REFERENCE-CYCLE AMPLITUDE IN — Millions of Dollars			AVERAGE REFERENCE-CYCLE AMPLITUDE IN — % of Changes in Gross Product or National Income			% of Reference-Cycle Bases		
	Millions of Dollars Per Year (2)	% of Gross Prod. or Nat. Inc. (3)	(4)	Ex-pan-sion (5)	Con-trac-tion (6)	Busi-ness cycles (7)	Ex-pan-sion (8)	Con-trac-tion (9)	Full cycle (10)	Ex-pan-sion (11)	Con-trac-tion (12)	Full cycle (13)	Ex-pan-sion (14)	Con-trac-tion (15)	Full cycle (16)
Wages and salaries	41,426	60.7	I–V	+100	+50	+100	+7,250	−6,060	+13,310	+51.4	−48.1	+49.9	+18.6	−14.0	+32.6
Income payments	65,415	95.8	I–V	+100	+50	+100	+12,270	−9,763	+22,033	+87.0	−77.5	+82.5	+19.8	−14.3	+34.1
Services	23,282	30.2	I–V	+100	−50	−14	+2,116	−733	+2,849	+14.0	−5.5	+10.0	+9.6	−1.5	+11.1
Interest	4,766	7.0	I–V	+50	0	−29	+125	+55	+70	+0.9	+0.4	+0.3	+2.5	+1.4	+1.1
Governmental savings	967	1.4	I–V	+50	0	+71	+606	−889	+1,495	+4.3	−7.1	+5.6	…	…	…

While gross capital formation averaged nearly $14 billion per annum, nearly $9 billion of that output were required to offset capital consumption, leaving less than $5 billion a year as 'net capital formation', or saving (col. 2). In other words, almost two-thirds of the capital goods produced was needed to offset capital used up, and little more than one-third remained as an addition to the country's stock. Capital consumption, which corresponds roughly to depreciation and its congeners, has relatively narrow amplitudes ($+12$, -7, $+19$) when measured in our standard fashion (col. 14–16). When this relatively stable series is subtracted from the much more variable series on gross capital formation (average amplitudes $+55$, -49, $+105$), the remainder, net capital formation, alternates between plus and minus values so often that we cannot measure its amplitude in the usual fashion. In other words, saving in the economy as a whole is a process especially sensitive to the cyclical tides.

Gross national product minus capital consumption equals national income (col. 2). Net capital formation, which makes up 6 percent of gross product, becomes 'total savings' in the second part of the table, where it forms 7 percent of national income. Kuznets ascertained from published accounts approximately how much American governments and corporations have saved annually since 1919, and he made rougher approximations for unincorporated businesses from the Department of Agriculture's studies of farm income and similar sources. When these types of savings are subtracted from 'net capital formation', whatever remains is taken to be the savings of individuals. Kuznets is emphatic that his estimates are "subject to fairly wide margins of error", and that what constitutes 'net capital formation' in his studies of gross product differs radically from what enterprises and individuals commonly reckon as savings. For example, his estimates exclude all gains and losses on sales of capital assets. On the other hand, they include accruals to individuals as depositors in savings institutions and as holders of life insurance policies. As Kuznets sums up:

. . . while the estimates . . . differ significantly from what enterprises and individuals conceive their savings to be; while they cannot be used to gauge the propensity of enterprises and individuals to save, they do reflect approximately the shares of net capital formation, i.e., of real investment financed from the current income of different groups of enterprises and individuals. In that sense they measure the contribution of various types of savings from current income to additions to the stock of the nation's capital goods.[35]

Kuznets' year-by-year figures indicate that outgo exceeded income among corporations in 1930–38, among unincorporated enterprises in 1922 and 1930–34, and among governments (federal, state, and local) in 1919, 1932–36, and 1938. Individuals were the only group to put by money every year. They were also the largest savers in every year covered by the estimates except 1919 and 1921. On the average (Table 15, col. 2) individual thrift contributed nearly four-fifths of total savings. This I take to be a larger fraction than would appear if the estimates could be carried backward several decades or brought down to date; for it is very doubtful that on the average of any other stretch of 18 years corporate savings were a minus quantity. But even if we confined our average to 'the prosperous' 1920's—which would err on the opposite side—the share of individuals in the national total of savings would be one-half and the share of corporations less than a seventh.

We cannot measure the reference-cycle amplitudes of corporate, entrepreneurial, or governmental savings in our standard fashion because of the intermixture of minus and plus items. Individual savings alone can be measured this way. They have amplitudes that are rather large for annual data: +40, −39, +79 (col. 14–16). These are nearly triple the amplitudes of the income of individuals (+16, −12, +28). People spend 94 percent of their incomes on consumer goods, and these expenditures rise and fall during business cycles nearly as much (+15, −10, +25) as incomes themselves. So the small fraction of individual income that is saved (6 percent in the average year, if we accept Kuznets' concepts and estimates) constitutes a flow of funds into the investment market more than three times as variable as the aggregate flow into the markets for consumer goods.

Much more variable still are the savings of other groups.

[35] *National Income and Its Composition*, Vol. I, p. 278.

Though they contribute on the average minor fractions of national savings, they are responsible for about three-quarters of the cyclical rise and fall in saving measured in millions of dollars (col. 8–10 of the table, and note *g* for governmental savings). Corporations contribute most to these fluctuations in savings, which is of course a sound reason for attending closely to them in studies of business cycles.

Summary and Supplement

So prominent is the role played by investing in the business-cycle drama that I commend to the reader's thoughtful study the following summary of the reference-cycle timing, conformity, and amplitudes of series representing this process from different viewpoints and at different stages.

Section A of Table 16 on stocks of industrial equipment in existence shows how little influence a typical business cycle has upon the numbers or the theoretical 'capacity' of the nation's mines, processing plants, transportation lines, and machines. The last few entries demonstrate that the use of monthly data would raise the amplitudes somewhat, but the most variable of these monthly series rises and falls only 6 percent. It is noteworthy, also, that not one of these series conforms perfectly to expansions, contractions, and full cycles, and not one has I–V timing. Indeed, the prevailing timing types are neutral, inverted, or irregular. None of these findings seems surprising when we recall how many years most of this equipment will last, how many months much of it takes to build, and at what stages of a business cycle the production of new equipment reaches the largest volumes.

Section B of the table deals with formal commitments to invest. Here the amplitudes run high, usually above 100, and the conformity is strikingly regular. Positive timing prevails with leads at one turn or both. The exceptions to these rules are few and (aside from the medium amplitudes of orders for Southern pine lumber) are confined to governmental construction.

Section C moves forward to the stage of production or ship-

Table 16

REFERENCE-CYCLE TIMING, CONFORMITY, AND AMPLITUDE OF SELECTED SERIES RELATING TO INVESTMENT

Series[a]	Period Covered[b]	No. of Reference Cycles	Expansion Stages	Index of Conformity to			Av. Reference-Cycle Amplitude		
				Expansion	Contraction	Business cycles	Expansion	Contraction	Full cycle[c]
A STOCKS OF INDUSTRIAL EQUIPMENT IN PLACE									
BY YEARS									
Coal and coke industries									
1 Anthracite coal mines, capacity	1891–1938	13	V–III	–38	–14	–38	–1.3	+2.3	–3.6
2 Bituminous coal mines, capacity	1891–1938	13	Irreg.	+69	–57	–8	+8.3	+2.5	+5.8
3 Bituminous coal, undercutting machines in use, no.	1897–1939	11	III–VII	+55	–9	+52	+12.2	+6.0	+6.2
4 Coke ovens, total, no.	1885–1939	15	V–IX	+7	–12	–33	+1.9	–0.8	+2.7
4 Coke ovens, total, no.	1885–1919	10	V–IX	+60	–64	–40	+9.0	+6.9	+2.1
4 Coke ovens, total, no.	1919–1939	5	V–IX	–100	+100	–33	–12.3	–16.2	+3.9
5 Beehive coke ovens, no.	1885–1919	10	V–IX	+60	–64	–50	+8.2	+6.6	+1.6
5 Beehive coke ovens, no.	1919–1939	5	V–IX	–100	+100	–33	–19.3	–23.3	+4.0
6 Byproduct coke ovens, no.	1894–1939	12	Irreg.	+83	–67	+22	+34.3	+20.0	+14.3
7 Byproduct coke ovens, capacity	1919–1939	5	Irreg.	+20	–67	–40	+5.6	+6.3	–0.7
Metal industries									
8 Pig iron capacity	1915–1939	6	III–VII	+57	+14	+69	+2.0	–0.2	+2.2
9 Steel ingot capacity	1915–1939	6	Irreg.	+67	–100	–33	+4.9	+4.4	+0.5
10 Copper refineries, capacity	1908–1939	8	III–VII	+56	–56	+29	+8.9	+4.8	+4.1
Cotton industry									
11 Spindles in place, total, no.	1908–1938	8	Irreg.	+25	–33	–31	–0.7	–0.02	–0.7
12 Spindles, cotton-growing states, no.	1914–1938	6	Irreg.	+67	–71	–33	+4.0	+2.2	+1.8
13 Spindles, noncotton-growing states, no.	1914–1938	6	Irreg.	0	+14	–33	–10.1	–5.5	–4.6

Table 16 (cont.)

Series[a]	Period Covered[b]	No. of Reference Cycles	Expansion Stages	Index of Conformity to			Av. Reference-Cycle Amplitude		
				Expansion	Contraction	Business cycles	Expansion	Contraction	Full cycle[^]
Railroads & other transport industries									
14 Locomotives, steam, available, no.	1891–1939	13	III–IX	+23	–57	–69	+0.2	+2.4	–2.2
15 Locomotives, steam, available, tractive power	1904–1939	9	III–VII	+60	–40	+47	+4.9	+2.3	+2.6
16 Locomotives, freight & passenger service, no.	1922–1939	4	Irreg.	–50	+100	–38	–6.6	–4.9	–1.7
17 Freight cars owned, no.	1922–1939	4	Irreg.	–50	+60	–50	–5.4	–2.6	–2.8
18 Freight cars on line, total, no.	1922–1939	4	III–VII	–50	+20	+12	–2.0	–3.8	+1.8
19 Freight cars on line, serviceable, no.	1922–1939	4	III–VII	0	+60	+75	+0.4	–6.3	+6.7
20 R.R., total track mileage	1891–1939	13	V–IX	+85	–79	–58	+3.0	+2.2	+0.8
21 Auto. registrations, truck, total	1908–1939	8	Irreg.	+100	–100	+65	+44.0	+40.7	+3.3
22 Auto. registrations, passenger car, total[f]	1897–1939	11	Irreg.	+100	–83	+27	+54.8	+50.8	+4.0
23 Merchant marine, total tonnage	1843–1938	24	Irreg.	+21	–42	–11	+4.6	+3.6	+1.0
Communications industry									
24 Western Union, wire mileage	1867–1939[d]	17	III–VII	+100	–88	+19	+10.8	+8.9	+1.9
24 Western Union, wire mileage	1867–1914	12	III–VII	+100	–100	+35	+13.9	+11.4	+2.5
24 Western Union, wire mileage	1919–1939	5	Irreg.	+100	–100	–11	+3.4	+3.1	+0.3
BY MONTHS									
Railroad industry									
25 Locomotives, frt. & pass. service, no.	1921–1938	4	VI–IX	–100	+50	–71	–8.2	–2.2	–6.0
26 Freight cars owned, no.	1921–1938	4	Irreg.	–50	+60	–25	–5.6	–2.1	–3.5
27 Freight cars on line, total, no.	1921–1938	4	IV–VII	0	+60	0	–5.2	–0.4	–4.8
28 Freight cars on line, serviceable, no.	1921–1938	4	II–VI	0	+60	+100	+0.9	–5.5	+6.4

Table 16 (cont.)

B CONTRACTS AND ORDERS FOR INVESTMENT GOODS

Contracts for construction work										
29	Total, value	1912–1938	7	VIII–IV	+71	+50	+86	+43	−30	+74
30	Residential buildings, value	1919–1938	5	VII–IV	+60	+67	+80	+37	−37	+74
31	Commercial buildings, value	1919–1938	5	VIII–V	+100	+60	+100	+58	−55	+112
32	Industrial buildings, value	1919–1938	5	VIII–V	+100	+100	+100	+116	−114	+230
33	Public & institutional buildings, value	1919–1938	5	VIII–V	+60	−20	+11	+30	−9	+38
34	Public utilities, value	1919–1938	5	I–VI	+100	+100	+100	+117	−109	+225
35	Public works, value	1919–1938	5	Irreg.	+100	−20	+78	+35	−15	+50
New orders for industrial equipment										
36	Machine tools & forging machinery, index	1919–1938	5	I–V	+100	+100	+100	+116	−121	+237
37	R.R. locomotives, no.	1870–1938	17	VIII–IV	+100	+100	+100	+93	−92	+185
38	R.R. freight cars, no.	1870–1938	17	VIII–IV	+100	+65	+100	+90	−82	+172
39	R.R. passenger cars, no.	1870–1938	17	VIII–IV	+76	+88	+94	+60	−59	+120
40	Rails	1870–1927	15	VI–IIIe	+87	+60	+72	+69	−52	+121
New orders for basic materials										
41	Merchant pig iron	1919–1924	2	VIII–IV	+100	+100	+100	+141	−121	+262
42	Fabricated structural steel	1912–1938	7	VIII–V	+71	+25	+57	+51	−59	+110
43	Steel sheets	1919–1933	4	VIII–III	+100	+100	+100	+60	−60	+121
44	Southern pine lumber	1919–1938	5	VII–IV	+20	+100	+100	+21	−30	+51
45	Oak flooring	1914–1938	6	VII–III	+67	+43	+83	+45	−38	+82
Unfilled orders										
46	U.S. Steel Corporation	1904–1933	8	I–V	+100	+100	+100	+44	−51	+95

Table 16 (cont.)

Series[a]	Period Covered[b]	No. of Reference Cycles	Expansion Stages	Index of Conformity to			Av. Reference-Cycle Amplitude		
				Expansion	Contraction	Business cycles	Expansion	Contraction	Full cycle[h]
C PRODUCTION OF INVESTMENT GOODS									
Production indexes									
47 Producer durables	1919–1938	5	I–V	+100	+100	+100	+44	−57	+101
48 Consumer durables	1919–1938	5	I–IV	+100	+100	+100	+48	−57	+105
49 Producer nondurables[f]	1919–1938	5	I–V	+100	+100	+100	+18	−22	+40
50 Consumer nondurables[f]	1919–1938	5	I–V	+100	+100	+100	+7	−11	+18
Industrial equipment, etc.									
51 Machine-tool shipments, index	1927–1933	1	Uncertain				+93	−187	+280
52 Woodworking mach., shipments, value	1919–1938	5	I–V	+100	+100	+100	+68	−80	+148
53 Industrial pumps, shipments, value	1919–1933	4	I–V	+100	+100	+100	+44	−60	+104
54 R.R. locomotives, shipments, no.	1919–1933	4	III–VI	+60	+60	+78	+58	−94	+152
55 R.R. freight cars, shipments, no.	1919–1938	5	I–V	+60	+100	+78	+95	−115	+210
56 R.R. passenger cars, shipments, no.	1919–1938	5	I–V	+20	+60	+33	+20	−20	+39
57 Auto. trucks, production	1914–1938	6	I–V	+100	+71	+100	+94	−65	+158
58 Auto. passenger cars, production	1914–1938	6	I–V	+100	+67	+82	+60	−45	+105
Production of basic materials									
59 Pig iron at merchant furnaces	1904–1938	9	I–V	+100	+100	+100	+59	−67	+126
60 Steel ingots	1900–1938	10	I–V	+100	+100	+100	+59	−55	+114
61 Steel sheets	1919–1938	5	VIII–V[c]	+100	+100	+100	+70	−70	+139
62 Southern pine lumber	1919–1938	5	I–IV	+60	+100	+80	+16	−29	+45
63 Oak flooring	1914–1938	6	VII–IV	+67	+43	+83	+40	−30	+71
64 Portland cement	1912–1938	7	I–V	+43	+14	+69	+20	−14	+33
65 Polished plate glass	1924–1938	3	I–V	+100	+100	+100	+69	−77	+146

Table 16 (cont.)

D EMPLOYMENT AND WAGES IN INVESTMENT GOODS INDUSTRIES

#	Series	Period	No.	Phase					+	−	+
	Employment indexes										
66	Factory, total	1914–1938	6	I–V	+100	+100	+100	+100	+22	−23	+45
67	Durable goods	1919–1938	5	I–V	+100	+100	+100	+100	+32	−38	+69
68	Nondurable goods[f]	1919–1938	5	I–V	+100	+60	+100	+100	+14	−15	+28
69	Iron & steel products	1919–1938	5	I–VI	+100	+100	+100	+100	+30	−33	+63
70	Machinery	1919–1938	5	I–VI	+100	+100	+100	+100	+37	−40	+77
71	Transportation equipment	1919–1938	5	I–V	+100	+60	+100	+100	+42	−46	+89
72	Building materials, total	1919–1938	5	I–V	+100	+100	+100	+100	+26	−31	+57
73	Lumber & products	1919–1938	5	I–V	+100	+100	+100	+100	+23	−31	+54
74	Cement, clay & glass	1919–1938	5	I–V	+100	+60	+100	+100	+23	−26	+49
	Payroll indexes										
75	Factory, total	1919–1938	5	I–V	+100	+100	+100	+100	+36	−40	+76
76	Durable goods	1919–1938	5	I–V	+100	+100	+100	+100	+52	−55	+107
77	Nondurable goods[f]	1919–1938	5	I–V	+100	+60	+100	+100	+26	−25	+51
78	Iron & steel products	1919–1938	5	I–VI	+100	+100	+100	+100	+54	−59	+113
79	Machinery	1919–1938	5	I–V	+100	+100	+100	+100	+55	−56	+111
80	Transportation equipment	1919–1938	5	I–V	+100	+60	+100	+100	+53	−58	+111
81	Building materials, total	1919–1938	5	I–V	+100	+100	+100	+100	+39	−44	+84
82	Lumber & products	1919–1938	5	I–V	+100	+100	+100	+100	+39	−46	+85
83	Cement, clay & glass	1919–1938	5	I–V	+100	+60	+100	+100	+33	−34	+67
	Other employment & wage series										
84	Wage earners, all construction work, Ohio	1914–1938	6	I–V	+100	+67	+82		+37	−33	+70
85	Av. hours worked per week, mfg. wage earners	1921–1938	4	I–V	+100	+100	+100		+8	−16	+25
86	Av. hourly earnings, 25 mfg. industries	1921–1938	4	I–VI	+100	−50	+71		+14	−5	+19

Table 16 (cont.)

Series[a]	Period Covered[b]	No. of Reference Cycles	Expansion Stages	Index of Conformity to			Av. Reference-Cycle Amplitude		
				Expansion	Contraction	Business cycles	Expansion	Contraction	Full cycle[A]
E BUSINESS INVENTORIES									
Metals									
87 Iron ore at furnaces	1919–1938	5	V–IX	−60	−33	−60	−5	+12	−17
88 Pig iron at merchant furnaces	1919–1924	2	V–IX	−100	−100	−100	−54	+93	−146
89 Steel sheets, sold	1919–1933	4	I–VI	+100	+100	+100	+45	−47	+92
90 Steel sheets, unsold	1919–1933	4	V–IX	+20	−50	−50	−49	+82	−130
91 Refined copper	1912–1938[d]	6	V–IX	−33	−43	−64	−49	+66	−116
92 Tin, total visible supply	1894–1938[e]	10	VIII–V	+60	+83	+90	+32	−25	+57
Building materials									
93 Portland cement	1912–1938	7	Irreg.	−14	−14	−23	−6	+17	−22
94 Southern pine lumber	1919–1938	5	V–IX	−100	−33	−60	−10	+7	−18
95 Oak flooring	1912–1933	6	III–VII	+100	+33	+67	+43	−12	+55
Rubber & products									
96 Crude rubber	1924–1938	3	V–IX	+33	−50	−67	−13	+58	−71
97 Pneumatic casings	1921–1938	4	I–VI	+100	+100	+100	+41	−28	+69
98 Inner tubes	1921–1938	4	I–V	+100	+100	+100	+41	−32	+74
Cattle hides & products									
99 Raw hides in all hands	1921–1938	4	I–IV	+50	+75	+100	+12	−24	+35
100 Raw hides at tanners	1924–1938	3	I–V	+33	+75	+33	+10	−15	+25
101 Leather in process	1921–1938	4	I–V	0	+100	+71	+2	−11	+13
102 Finished leather in all hands	1921–1938	4	Irreg.	−50	+100	−43	−16	−5	−11
103 Finished leather at tanners	1924–1938	3	Irreg.	−33	−33	−20	−26	+6	−32

Table 16 (cont.)

Cotton									
104 Visible supply	1870–1938	17	V–II	−41	−44	−59	−10	+26	−36
105 In public storage & at compresses	1914–1938	6	V–IX	−33	−43	−50	−22	+42	−63
106 At mills	1914–1938	6	I–V	+67	+100	+100	+24	−18	+42
Newsprint paper									
107 At mills	1919–1933	4	V–IX	−60	−100	−100	−35	+53	−88
108 At publishers & in transit to them	1919–1933	4	III–VII	+80	+60	+78	+18	−7	+24
Department store stocks									
109 Dollar volume, index	1919–1938	5	I–VI	+60	+40	+56	+15	−15	+30
F SECURITY ISSUES AND INCORPORATIONS									
110 Cash from new issues on N.Y. Stock Exchange	1868–1921	14	VIII–V	+87	+73	+93	+58	−39	+97
111 Corporate issues, including refunding	1908–1938	8	VIII–IV	+100	+50	+60	+47	−46	+93
112 New corporate issues, total	1919–1938	5	I–V	+100	+20	+33	+78	−52	+130
113 New issues, stocks	1919–1938	5	I–V	+100	+60	+78	+135	−113	+248
114 New issues, short-term bonds & notes	1919–1938	5	I–V	+60	+60	+56	+136	−119	+255
115 New issues, long-term bonds & notes	1919–1938	5	I–VI	+60	−20	+33	+51	−26	+78
116 Refunding issues	1919–1938	5	VII–IV	+100	+60	+56	+61	−68	+129
117 Incorporations, no.	1861–1938	19	VIII–V	+68	+60	+84	+27	−10	+37
G STOCK MARKET OPERATIONS									
Trading on N.Y. Stock Exchange									
118 Shares sold, no.	1879–1938	16	VIII–IV	+88	+75	+94	+41	−36	+77
119 Bond sales, par value	1888–1938	14	VII–II	−57	−71	−70	−15	+35	−50
Price indexes of securities									
120 Common stocks	1879–1938	16	VIII–IV	+88	+65	+88	+27	−20	+47
121 R.R. bonds	1858–1933	19	VII–III^c	+60	+37	+63	+6	−3	+9

Table 16 (cont.)

H BANK LOANS AND INVESTMENTS

Series[a]	Period Covered[b]	No. of Reference Cycles	Expansion Stages	Index of Conformity to			Av. Reference-Cycle Amplitude		
				Expansion	Contraction	Business cycles	Expansion	Contraction	Full cycle[a]
Bank loans									
National banks									
122 New York City	1868–1914	12	VII–IV	+100	+17	+52	+15	–1	+16
123 Reserve cities other than central	1885–1914	9	VIII–V	+100	–11	+88	+18	+1	+17
124 Country districts, total	1879–1914	10	I–VI	+100	–20	+89	+19	+1	+18
125 Country districts, per bank	1879–1914	10	I–VI	+100	+60	+100	+11	–5	+17
126 All national banks	1879–1914	10	VIII–V	+100	–40	+100	+18	+2	+16
Member banks, Fed. Res. System									
127 Total loans	1921–1938	4	I–VI	+100	0	+14	+9	–14	+23
128 Loans on securities	1921–1938	4	I–V	+50	+20	+50	+7	–14	+21
129 All other loans	1921–1938	4	I–VI	+50	+60	+75	+8	–13	+21
Bank investments									
National banks									
130 New York City	1879–1914	10	VII–III	+100	–30	+37	+16	+10	+6
131 Reserve cities other than central	1885–1914	9	VII–III	+100	–11	+59	+25	+5	+19
132 Country districts	1879–1914	10	VII–IV	+100	–70	+63	+24	+8	+16
133 All national banks	1879–1914	10	VII–IV	+100	–40	+58	+24	+7	+18
Member banks, Fed. Res. System									
134 Total investments	1921–1938	4	VII–III	+100	0	+71	+20	+9	+11
135 Investments other than 'governments'	1921–1938	4	VII–IV	0	0	+14	+5	+5	0

Table 16 (concl.)

I INTEREST RATES AND BOND YIELDS

Series	Period		Reference cycles[b]	Conformity			Amplitude		
				Exp.	Contr.	Cycle	Exp.	Contr.	Cycle
Open-market rates									
136 Call money, N.Y.C.	1858–1914	14	I–V	+71	+100	+100	+90	−91	+181
137 Commercial paper, N.Y.C.	1858–1914	14	II–VI	+86	+73	+93	+31	−34	+65
138 90-day time money, N.Y.C.	1891–1914	7	I–VI	+100	+75	+86	+45	−51	+96
136 Call money	1919–1938	5	I–V	+20	+80	+78	+23	−59	+82
137 Commercial paper	1919–1938	5	II–VI	+60	+60	+100	+3	−32	+35
138 90-day time money	1919–1938	5	I–VI	+20	+80	+78	+11	−36	+47
139 Weighted av., open-market, N.Y.C.	1919–1938	5	I–V	+20	+100	+78	+8	−47	+55
Customer rates									
140 New York City	1919–1938	5	II–V	+20	+100	+56	−2	−14	+13
141 8 northern & eastern cities	1919–1938	5	II–VI	+20	+100	+33	−3	−8	+6
142 27 southern & western cities	1919–1933	4	III–VI	+20	+50	+75	+3	−8	+11
Bond yields									
143 Railroads	1858–1933	19	III–VII[e]	+37	+60	+58	+3	−6	+9
144 New England municipals	1858–1911	13	III–VII	+57	+57	+70	+4	−5	+8
145 High grade corp. & municipal	1900–1933	9	III–VII	+40	+40	+68	+5	−6	+11
146 Corporate, lowest rating	1919–1938	5	IV–VIII	−20	−20	−78	−21	+16	−37

[a] For sources of data, see Appendix B.

[b] Identifies the complete reference cycles covered by the series. This period, however, may differ somewhat from that covered by one or more of the conformity indexes. See *Measuring Business Cycles*, Ch. 5, Sec. X.

[c] For a few series an alternative expansion period is equally acceptable. The results follow:

	Conformity			Amplitude		
	Exp.	Contr.	Cycle	Exp.	Contr.	Cycle
Steel sheet production, I–V	+100	+100	+100	+68	−65	+133
R.R. bond prices, VI–III	−47	−30	−68	−4	+7	−11
R.R. bond yields, III–VI	+47	+30	+68	+4	−6	+10

[d] Omits 1914–19.

[e] See Ch. 6, note 7.

[f] Introduced in table for comparative purposes.

[g] Omits 1914–21.

[h] In this table, as elsewhere in the volume, rounding of numbers occasionally produces a slight discrepancy between the phase amplitudes and the full-cycle amplitude.

ment of equipment, or of basic materials used in construction work and machine building. Here also the amplitudes and conformity indexes run high, but there are not so many leads at the cyclical turns as in the series on contracts and orders; for, in these branches of business, production follows sales. For the sake of contrast—and the contrast in amplitude is striking —two indexes of nondurable goods production are introduced.

Section D shows the effects of the highly variable demand for production of capital goods upon employment and consumer purchasing power. Again the contrast in cyclical variability between durable and nondurable goods industries is brought out by index numbers. Then it is shown that the average length of the working week, and average rates of pay per hour fluctuate with employment, though less violently. The result is that payrolls attain amplitudes decidedly higher than the corresponding employment series, and comparable with the amplitudes prevailing in the production of durable goods.[36]

Section E, devoted to inventories, illustrates the diversity of cyclical behavior characteristic of this highly important factor in business, but only in that sense does it offer a summary. The timing varieties of inventories have been stressed in Chapter 5; they are explored far more fully in Abramovitz' monograph, which analyzes the cyclical movements of additions to inventories as well as of inventories proper. Here I note only that the durability of goods, or their ultimate destination as ingredients of capital, seems not to rule the amplitudes of inventories so strictly as the amplitudes of production and employment.

In Section F we turn from the realms of industry and commerce to the realm of finance. Issues of corporate securities have amplitudes corresponding to those of contracts and orders; even the steadiest series of the lot (long-term bonds and notes) rises and falls 78 percent. The conformity to business cycles is lower on the whole than many may expect, but that disappointment may arise from thinking of security dealing as the quintessence of American business.

Section G gives a condensed view of activities at this focus of financial interests. The picture is not sensational. Even the

[36] Cf. Table 13.

most volatile of these series—the number of shares sold on the New York Stock Exchange—has amplitudes decidedly lower than those in Section C for the production of durable goods.[37] And stock prices, according to what we have chosen as the most representative long-range index number, have much lower amplitudes than shares sold. The most important behavior traits of bond sales and prices are their quasi-inverted timing and modest or low amplitudes.

Section H suggests that the Federal Reserve System did not alter radically the relations between banks and their customers. The reference-cycle amplitudes of both loans and investments remain low. Here, of course, we are measuring the volume of loans outstanding; that is, the measures correspond logically to those of Section A on stocks of industrial equipment, and differ from the measures of contracts, orders, production, etc. in later sections. In bank loans there is a marked shift in the *trend* component from a rapid rise before World War I to decline since then; but the *cyclical* component, which is best represented by the full reference-cycle amplitude, remains much as it was. Investments, we noted above, grew even faster than loans under the National Banking System, and their secular rise has been if anything expedited since loans began to shrink. Bank investments are especially interesting because of their cyclical leads. But this and various other features of the exhibit will mean more to us at a later stage of the investigation.

The last section of the table, interest rates, reveals an unusually wide diversity of cyclical behavior, and demonstrates how inadequate was the happily obsolescent practice of treating 'the' interest rate as a factor in cyclical movements. The durability of a loan clearly does not affect the cyclical amplitudes of interest rates as the durability of commodities affects the cyclical amplitudes of orders, employment, and production. On the contrary, the shortest of loans have the most variable interest rates. But that is not so much because the loans

---

[37] Taking the amplitudes for the period common to both series, 1919–38, would not reduce the difference much. On that basis we have +42, −40, +82 for shares sold, and +44, −57, +101 for the production of durable producer goods.

are payable on call, as because they are made with marginal banking funds, and to clients whose credit needs have been subject to sharp fluctuations. All open-market rates have been much steadied by the changes in banking organization effected by the Federal Reserve System, but the contrast between open-market and customers' rates remains striking in 1919–38. Customers' rates are what we should have in mind when thinking about the rates paid by the mass of business enterprises and individuals for bank loans. As it happens, the secular decline in bank loans has been accompanied by a secular decline in rates. This decline seems more striking in bank rates than in the yields of bonds, but that is because of differences in the periods covered by the two sets of series.[38] The last entry in the table reminds us of a feature too often slighted in cyclical studies—the risk factor in the interest rates of practical business. Where risk is believed to be considerable, bond yields attain relatively large amplitudes; and their cyclical timing shifts from the standard neutral pattern of expansion in stages III–VII to the definitely inverted pattern of expansion in stages IV–VIII. Of course, rising bond yields mean falling bond prices; inversion is to be expected in the mathematically indicated yields of risky investments.

F CYCLICAL AMPLITUDES OF PRICES AND PRODUCTION

In preceding sections we have given only passing attention to the relation between the cyclical patterns of prices and production. This relation poses an interesting problem. We know that increases in supply tend to depress prices and that increases in demand tend to raise them; but how will prices behave in a cyclical expansion when both supply and demand rise, or in a contraction when both supply and demand shrink? It is in this theoretically indeterminate form that price problems confront students of business cycles. What to expect we learn from experience: most prices rise and fall with the cyclical

[38] For example, the average reference-cycle amplitudes of the series on high grade corporate and municipal bond yields during 1919–33 are +1.3, −9.4, +10.7.

tides of business activity most of the time—not always. For example, the best American index of wholesale prices fell in the expansions of 1891–93 and 1927–29; it rose in the contraction of 1899–1900; in the other 23 cyclical phases from 1890 to 1938 prices moved in the same direction as production. A keen British· theorist, noting similar movements in England, has remarked:

This fact, that prices rise when goods are turned out in greater abundance and fall in the opposite situation, is a striking paradox and requires to be seen to be believed. It is one of the very few generalizations vouchsafed by empirical observation in economics; and it is probably the best established of any.[39]

Our evidence on the cyclical behavior of prices and production consists not merely of comprehensive index numbers, but also of numerous series representing single commodities, which we can classify by various criteria. For some 60 commodities we have both price and production records covering identical periods, which enables us to make more than usually exact comparisons.[40] The considerable size and varied composition of our sample put us in a position, not only to confirm the basic generalization of which Harrod writes, but also to improve it by a qualification, and to supplement it by certain related generalizations of scarcely less moment.

To begin with the direction of price movements during business-cycle phases: 87 percent of the 147 price series in our standard sample have positive timing; that is, they characteristically rise when activity expands and fall when activity contracts. This is a higher ratio than we find among our 188 series on production, of which less than 82 percent have positive timing—a difference that is significant because 35 percent of the price series and only 25 percent of the production series represent agricultural products. Irregular cyclical timing is less common among price than among production series, despite the

[39] R. F. Harrod, *The Trade Cycle* (Oxford, Clarendon Press, 1936), p. 41.
[40] These paired series are being intensively studied by Frederick C. Mills, whose monograph *Price-Quantity Interactions in Business Cycles* (National Bureau, 1946), will be followed by further instalments.

larger proportion of foods and other farm products in the sample of prices.[41]

Mills provides fuller detail regarding his 64 pairs of series on prices and quantities. In expansion he finds that both prices and quantities rise on the average in 47 pairs, that one rises and the other falls in 13 pairs, and that one shows no net change while the other does change in 4 pairs. In contraction prices and quantities both fall in 42 pairs, while in 22 they move in opposite directions. Of the 13 pairs showing opposite movements in expansion, 10 pairs represent foods or other farm products; so also do 20 of the 22 pairs showing opposite movements in contraction.[42] Thus the empirical generalization that prices rise when goods are turned out in greater abundance, and vice versa, should be confined to industries in which producers have effective short-period control over output. The rule fails about as often as it holds with respect to farm products. Another qualification suggested by our evidence, though less emphatically, is that the rule applies better to competitive than to administered prices. The prices of plate glass, asphalt, passenger automobiles, and iron ore do not rise on the average in the expansions covered by Mills' analyses.

When producers lack effective short-run control over output, prices conform better than production to business cycles, and have higher reference-cycle amplitudes. When producers possess such control, production conforms better than prices and has higher reference-cycle amplitudes. Table 17[43] sums

41 The timing types of our price and production series are as follows:

| | NUMBER OF SERIES | | PERCENTAGES | |
TYPE OF TIMING	Prices	Production	Prices	Production
Positive	128	154	87.1	81.9
Neutral	1		0.7	
Inverted	5	7	3.4	3.7
Irregular	13	27	8.8	14.4
Total	147	188	100.0	100.0

42 Mills, *ibid.*, Table 8, Part 2, pp. 32–3.

43 The sample of paired series used here was arranged by Geoffrey H. Moore, and is almost identical with the sample used above in Chapter 6, note 5. For my purposes it is better suited than Mills' similar sample, because the amplitudes are directly comparable with those shown in other tables, war cycles have been omitted from the averages, and the ratio of foodstuffs and other farm products to all pairs of commodities is 30 instead of 58 percent (see Mills, *ibid.*, p. 118).

Table 17

REFERENCE-CYCLE CONFORMITY AND AMPLITUDE OF SERIES ON PRICES AND PRODUCTION

	Number of Series		Mean Index[a] of Conformity to Business Cycles		Mean Reference-Cycle Amplitude[a]	
	Full sample[b]	Paired series	Full sample	Paired series	Full sample	Paired series[c]
ALL SERIES						
Prices	147	60	60	66	26	35
Production	188	60	74	66	58	47
COMPREHENSIVE SERIES[d]						
Broadest index						
Prices	1	1	100	100	18	27
Production	1	1	100	100	53	55
Farm products						
Prices	1	1	43	14	21	40
Marketings	1	1	33	14	2	2
Nonagricultural products						
Prices	1	1	100	100	25	25
Production	1	1	100	100	68	72
FARM PRODUCTS AND FOODS						
Prices	51	17	52	55	25	33
Production	47	17	42	38	15	13
OTHER PERISHABLES						
Prices	22	11	63	69	30	40
Production	29	11	83	82	51	43
SEMIDURABLES						
Prices	18	10	52	52	24	33
Production	29	10	79	70	48	45
DURABLES						
Prices	45	19	65	81	26	35
Production	57	19	82	80	101	82

[a] All averages are taken without regard to sign.

[b] The full number of series on prices (147) includes 8 indexes, besides the three listed, that cannot be classified according to durability. Likewise, the full number of series on production (188) includes 23 indexes, besides the three listed, that cannot be thus classified.

[c] Based on movements between stages I–V and V–IX. Means in the three preceding columns are based on characteristic stages of expansion and contraction.

[d] The comprehensive series used are as follows:

Bureau of Labor Statistics index of wholesale prices, 'all' commodities: 11 cycles, 1891–1914 and 1921–38, in columns for full sample; 4 cycles, 1921–38, in columns for paired series.
Federal Reserve Bank of New York index of production: 5 cycles, 1919–38, in columns for full sample; 4 cycles, 1921–38, in columns for paired series.

Bureau of Labor Statistics index of wholesale prices of farm products: 11 cycles, 1891–1914 and 1921–38, in columns for full sample; 4 cycles, 1921–38, in columns for paired series.
Department of Commerce index of agricultural marketings: 5 cycles, 1919–38, in columns for full sample; 4 cycles, 1921–38, in columns for paired series.

Bureau of Labor Statistics index of wholesale prices of nonagricultural commodities: 4 cycles, 1921–38, in both comparisons.
Federal Reserve Board index of industrial production: 5 cycles, 1919–38, in columns for full sample; 4 cycles, 1921–38, in columns for paired series.

up the evidence for this double-barreled generalization, and also demonstrates that the durability of goods has far less influence upon the cyclical amplitudes of prices than of production.[44]

Judged by the amplitudes of their reference-cycle movements, prices are tied together more closely than are physical outputs. This difference can be seen in the group averages of Table 17. It stands out more boldly among individual series. The highest reference-cycle amplitude of any price in our sample (steel scrap) is 87; that figure is exceeded by more than a fifth of our production series. On the basis of a still wider survey Mills reports:

> The median advance of 241 production series between reference-cycle stages I and V was 20.3 (in reference-cycle relatives); the median advance of 132 price series was 8.0 (war cycles were excluded . . .). The price movements were much more compact and uniform than the production movements, a condition evidenced by an interquartile range of 5.8 for the price series, at stage V, and a corresponding interquartile range of 17.0 for the production series.[45]

In these few paragraphs we have flushed a rather terrifying list of theoretical problems. Why should most commodity prices rise when supply is being enlarged and fall when supply is being reduced? Why should the reference-cycle amplitudes of prices be greater than the corresponding amplitudes of production when producers cannot adjust output to current demand, and why should prices fluctuate less than production when producers can control output? Why should the cyclical movements of prices be more uniform than the cyclical movements of production, and yet have on the whole lower indexes of conformity to business cycles?

Price theory may be the most highly developed section of

[44] I may note that if coke were transferred from 'other perishables' to 'durables', as it might be in view of its chief use, the amplitudes of the production groups in the table would fit our earlier analysis somewhat better. That transfer would reduce the amplitude of other perishables from 51 to 50 in the full sample, and from 43 to 39 in the sample of paired series. In prices, the corresponding shifts would be from 30 to 27 in the full sample and from 40 to 36 in the sample of paired series.

[45] *Ibid.*, p. 32, footnote. See also pp. 76, 77, 108.

economics, but it has not been designed to raise or to settle problems of this character. Quite obviously these problems involve the relations of present prices to past prices of the same goods; the relations of present prices of different goods to prospective profits and family comfort, and the relations of all prices to the supply of 'money'—the most ambiguous of economic terms, and therefore perfectly adapted to use in a list of unknowns. Not until we enter upon our full analysis of what happens from stage to stage of a business cycle will it be prudent to attack these complications.

V The Problem of Comparing and Combining Reference-Cycle Amplitudes

In comparing reference-cycle amplitudes of different processes in this chapter, we have glossed over some conceptual problems that should be faced explicitly. The three ways of comparing reference-cycle amplitudes used in Table 17 will serve our purpose. The first involves averaging the amplitudes of all price series belonging to a given group or combination of groups, then making corresponding averages for production. In the second only commodities and periods are included for which both price and production records have been analyzed. The third relies upon comprehensive indexes. The three methods yield broadly similar results, but there are also numerous differences, of which some are considerable. How should these differences be interpreted? Should we take them as warnings that all measures in this field are exceedingly rough? Or should we conclude that one method of comparing amplitudes is right and the others are wrong? Or do the differences have economic meanings that, when grasped, illuminate the subject and increase our confidence in the measures?

A AMPLITUDES OF COMPREHENSIVE SERIES AND THEIR COMPONENTS

Consider first the comprehensive series. In the last section of Chapter 6 we observed that wide coverage tends to raise the numerical value of conformity indexes, because the larger the number and greater the variety of activities represented by a series the more chances have irregular movements to offset one another. Table 17 illustrates this effect afresh—perfect conformity to business cycles appears only in the most comprehensive indexes of prices and production, and in the indexes covering all nonagricultural products. But the table suggests that inclusiveness has the opposite effect upon reference-cycle amplitudes: the broader an index number or aggregate, the lower tends to be its reference-cycle amplitude in relation to the mean amplitude of its component series.

This generalization can be deduced from our method of computing reference-cycle amplitudes and what we know about varieties of cyclical timing. When analyzing a series, we measure its net rise from the first to the last of the stages that we have judged to be characteristic of its expansions, and we measure its fall in similar fashion—unless the cyclical timing is irregular, in which case we measure the rise from stage I to stage V and the fall from V to IX. The average group amplitudes for full samples in Table 17 are simple averages of measures made in this way, taken without regard to sign.

The amplitude of an index or aggregate would equal the similarly weighted mean of the amplitudes of its component series, provided all components had the same variety of cyclical timing. But if the components reach their peaks in different stages, the highest point in the pattern of the comprehensive series will not be so high as the similarly weighted average of the peaks of the individual components. Nor will the trough of the comprehensive series be so low as the similarly weighted mean of the troughs of the component series, when these troughs are scattered among different stages. Of course lowering peaks and raising troughs diminishes amplitudes. The wider the variety of timing in a group of series, the lower tends to be the amplitude of an aggregate or index that covers the whole group in relation to the mean amplitude of the individual series. The difference in Table 17 between the amplitude of the Bureau of Labor Statistics index of wholesale prices (18) and the mean amplitude of all our 147 series on prices (26) illustrates this effect, and so also does the difference between the amplitude of the New York Federal Reserve Bank index of production (53) and the mean of all our series on production (58); though in neither case are all the individual series components of the index, and though both indexes have components not separately included in our sample.

Such differences in results are not discrepancies. The means compared are measures of two distinct aspects of business cycles: (1) the mean cyclical fluctuations in national output and in what is called the price 'level', (2) the mean cyclical fluctuations to which individual prices and industries are exposed. We should not ask which of the two measures is better, for they serve different purposes, both important. For example, when we ask how violent are the cyclical fluctuations in aggregate demand for labor, we want the answer given by the most comprehensive index available. When we ask what is the average unemployment hazard in American industries, we want the higher answer yielded by a properly weighted mean of the amplitudes of many series. If a similar question were asked about the average enterprise, or average union, or average individual, we should want the still higher figures that could be had only from far more detailed information than is currently published.

B AMPLITUDES OF PAIRED SERIES AND FULL SAMPLES

In Table 17 the shift from full samples to paired series raises the reference-cycle amplitudes of prices and reduces the amplitudes of production.[46] Is this curious difference an inscrutable matter of chance, or has it a lesson to teach?

The comparisons confined to paired series in Table 17 involve three sacrifices of information. (1) All price series not matched by records of production, and all production series not matched by price records, must be dropped. Manifestly, the 60 price series in our sample of pairs do not represent the

---

[46] This observation applies to all the group averages in the table, but not to all series in the groups. Nor does it apply to the comprehensive series in the table.

cyclical behavior of prices so adequately as do the 147 price series in our full sample, and the like is true of the production data. (2) From the price series kept in the sample of pairs all months are dropped that are not matched in the corresponding production record, and vice versa. When there is a difference in the number of cycles covered, the full-sample average of a series is more representative than the paired-sample average. (3) In making the paired-sample averages of Table 17, we base all amplitudes on movements between stages I–V and V–IX. For most purposes, we prefer the amplitudes that take account of leads and lags, as do those of the full samples.

While it may be readily granted that the full samples represent the cyclical behavior of prices and production more adequately than do the paired samples, that does not mean that the full samples provide more trustworthy *comparisons* of the cyclical amplitudes characteristic of prices and production. (1) Price amplitudes differ widely from one commodity to another; production amplitudes differ still more. Hence, full-sample comparisons will be swayed by dissimilarities in the lists of commodities for which there are price and production records. (2) Successive business-cycle expansions and contractions differ widely in intensity, which means among other things, differences in the amplitude of the price and production movements they excite. Full-sample amplitudes aim to *minimize* the effect of these intercycle differences by basing the averages upon all the acceptable cycles in the price series, and also all the acceptable cycles covered by the output data. The paired samples aim to *equalize* the effect of intercycle differences upon prices and production by making the lists of cycles identical. Is not this aim more attainable than the other? (3) Differences in cyclical timing can be taken into account when dealing with paired series as readily as when dealing with full samples, provided stress is not laid upon strict identity of the period covered.

Table 18 shows how the first two factors bear upon the results presented by Table 17. The chief reason why the mean amplitudes of prices are higher in the paired than in the full

Table 18

ANALYSIS OF DIFFERENCES BETWEEN MEAN REFERENCE-CYCLE AMPLITUDES OF FULL SAMPLES AND PAIRED SERIES IN TABLE 17

	NUMBER OF SERIES			MEAN NUMBER OF REFERENCE CYCLES COVERED BY			MEAN REFERENCE-CYCLE AMPLITUDE[a]			
				Paired Series		Other Series in Full Sample	Paired Series		Other Series in Full Sample	All Series in Full Sample
PRICES	Paired series	Other series	Full sample[a]	As used in price-quantity comparison	As they come in full sample		As used in price-quantity comparison	As they come in full sample		
Farm products & foods	17	37	51	5.6	10.6	7.2	33.2	27.9	23.3	24.9
Other perishables	11	11	22	4.4	7.9	6.0	40.1	34.5	24.5	29.5
Semidurables	10	10	18	3.5	9.1	10.3	33.1	23.2	24.1	24.1
Durables	19	27	45	4.4	9.6	8.4	35.4	27.1	25.9	26.3
All price series[b]	57	96	147	4.6	9.5	7.8	35.3	28.1	24.1	25.7
PRODUCTION										
Farm products & foods	17	30	47	5.6	8.4	6.8	13.0	14.9	15.5	15.3
Other perishables	11	18	29	4.4	5.9	6.1	42.6	42.9	56.6	51.4
Semidurables	10	19	29	3.5	4.3	4.7	45.2	47.1	47.8	47.6
Durables	19	39	57	4.4	6.1	4.3	82.0	81.4	110.5	100.8
All production series[b]	57	132	188	4.6	6.4	5.3	47.4	48.2	62.2	57.7

[a] Amplitudes are taken without regard to sign. In the column headed 'price-quantity comparison', the amplitude measures are all based on movements between stages I–V and V–IX. In the remaining three columns they are based on movements during characteristic stages of expansion and contraction.

[b] See Table 17, note b.

[c] The total of paired and other series can exceed the number of series in the full sample because in setting up pairs we have several times compared one price series with two production series, and once compared a production series with two price series.

179

sample is a cultural lag—the long delay in collecting statistics of production—coupled with the world developments responsible for the unusual violence of economic fluctuations in 1919–38. Prices are easier to ascertain than output in most branches of business; and they have been systematically recorded from earlier dates. A large part of our price collection is taken from the Bureau of Labor Statistics and runs back to 1890; there was no comparable effort to collect production statistics until World War I had given a costly demonstration of the nation's need of fuller industrial records. Table 3 shows that in our basic sample, 59 percent of the 147 series on commodity prices cover more than 5 reference cycles; only 28 percent of the 188 series on production have such a span. Hence when we pair series on prices and production, we have to discard part of the price record far more often than part of the production record. Table 18 shows that the 57 price series that are paired with series on production cover 9.5 reference cycles on the average in the full sample, but are cut to only 4.6 cycles on the average in the paired sample, while the corresponding cut in production series is only from 6.4 to 4.6 cycles. Of course, it is usually the earlier cycles that are cut off. Evidence that reference-cycle amplitudes have been higher on the average since World War I than before was presented in the second section of this chapter. Hence, discarding part of the record to fit the shorter member of a pair tends to raise mean reference-cycle amplitudes, and, as matters stand, this effect is felt much more keenly by prices than by production.

The use of I–V timing in measuring amplitudes of all series in the paired sample (as opposed to whatever timing is judged to be characteristic of the series) exercises an influence opposed to that of amputating cycles, tending to make the mean amplitudes smaller in the paired than in the full samples. This effect is felt much more by the series on production than by those on prices; for of the 57 paired series only 10½ price series[47]

---

[47] Sometimes we cannot decide which of two timing schemes fits a series better; then we use both and take an average of the two sets of conformity or amplitude measures. Hence the fraction.

and just twice as many production series have other than I–V timing.[48]

The main issue remains: How do the series in the paired sample compare with those in the full sample? There is a difference of only 4 points between the mean amplitude of the 57 price series used in the paired sample, when computed for the full ranges of cycles covered, and of the mean amplitude of the 96 other series on commodity prices we have analyzed. The corresponding difference between the amplitudes of the 57 production series in the paired sample and of the 132 other series is 14 points. The latter difference occurs mainly in durable goods, where the paired series have a mean amplitude of 81, while 39 other series have a mean amplitude of 110. The discrepancy of 29 points arises chiefly because of another cultural lag. We have not yet learned how to make satisfactory price records of the complicated durable goods we fabricate from lumber, cement, glass, and metals, though we can make clumsy production records by casting up the square feet of floor space represented by construction contracts, or by counting the number of motor vehicles, industrial pumps, railroad locomotives, etc. that we turn out. In our full sample there are 16 series on the output of vehicles, of industrial equipment, and the volume of construction work in process. These production series are matched by a single curious series on the price of passenger automobiles. While the 41 series on production of durable materials and fittings have a mean reference-cycle amplitude of 79, the 16 series on the elaborate products typically made from these materials have a mean amplitude of 157. It is primarily the virtual omission of these most characteristic products of our industrial age from our paired sample for lack of price data that makes the amplitudes of production in our paired sample 10 points lower than its amplitude in the full sample.

This analysis shows, I think, that to achieve the best comparisons of the cyclical behavior of prices and production we

---

[48] Strictly speaking, other than I–V or irregular timing; but irregular and I–V timing come to the same thing in measuring amplitudes.

should use both our paired samples and our full samples. Each method has something to tell us that the other tells less well or not at all. And this remark applies to many other comparisons we shall have to make among economic variables. Yet evidence upon differences between measures made in different ways, and the confidence-inspiring fashion in which these differences often turn out to be significant when traced to their sources, should not blind us to the residual differences we cannot yet explain. Nor should an anxious concern with minor differences, whether accounted for or not, dull us to broad similarities among measures that do not, and should not, agree closely.

Finally, this experiment with prices and production illustrates the advantages of having at our disposal numerous series to use in treating problems that could not have been foreseen in detail when we began compiling our sample of time series. No collection of general indexes or aggregates, however skilfully manipulated, could tell us what we have learned by very simple operations upon good sized samples of series on prices and production.

C THE AMPLITUDES OF BUSINESS CYCLES

At the outset of this chapter I put the reference-cycle amplitudes of all 794 series included by our full sample into a single chart and table. The latter presents medians and arithmetic means of the whole array. Then I ranked 29 groups of series in Table 11 according to their mean amplitudes, and later swept these groups together into a few much broader classes.

While useful for exhibiting the range and distribution of reference-cycle amplitudes, these statistical compilations do not yield averages into which we can read much economic meaning. The lack of systematic weighting, while a grievous fault, is less fundamental than the fact that the series do not all stand in an additive relation to one another. Even the fairly homogeneous groups of Table 11 sometimes jumble together broad series and their components. What sense is there in an average amplitude that includes a general index and a dozen series from which the index itself has been computed? The broader classes of Table 11 and the full arrays of Table 10 suggest worse absurdities. We do not add the prices and the output of pig iron; we multiply one by the other. Then why should we include the amplitudes of price and output series in a single average? When Frederick Mills multiplies quantities supplied by unit prices to get 'buyers' outlays' or 'sellers' revenues', he contributes a fresh set of series to our records—a set that has meaning, and that, among other advantages, enables him to determine the relative influence exercised by changes in prices and in quantities upon the amplitude of their joint product.[49] Once again, it produces little except confusion to average bank loans *outstanding* with monthly issues of securities, or tonnage of vessels under construction with building contracts let. The fluctuations in a stock of goods in existence and the fluctuations in the stream of goods flowing into or out of that stock can be made to illuminate one another, but not by simple averaging.

So it goes throughout our sample. Yet the hypothesis that all economic activities are interrelated, at every moment of time and over time, implies that the reference-cycle amplitudes of all the series in our sample, and of the vastly larger number that would be needed to complete it, are functionally related to one another. It is not absurd to think of all these amplitudes as constituting a system of mutually determining members. Indeed, the chief job before us may be defined as that of learning what we can about the ways in which the cyclical fluctuations characteristic of many segments of the economy arouse, reenforce, deaden, and reverse one another. Somehow the whole congeries of squirming entities manages to swell in volume for a while; then to shrink for another while, only to repeat once more what it has already done time and again. Obviously, our very concept of general tides implies overall amplitudes. Thus we are left confronting an important problem: How can we sum up movements in the whole economy, and how can we measure their amplitudes? But that is

[49] See his *Price-Quantity Interactions in Business Cycles*.

obviously a problem for Part III, The Consensus of Cyclical Behavior. What Part II on Varieties of Cyclical Behavior contributes is a warning not to mistake the average reference-cycle amplitudes of our sample for measures of the cyclical tides that sweep over the American economy.

CHAPTER 8

Cycle-by-Cycle Variability in Cyclical Behavior

I PROBLEMS RAISED BY CYCLE-BY-CYCLE VARIABILITY

So far we have dealt almost exclusively with the average cyclical behavior of individual series, or groups of series. Chapter 4 presents average reference-cycle patterns; Chapter 5 treats 'characteristic' cyclical timing; Chapter 6 considers indexes of conformity to all the business cycles covered by a series; Chapter 7 takes up average reference-cycle amplitudes. The variability in cyclical behavior on which stress has been laid is variability *among* series in average behavior. Little has been said about a more fundamental type of variability—that found from cycle to cycle *within* series.

An ultrasimple measure of this behavior trait is presented by the vertical lines accompanying each reference-cycle pattern of Chart 1 that covers more than a single cycle. We shall now inquire into the economic meaning of these bleak symbols. They are briefly referred to in Chapter 4 as representing the average deviations of the standings of a series in individual cycles from the mean standings that constitute the average reference-cycle pattern. That is an accurate but not an illuminating statement. Before we begin using average patterns as prefabricated materials for constructing a model business cycle, we should learn what we can about the relations between average cyclical behavior and cycle-by-cycle behavior.

What types of movement are responsible for the average deviations from our reference-cycle patterns? Why do the average deviations differ so widely from one series to another? What bearing have they upon the use of our cyclical patterns and of the measures derived from them—the reference-cycle amplitudes and the average rates of change per month from stage to stage of business cycles?

II   Cycle-by-Cycle Variability within Series

A   COMPONENTS OF AVERAGE DEVIATIONS

The single-cycle patterns of a series, therefore the average reference-cycle pattern, and the average deviations from the latter may include contributions from all types of movement recognized by time-series analysis.

1) Our efforts to remove seasonal variations from our series before converting the original data into reference-cycle relatives are fallible. Doubtless the adjustments are here too large, there too small. Probably we have failed to recognize some genuine cases of seasonality, and perhaps we have introduced spurious seasonal movements into some series by making adjustments when none are needed. Once committed, errors of all these kinds are carried into the single-cycle patterns, are reflected at least faintly in the average pattern, and reappear in the average deviations.

2) Errors in the reference dates have similar effects. They do most damage to reference-cycle standings at stages I, V, and IX—also, of course, to leads, lags, and decisions about the variety of cyclical timing. A wrong peak date will warp the reference-cycle pattern of virtually every series in our whole collection that includes the date in question, while a wrong trough date will warp the patterns of two cycles.[1]

3) Grouping months into reference-cycle stages is a 'smoothing' operation with a variable span—seldom less than 3 months or more than 15.[2] Smoothing is the standard device for 'eliminating' irregular movements from time series; more accurately, for redistributing irregularities among the entries according to some scheme set by the smoothing formula employed. Of course, we cannot assume that the variable-span smoothing incident to the preparation of our single-cycle patterns disposes of the most formidable difficulty in time-series

[1] The text refers to cycles taken as units running from one trough to the next. If a peak-to-peak analysis is used, errors in trough dates disturb the pattern of one cycle and errors in peak dates of two cycles.

[2] For full details, see *Measuring Business Cycles*, Appendix A.

analysis. Irregular movements must be prominent components of the average deviations in many series, if not also of many average patterns.

4) Reasons will be shown presently for thinking that virtually all of the intracycle trends retained in our reference-cycle patterns change over time. If so, they too give rise to differences among single-cycle patterns. When these secular shifts become prominent in comparison with the cyclical movements, we break a series into segments, and strike two or more sets of averages. But within each segment there remain cycle-by-cycle differences in the trend component.

5) Along with all these other elements, wanted and unwanted, the single-cycle patterns include what we call 'cyclical movements'—the changes in individual series that correspond to (and, when taken all together, constitute) business cycles. We have no assurance that these cyclical movements tend to be uniform. Possibly they tend to grow progressively more violent, as Karl Marx predicted; possibly they tend to subside into brief and mild expansions followed by long and moderate contractions, as Thorstein Veblen surmised; perhaps they tend to alternate in character according to a rhythm of their own, as suggested by some long-cycle theorists; perhaps they tend to vary in ways and for reasons yet unguessed. Whatever the future may teach us, for the present we should not exclude the hypothesis that our average deviations are traceable in part to cycle-by-cycle variations in the movements the average reference-cycle patterns are meant to represent.

6) We know that sudden shifts occasionally occur from one well established cyclical pattern to another, which is then followed consistently for a while. Major discontinuous shifts of this sort lead us to subdivide series; for minor discontinuities we make no adjustment. Presumably the minor discontinuities are numerous, and leave their imprint on the cyclical patterns.

7) While the inquiry into "Cyclical Changes in Cyclical Behavior" in Chapter 11 of *Measuring Business Cycles* did not yield any satisfactory evidence that the fluctuations marked off by our reference dates are integral parts of long cycles, we

are satisfied that long waves occur in the building industry and certain other processes. Further, we suppose that diligent inquiry and the use of special tools would lengthen the list of activities in which long waves are found. Presumably our patterns of single cycles in many series tend to differ according as the 'long range' conditions that affect building construction favor a rise or a fall. We shall not know how common or how important such influences are until a thorough search for long cycles has been made, and the timing relations among the waves in different sectors of the economy established.

Thus, any single-cycle pattern in any series may be the net resultant of at least six or seven factors. As long as we confine attention to a single cycle, we cannot do much more toward segregating these components than has already been accomplished by adjusting for seasonals, eliminating the intercycle component of trends, and smoothing out some irregularities. For example, who could say what cyclical behavior is characteristic of imports and exports, of steel production and sugar refining, of stock sales and call loan rates, if he had only the reference-cycle patterns of 1927–33 or only those of 1933–38 at his disposal? And how would hypotheses based exclusively upon single-cycle studies of the first of these cycles compare with hypotheses based solely upon the second?

It was this inscrutability of single cycles that forced upon us the arduous task of collecting data covering as many cycles as feasible, and of devising ways of finding what happens on the average. We argued in the final chapter of *Measuring Business Cycles* that movements peculiar to single cycles, from whatever source they arise, tend to fade out of cyclical averages, while movements common to the species become more prominent the more cycles we cover. So far as averaging achieves this end of clarifying the combined cyclical and intracycle trend movements, it may be made to clarify also our views about the other factors that make single-cycle patterns what they are.

Of course the deviations of a single-cycle pattern from an average pattern are net resultants of numerous movements, and hardly less inscrutable than the single-cycle reference patterns. But, once again, averaging what happens in successive cycles enables us to take a long stride toward segregating elements that we might never pry apart so long as we dealt with single cases. Just as average cyclical patterns have much higher value for economic analysis than single-cycle patterns, so average deviations have much higher value than single-cycle deviations. Indeed, certain mathematical implications of our technique, plus the relative richness of our sample, enable us to learn more than we foresaw about the noncyclical features of economic changes, and in the process to learn more also about the cyclical features.

B CONTRIBUTION OF IRREGULAR MOVEMENTS

What we have learned about the residue of irregular movements in our measures stems mainly from the experiments reported in Chapter 8 of *Measuring Business Cycles*. Realizing that the variable-span averages of our nine-point cyclical patterns merely moderate the irregularities of monthly series, we probed the effect of smoothing the original data before beginning our analysis. An earlier National Bureau investigation supplied excellent materials. In his studies of interest rates, bond yields, and stock prices, Frederick R. Macaulay developed a method of "graduating monthly data in such a manner as to eliminate seasonal and erratic fluctuations and at the same time save all trend and the nonseasonal cyclical swings".[3] We chose four long series that Macaulay had smoothed—series characterized by wide differences in cyclical behavior—analyzed his form of the figures in our usual fashion, and compared the results with the measures we had obtained from what we called by way of contrast the 'raw' data. Chart 6 and Table 19 present the results of chief immediate interest.

The chart shows that the effects of systematic smoothing on

---

[3] Macaulay's formula is a "43-term summation, approximately fifth-degree parabolic graduation". For methods of computing and weight diagram, see his *Smoothing of Time Series* (National Bureau, 1931), especially pp. 24–6, 73–5, and the references there given.

Chart 6
Average Reference-Cycle Patterns of Raw and Smoothed Data of Four Series

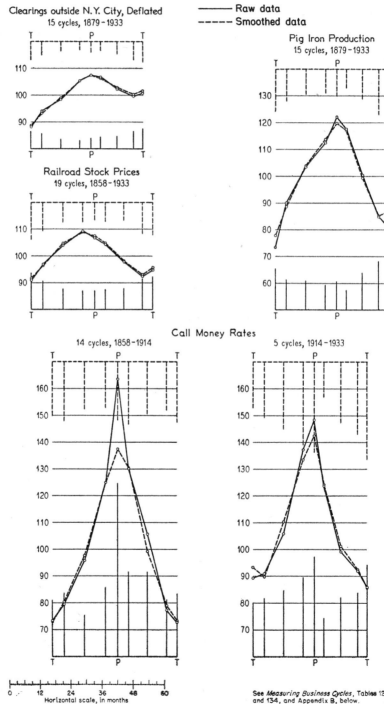

Clearings outside N.Y. City, Deflated
15 cycles, 1879–1933

——— Raw data
----- Smoothed data

Pig Iron Production
15 cycles, 1879–1933

Railroad Stock Prices
19 cycles, 1858–1933

Call Money Rates

14 cycles, 1858–1914

5 cycles, 1914–1933

0   12   24   36   48   60
Horizontal scale, in months

See *Measuring Business Cycles*, Tables 128 and 134, and Appendix B, below.

Table 19

EFFECTS OF SMOOTHING FOUR MONTHLY SERIES UPON THEIR
AVERAGE REFERENCE-CYCLE PATTERNS AND THE AVERAGE
DEVIATIONS FROM THEM

(Effects measured in percentages of reference-cycle bases)

SERIES[a]	REFERENCE-CYCLE STAGES								
	I	II	III	IV	V	VI	VII	VIII	IX
Clearings outside N.Y.C., deflated, 15 cycles, 1879–1933									
Mean duration of stage, mos.	3.0	7.6	7.1	7.6	3.0	6.2	6.5	6.2	3.0
Change made by smoothing in									
Av. standing	+0.5	−0.9	+0.5	0 0	0.0	−0.5	+0.5	+0.6	+0.9
Av. deviation	+0.2	−0.5	+0.1	0.0	+0.2	−1.0	0.0	+0.3	+0.2
R.R. stock prices, 19 cycles, 1858–1933									
Mean duration of stage, mos.	3.0	8.1	7.6	8.1	3.0	6.9	7.3	6.9	3.0
Change made by smoothing in									
Av. standing	+0.7	−0.5	+0.7	−0.1	+0.6	+0.3	+0.1	+0.5	+1.0
Av. deviation	+0.3	+0.1	−0.2	+0.4	−0.3	−0.2	−1.0	+0.3	+0.1
Pig iron production, 15 cycles, 1879–1933									
Mean duration of stage, mos.	3.0	7.6	7.1	7.6	3.0	6.2	6.5	6.2	3.0
Change made by smoothing in									
Av. standing	+4.5	−1.4	+0.3	+1.3	−2.4	−0.5	−1.1	+0.2	+5.6
Av. deviation	+0.6	+0.8	−1.2	−0.4	−0.6	−0.1	−2.6	−1.0	−1.1
Call money rates, 14 cycles, 1858–1914									
Mean duration of stage, mos.	3.0	8.2	7.7	8.2	3.0	7.2	7.4	7.2	3.0
Change made by smoothing in									
Av. standing	−0.2	+1.0	+1.9	0.0	−26.2	+0.1	−6.4	+1.7	+0.5
Av. deviation	−1.1	−1.5	+2.3	−8.6	−43.0	−8.3	−12.0	−3.1	−1.0
Call money rates, 5 cycles, 1914–1933									
Mean duration of stage, mos.	3.0	7.6	7.4	7.6	3.0	6.2	6.8	6.2	3.0
Change made by smoothing in									
Av. standing	+4.0	−1.2	+4.5	−3.7	−6.0	+0.3	+2.0	+0.4	−0.1
Av. deviation	−2.9	−0.9	−0.4	+1.4	−3.7	−1.1	+0.8	+3.4	+2.3

[a]See Appendix B for sources of data.

average reference-cycle patterns are negligible in deflated clearings and railroad stock prices. In iron production, smoothing raises the troughs about 5 points and reduces the peak half as much. (A 'point' here is 1 percent of the cycle bases.) At other stages the maximum effect is 1.4 points. But in call loan rates before 1914 smoothing reduces the peak of the average pattern by 26 points. Under the Federal Reserve System this reduction is still 6 points. In other stages, smoothing shoves the call loan pattern up or down by an average of 1.5 points in 1858–1914, and of 2 points in 1914–33. To what are these wide differences in the effects of smoothing due?

Any moving average with a considerable span will change raw data patterns much or little according as the latter present brief and violent or long and gentle movements. Macaulay's formula raises the troughs of the pig iron pattern appreciably because these troughs are frequently V-shaped. It affects the troughs of call loan rates relatively less because these troughs are typically U-shaped. It affects the pig iron peak less than pig iron troughs because the slopes on the two sides of the peak are somewhat less precipitous than those on the two sides of the troughs. It reduces the peak of call loan rates before 1914 drastically because this peak is a veritable spike in the raw data, shooting up 38 points in the 4.6 months of stage IV–V and falling 33 points in the 4.1 months of stage V–VI. It affects the call loan peak after 1914 much less than before, but still considerably, because the movements of the raw data pattern in stages IV–V and V–VI, though moderated, remain large (+11, −25). It makes little change in the reference-cycle patterns of deflated clearings and railroad stock prices at any stage because their raw data patterns have few violent movements to be rounded off.[4]

Now brief and violent movements in an *average* reference-cycle pattern are likely to be cyclical phenomena, especially when the series in question covers a dozen or more cycles and a considerable volume of transactions. It would be strange indeed if a violent random perturbation recurred in the same form in a long series of broad coverage within the same stage of enough reference cycles to produce such a spike in the average pattern as we find in call loans, or even such troughs as we find in pig iron. And when, as in these cases, cyclical explanations of the brief but violent movements are at hand, we may be confident that the smoothing is not to be credited with mitigating an erratic movement, but debited with blunting cyclical turns.[5]

[4] For a fuller analysis, see *Measuring Business Cycles*, Ch. 8, especially Sec. IV.

[5] The explanation of the call loan spike before 1914, for example, runs as follows: Whenever the country's banks needed additional currency in large amounts, their demands centered upon a small number of banks in New York City. The first recourse of these banks when demands for currency were large was to call in their loans to stockbrokers. The brokers, threatened with ruinous losses if many of their customers had to sell securities all at once, bid desperately for funds, and the rates they are reported to have paid sometimes shot up above 100 percent for a few hours or days.

Let us examine next the effects of smoothing on average deviations. When they are averaged over all of the 9 stages of reference cycles, we find that smoothing has effected a net reduction equal to 0.1 percent of the reference-cycle bases in clearings, railroad stock prices, and call loans after 1914, 0.6 percent in iron production, and 8.5 percent in call loans before 1914. What makes all except the last of these changes slight is that at some stages smoothing increases the average deviations instead of reducing them. Increases occur at five stages of the patterns for clearings and railroad stock prices, at four stages of the call money pattern after 1914, at two stages of the iron pattern, and even at one stage of the earlier pattern for call money. Altogether, Table 19 shows 26 decreases in average deviations, 2 cases of no change, and 17 increases.

We are prone to think of smoothing as operating chiefly upon random movements, and of random movements as brief

---

Such rates did not bankrupt the borrowers, because call loans could be refunded at lower rates as soon as the stringency relaxed (100 percent interest for 3.65 days is only 1 percent of a loan).

Heavy demands for money to move the crops were made on New York every autumn; but they could be foreseen and prepared for. Such effects as these seasonal requirements had upon call rates are virtually eliminated before our raw data patterns are computed. Not so the effects of the panicky demands for currency that frequently accompanied business-cycle recessions in those days. It is these movements that produce the call money spike at stage V. Even our customary 3-month averages at the peaks understate the average cyclical rise of call loan rates.

I may add that the average pattern before World War I is much influenced by the extraordinary peak of October 1873 when the autumnal demand for crop moving funds coincided with a severe financial panic. But the omission of that cycle from the average would leave a 22 point rise between stages IV and V (instead of 38) and a 26 point fall between stages V and VII (instead of 58).

The less lofty but still considerable raw data peak of the pattern for 1914–33 also has a simple economic explanation. The structural change in banking effected by the Federal Reserve System has greatly reduced, but not wholly removed, money market stringencies in New York at times of recession. The peak reference-cycle standing of call loans in 1929 was 215.

Finally, our series on call money rates is compiled from monthly averages, and does not reveal the extreme fluctuations of the daily quotations. Our highest entry is 61.23 percent in September 1873; entries above 10 percent occur in 36 months scattered over 22 years from 1857 to 1920. The highest entry of later date is 9.23 percent in July 1929. For our data up to January 1937, see F. R. Macaulay, *Interest Rates, Bond Yields and Stock Prices in the United States since 1856* (National Bureau, 1938), pp. A142–61.

perturbations not closely correlated with one another. On this basis, probability theory suggests that smoothing will reduce average deviations most at stages I, V, and IX of our reference-cycle patterns. At these turning stages our standard measures span only 3 months, while at the other six stages they span on the average more than twice as many months, and so give much better chances for the mutual offsetting of brief random movements. In the data that have been smoothed in advance by Macaulay's 43-term formula, this disparity in the duration of stages counts for little; certainly for much less than in our standard measures. Hence one might expect that the reductions in the average deviations effected by smoothing would be appreciably greater on the average at stages I, V, and IX than at stages II–IV or VI–VIII. But that is not what Table 19 tells us. In clearings, railroad stock prices, and iron production, smoothing reduces the average deviations rather less on the whole at the turning stages than at the stages dominated by expansion and by contraction.[6] Only in call

[6] The following table tells its own story.

EFFECTS OF SMOOTHING AT THREE GROUPS OF STAGES UPON AVERAGE
DEVIATIONS FROM AVERAGE REFERENCE-CYCLE PATTERNS

	REFERENCE-CYCLE STAGES		
	I, V, IX	II, III, IV	VI, VII, VIII
Deflated clearings			
Signs regarded	+0.20	−0.13	−0.23
Signs disregarded	0.20	0.20	0.43
R.R. stock prices			
Signs regarded	−0.03	+0.10	−0.30
Signs disregarded	0.23	0.23	0.50
Iron production			
Signs regarded	−0.37	−0.27	−1.23
Signs disregarded	0.77	0.80	1.23
Call money before 1914			
Signs regarded	−15.03	−2.60	−7.80
Signs disregarded	15.03	4.13	7.80
Call money after 1914			
Signs regarded	−1.43	+0.03	+1.03
Signs disregarded	2.97	0.90	1.77

As in Table 19, from which the summary is compiled, the measures are expressed in percentages of reference-cycle bases.

Striking separate averages for the trough and peak stages would bring out again what has already been said about the unlike effects of smoothing upon call money peaks and troughs. In the other 3 series this elaboration would show inconsequential differences. The mathematically instructed will find the results of our smoothing tests easier to grasp if they read Millard Hastay's algebraic analysis in the first Technical Note appended to this chapter.

money is the expectation borne out by the figures, and there we have shown that the movements chiefly affected by smoothing are cyclical in character.

We do not conclude from these experiments that irregular movements are a minor factor in economic fluctuations, or that our standard analysis eliminates all but a small percentage of irregular movements from reference-cycle patterns and average deviations. The lesson is rather that we should discriminate between two types of irregular movements—those which last only a month or two, and those which persist for several quarters or even years.

Brief movements are virtually erased when they are mild, and much modified when they have considerable amplitudes, by the simple smoothing involved in our technique, so that only slight residues are left for more systematic smoothing to iron out. If a brief random movement during a cycle is so violent that it would distort the average reference-cycle pattern of a series, we exclude that cycle.

Long-continued irregular movements, on the other hand, survive not only the variable-span smoothing of our standard analysis, but also more systematic smoothing, provided the latter is not so drastic as to erase almost all cyclical movements. For example:

Smoothing by Macaulay's method will not remove the great bulges in American price and value series in 1862–67 and 1915–21. It will moderate the effects of two bad harvests upon agricultural prices less than it will moderate the effects of speculative maneuvers associated with monthly crop reports, or even the effects of two bad seasons separated by a good season. Random effects of considerable size thus remain in the smoothed forms of the series we have used in our tests, and contribute toward making the average deviations nearly as large in the results obtained from the smoothed as in those obtained from the raw data.[7]

A methodological conclusion follows: If major wars and two bad harvests in succession typify the irregular movements that cut a considerable figure in the average deviations from

[7] *Measuring Business Cycles*, p. 362.

mean reference-cycle patterns made from smoothed data, and *a fortiori* in the deviations from our standard patterns, we should be able to formulate specific hypotheses concerning the irregularities of most moment to us. We need not give up the concept that every economic activity is influenced at all times by a host of factors that cannot be classified as seasonal, cyclical, or secular; but we can suppose that the net effects of this host upon our standard measures of time series as comprehensive as the four used in our test are relatively slight in comparison with the effects produced by identifiable events. Then we can concentrate upon the latter.[8]

It should be observed that the conclusions of this section rest upon a narrow statistical base. Only 4 series were used in our smoothing tests. However, the average deviations from their reference-cycle patterns run the gamut from 3 percent of the reference-cycle bases at stage IV of the clearings pattern to 65 percent at stage V of the pattern for call money before 1914. All 4 series are exceptionally long—a circumstance that favors regularity in reference-cycle patterns. But the call money pattern after 1914 covers only 5 cycles, and when we broke each of the long series into three segments we found no reason to change our conclusions materially.[9] Yet it is fortunate that the next two sections, which will lead by a roundabout path back to the irregular component in average deviations, have a much broader foundation.

C   CONTRIBUTION OF SECULAR MOVEMENTS

Our method of eliminating the portion of a secular trend that represents shifts in the level about which a series fluctuates from one cycle to the next "implies that if the secular trend were represented . . . by a continuous line, that line would be

---

[8] Certainly our smoothing tests lend little support to the assumption that the irregular component of our average deviations varies inversely as the duration of reference-cycle stages. Presumably there is some such effect; but our efforts to demonstrate it have so far been unavailing.

[9] See Chart 51 in *Measuring Business Cycles* and the textual comments upon it.

a flexible curve cutting through successive specific cycles".[10]
We do not draw such lines, but we do measure the intercycle
component of trend by computing percentages of change per
month from one specific-cycle base to the next. These measures
vary from cycle to cycle within series, and also among series,
in much the same fashion as do our measures of cycle durations
and amplitudes. The transfer from specific-cycle to reference-
cycle analysis changes the individual cycle bases little or much
according as a series conforms closely or loosely to business
cycles and I–V timing; but the transfer does not diminish the
differences among shifts from one cycle base to the next.
Finally, the readily demonstrable variability in the intercycle
component of trend implies corresponding variability in the intracycle component; for the intracycle component is the full
trend of a series between stages I and IX of a cycle, just as the intercycle component is the full trend from one cycle to the next.
Thus our reference-cycle standings include a trend component
that is far more variable from cycle to cycle than the term
'secular trend' suggests to many minds. What are for our purposes secular movements must cut a considerable figure in the
average deviations from our average measures of cyclical behavior.[11]

   Geoffrey H. Moore has found a way to determine approximately how much the intracycle trend component contributes
to the average deviations from average specific-cycle or average reference-cycle standings.[12] His method rests upon the

10 *Measuring Business Cycles*, p. 39, note 5.

11 How we come to use what are in effect highly flexible trends is set
forth in Technical Note II appended to this chapter. The gist of the matter
is that shifts in cycle bases are to us secular movements. Presumably these
highly variable shifts are influenced by all the 'forces', or 'factors', or 'movements' that affect the monthly, quarterly, or annual data used in computing
bases. To account for the alterations, large or small, in the levels on which
successive specific and successive business cycles run is a problem of the
first magnitude. When economists get around to treating this problem, or
group of problems as it will probably turn out to be, they may find the
National Bureau's specific-cycle bases a highly valuable collection of observations. Perhaps even more useful will be the corresponding collection of
reference-cycle bases.

12 A similar method was suggested independently by Simon Kuznets.

fact that our standard analysis tends to make the secular contribution to the average deviations largest at the 'ends' of the cycles and smallest in their middles.

The reason is simple. In effect, we represent the trend of a series, not by a continuous line, but by a succession of horizontal base lines, each one cycle long. When the trend rises, each base line is higher than its predecessor; when the trend falls the lines are progressively lower.[13] In series with rising trends, each base line tends to be farthest above the corresponding continuous trend line at the beginning of a cycle, to coincide with the continuous trend at the cycle's midpoint, and to be farthest below the continuous trend at its end. With appropriate reversals, this rule holds also for declining trends. The rule applies most clearly and strictly to linear trends; virtually it applies also to most curvilinear trends met in practice, for the intracycle segments of such trends seldom differ so much from straight lines as to alter the stages of maximum and minimum divergence from our horizontal bases. What is more to the point, the rule applies roughly even to the highly flexible trends that correspond to the ever varying shifts in our cycle bases.

Whatever cycle-by-cycle changes occur in the intracycle trend component influence our measures most at the stages where our horizontal base lines diverge most from flexible but continuous trend lines, and influence our measures least where the divergence is least. Theoretically, indeed, the trend component should be wholly eliminated from our reference-cycle measures at the points where the 'true' trend coincides with our horizontal cycle bases; that is, the secular component in the average deviations should be zero at these points of intersection. The longer a cycle is, the greater tends to be the difference between the value of the trend component at the midpoint of the cycle and at its 'ends'.

Our practice of marking off business cycles by their troughs makes troughs the 'ends' of a cycle, while the peak stage more

---

[13] For illustrations see Charts 14 and 18 of *Measuring Business Cycles*, which represent the derivation of specific- and reference-cycle patterns.

often than any other approximates the midpoint. If we mark off cycles by successive peaks, these peaks become the 'ends', and the midpoints are more likely to occur in troughs than in any other stage. Appendix Tables B3 and B4 in *Measuring Business Cycles* give the cycle-by-cycle patterns of 7 series covering 14 or more reference cycles both on a trough-to-trough (T–T) and on a peak-to-peak (P–P) basis. As Table 29 (see Technical Note II at the end of the chapter) shows, the shift from a T–T to a P–P basis has one of the expected effects: without exception, P–P analysis reduces the average deviations at troughs and raises them at peaks. But the test does not show a second expected effect: average deviations are not smallest at cyclical peaks on the T–T basis, or smallest at the troughs on the P–P basis, as they would be if trends were the sole or the controlling factor at work. Only in railroad stock prices do the minimum deviations occur at the T–T peak; in no series does the minimum occur at the trough in either form of analysis. Thirteen out of 14 times the influence of trends upon the location of *minimum* deviations is blocked by some other factor; but 12 times out of 14 the *maximum* deviations occur in the stage where trends tend to place them—at the trough in T–T, at the peak in P–P analysis.[14]

D CONTRIBUTION OF CYCLICAL MOVEMENTS

This striking difference is due to another feature of our technique. Whether the analysis is T–T or P–P, our reference-cycle relatives tend to minimize the deviations arising from conforming cyclical movements at the midpoints of expansions and contractions, and to maximize them at troughs and peaks impartially.

Suppose (1) that the T–T pattern of every series in every cycle consists of a straight line sloping upward from trough to peak and a straight line sloping downward from peak to

[14] One of the exceptions to the latter rule is that call money rates have their maximum average deviation in stage V, even in the T–T analysis; another is that pig iron production has its maximum deviation in stage VI in the P–P analysis. In the T–T analysis, the deviation of outside clearings in stage II equals that at the trough.

trough; (2) that the standings at the initial and terminal troughs of a cycle are identical; (3) that the slopes of these lines, and therefore the amplitude of rise and fall, differ from cycle to cycle; and (4) that, while the durations of successive cycles differ, expansion and contraction are of equal length in each cycle.

It follows from our assumptions that in every cycle covered by a series, the stage standing is farthest below the cycle base at the troughs and farthest above it at the peak. The maximum differences among the standings occur where the standings themselves diverge most from the horizontal base. But in rising from their low values at stage I to their high values at V, all the straight lines intersect the base in the middle of expansion, and the down-sloping lines from V to IX intersect the base in the middle of contraction. That is, in stages III and VII the standings in every cycle are 100, and the average deviations zero. This argument applies also to straight-line patterns that on the T–T basis fall from stage I to V and rise from V to IX, that is, to inverted series.

Of the assumptions used here, the third is true to fact: the rise and the fall of reference-cycle relatives differ from one cycle to another. The other assumptions distort the observed facts. The movements from I to V and from V to IX seldom follow straight lines; often stages I and IX are not troughs and stage V is not the peak of a pattern; some series have reference-cycle patterns so irregular that one cannot identify either peaks or troughs; expansions and contractions differ in duration; and the standings at stages I and IX commonly diverge. Yet the movements we observe during successive reference cycles in the many series of our sample seem to be distributed not very unevenly around the ultrasimple model we have assumed. If the cyclical component in cycle-by-cycle variability stood in splendid isolation, the average deviations would be least in stages III and VII, greatest in stages I, V, and IX.

E STATISTICAL TESTS

As the reader may have remarked, the effects of cycle-by-cycle changes in intracycle trends and in cyclical amplitude upon the average deviations agree at the troughs and oppose each other at the peaks of business cycles, when we analyze series on our standard T–T plan. At the troughs our methods tend to maximize the deviations of both components; at the peaks they tend to maximize cyclical and minimize secular deviations. These tendencies are frequently overborne by irregular movements; but such 'disturbing circumstances' are as likely to reenforce as to counteract the systematic effects of our technique. Hence in fairly long series, such as were used in our tests, or in a considerable collection of short series, we may expect to find the maximum deviations most frequently in stages I and IX, but we do not know whether to expect the minimum deviations in stages III and VII, where the cyclical component tends to put them, or in stage V, which is favored by the secular component, or perhaps in one or another of the intermediate stages.

Our 7 test series in Table 29 are too small a sample to settle the open issue. Their T–T analyses scatter the minimum deviations over all the stages from III to VII with fine impartiality.[15] So we turn to the full sample of 794 series presented in Table 3, or rather, this sample minus the 6 series that cover only one cycle and so have no cycle-by-cycle differences to measure. These numerous T–T analyses give a definite answer. Table 20 shows that averages of the average deviations are smallest in stages IV and VI. They decline regularly from one maximum in stage I to a minimum at IV, rise rather sharply in V, fall as sharply to a second minimum in VI, then rise regularly to a second maximum in IX. Of course, departures from this average scheme appear among the 29 groups for which we have computed separate averages. For example, maximum devia-

[15] The minimum deviations appear at the following stages in the several series:

III	Call money rates
IV	Clearings outside N.Y.C., deflated
V	Railroad stock prices
VI	Pig iron production and shares traded
VII	Freight car orders
IV, VI	Railroad bond yields

For full details, see Technical Note II, Table 29.

Table 20

MEAN AVERAGE DEVIATIONS FROM AVERAGE REFERENCE-CYCLE PATTERNS, BY GROUPS OF SERIES

Group	No. of Series[a]	Mean Average Deviation at Reference-Cycle Stages								
		I	II	III	IV	V	VI	VII	VIII	IX
Retail sales	10	6.2	5.4	4.4	4.9	4.9	3.6	3.8	7.6	9.6
Wholesale sales	14	11.2	9.7	9.1	7.5	10.0	8.5	8.2	11.2	12.6
New orders from manufacturers	17	28.8	32.1	25.5	31.9	40.9	22.1	27.6	22.4	29.5
Construction contracts										
Private	26	36.3	38.1	36.4	29.6	47.3	32.1	26.4	30.9	32.4
Public	16	30.7	18.9	17.9	12.4	24.7	20.2	15.4	27.2	37.3
Inventories										
Positive timing	18	13.3	11.5	10.0	12.2	10.9	7.6	11.9	14.5	16.4
Irregular timing	18	21.7	16.6	11.0	10.0	13.5	13.1	12.6	16.7	20.6
Inverted timing	24	22.6	18.1	14.6	12.0	11.0	13.3	16.8	20.1	24.9
Production										
Foodstuffs	47	10.8	8.4	6.1	5.6	7.0	6.7	7.7	8.4	9.5
Other perishables	29	10.9	8.0	8.0	6.3	9.6	8.4	7.3	11.6	11.4
Semidurables	28	14.1	9.5	8.9	8.9	9.3	5.0	10.9	11.2	11.7
Durables	53	25.5	20.4	18.2	14.3	18.1	17.0	16.5	22.6	22.6
Employment										
Perishable goods industries	8	8.5	5.5	4.6	4.2	3.9	3.6	3.4	6.2	6.4
Semidurable goods industries	13	9.0	5.9	4.9	4.4	4.5	2.9	5.0	5.9	6.7
Durable goods industries	9	18.1	12.8	10.4	7.9	10.6	8.5	10.3	14.8	14.4
Hours of work per week	9	5.5	4.3	4.1	3.4	4.0	2.3	2.2	5.2	5.8
Earnings per week, month, or year	10	5.8	4.8	3.1	2.9	4.9	5.2	5.9	7.9	9.1
Payrolls										
Perishable goods industries	8	12.0	8.5	5.9	5.4	6.5	6.2	5.8	11.3	13.5
Semidurable goods industries	13	17.4	10.4	8.1	7.5	8.5	5.7	6.0	10.8	13.3
Durable goods industries	6	23.8	19.3	15.4	14.2	19.1	13.5	14.7	21.6	22.8

Table 20 (concl.)

Prices of commodities										
Farm products & foods	51	16.0	12.4	9.1	8.4	10.1	8.9	7.8	11.3	13.6
Other perishables	22	10.6	8.7	8.0	6.8	8.1	7.5	7.6	8.9	9.9
Semidurables	18	14.4	10.5	8.7	7.3	8.2	7.0	8.3	9.8	10.9
Durables	45	11.5	9.0	6.4	5.3	6.4	6.3	7.6	9.2	9.4
Interest rates										
Short-term	11	30.7[b]	13.0	13.2	15.4	18.7	8.2	15.6	12.9	13.9
Long-term & bond yields	12	7.9	5.6	3.0	3.0	3.2	3.3	3.6	4.8	4.6
Security issues, corporate	14	41.6	32.4	35.5	45.2	56.4	41.3	26.5	43.0	53.1
Bank clearings or debits	8	10.4	10.0	7.6	9.1	9.3	7.3	7.6	13.1	16.2
Indexes of business activity	11	8.2	6.6	5.8	5.1	6.1	4.7	5.4	8.3	8.8
Summaries										
All series on										
Construction contracts or permits	58	31.0	28.2	26.0	21.2	33.1	23.8	20.8	27.8	31.4
Production	183	15.8	12.2	10.9	9.1	11.2	9.6	10.5	13.7	13.9
Employment	37	11.3	7.8	6.2	5.1	6.0	4.6	6.1	8.5	8.7
Payrolls & other income payments	30	17.0	11.8	9.0	8.4	10.4	7.7	8.0	13.6	15.7
Prices of commodities	147	13.1	10.1	7.8	6.8	8.0	7.3	7.5	9.8	11.0
All series on										
Flow of commodities, services, or income	472	17.7	14.6	12.6	11.2	14.3	11.3	11.9	15.6	17.6
Prices of commodities or services	168	12.1	9.4	7.1	6.2	7.5	6.9	7.1	9.3	10.5
Financial activities	135	17.6	12.3	10.3	11.5	13.9	11.3	11.5	14.7	17.4
General business activity	13	8.7	7.3	6.2	5.9	6.8	5.2	5.8	9.5	10.5
All series in sample	788	16.4	13.0	10.9	10.1	12.7	10.2	10.7	14.0	15.9

[a] See Table 8, note a. Six series that cover only one cycle are omitted here.

[b] The high figure at this stage is largely due to the sharp decline of short-term interest rates after 1933. Their level at the 1933 trough, when expressed as a percentage of the 1933–38 cycle, is far above the standing at stage I in previous cycles.

tions appear at stage V in new orders from manufacturers, contracts for construction (all series and the private subgroup), and issues of corporate securities—three groups that relate to investments and in which cyclical are much larger than secular changes. In one group, production of perishable goods other than foods, the maximum occurs in stage VIII. In all the other groups we have averaged, the maximum occurs in one of the troughs. A similar concentration appears in the location of the minimum deviations: in the 29 groups they occur 22 times in stages IV or VI, 5 times in stage VII, once in stages III and IV, and once in stage V. Thus the evidence of the groups amply supports that of the grand average of all series, and so also does that of the groups of groups near the end of the table.

F   DECOMPOSITION OF AVERAGE DEVIATIONS

When pushed to its logical limits, the preceding analysis enables us to decompose the average deviations from the average reference-cycle patterns of our full sample into their irregular, secular, and cyclical components. This operation strains one's credulity; but let us perform it hardily and assess the results later.

By way of preparation we enter under each reference-cycle stage the full average deviation we shall presently break into parts. Below these figures we put down the way in which each component is supposed to behave 'under the bludgeonings of chance' and the pressures of our analytic methods.

Table 21

MEAN AVERAGE DEVIATIONS FROM AVERAGE REFERENCE-CYCLE
PATTERNS OF FULL SAMPLE, AND THEORETICAL EXPECTATIONS
CONCERNING STAGE-BY-STAGE CHANGES IN THEIR COMPONENTS [a]

	REFERENCE-CYCLE STAGES								
	I	II	III	IV	V	VI	VII	VIII	IX
Av. deviation	16.4	13.0	10.9	10.1	12.7	10.2	10.7	14.0	15.9
Component									
Irregular	C	C	C	C	C	C	C	C	C
Secular	M	F	F	F	O	R	R	R	M
Cyclical	M	F	O	R	M	F	O	R	M

[a] C stands for constant, M for maximum, F for falling, R for rising, and O for zero.

Note first how symmetrically the average deviations are arrayed on either side of the reference-cycle peak. The following rearrangement of the figures makes this symmetry clearer.

| REFERENCE-CYCLE STAGES | AVERAGE DEVIATIONS | DIFFERENCE BETWEEN AV. DEVIATIONS AS % OF | |
		Reference-Cycle Bases	Mean of Deviations
I and IX	16.4 and 15.9	0.5	3.1
II and VIII	13.0 and 14.0	1.0	7.4
III and VII	10.9 and 10.7	0.2	1.9
IV and VI	10.1 and 10.2	0.1	1.0
Average	12.6 12.7	0.4	3.4

This close approach to perfect balance fits neatly the theoretical expectations set forth in preceding sections and summarized in Table 21. If the implications of our theoretical model were fully realized, and if the stage-by-stage changes in the average deviations proceeded at uniform rates per month, we could start with stage V and argue as follows: Since the rise in the secular component of the average deviations from zero at the cyclical peak to a maximum value at stage IX matches in rate and duration the preceding fall from a maximum at stage I to zero at the peak, the maximum secular values at stages I and IX are equal, and so also are all intermediate secular values equidistant from stage V. On the same assumptions, a similar argument applies to the cyclical component. Since the fall in this component from a maximum value at the peak to zero at stage VII is supposed to equal in rate and duration the preceding rise from zero at stage III to the maximum at V, the intervening cyclical values at VI and IV are equal. So also are the cyclical values at stages VIII and II, and at IX and I; for the rise from zero at VII to a maximum at IX is supposed to equal in rate and duration the fall from a maximum at I to zero at III.

The perfect balance thus theoretically maintained on the two sides of the cyclical peak by each component insures that the two components combined maintain such a balance. But the preceding argument does not explain why the *full* average deviations should be so nearly equal at the stages paired as the above figures show them to be. For this argument tells us nothing about the average deviations arising from irregular movements, which may well exceed the deviations arising from both of the other components combined. Our assumption that the irregular component remains constant from stage to stage of reference cycles rests upon an independent foundation. This component includes all changes in economic activities that are not correlated with the secular-cyclical fluctuations in which our interest centers.[16] To say that these movements are not correlated in time with the movements we are trying to measure is to say that we have no reason to expect that the irregular component in the average deviations will be larger at some stage of business cycles than at other stages; which is equivalent to the expectation that this component will have the same value at all stages.[17]

While this expectation is independent of our expectations concerning the other components, the evidence at hand seems to confirm it. A restatement of the preceding findings makes this clear. The stage-by-stage changes in the full average deviations comply so closely with theoretical expectations concerning the secular and cyclical components, taken by themselves, that only small changes are left to be explained by other factors. Apparently, all nonsecular-cyclical movements have a small part in producing stage-by-stage differences in average

[16] In terms of Section A above, we classify with irregular movements in the usual sense (if there be one) seasonal residues and overadjustments, the effects of reference-date errors, elements of long cycles and discontinuous changes in cyclical behavior, and perhaps other kinds of nonsecular-cyclical movements that may some day win names and recognition.

[17] To assume that the irregular component is unevenly distributed over reference-cycle stages would not be inconsistent with our assumption that the irregular component tends to be distributed evenly over time. For these stages are unequal in duration; and, when we are dealing with samples that are limited in both economic coverage and time, departures from uniform distribution will occur, and are most likely when irregular movements have least chance of canceling one another—that is, in the short stages I, V, and IX. But in Section B above we found evidence that, in practice, the average deviations are not appreciably influenced by the duration of stages, apart from the deviations due to certain violent cyclical movements. And this observation is made less surprising by Hastay's theoretical analysis in Technical Note I, at the end of the chapter.

deviations, however large a part they may have in producing these deviations at every stage.

One other feature of our technique should be noted before we try to determine the actual magnitudes of the three components. The difference between the average deviations at the stages I have paired increases from 0.1 percent of the reference-cycle bases at stages IV and VI to 0.2 percent at III and VII, and to 1.0 percent at II and VIII; then the difference drops to 0.5 percent at stages I and IX. This drop is due to our practice of taking the terminal trough of one cycle as the initial trough of its successor; that is, the same seasonally-adjusted data are used in computing the reference-cycle standing of a series at stage IX of a cycle and stage I of the following cycle. It may seem, in view of this technical fact, that the average deviations at stages I and IX should be even closer than we find them. However, two factors oppose equality. (1) The standing at stage I of the first cycle in a series has no mate at a preceding stage IX, and the standing at stage IX of the last cycle has no mate at stage I of a subsequent cycle. In short series these non-overlapping entries have a considerable influence, and Table 3 shows that over half the series in our sample cover less than six cycles. When in longer series we have to drop a cycle or two between the first and last one covered, at least two standings in stage I have no mates in IX, and at least two in IX are without mates in I. (2) Every change in cycle bases produces a difference between the standings at stage IX of one cycle and at stage I of the next cycle; for these two standings are ratios of the same magnitude to unequal magnitudes. The last section of Technical Note II, appended to this chapter, shows how large these effects can be and frequently are.[18]

G ESTIMATES OF COMPONENTS

We can get a basal estimate of the secular component of the average deviations by subtracting the average deviation at stage V from the average deviations at stages I and IX. The

[18] The average deviations from average reference-cycle standings are lower at stage IX than at stage I in 16 of the 29 minor groups in Table 20, and higher in 13 of these groups.

cyclical component is supposed to be at its maximum (that is, at the same value) in all three stages and the irregular component is supposed to remain constant from stage to stage; the only difference is that the secular component is zero in V and at its maximum values in I and IX. Thus the differences between the full average deviations at the peak and at the two troughs, 3.7 and 3.2 percent respectively of the reference-cycle bases, express the maximum deviations due to changes in intracycle trends (Table 21).

By accepting these figures and the corresponding value of zero at the peak, assuming that the stage-to-stage changes proceed at a uniform rate per month, and choosing an appropriate measure of business-cycle durations, we can estimate the numerical value of the secular components in the mean average deviations from the average reference-cycle patterns of our full sample at each of the nine stages. The most inclusive of our monthly duration measures, based upon the American reference dates from 1854 to 1938, gives an average of 47.7 months. Within that span, let us say, the secular component falls from 3.7 percent of the reference-cycle bases to zero and then rises to 3.2 percent, a total movement of 6.9 percent, which means a shift of 0.145 percent each month. The monthly intervals between stages are:

I–II	II–III	III–IV	IV–V	V–VI	VI–VII	VII–VIII	VIII–IX
4.8	8.3	8.3	4.8	3.9	6.9	6.9	3.9

Thus estimated, the secular component of the mean average deviations of our full sample, expressed in percentages of reference-cycle bases, comes out as follows:

I	II	III	IV	V	VI	VII	VIII	IX
3.7	3.0	1.8	0.6	0.0	0.7	1.6	2.6	3.2

Next we estimate the irregular component. That is easily done now that we have the secular estimates. Since the cyclical component is supposed to be zero at stages III and VII, the irregular component at these stages will be the full average deviation minus the secular component:

STAGE	FULL AVERAGE DEVIATION	SECULAR COMPONENT	IRREGULAR COMPONENT
III	10.9	1.8	9.1
VII	10.7	1.6	9.1

Of course, the results accord well with our assumption that the irregular component is uniform from stage to stage.

To complete the operation, we obtain the cyclical component by subtracting the sum of the above estimates of the secular and irregular components from the full average deviations at each stage.

Table 22

ESTIMATES OF THE SECULAR, CYCLICAL, AND IRREGULAR COMPONENTS IN MEAN AVERAGE DEVIATIONS FROM AVERAGE REFERENCE-CYCLE PATTERNS OF FULL SAMPLE

	I	II	III	IV	V	VI	VII	VIII	IX
				REFERENCE-CYCLE STAGES [a]					
Av. deviation	16.4	13.0	10.9	10.1	12.7	10.2	10.7	14.0	15.9
Component									
Irregular	9.1	9.1	9.1	9.1	9.1	9.1	9.1	9.1	9.1
Secular	3.7	3.0	1.8	0.6	0.0	0.7	1.6	2.6	3.2
Cyclical	3.6	0.9	0.0	0.4	3.6	0.4	0.0	2.3	3.6

[a] All entries are expressed in percentages of reference-cycle bases.

H SOME CONCLUSIONS

It would be easy to refine and enlarge upon Table 22. For example, the procedure followed in making it throws what stage-by-stage departures from regularity there are in the average deviations of our full sample into the cyclical component. They might more plausibly be assigned to the irregular component. Also, the differences between the deviations at troughs and peaks are ascribed wholly to the trend component—a position that taxes credulity. We might try several duration scales, derivable from our reference dates or by averaging the time span of the series in our samples. We might make calculations like those in Table 22 for various parts of our sample—say for all series on physical production, all on commodity prices, etc. But such betterments and additions would carry us into the realm of rapidly diminishing returns and, what is worse, suggest an unwarranted confidence in the representative value and precision of our results.

Table 22 rests upon a set of bold assumptions and an imperfect set of data. At best, the assumptions represent central tendencies that should appear in a large and properly drawn sample of measures made by our methods from time series subject to cyclical fluctuations, to shifts in the levels about which successive cycles occur, and also to ever changing complexes of other movements that bear irregular relations in time to the cyclical-secular complex. The statistical observations show clearly certain effects logically to be expected from the secular and cyclical components. They do not demonstrate the zero influence of secular changes at stage V, or the uniform rate of change in the secular factor from I to V and from V to IX, or the zero influence of cyclical changes at stages III and VII, or their maximum influence at troughs and peaks. These features of the scheme are deduced from certain properties of secular and cyclical movements, from the mathematical implications of our technique, and the observation that the modal type of timing among our series is that which fits the reference dates. From the statistical side, all we can say is that the evidence is compatible with broad expectations. If so much is granted, we can add that observation gives some warrant for the uniform distribution of noncyclical-secular effects among the nine stages. Thus our neat scheme, while not a set of actual measures, is more than a flight of fancy.

We may sum up the findings in the following propositions: The cyclical component varies from cycle to cycle; its variability declines sharply from stage I to stage III, rises sharply in III–V, then falls again in V–VII and rises in VII–IX. Intracycle trends also vary from cycle to cycle. Their contribution to the average deviations from reference-cycle patterns declines from stage I to stage V and rises from V to IX. Other types of cycle-by-cycle differences in our measures are not closely correlated with the changes in cyclical-secular movements, and tend to be evenly distributed among the nine stages. In magnitude they seem to exceed the differences attributable to the cyclical and secular components taken together, but the excess shown by

Table 22 cannot be taken at face value.[19] In any case it is not large at the troughs of the cycle where our methods maximize the variability of both the cyclical and secular components.

Since the stage-by-stage differences in average deviations arise in large measure from technical features of our analytic methods, we must be cautious about reading economic meanings into them. For example, the fact that these deviations reach major maxima at stages I and IX, and a minor maximum at stage V, does not prove that cyclical behavior is more variable from cycle to cycle at troughs than at peaks, and more variable at peaks than during expansions and contractions. Yet, by taking due precautions, we can make the stage-by-stage differences in average deviations yield economically significant information. An example of how that may be done is afforded by Table 23, which was drawn up by Geoffrey H. Moore. Since our methods are applied in virtually uniform fashion to all monthly and quarterly series, differences from series to series in the results must be due to the unlike ways in which different sets of data respond to the same treatment. To be

[19] Our calculations assume that the several components of variation can be treated as additive, whereas in fact such a relation does not hold in general among average deviations. However, an additive relation does hold among variances, provided the several components of variation can be treated as uncorrelated; and this suggests that a better approach would be to square the mean average deviation for each of the nine stages, then perform the decomposition described in the text, finally, extract square roots to put the results on an average deviation basis. Using this approach, Millard Hastay obtained the following interesting results:

TYPE OF COMPONENT	REFERENCE-CYCLE STAGES								
	I	II	III	IV	V	VI	VII	VIII	IX
Irregular	8.2	8.2	8.2	8.2	8.2	8.2	8.2	8.2	8.2
Secular	10.4	9.4	7.3	4.3	0.0	4.2	6.8	8.7	9.6
Cyclical	9.7	3.8	0.0	4.1	9.7	4.4	0.0	7.3	9.7

Of course, it is not strictly permissible to pass directly from average deviations to variances. Further, the new results may differ markedly from those we would get if we worked throughout with standard deviations for individual series.

Table 23

RATIOS OF MEAN AVERAGE DEVIATIONS AT REFERENCE PEAKS TO MEAN AVERAGE DEVIATIONS AT REFERENCE TROUGHS, BY GROUPS OF SERIES[a]

GROUP	NO. OF SERIES	MEAN AV. DEVIATION AT STAGE V AS RATIO TO THAT AT Stage I	MEAN AV. DEVIATION AT STAGE V AS RATIO TO THAT AT Stage IX	MEAN RATIO	RANK OF MEAN RATIO
Retail sales	10	.79	.51	.65	9
Wholesale sales	14	.89	.79	.84	24
New orders from manufacturers	17	1.42	1.39	1.40	29
Construction contracts					
Private	26	1.30	1.46	1.38	28
Public	16	.80	.66	.73	18.5
Inventories					
Positive timing	18	.82	.66	.74	20
Irregular timing	18	.62	.66	.64	8
Inverted timing	24	.49	.44	.46	1
Production					
Foodstuffs	47	.65	.74	.70	14
Other perishables	29	.88	.84	.86	25
Semidurables	28	.66	.79	.72	16.5
Durables	53	.71	.80	.76	21
Employment					
Perishable goods industries	8	.46	.61	.54	3
Semidurable goods industries	13	.50	.67	.58	6
Durable goods industries	9	.59	.74	.66	10.5
Hours of work per week	9	.73	.69	.71	15
Earnings per week, month, or year	10	.84	.54	.69	13
Payrolls					
Perishable goods industries	8	.54	.48	.51	2
Semidurable goods industries	13	.49	.64	.56	4.5
Durable goods industries	6	.80	.84	.82	23
Prices of commodities					
Farm products & foods	51	.63	.74	.68	12
Other perishables	22	.76	.82	.79	22
Semidurables	18	.57	.75	.66	10.5
Durables	45	.56	.68	.62	7
Interest rates					
Short-term	11	.61	1.35	.98	26
Long-term & bond yields	12	.41	.70	.56	4.5
Security issues, corporate	14	1.36	1.06	1.21	27
Bank clearings or debits	8	.89	.57	.73	18.5
Indexes of business activity	11	.74	.69	.72	16.5

[a] Based upon Table 20; see notes attached to that table.

Table 23 (concl.)

Summaries	NO. OF SERIES	MEAN AV. DEVIATION AT STAGE V AS RATIO TO THAT AT		MEAN RATIO
		Stage I	Stage IX	
All series on				
Construction contracts or permits	58	1.07	1.05	1.06
Production	183	.71	.81	.76
Employment	37	.53	.69	.61
Payrolls & other income payments	30	.61	.66	.64
Prices of commodities	147	.61	.73	.67
All series on				
Flow of commodities, services, or income	472	.81	.81	.81
Prices of commodities or services	168	.62	.71	.66
Financial activities	135	.79	.80	.80
General business activity	13	.78	.65	.72
All series in sample	788	.77	.80	.78

RANKING OF GROUPS OF SERIES ACCORDING TO MEAN RATIO JUST GIVEN

Minor group	Mean ratio	Major group	Mean ratio
Inventories, inverted timing	.46		
Payrolls, perishables	.51		
Employment, perishables	.54		
Interest rates, long-term	.56		
Payrolls, semidurables	.56		
Employment, semidurables	.58		
		Employment	.61
Prices, durables	.62		
Inventories, irregular timing	.64	Payrolls & other income payments	.64
Retail sales	.65		
Employment, durables	.66	Prices of commodities or services	.66
Prices, semidurables	.66		
		Prices of commodities	.67
Prices, farm & food	.68		
Earnings per week, etc.	.69		
Production, foodstuffs	.70		
Hours of work per week	.71		
Production, semidurables	.72		
Indexes of business activity	.72	General business activity	.72
Construction contracts, public	.73		
Bank clearings or debits	.73		
Inventories, positive timing	.74		
Production, durables	.76	Production	.76
		ALL SERIES IN SAMPLE	.78
Prices, other perishables	.79		
		Financial activities	.80
		Flow of commod., serv., or incomes	.81
Payrolls, durables	.82		
Wholesale sales	.84		
Production, other perishables	.86		
Interest rates, short-term	.98		
Security issues, corporate	1.21		
Construction contracts, private	1.38	Construction contracts or permits	1.06
New orders from manufacturers	1.40		

more specific: our statistical operations tend to make the average deviations larger at the troughs than at the peaks of business cycles. But the degree in which this tendency manifests itself in the results varies from series to series according to individual trends, individual cyclical movements at peaks and at troughs, and according to the irregular factors that impinge upon individual series at these stages. Hence, when we compute the *ratios* of average deviations at peaks to average deviations at troughs, we find differences from series to series that are not mathematical consequences of our method. They must be due to dissimilarities of secular, cyclical, or irregular movements, taken in the senses assigned to these categories by our analytic technique. And when we compute these ratios, not for single series but for groups, we can go further and claim that the differences among groups are less the result of chance irregularities than of differences in the combined cyclical-trend components in which our interest centers.

Thus interpreted, Table 23 becomes highly interesting. For example, the last column shows that the groups having the highest variability at business-cycle peaks in relation to their variability at troughs are three representing the volume of investments to which private parties are committing themselves in the near future. How significant that finding may be for the theory of cyclical recessions and for the theory of revivals must be left for the present to the reader's imagination. Hardly less interesting is it to find the maximum variability at troughs in relation to peaks in inverted inventories—a business factor that makes the most trouble at the end of contractions. The difference between the role played by the durability of commodities in determining the cyclical behavior of series on prices and production, to which attention was directed in the chapter on reference-cycle amplitudes (Sec. IVF), reappears in this table on deviations. And this is only a beginning of the seemingly significant results that the reader can find in Table 23 if he observes with care. Our own efforts to exploit these materials, explaining what the table shows and making it explain other features of business cycles, will come later—when we shall be journeying round the cycle stage by stage. Still more useful will such studies of the average deviations prove when someone undertakes a systematic investigation of differences among business cycles. What is pertinent—and important—here is merely the demonstration that the technical effects of our analytic procedure upon the average deviations from mean reference-cycle standings do not render these measures useless. On the contrary, we can observe in them features of cyclical behavior that might otherwise escape attention—features that will enrich and enlarge our knowledge of what happens during business cycles.

What we have learned about the average deviations should reduce our troublesome misgivings concerning the representative value of reference-cycle patterns. Both the cyclical and the secular components in average deviations appear clearly, not only in the full sample, but also in most of the 29 groups. This finding means that, even in fairly small groups, the noncyclical-secular components are usually distributed evenly enough to let the systematic effects shine through. If this 'evening out' of irregular movements occurs among the nine stages of reference cycles, a 'canceling out' will probably occur when standings at the same stage of different cycles are combined to get one point of an average reference-cycle pattern. Indeed, the noncyclical-secular components of standings at the same stage of successive cycles are less likely to be intercorrelated than are these components of successive stages in the same cycle; that is, 'canceling out' is likely to be fuller than 'evening out'. And when we rise above the 29 groups to the full sample, we find some evidence of virtual stage-by-stage equality in the obscuring factors—evidence that is more impressive when coupled with 'evening out' in the group averages. But, once again, these reassuring conclusions apply in full force only to considerable samples of reference-cycle patterns. The representative value of the patterns of individual series we have still to consider.

So far the discussion has been confined to deviations from average standings at successive reference-cycle stages. A word should be added concerning the average deviations of the two sets of measures we derive from these standings.

Reference-cycle amplitudes are computed by taking the differences between the average standing of a series at whatever stage its timing variety indicates as the characteristic location of its peak and its standings in whatever preceding and following stages are indicated as its troughs. Obviously, the cycle-by-cycle variability of these differences depends upon the cycle-by-cycle variability of the standings at whatever may be the peak and trough stages of a series. Mathematical analysis suggests that the average deviation from the average amplitude of rise or fall may be approximately equal to the square root of the sum of the squares of the average deviations at the trough and peak standings, and hence larger than either the trough or the peak average deviation.

The mathematical grounds for this expectation have been stated at my request by Millard Hastay in Technical Note III, appended to this chapter. By way of seeing how our results fit the mathematical argument, we computed the average deviations from the average reference-cycle amplitudes of seven series in two ways: first, by direct computation, that is, measuring the amplitude of each cycle, casting up the sum, striking an average, and comparing with it the amplitudes of the individual cycles so as to get their average deviation; second, by squaring the average deviations at each of the two stages involved and taking the square root of the sum.[20]

Table 24 shows rather close agreement between expectations and observations. In most instances the average deviation from the mean amplitude is larger than the average deviation from

[20] For a more precise statement of this indirect method, see Technical Note III.

Table 24

AVERAGE DEVIATIONS FROM AVERAGE REFERENCE-CYCLE AMPLITUDES OF SEVEN SERIES COMPUTED DIRECTLY AND INDIRECTLY

SERIES[a]	NO. OF CYCLES	EXPANSION STAGES	AVERAGE DEVIATION FROM AV. STANDING AT STAGE OF			AV. DEVIATION FROM AV. REFERENCE-CYCLE AMPLITUDE COMPUTED BY					
						Direct Method			Indirect Method[b]		
			Initial Trough	Peak	Terminal Trough	Expansion	Contraction	Full cycle	Expansion	Contraction	Full cycle
Clearings outside N.Y.C., deflated, 1879–1938	16	VIII–V	6.7	4.0	6.2	7.6	7.1	9.8	7.8	7.4	12.1
Pig iron production, 1879–1938	16	I–V	17.1	13.3	19.5	21.3	28.3	37.1	21.7	23.6	37.2
Freight car orders, 1870–1938	17	VIII–IV	34.8	38.2	38.2	52.1	58.7	85.2	51.7	54.0	92.2
Shares traded, N.Y. Stock Exchange, 1879–1938	16	VIII–IV	22.3	12.4	15.1	18.7	21.7	25.7	25.5	19.5	36.6
R.R. stock prices, 1858–1933	19	VIII–IV	16.5	7.0	11.5	15.8	16.7	26.8	17.9	13.5	24.5
Call money rates, 1858–1938	20	I–V	29.4	55.5	26.3	59.9	59.8	115.0	62.8	61.4	117.8
R.R. bond yields, 1858–1933	19	III–VII	3.3	3.2	8.0	6.2	6.3	6.7	4.6	8.6	10.8

[a] See Appendix B for sources of data.

[b] This involves squaring of average deviations of the standings at peaks and troughs, as explained fully in Technical Note III.

either of the average standings at the corresponding trough or peak. The two methods of computing the average deviation from the average amplitude yield results that, as a rule, are not far apart. The largest absolute discrepancies occur in the series on freight car orders and shares traded. Five of the 21 discrepancies are less than 1.0 percent, and 18 are less than 5 percent.

What has been said about the average deviations from reference-cycle amplitudes applies also, though with an important exception, to the average deviations from average rates of change per month from one reference-cycle stage to the next. One of the assumptions underlying the expectation that the average deviation of the reference-cycle amplitudes will approximate the square root of the sum of the squares of the average deviations at trough and peak stages is that variations in peak and trough standings are uncorrelated in combinations of successive peaks and troughs. (See Technical Note III.) Such an assumption is less likely to be approximated when the arrays of standings involved in the computation are at adjacent stages than when the arrays are separated by the full or approximate duration of a reference expansion or contraction. Hence we cannot expect that the average deviations from the average rates of change per month will bear as close a relation to the average deviations from the standings at the stages compared as Table 24 suggests.

III Cycle-by-Cycle Variability among Series

So far our interest has focused on average deviations of single series or groups of series. We have inquired what types of time-series movements contribute to the average deviations of reference-cycle patterns, what is the relative importance of three types of movements, and how the deviations differ from stage to stage. On turning from differences within series to differences among series in cycle-by-cycle behavior, we must ask two more questions about average deviations. Instead of dissecting deviations, we now accept them as wholes in an effort to learn how and why they differ from series to series, and what bearing their varying magnitudes have upon the representative value of average reference-cycle patterns and their derivatives.

A INFLUENCE OF AVERAGE AMPLITUDES

Among the factors that influence the size of full average deviations from average reference-cycle standings, first place belongs to specific-cycle amplitudes. Obviously, a series that rises and falls by only a few percent of its average value in successive cycles can show only small differences among its cycle-by-cycle standings at its initial troughs, its peaks, and its terminal troughs. An erratic movement at some other stage may produce a greater deviation; but large departures from their characteristic behavior are rare among series with low amplitudes, aside from war-begotten price gyrations, and these we exclude from the averages. On the other hand, series that typically rise and fall by 50 or 100 percent of their average value during a cycle are likely to show correspondingly large differences in cycle-by-cycle standings as we measure them, both at the turning and the intermediate stages.

This relation between average deviations and average amplitudes in the specific-cycle analysis persists with certain modifications when series are analyzed on a reference-cycle basis. That reference-cycle amplitudes and average deviations are correlated can be seen by glancing over the reference-cycle patterns of Chart 1. So close is the connection between the two variables that what was done in Chapter 7 toward explaining differences among series in amplitude applies in large part to the deviations also.

So, too, does what was said in the second section of that chapter concerning the problem of bias in our sample. The fact that about half of the series we have analyzed cover only the period between the two world wars, or parts of it, means not only that our results give an exaggerated impression of the violence of cyclical fluctuations in the American economy since the 1850's, but also that the results exaggerate long-run differences in cycle-by-cycle behavior.[21]

B INFLUENCE OF REGULARITY IN CYCLICAL TIMING

While amplitudes dominate deviations from average reference-cycle patterns, their sway is modified by other factors, of which degree of regularity in cyclical timing seems to be the most pervasive. Regular cyclical timing cannot confer large specific-cycle amplitudes upon a series, but it tends to preserve most of these amplitudes, whether large or small, when the series is analyzed on a reference-cycle basis. At the same time, the regularity that tends to keep reference-cycle amplitudes up to the specific-cycle level tends to keep average deviations from reference-cycle patterns down to the level of average deviations from specific-cycle patterns. Irregular timing, on the contrary, tends to make reference-cycle amplitudes decidedly lower and reference-cycle deviations higher than their specific-cycle counterparts.

The reasons why reference-cycle analysis changes specific-cycle amplitudes and deviations in opposite ways are simple. We have previously shown that irregular timing with respect to business cycles means that the specific-cycle peaks of a series are scattered among the nine reference-cycle stages in haphazard fashion.[22] Hence, no reference stage has as high an

---

[21] This effect is illustrated by the series used in our smoothing tests (see above, Sec. IIB). In call money rates the variability is smaller after than before 1914 because the passage of the Federal Reserve Act led to a 'structural change' in the New York money market. See above, note 5.

MEAN AV. DEV. FROM AV. REFERENCE-CYCLE STANDINGS AT ALL NINE STAGES

| | BEFORE WORLD WAR I | | | AFTER WORLD WAR I | | |
	Period	No. of cycles	Mean av. dev.	Period	No. of cycles	Mean av. dev.
Deflated clearings	1879–1914	10	4.1	1919–1938	5	6.2
R.R. stock prices	1858–1914	14	6.6	1919–1933	4	18.1
Pig iron production	1879–1914	10	9.0	1919–1938	5	19.7
Call money rates	1858–1914	14	29.6	1919–1938	5	22.2

Here, as elsewhere, stages I and IX are given a weight of one-half each in striking nine-stage averages of the average deviations.

[22] See above, Ch. 7, Sec. IVA.

average standing as stage V of the specific cycles. Similarly, the specific-cycle troughs are scattered among several or all the reference-cycle stages, and none of the latter has an average standing so low as stages I and IX of the specific cycles. Lower peaks and higher troughs in the reference-cycle pattern yield lower amplitudes. But the scattering of the specific-cycle peaks and troughs among the nine reference-cycle stages means that each stage is likely to include some very low and some very high standings along with a larger number of intermediate size. Then the average deviation from the average standing at each stage tends to be larger than when all the initial troughs are assembled in a single stage, all the peaks in a second stage, all the terminal troughs in a third; and when each of the three steps between the initial trough and the peak, also each of the three steps between the peak and the terminal trough, is put with its fellows from other cycles.

How all this works out in practice may be illustrated by comparing a series with highly regular and one with decidedly irregular timing. Pig iron production has conformity indexes of +100, +100, +100, and its specific-cycle turns correspond invariably to our reference dates. Despite an average lead of three months at revivals and an average lag of two months at recessions, we treat the series as having I–V timing. Regular as is the behavior of iron production on this timing basis in cycle after cycle, only 8 of the 17 specific-cycle troughs occur within the three months centered on a reference-cycle trough date, and only 6 of the 16 specific-cycle peaks occur in stage V of a reference cycle. The value of total exports from the United States has much less regular timing; its indexes of conformity are +62, 0, +27. It undergoes 21 specific cycles in approximately the time occupied by 16 business cycles. Of its specific-cycle troughs only 11 correspond to reference troughs, and of these only 3 occur in stage I (or IX) of a reference cycle. Of its 21 specific-cycle peaks, 6 correspond to reference peaks and only 1 of them comes in reference-stage V.[23]

[23] For our technical rules concerning correspondence between specific-cycle and reference turns, see *Measuring Business Cycles*, pp. 118–26.

When these series are analyzed on a reference-cycle basis, both have their amplitude reduced and the average deviations from their cyclical patterns increased. In the series with regular timing, the reduction in amplitudes is from a rise and fall of 128 percent of the specific-cycle bases to a rise and fall of 99 percent of the reference-cycle bases—a decline of 23 percent of the larger amplitude. In the series with irregular timing, the reduction is from a rise and fall of 62 to one of 16—a decline of 74 percent. The average deviations from the average standings in the nine stages of the specific cycles of iron production are 12.8 percent of the cycle bases; the corresponding figure in the reference-cycle analysis is 13.7—an increase of 7.0 percent. In total exports the increase is from average specific-cycle deviations of 7.9 to average reference-cycle deviations of 10.6 —an increase of 34.2 percent. It should be noted that the increase in average deviations produced by the shift from specific to reference cycles is much smaller than the concomitant decrease in amplitudes, not only when measured in percentages of cycle bases, but also when measured in percentages of the specific-cycle results. A casual survey—no close examination has yet been made—suggests that in this respect iron production and exports are typical.

Identity of average amplitude and conformity does not guarantee identity of average deviations. Table 25 shows the average deviations from average reference-cycle standings at all nine stages for series with virtually perfect conformity and with amplitudes that round off at 25, at 50, and at about 100 percent of the reference-cycle bases. Within each of the three identical amplitude-conformity groups there are appreciable differences in the column for average deviations. The main reason for the differences is obvious. When the average amplitude is small and the cyclical timing regular, large average deviations cannot occur in the peak and trough stages of a series. But the opposite is not true: small average deviations can occur in the peak and trough stages when the average amplitude is large. The relation between average amplitudes and average deviations is likely to be especially loose in short

Table 25

MEAN AVERAGE DEVIATIONS FROM AVERAGE REFERENCE-CYCLE
PATTERNS OF THREE GROUPS OF SERIES HAVING VIRTUALLY
IDENTICAL REFERENCE-CYCLE AMPLITUDES AND CONFORMITY

	SERIES[a]	PERIOD COVERED	NO. OF CYCLES	AV. AMPLI-TUDE	MEAN CON-FORMITY[c]	MEAN AV. DEVIATION AT REF.-CYCLE STAGES[d]
1	Cotton spindles active, noncotton-growing states	1914–38	6	25.4	84	7.7
2	Av. hours worked per week, males, skilled & semiskilled, mfg.	1921–38	4	25.3	100	4.9
3	Av. hours worked per week, mfg., total	1921–38	4	24.8	100	4.6
4	Factory payrolls, boots & shoes	1919–38	5	50.4	100	6.7
5	Mining production index, total	1914–27	4	50.2	100	7.0
6	Wholesale prices, lumber	1921–38	4	50.1	100	7.5
7	Wholesale sales, hardware	1919–27	3	49.7	100	6.5
8	Mining production index, metals	1914–38	6	102.8	100	18.8
9	Suspended commercial banks, no.	1921–33	3	101.8[b]	100	28.2
10	Production index, dur. producer goods	1919–38	5	101.3	100	15.2
11	Production, tin & terne plate	1924–38	3	100.9	100	10.1
12	Production index, durable goods, total	1919–38	5	100.3	100	15.9
13	Shipments, steel sheets	1919–33	4	100.3	100	18.0
14	Constr. contracts, total bldg., floor space	1919–38	5	100.2	100	27.5
15	Production, pig iron	1879–38	16	99.1	100	13.6

[a] See Appendix B for sources of data.
[b] Average of 2 reference cycles, with III–VII as the expansion stages.
[c] Average of indexes of conformity to reference expansions and reference contractions.
[d] Average deviations of standings at stages I and IX receive a weight of one-half each.

series covering periods affected by powerful irregular factors
—such as are heavily represented in Table 25.[24] Yet it may be
noted that Table 25, devised to show differences in average
deviations among series having virtually identical average amplitudes and conformity, itself bears witness to the dominant
influence of the factors whose omnipotence it denies. The
mean average deviation of the 25 percent amplitude group is
5.7, that of the 50 percent group 6.9, and that of the 100 percent group 18.4. Only one series in the table has deviations that
belong in the next higher group, and that is the only series with
less than perfect conformity.

[24] To illustrate: Tin and terne plate production gets its average of 100.9
from three reference cycles with amplitudes of 72.5, 73.9, and 156.3. The
number of suspended banks, with the unusual timing scheme III–VII, allows
us to measure the patterns of three reference cycles but the amplitudes of

C STATISTICAL TESTS

More systematic evidence concerning the relations among deviations, amplitudes, and conformities is offered by Table 26. In making this table the 29 groups of series used in Table 20 were ranked, first according to their average deviations, second according to their average amplitudes, third according to their ratios of average deviations to amplitudes, and fourth according to their mean conformity to reference expansions and contractions. In each ranking all four measures of the groups were recorded. Then the 29 groups were divided into 3 nearly equal sets. The table presents averages of these sets, and the ranges of the measures from which the averages are

---

only two. The first (1921–24) was accompanied by a severe epidemic of bank failures; the second cycle (1924–27) was marked by relative banking tranquility. The amplitudes of bank suspensions in these two cycles (168.7 and 34.9) yield an average (101.8) that is 0.9 points higher than for tin and terne plate production; but the average deviations are more than twice as large (28.2 compared with 10.1). Needless to say, the averages of these very short series, though better than no information (especially when supplemented by other series of similar character), have slight claim to representative value.

Another illustration that may be helpful concerns the effects of irregular timing upon the relation between average deviations and average amplitudes. The following figures are nearly self-explanatory.

	IRREGULAR INVENTORIES	POSITIVE INVENTORIES	INVERTED INVENTORIES
Number of series	18	18	24
Av. reference-cycle amplitude [a]	33.6	44.3	68.2
Av. index of conformity to business cycles [a]	24	69	64
Mean av. deviation at reference-cycle stages [b]	14.3	11.7	16.2
Mean av. deviation as % of av. amplitude	42.6	26.4	23.8

[a] Taken without regard to sign.
[b] Average deviation at stages I and IX receive a weight of one-half each

The irregular inventories have larger deviations than the positive, despite the fact that the latter have substantially higher reference-cycle amplitudes. But the effect of irregular timing in raising deviations cannot equal the effect of a doubling of reference-cycle amplitudes, which appears on comparing the irregular with the inverted inventories. In the last line of the table, however, the *ratio* of deviations to amplitudes is lowest in the inverted and much the highest in the irregular group.

made, so that one can judge how much or how little the sets overlap one another. Correlation coefficients at the end of the table summarize the relations among the rankings in a more compact way.

The first ranking indicates a close association between average deviations and average amplitudes, but not between average deviations and the other two behavior traits taken separately.

The ranking by average amplitudes shows again, from the opposite viewpoint, the close association between amplitudes and deviations. But amplitudes are somewhat more closely related than deviations to the other two measures. The larger the amplitudes the higher tend to be the mean conformity indexes and the lower tend to be the ratios of average deviations to amplitudes. However, these tendencies are often balked by other factors.

The ranking by ratios of average deviations to average amplitudes confirms the moderately inverse relation to amplitudes. The new feature is the close inverse relation to conformity indexes. This finding confirms the foregoing observation that close conformity to business cycles has opposite effects upon reference-cycle amplitudes and deviations from reference-cycle patterns, for close conformity tends to preserve full specific-cycle amplitudes in the reference-cycle analysis and to minimize cycle-by-cycle deviations from average standings. Of course, holding amplitudes up and deviations down is equivalent to decreasing the ratio of deviations to amplitudes.

The fourth ranking—that by conformity indexes—merely repeats in turn what the previous rankings told us. Conformity indexes, taken by themselves, have no regular relation with average deviations, a positive relation with average amplitudes, but a close inverse relation with ratios of the first to the second.

The coefficients of rank correlation at the end of the table put the preceding conclusions in so precise a form that they tempt one to overrate the representative value of the findings. But they add one interesting item: the relations among the traits we have been studying appear to be substantially closer when one correlates deviations with amplitudes and conform-

Table 26

Summary of Relations among Average Deviations of Reference-Cycle Patterns, Average Amplitudes, and Regularity of Cyclical Timing in 29 Groups of Series[a]

	Av. deviation of reference-cycle pattern[b]	Av. reference-cycle amplitude	Percentage ratio of av. deviation to av. amplitude	Mean conformity[c]
1) Groups ranked by av. deviations				
Averages				
Lowest 10 groups	5.8	24.8	25.6	69.9
Middle 10 groups	9.7	43.4	24.7	67.5
Highest 9 groups	23.1	91.0	28.8	63.4
Ranges				
Lowest 10 groups	3.9– 7.8	12.8– 46.3	13.6–49.0	40–100
Middle 10 groups	8.2–11.7	24.1– 62.8	16.2–41.8	40– 92
Highest 9 groups	14.3–41.0	33.6–166.0	18.5–50.1	33– 96
2) Groups ranked by av. amplitudes				
Averages				
Lowest 10 groups	6.3	22.0	29.7	61.3
Middle 10 groups	11.3	41.7	27.7	64.3
Highest 9 groups	20.7	96.0	20.8	76.6
Ranges				
Lowest 10 groups	3.9–10.4	12.8– 27.8	19.1–49.0	40–100
Middle 10 groups	6.3–21.3	29.5– 49.5	13.6–50.1	33– 98
Highest 9 groups	8.8–41.0	51.4–166.0	16.2–32.8	55– 96
3) Groups ranked by ratios of av. deviation to av. amplitude				
Averages				
Lowest 10 groups	10.6	58.4	18.0	84.1
Middle 10 groups	12.7	56.4	23.6	69.0
Highest 9 groups	14.5	39.3	38.4	46.0
Ranges				
Lowest 10 groups	3.9–29.0	20.4–147.6	13.6–19.6	68–100
Middle 10 groups	4.9–34.4	18.2–166.0	20.5–27.8	55– 80
Highest 9 groups	4.1–41.0	12.8–124.9	28.9–50.1	33– 62
4) Groups ranked by mean conformity				
Averages				
Lowest 10 groups	11.4	32.6	36.4	46.3
Middle 10 groups	12.3	50.4	23.3	70.3
Highest 9 groups	14.0	74.5	18.4	86.6
Ranges				
Lowest 10 groups	4.1–21.3	12.8– 68.2	23.8–50.1	33– 58
Middle 10 groups	4.9–41.0	18.2–124.9	17.1–32.8	62– 74
Highest 9 groups	3.9–34.4	20.4–166.0	13.6–20.7	76–100

Table 26 (concl.)

Coefficients of rank correlation for the 29 groups of series, when the factors related are:

Average deviations and
    Average amplitudes   .79
    Ratios of average deviations to average amplitudes   .15
    Mean indexes of conformity   −.08

Average amplitudes and
    Ratios of average deviations to average amplitudes   −.43
    Mean indexes of conformity   .42

Ratios of average deviations to average amplitudes and
    Mean indexes of conformity   −.88

Average deviations and average amplitudes, with effect
    of mean indexes of conformity eliminated   .91

Average deviations and mean indexes of conformity, with
    effect of average amplitudes eliminated   −.74

Average deviations and both average amplitudes and mean
    indexes of conformity   .91

[a] For a list of the groups, see Table 20.

[b] Average deviations at stages I and IX receive a weight of one-half each.

[c] Average of indexes of conformity to reference expansions and reference contractions.

[d] This coefficient is larger by less than a half unit in the second decimal place than the coefficient which eliminates the effect of mean conformity.

ity together. It was with this last combination that the preceding analysis began.

IV   THE REPRESENTATIVE VALUE OF CYCLICAL PATTERNS

Though the preceding analyses offer merely a rough sketch of a field that should be surveyed thoroughly, they demonstrate that the deviations from reference-cycle standings have a rationale of their own, and can be made to contribute toward the understanding of business cycles. These deviations correspond to the 'disturbing circumstances' economic theorists impound in *ceteris paribus* clauses, or exclude by discussing what happens 'in the long run'. For such logical devices a statistical inquirer substitutes averages that he hopes bring out the central tendencies of his arrays. There is, however, an important psychological difference between the two procedures. 'Disturbing circumstances' is too vague a concept to excite much interest. Seldom does a theorist feel impelled to hunt for the exceptions to his rules and inquire how they come about. Of course a statistician may rest content with what his averages tell. But in the statistical approach deviations from averages constitute a standing challenge to scientific curiosity, inciting further explorations, which may lead to the discovery of unsuspected regularities among what had seemed annoying exceptions to orderly relations. Presently the newly discovered regularities may be incorporated into the older generalizations; this more adequate formulation stimulates fresh inquiries into the discrepancies that still appear between 'theory' and 'fact', and the spiral of research mounts to a higher level.

At present I can follow only one round of this spiral. Having shown that the average deviations are complexes made up of cyclical and secular as well as irregular elements, and pointed out the chief factors that influence the magnitude of the deviations, I pass on to the study of averages. Later I should return to cycle-by-cycle differences, and use whatever the averages have taught in an effort to find out how business cycles come to differ from one another so much as they patently do. But that task remains for later times and other hands.

Meanwhile what we can discover here and now about average behavior should be the richer and the truer for our brief study of deviations from it. First and foremost we should keep in mind that cycle-by-cycle variability is the one trait most typical of cyclical behavior. In the coming comparisons of reference-cycle patterns and summaries of reference-cycle standings or amplitudes, I shall seldom include the average deviations, for a reconnaisance survey of a complicated province must be confined to salient features. But the reader should remember that the real terrain is not so simple as my sketch maps make it look. Second, this study of average deviations has provided a practical demonstration of the tests of consilience on which such heavy stress was laid in the last chapter of *Measuring Business Cycles* and in Chapter 3 of this book. Rather subtle implications of our technique that can seldom be traced in individual series began to appear when we assembled series in relatively homogeneous groups, and became clearer still when we combined all the heterogeneous groups that constitute our sample. That experience should warn us against relying exclusively upon what we might infer from a few series, however comprehensive they may be. Rather must we put our trust in findings borne out by groups of series, the broader and more varied the better. Third, close agreement between the average deviations in stages at which the cyclical-secular components are similar (I and IX, II and VIII, III and VII, IV and VI) indicates a remarkable degree of 'evening out' of noncyclical-secular components at different stages in our whole sample, and a similar effect can be traced, though with less confidence, in numerous groups. We drew, and now have use for, the conclusion that the chances are better still of a 'canceling out' of noncyclical-secular components when standings during the same stage of successive cycles are averaged. Fourth, on turning to averages of average deviations at all stages, we noted that their magnitude rises with, but on the whole more slowly than, the average amplitude. That is, deviations so large as to arouse grave misgivings about the representative value of a reference-cycle pattern are often (by no means always) moderate in comparison with the average rise and fall. On the other hand, small deviations are sometimes large percentages of modest amplitudes. But on this crucial topic I should be more specific.

The reference-cycle patterns are meant to approximate the combined cyclical and intracycle trend components in economic fluctuations; that is, to extricate from their matrices the movements attributable to the alternating tides of expansion and contraction acting upon elements of the economy that keep changing the levels about which they fluctuate. Always the cyclical tides flow and ebb in a complex of conditions peculiar to the national and international scene during some segment of history—conditions that affect different factors in the economy in unlike ways and degrees. It is precisely because the movements of a series during successive business cycles are not alike that, to approximate cyclical behavior, we adopt the laborious method of averaging movements in as many cycles as feasible. The greater the cycle-by-cycle diversity of movements, the more do we need an average to help us judge whether a 'central tendency' toward cyclical regularity can be descried in the jumble. When such a tendency does appear, the larger the average deviations from the average pattern, the more trustworthy is this pattern as a measure of cyclical behavior in comparison with the movements during any single cycle.

Yet it is also true that the larger the average deviations, the harder it is to derive a trustworthy measure of the cyclical-secular component of economic movements. Distrust of a reference-cycle pattern subject to large average deviations is justified, not because the average pattern differs widely from the movements in individual cycles, but because the average may be too much like the pattern of some one or two especially violent cycles. Under these circumstances, we become more eager than ever to cover more cycles and to find closely related series for comparison. Even when the quest for further evidence succeeds, we sometimes end with the conviction that the best measures we can make are exceedingly rough approximations. Yet, at worst, it is no small advantage to have measures that tell what economic activities are unpredictable in cyclical behavior and what have responded to successive cycles in a relatively uniform fashion.

Technical Note I

EFFECT OF MACAULAY'S SMOOTHING FORMULA
ON THE VARIATION OF A RANDOM SERIES

In discussing my observations upon the way in which smoothing alters the average deviations from mean reference-cycle standings, Millard Hastay suggested that the effect of Macaulay's formula on the variation of a random series might be investigated algebraically. At my request, he worked out this suggestion, and summarizes his findings below.

Memorandum by Millard Hastay
Consider first a purely random time series without trend or cycles or other systematic component. The argument is simplified without affecting the conclusions by assuming that the average level of this series is zero. Assume further that the variability of the observations tends to remain constant through time. We may then represent the series as follows:

$$\ldots, x_{-1}, x_0, x_1, x_2, x_3, \ldots, x_i, \ldots, x_n, \ldots$$

where the time origin is taken at any convenient point and our assumptions imply the following expected values (E):

(1) $E(x_i) = 0$ for all i (zero trend level)
(2) $E(x_i^2) = \sigma^2(x_i) = \sigma^2$ for all i (constant variation)
(3) $E(x_i x_j) = 0$ if $i \neq j$ (simple randomness)

Suppose such a series to be smoothed by a weighted moving average with weights $w_{-n}, \ldots, w_0, \ldots, w_n$ and period $2n + 1$. (The assumption of an odd period is not essential, and is made simply in view of the application to Macaulay's formula below.) In this fashion a new series $X_0, X_1, X_2, \ldots$ is generated, where

$$X_0 = w_{-n}x_{-n} + w_{-n+1}x_{-n+1} + \cdots + w_{-1}x_{-1} + w_0x_0 + w_1x_1 + \cdots$$
$$+ w_ix_i + \cdots + w_nx_n$$
$$X_1 = w_{-n}x_{-n+1} + w_{-n+1}x_{-n+2} + \cdots + w_{-1}x_0 + w_0x_1 + w_1x_2 + \cdots$$
$$+ w_ix_{i+1} + \cdots + w_nx_{n+1}$$

.
.
.

$$X_i = w_{-n}x_{-n+i} + w_{-n+1}x_{-n+1+i} + \cdots + w_0x_i + \cdots + w_{n-i}x_n$$
$$+ \cdots + w_nx_{n+i}$$

etc.

Like the original series, this series will have average level zero, for

$$E(X_i) = E\left(\sum_{j=-n}^{n} w_j x_{j+i}\right) = \sum_{j=-n}^{n} w_j E(x_{j+i}) = 0$$

The variance is therefore easily computed

$$\sigma^2(X_0) = E(X_0^2) = E\left(\sum w_j x_j\right)^2$$

$$= E\left[\sum_{j=-n}^{n} w_j^2 x_j^2 + 2 \sum_{j=i+1}^{n} \sum_{i=-n}^{n-1} w_i w_j x_i x_j\right]$$

$$= \sum w_j^2 E(x_j^2) + 2 \sum_{i<j} w_i w_j E(x_i x_j)$$

But by assumption
$$E(x_j^2) = \sigma^2$$
$$E(x_i x_j) = 0, \quad i \neq j$$

Thus

(4)
$$\sigma^2(X_0) = \sigma^2 \sum_{j=-n}^{n} w_j^2$$

Since X_0 might be any term of the series, this result is plainly general, whence the smoothed series too exhibits homogeneous variation over time.

However, the third feature of the original series is not reproduced in the smoothed one, for successive items are serially correlated. Since the smoothed series varies homogeneously with time, the serial correlations will be a constant multiple [namely, $1/\sigma^2(X)$] of the corresponding covariances and it therefore suffices to determine the latter. By the definition of covariance with lag i months

$$(5) \quad \sigma(X_0 X_i) = E(X_0 X_i) = E\left[\left(\sum_{j=-n}^{n} w_j x_j\right)\left(\sum_{j=-n}^{n} w_j x_{j+i}\right)\right]$$

$$= E\left[\sum_{j=-n}^{n-i} w_j w_{j+i} x_{j+i}^2 + \sum_{j=-n}^{n}\sum_{\substack{k=-n\\j\neq k+i}}^{n} w_j w_k x_j x_{k+i}\right]$$

$$= \sum_{j=-n}^{n-i} w_j w_{j+i} E(x_{j+i}^2) + \sum_{j}\sum_{\substack{k\\j\neq k+i}} w_j w_k E(x_j x_{k+i})$$

$$= \sigma^2 \sum_{j=-n}^{n-i} w_j w_{j+i}, \quad \text{since} \quad \underset{j\neq k+i}{E}(x_j x_{k+i}) = 0$$

This argument is plainly independent of the term chosen as X_0, while the lag i might be anything from one to $2n$ months. Thus the serial correlations of the smoothed series are independent of the time origin; i.e., for a fixed lag they tend to be the same anywhere in the series.

Formulas (4) and (5) have been used to compute the variance and lagged covariances of a series derived by smoothing a purely random series with Macaulay's "43-term approximately 5th-degree parabolic graduation", utilizing the implicit weights given in Table A.

Table A

WEIGHTS IMPLIED BY MACAULAY'S 43-TERM APPROXIMATELY
5TH-DEGREE PARABOLIC GRADUATION FORMULA

Month	Weight	Month	Weight
0	+.12042	−11, +11	−.02135
−1, +1	+.11739	−12, +12	−.01854
−2, +2	+.10937	−13, +13	−.01271
−3, +3	+.09667	−14, +14	−.00625
−4, +4	+.07917	−15, +15	−.00083
−5, +5	+.05854	−16, +16	+.00292
−6, +6	+.03750	−17, +17	+.00469
−7, +7	+.01698	−18, +18	+.00417
−8, +8	−.00063	−19, +19	+.00312
−9, +9	−.01323	−20, +20	+.00187
−10, +10	−.01979	−21, +21	+.00073

No essential generality is lost by assuming that the random series has variance $\sigma^2 = 1$; in fact, the results for this case, summarized in Table B, constitute a kind of canonical form for all random series such that

$$\sigma(x_i x_j) = 0, \quad i \neq j$$
$$\sigma^2(x_i) = \sigma^2 \quad \text{for all } i$$

when Macaulay's formula is used in the graduation.

Table B

VARIANCE AND LAGGED COVARIANCES OF A SMOOTHED SERIES DERIVED
BY GRADUATING A PURELY RANDOM SERIES OF UNIT VARIANCE
WITH MACAULAY'S 43-TERM FORMULA

$\sigma^2(X_i)$ = 0.1107	$\sigma(X_i X_{i+4})$ = 0.0647
$\sigma(X_i X_{i+1})$ = 0.1082	$\sigma(X_i X_{i+5})$ = 0.0594
$\sigma(X_i X_{i+2})$ = 0.1010	$\sigma(X_i X_{i+6})$ = 0.0452
$\sigma(X_i X_{i+3})$ = 0.0898	$\sigma(X_i X_{i+7})$ = 0.0268

Consider next the effect of averaging successive items in a smoothed series of the above type. Let the average be denoted

$$\xi = \frac{X_1 + \cdots + X_N}{N}$$

Then by definition of the variance of a simple average

$$(6) \qquad \sigma^2(\xi) = \frac{1}{N^2} E(X_1 + \cdots + X_N)^2$$

$$= \frac{1}{N^2} E\left[\sum_{i=1}^{N} X_i^2 + 2 \sum_{j=i+1}^{N} \sum_{i=1}^{N-1} X_i X_j \right]$$

$$= \frac{1}{N^2} \left[N\sigma^2(X) + 2 \sum_{j=i+1}^{N} \sum_{i=1}^{N-1} \sigma(X_i X_j) \right]$$

$$= \frac{1}{N^2} \left[N\sigma^2(X) + 2 \sum_{j=1}^{N-1} \sum_{i=1}^{N-j} \sigma(X_i X_{i+j}) \right]$$

$$= \frac{\sigma^2(X)}{N} + \frac{2}{N^2} \sum_{j=1}^{N-1} (N-j)\sigma(X_0 X_j)$$

This expression depends upon the N^2 possible variances and covariances between N successive items of the smoothed series; N of these equal the variance of a single smoothed item, $2(N-1)$ equal the covariance with lag $1, \ldots, 2(N-j)$ equal the covariance with lag j, etc.

As a sample calculation, suppose $N = 3$ and the variance and covariances of the smoothed series are as in Table B. Then $\xi = (X_1 + X_2 + X_3)/3$ and

$$\sigma^2(\xi) = \tfrac{1}{9} [3\sigma^2(X) + 4\sigma(X_i X_{i+1}) + 2\sigma(X_i X_{i+2})]$$
$$= \tfrac{1}{9} [3(0.111) + 4(0.108) + 2(0.101)]$$
$$= 0.107$$

Formulas (4), (5), and (6) permit us to study the relative effects of smoothing, of averaging, and of smoothing with subsequent averaging, on a purely random series. As before, it is convenient to assume that the random series has variance $\sigma^2 = 1$; also, in order that the results may be directly applicable to the effect of averaging over reference-cycle stages of different duration, we consider averages of 3, 6, and 7 successive items. The relevant findings are summarized in Table C.

Table C

VARIANCES OF ORIGINAL AND SMOOTHED TIME SERIES AND OF AVERAGES
OF SUCCESSIVE ITEMS FROM THEM

Variance of	Original series	Smoothed series
Single item	1.00	0.111
Average of 3 successive items	0.33	0.107
Average of 6 successive items	0.17	0.096
Average of 7 successive items	0.14	0.092

As a measure of the effect of smoothing alone, we find that the variance of a single smoothed item is only 11.1 percent of the variance of an item in the unsmoothed series. The gain from subsequent averaging is relatively small. Averaging 3 successive items of the smoothed series achieves a further reduction of variance of only 4 percent; averaging 6 items, only 14 percent; averaging 7 items, 17 percent. In the original series the corresponding reductions, which measure the influence of averaging alone, reflect the rule that the variance of the average of successive items in a random series varies inversely as the period spanned. These reductions are:

3 items, 67 percent
6 items, 83 percent
7 items, 86 percent

The largest of these reductions is only slightly less than that achieved by the 43-item weighted average, namely, 89 percent.

These results are somewhat more intelligible when translated into terms of standard deviations, as is readily accomplished by taking square roots of the items in Table C. We find that smoothing alone reduces the standard deviation of the original series by 67 percent, while the effects of averaging on the standard deviations of the original and smoothed series are as shown in Table D. Application

Table D

PERCENTAGE REDUCTION OF STANDARD DEVIATION DUE TO AVERAGING

Average of	Original series	Smoothed series
3 successive items	43	2
6 successive items	59	7
7 successive items	63	9

of these results to the average deviation is immediate if we may assume that the average deviation tends to be a fixed multiple of the standard deviation. Such a relation is readily demonstrated for the normal distribution and seems to hold with good approximation for symmetrical distributions that do not depart too widely from the normal type.

Now suppose that the original series had involved serial correlations, at least for lags of a few months. This would mean that the assumption $E(x_i x_j) = 0$ for $i \neq j$, on which formulas (4) and (5) are based, no longer holds for $(j - i)$ less than some small integer d, say 3 or 4. The usual conception of these correlations suggests that they be considered positive. If, then, we assume

$$Ex_i x_j > 0, \quad (j - i) < d$$

it follows that
$$\sigma^2(X) > 0.111$$

and that $\sigma(X_i X_j)$ will exceed the corresponding covariances in Table B. In other words, smoothing the original series would reduce its variance by less than 89 percent—by substantially less if the serial correlations of low order were fairly strong. The effectiveness of averaging the smoothed series would likewise be reduced, so that the variance of the average of 7 items might be little different from the variance of a single smoothed item.

To a lesser degree, a similar influence on averaging would appear in the original series; averages of short duration might be little less variable than a single item; those of longer duration would be affected to lesser extent by serial correlations but their variability would still be reduced by less than the rule of inverse proportion to duration suggests. For example, if the original series were constituted with serial correlations as high as those of a random series smoothed by Macaulay's formula, the standard deviation of a seven-item average would be only 7 percent less than that of a three-item average.

Technical Note II

CYCLE-BY-CYCLE VARIABILITY IN THE TREND COMPONENTS
OF AVERAGE REFERENCE-CYCLE STANDINGS

1 *Type of Secular Trend Implied by National Bureau Measures*

In 1934 Edwin Frickey illustrated the "basic logical difficulty connected with the separation of secular and cyclical variations" by presenting "a list of the various mathematically-fitted secular trends which have . . . been calculated" for pig iron production in the United States. His list includes 23 such efforts, ranging from straight lines fitted to the data for different periods to such constructions as a third degree parabola fitted to logarithms of the data. To these mathematically fitted lines he added 6 moving-average trends with periods running down from 20 to 3 years.

With these materials in hand, Frickey determined the number and duration of the 'cycles' in pig iron production by "observing the number of complete swings" of the data about each trend line. The average duration of these 'cycles' varied between 3.3 and 40–45 years. The conclusion he drew was not that the 29 trends "are lacking in statistical or economic significance". On the contrary, Frickey believed that "many of them unquestionably possess such significance", though he did not try to determine which trends are useful for what purposes, or to discuss criteria for choosing among competitors for a given use. His positive conclusions were:

first, that the average length of 'cycle' for a series—and for that matter, the whole form of the supposed cyclical picture—may exhibit great variation depending upon the kind of secular trend which has *previously* been fitted; second, that the discovery, about a particular trend representation which has been set up for a given economic series, of oscillations which may conform more or less closely to a certain average length cannot in itself be taken as establishing the statistical or economic validity of such movements as cycles.[1]

By way of contrast, this notable paper facilitates understanding of the National Bureau's treatment of trends. Instead of first fitting lines of secular trend to time series, and afterwards observing the number and duration of specific cycles, we first identify the specific cycles in a series, and afterwards measure the secular movements indicated by the cycles. We can follow this order because our working definition of business cycles tells us the basic characteristics of the specific cycles we wish to observe in many series —"and for that matter, the whole form of the supposed cyclical picture". These specific cycles are "recurrent sequences of expansion, recession, contraction, and revival, lasting more than one year but not more than ten or twelve years" (*Measuring Business Cycles*, p. 11). Their statistical and economic 'validity' is involved in that of the basic concept we are testing.

Having found such cycles in a series, we wish to distinguish them from the seasonal, irregular, and secular movements with which they are intertwined. As part of this effort, we convert the original data of a series during each of its specific cycles into percentages of their average value during that cycle. It is from these averages— cycle bases in our jargon—that we make 'measures of secular movements'. We usually find rather marked variability in the percentage change per month from one cycle base to the next. Passing from specific to reference cycles does not make these secular changes any more uniform. In short, our 'secular' measures give firm statistical support to the statement in the text that, if the secular trend implied by our procedure were represented by a continuous line, that line would be a flexible curve. Yet our implicit

[1] My italics. See Edwin Frickey, "The Problem of Secular Trend", *Review of Economic Statistics*, October 15, 1934, pp. 199–206.

trend of pig iron production is no more flexible than some half dozen of the trends listed by Frickey, if we may judge flexibility by the average duration of the 'cycles' found by Frickey and by us.

2 Effects of Preliminary Trend Adjustments upon Cycle Bases

As the preceding section suggests, the usual methods of 'eliminating' secular trends from time series accomplish only a partial separation of cyclical fluctuations from shifts in the levels upon which these fluctuations occur. Experience in analyzing data that others have adjusted for trend has taught us to expect cycle-by-cycle differences in both their specific-cycle and reference-cycle bases. For our purposes, such differences are remnants of trends, and to dispose of them we must go through all the operations we perform upon unadjusted data. Meanwhile, the preliminary trend adjustment wipes out part of the intracycle components that we wish to retain in our measures.

By way of illustration, consider Table 27, which presents the reference-cycle bases of pig iron production before and after adjustment for trend by Frederick R. Macaulay. The chart of Macaulay's trend on page 272 of *Measuring Business Cycles* shows that it fits the data well, at least up to the 1930's, and to give the trend every advantage I omit the last cycle from the averages.[2] The manner in which the adjusted bases run now somewhat above, then somewhat below 100 percent of the mathematical trend is further testimony to the goodness of Macaulay's fit for some 50 years; the average of all the bases up to 1927 is 99.5 percent. Nevertheless, not much less than half of the cycle-by-cycle shifts in reference-cycle bases remain in the trend-adjusted figures, and have to be taken out for our purposes by a second operation.

Removing secular trends in two stages instead of one would have substantial advantages if we had clearer ideas about what fitted

[2] In *Interest Rates, Bond Yields and Stock Prices in the United States since 1856*, Macaulay wrote: "The mathematical equation used to describe the trend of pig iron production was fitted to the data fifteen or sixteen years ago. Upon taking up the series for the purposes of this book, we decided to use the curve already fitted, not only because it had remained so astonishingly good but also because of the interest attaching to it as an illustration of how growth curves seem sometimes to be more than mere fits to existing data" (p. 209, note).

Whether an extrapolation of the trend would fit the data for the 1940's better than the data for the early 1930's is doubtful. One convenience of the National Bureau's method of treating trends is that its cycle bases are less likely to be altered radically with the passage of time than the equations of trend lines.

Table 27

CHANGES IN THE REFERENCE-CYCLE BASES OF PIG IRON PRODUCTION
BEFORE AND AFTER ADJUSTMENT FOR SECULAR TREND

	REFERENCE-CYCLE BASE		% CHANGE FROM PRECEDING BASE	
	Unadj. data	Adj.		
	(thous.	data		
REFERENCE CYCLE	gross tons	(% of	Unadj.	Adj.
(trough-to-trough)	per day)	trend)	data	data
March 1879 — May 1885	9.77	106.0	. . .	. . .
May 1885 — April 1888	14.20	104.3	+45.3	−1.6
April 1888 — May 1891	19.71	113.7	+38.8	+9.0
May 1891 — June 1894	20.76	95.1	+5.3	−16.4
June 1894 — June 1897	23.16	83.7	+11.6	−12.0
June 1897 — Dec. 1900	33.84	96.8	+46.1	+15.7
Dec. 1900 — Aug. 1904	45.11	102.7	+33.3	+6.1
Aug. 1904 — June 1908	61.02	111.7	+35.2	+8.8
June 1908 — Jan. 1912	65.79	99.2	+7.8	−11.2
Jan. 1912 — Dec. 1914	76.33	100.2	+16.0	+1.0
Dec. 1914 — April 1919	98.99	114.0	+29.7	+13.8
April 1919 — Sept. 1921	77.24	82.4	−22.0	−27.7
Sept. 1921 — July 1924	85.81	86.8	+11.1	+5.3
July 1924 — Dec. 1927	99.58	96.5	+16.0	+11.2
Dec. 1927 — March 1933	73.60	69.1	−26.1	−28.4
Average, excluding last cycle				
Regarding signs			+21.1	+0.15
Disregarding signs			24.5	10.8

trend lines represent. For example, if we could believe that Macaulay's trend (or any of its numerous rivals) represents the net effects of the secular 'forces' impinging upon the iron-steel industry, or its 'secular growth', we might ascribe differences between the shifts in cycle bases computed from trend-adjusted data and the shifts in cycle bases computed from unadjusted data to nonsecular factors and start hunting for them. Perhaps an investigation along these lines would yield valuable results even now despite the vagueness of the secular concept, especially outside the realm where the biological notion of growth is appropriate. But we cannot take on this adventure as a side issue of cyclical studies. What we do in effect is to throw into the box labeled 'secular movements' all changes in cycle bases from one specific or reference cycle to the next. In a statistical sense, this practice gives an unwonted definiteness to the secular concept—a definiteness limited only by the fuzzy edges surrounding our concepts of seasonal variations, specific cycles, and business cycles. If it does nothing else, this practice at least discloses the shifting levels on which business cycles and their component specific cycles run their rounds.

3 Effects of Preliminary Trend Adjustments upon Average Deviations from Reference-Cycle Standings

As remarked above, converting the data of a time series into percentages of a secular trend tends to reduce the intracycle trend component that we wish to retain in our measures. The plainest sign of this change is usually that cyclical patterns are made more nearly horizontal. We have analyzed 9 series before and after the data have been adjusted for trend by competent statisticians, and this effect appears in 7 of them.[3]

An operation that reduces cycle-by-cycle differences in any type of movement covered by our measures should reduce the average deviations of reference-cycle standings, unless it has an offsetting effect upon the variability of other components. Seeing no reason to suppose that converting data into percentages of the ordinates of a trend line will systematically increase the variations we classify as cyclical or irregular, we may expect that a series will usually have smaller average deviations after than before it is

---

[3] The change in the tilt of the patterns made by adjusting for trend should appear numerically as an alteration in the difference between the reference-cycle standings at stages I and IX. In practice this difference may be seriously influenced by the relative depths of the initial and terminal troughs covered by a series. The differences before and after adjusting for trend are as follows in the 9 series:

| SERIES | AV. REFERENCE-CYCLE STANDING | | | | DIFFERENCE BETWEEN STANDINGS AT I AND IX | |
| | Stage I | | Stage IX | | | |
	U	A	U	A	U	A
Pig iron production	73.3	80.0	81.1	73.7	+7.8	−6.3
Electric power production	85.6	98.2	103.2	91.5	+17.6	−6.7
Department store sales, deflated	93.0	96.3	93.2	92.8	+0.2	−3.5
Clearings outside N.Y.C., deflated	88.1	95.6	100.6	92.9	+12.5	−2.7
Clearings, 7 cities, Frickey	83.5	91.6	101.1	92.2	+17.6	+0.6
AT&T index, 1932 revision	86.8	92.1	90.8	85.7	+4.0	−6.4
AT&T index, 1944 revision	82.8	88.3	90.8	85.2	+8.0	−3.1
Axe-Houghton index	83.2	87.7	95.7	89.1	+12.5	+1.4
R.R. bond yields	102.0	100.3	100.2	100.8	−1.8	+0.5

U = unadjusted data; A = trend-adjusted data.

For fuller titles of several series and the time coverage of all, see Table 28.

adjusted for trend. But this effect is not likely to be very pronounced. For, as the text shows, the trend component in average deviations is supposed to approximate zero at stage V, and to be not far removed from zero at stages IV and VI. If the estimates of Table 22 are not grievously wrong, the trend component is a minor part of the whole even in stages I and IX—when it is at a maximum. And if a trend adjustment merely reduces the intracycle trend component by a fraction, as our pig iron illustration suggests, this alteration in a minor factor may not stand out clearly in a small sample. To repeat, our sample includes only 9 series in both trend-adjusted and unadjusted form.

The results presented in Table 28 answer expectations tolerably well. If we include all 9 stages in all 9 series, eliminating the trend reduces the average deviations in 54 percent of the stages and increases them in 40 percent (in 6 percent there is no change). But if we take only the stages in which the trend component has most effect (I and II, VIII and IX) the reductions rise to 72 percent; and if we take only the stages where the trend component has least effect (III, IV, V, VI, and VII) the reductions fall to 40 percent.

How the effects of removing the trend differ from series to series can be seen most readily in the following ranking.

SERIES	CHANGE IN AVERAGE DEVIATIONS, ALL STAGES	NO. OF STAGES IN WHICH AVERAGE DEVIATIONS ARE		
		Reduced	Unchanged	Raised
R.R. bond yields	−1.4	9	..	..
Clearings, 7 cities, Frickey	−0.6	8	1	..
Pig iron production	−0.4	6	..	3
Clearings outside N.Y.C., deflated	−0.3	6	1	2
Department store sales, deflated	+0.1	4	..	5
AT&T index, 1932 revision	+0.1	4	..	5
AT&T index, 1944 revision	+0.1	2	2	5
Axe-Houghton index	+0.2	3	1	5
Electric power production	+0.9	2	..	7
Total		44	5	32

Perhaps these differences have an economic meaning, but I think it more probable that they arise from differences in statistical procedure by the trend fitters and perhaps in the period covered.

4 Intracycle Trend Component in Average Deviations from Average Reference-Cycle Standings

Moore's method of approximating the intracycle trend component in average deviations from average reference-cycle patterns is ex-

Table 28

Average Deviations from Average Reference-Cycle Patterns of Nine Series Before and After Adjustment for Secular Trend

SERIES[a]	PERIOD COVERED	FORM OF DATA[b]	AVERAGE DEVIATION[c] AT REFERENCE-CYCLE STAGES									All Stages[d]
			I	II	III	IV	V	VI	VII	VIII	IX	
1 Pig iron production	1879-1933	U	15.5	11.4	10.9	9.4	10.7	7.3	13.9	18.2	19.0	12.4
		A	15.4	11.0	9.9	9.6	12.1	7.5	13.1	16.6	16.7	12.0
2 Electric power production	1919-1933	U	5.6	4.4	2.4	2.7	2.3	0.9	4.7	9.0	8.7	4.2
		A	7.2	6.5	4.8	3.4	3.2	2.4	3.4	8.4	9.6	5.1
3 Department store sales, deflated	1921-1938	U	5.9	4.2	3.1	2.9	1.5	1.0	1.2	6.4	8.9	3.5
		A	6.2	3.8	3.8	3.2	2.6	1.8	0.6	5.6	7.9	3.6
4 Clearings outside N.Y.C., deflated	1879-1933	U	6.6	5.7	3.7	3.2	4.0	4.5	4.8	6.6	7.6	5.0
		A	6.2	5.7	3.8	3.8	3.1	3.5	4.3	6.3	7.5	4.7
5 Clearings in 7 cities outside N.Y.	1879-1914	U	6.9	5.4	4.2	3.2	2.8	4.1	6.5	6.0	7.6	4.9
		A	6.1	4.8	4.0	3.2	1.6	2.7	6.0	5.7	7.3	4.3
6 A T & T index of industrial activity, 1932 revision	1900-1933	U	9.1	7.0	6.0	5.3	7.0	5.4	4.8	9.6	9.5	6.8
		A	9.0	7.4	5.8	5.8	7.6	5.5	5.1	9.3	8.9	6.9
7 A T & T index of industrial activity, 1944 revision	1900-1938	U	9.3	6.0	5.2	6.0	7.5	6.0	4.5	9.0	9.1	6.7
		A	9.9	6.5	5.2	6.0	7.9	6.2	4.8	8.9	8.7	6.8

242

Table 28 (concl.)

8 Axe-Houghton index of trade & industrial activity	1879–1927	U	5.8	4.6	4.3	3.2	3.2	3.4	4.4	7.7	8.5	4.7
		A	5.9	4.6	4.4	3.7	3.3	3.0	5.6	7.6	8.1	4.9
9 R.R. bond yields	1858–1933	U	5.1	4.0	3.3	2.6	3.1	2.5	3.2	3.8	4.7	3.4
		A	2.5	1.9	1.6	1.6	2.1	1.8	2.6	2.2	2.1	2.0
No. of cases in which trend adjustment												
Reduces av. deviation			5	4	4	1	3	4	6	9	8	44
Does not change av. deviation			..	2	1	2	..	..	..	..	..	5
Raises av. deviation			4	3	4	6	6	5	3	0	1	32

a For fuller identification of series, see Appendix B.
b U=unadjusted data; A=trend-adjusted data.

c Expressed in percentages of reference-cycle bases.
d Average deviations of standings at stages I and IX receive a weight of one-half each.

243

Table 29

EFFECT OF SHIFT FROM T-T TO P-P ANALYSIS UPON AVERAGE DEVIATIONS FROM
AVERAGE REFERENCE-CYCLE PATTERNS OF SEVEN SERIES

SERIES[e]	PERIOD COVERED	NO. OF CYCLES	TYPE OF ANALYSIS[c]	AVERAGE DEVIATION[f] AT REFERENCE-CYCLE STAGES							
				I	II	III	IV	V	VI	VII	VIII
Clearings outside N.Y.C., deflated	1882–1929	14	T-T	5.4[a]	5.4	3.5	3.2	3.7	4.3	4.6	5.0
			P-P	2.6	2.6	2.2	3.3	5.4[b]	4.2	2.6	2.7
Pig iron production	1882–1929	14	T-T	15.2[a]	11.5	11.2	9.5	7.7	5.8	12.4	14.6
			P-P	11.1	8.2	6.4	11.6	11.9[b]	12.0	11.1	11.3
Freight car orders	1873–1929[d]	12	T-T	46.5[a]	21.3	25.5	28.5	39.7	22.5	21.0	24.7
			P-P	37.2	19.5	35.5	40.0	55.3[b]	17.7	25.9	23.4
Shares traded, N.Y. Stock Exchange	1882–1929	14	T-T	30.8[a]	26.6	12.5	13.9	19.1	9.5	14.4	14.4
			P-P	18.6	19.9	17.5	14.5	27.8[b]	25.0	15.4	14.9
R.R. stock prices	1860–1929	18	T-T	11.9[a]	11.2	7.6	7.3	4.7	5.1	7.5	8.5
			P-P	6.3	5.0	6.2	11.1	11.2[b]	9.5	8.5	8.6
Call money rates	1860–1929	18	T-T	24.4[a]	23.5	18.8	27.6	57.4	28.7	27.6	22.0
			P-P	18.0	21.2	16.9	25.0	59.8[b]	29.6	36.4	18.3
R.R. bond yields	1860–1929	18	T-T	5.0[a]	4.2	3.3	2.6	3.1	2.6	3.0	3.7
			P-P	2.6	2.0	3.5	4.6	4.9[b]	4.1	3.4	2.5
No. of series in which shift from T-T to P-P analysis											
Reduces av. deviations				7	7	4	1	0	2	2	5
Raises av. deviations				0	0	3	6	7	5	5	2

[a] Average of the two entries for troughs.
[b] Average of the two entries for peaks.
[c] T-T means trough-to-trough, P-P means peak-to-peak.
[d] 1913-23 omitted.
[e] The sources are the same as for Table 24.
[f] Expressed in percentages of reference-cycle bases.

244

plained and the results of applying it to seven test series are summarized in the body of the chapter (Sec. IIC). Table 29 gives full
details of the test and needs no further explanation.

5 Effects of Reference-Cycle Bases upon Average Standings and Deviations at Stages I and IX

The relations between average standings and deviations from them
at stages I and IX are peculiar because stage IX of one reference
cycle is also stage I of its successor. To illustrate these relations I
have chosen a series in which sharp changes in reference-cycle
bases are not uncommon: namely, the number of shares sold
monthly on the New York Stock Exchange. Column (1) of Table
30 shows our reference dates for five business-cycle troughs, and
column (2) the average sales during the three months centered
on each of these dates. The three months centered on April 1888

Table 30

ILLUSTRATIONS OF RELATIONS BETWEEN STANDINGS AT STAGES IX AND I
OF ADJACENT REFERENCE CYCLES IN SHARES TRADED ON NEW YORK
STOCK EXCHANGE

	MILLION SHARES TRADED PER MONTH DURING			REFERENCE-CYCLE STANDING AT		DEVIATION FROM AV. STANDING AT	
REFERENCE TROUGH	Trough Stage [a]	Cycle in Which Trough Is					
		Stage IX	Stage I	Stage IX	Stage I	Stage IX	Stage I
(1)	(2)	(3)	(4)	(5)	(6)	(7)	(8)
April 1888	6.65	7.55	5.82	88.1	114.2	−7.5	+30.9
June 1897	6.29	4.73	11.23	133.0	56.0	+37.4	−27.3
June 1908	16.15	20.05	14.53	80.6	111.2	−15.0	+27.9
Jan. 1912	8.98	14.53	8.33	61.8	107.8	−33.8	+24.5
April 1919	24.94	15.25	21.28	163.6	117.2	+68.0	+33.9
Average, 16 cycles, 1879–1938				95.6	83.3	37.0	23.6

[a] Includes three months centered on reference date.

constitute stage IX of the reference cycle dated May 1885–April
1888 and also stage I of the cycle dated April 1888–May 1891. In
the earlier cycle, average monthly sales were 7.55 million shares;
in the later cycle 5.82 million. Average sales during the three
months centered on April 1888 were 6.65 million per month. This
figure is 88.1 percent of 7.55 million (the earlier cycle base) and
114.2 percent of 5.82 million (the later base). The analysis of
shares sold covers 16 reference cycles from 1879 to 1938. On the

average, reference-cycle standings were 95.6 percent of the cycle bases at stage IX and 83.3 percent at stage I. Hence the deviation of the standing at the April 1888 trough considered as stage IX of the 1885–88 cycle was $88.1 - 95.6 = -7.5$; but the deviation at this trough considered as stage I of the 1888–91 cycle was $114.2 - 83.3 = +30.9$. The entries at other troughs are to be read similarly.

The point of present moment is that our use of the same seasonally-adjusted data in computing reference-cycle standings at stages IX and I of adjacent cycles, though establishing a relationship between standings and between deviations at these stages, does not preclude the occurrence of considerable differences when the cycle bases fluctuate in the irregular fashion characteristic of pig iron production, shares sold, and, I may add, many other series.

Technical Note III

Average Deviations of Measures Based upon Differences between Reference-Cycle Standings

The relation suggested in the text, and explored in Table 24, between the average deviation from the mean reference-cycle amplitude of a series and the average deviations from its average standings at the peak and trough stages indicated by its timing variety is predicated upon two basic assumptions:

a) that variations in peak and trough standings are uncorrelated in combinations of successive peaks and troughs

b) that the average deviation tends to be a constant multiple of the standard deviation calculated from the same data, the multiple being about $4/5$. Call this constant $1/c$.

Now, let us denote the *population* standard deviation of a chance variable X by σ_x, and the *sample* standard deviation based on any finite sample of observations on X by s_x. Denote the corresponding sample average deviation by $(a.d.)_x$; and designate peak and trough standings by p and t, respectively. Then, given assumption (a), we know that

$$\sigma_{p-t}^2 = \sigma_p^2 + \sigma_t^2$$

Assumption (b) implies that the following relation *tends* to be fulfilled

$$c^2(a.d.)_{p-t}^2 = c^2(a.d.)_p^2 + c^2(a.d.)_t^2$$

Factoring out c^2 and taking square roots of both sides, we get the formula

$$(a.d.)_{p-t} = \sqrt{(a.d.)_p^2 + (a.d.)_t^2}$$

A similar argument leads to the following formula for the average deviation of full-cycle amplitudes

$$(a.d.)_{2p-t_1-t_2} = \sqrt{4(a.d.)_p^2 + (a.d.)_{t_1}^2 + (a.d.)_{t_2}^2}$$

where t_1 denotes initial trough and t_2 denotes terminal trough. Here there is the additional assumption that the standings in t_1 and t_2 are uncorrelated.

It should be noted that the truth of assumption (a) does not guarantee even that

$$s_{p-t} = \sqrt{s_p^2 + s_t^2}$$

for *finite* samples. Thus we must be prepared to see the formula

$$(a.d.)_{p-t} = \sqrt{(a.d.)_p^2 + (a.d.)_t^2}$$

hold only approximately even when assumptions (a) and (b) are fulfilled.

A test of the reasonableness of assumption (a) has been made by correlating the standings at turning points in successive cycles of the seven test series employed in Table 24. Few of the correlations

COEFFICIENTS OF CORRELATION BETWEEN REFERENCE-CYCLE STANDINGS
AT CHARACTERISTIC TURNING POINTS WITHIN REFERENCE CYCLES

| | | CORRELATION BETWEEN | | |
SERIES	NO. OF CYCLES	Initial trough and peak	Terminal trough and peak	Initial and terminal trough
Deflated clearings	16	+.25	−.27	−.72
Pig iron production	16	+.03	−.57	−.57
Freight car orders	17	+.04	−.17	−.43
R.R. stock prices	19	+.15	−.72	−.63
Shares traded	16	+.47	−.37	−.53
Call money rates	20	+.17	−.05	+.06
R.R. bond yields	19	−.82	+.70	−.68

are large, but they reveal a tendency to be positive for the turning points of expansions, and negative for the turning points of contractions and full cycles.

Of course, assumption (b) is strictly true only for a limited class of distributions, the chief of which is the Gaussian distribution; but it is well established empirically also for symmetrical distributions that do not depart widely from the Gaussian form. That assumption (b) does not hold precisely in our seven series is clear from the fact that we do not always get the discrepancies between directly and indirectly computed average deviations of amplitudes which we should expect from the above correlations.

Some idea of the variation in the relative size of average and standard deviations can be had from the accompanying table, which gives ratios of average to standard deviations for each class of turning points in our seven test series. Considering the small number of cyclical observations (16 to 20) in each series, the variation in these ratios does not seem excessive.

RATIOS OF AVERAGE DEVIATIONS OF TURNING-POINT STANDINGS
TO CORRESPONDING STANDARD DEVIATIONS

| | RATIOS RELATING TO | | |
SERIES	Initial troughs	Peaks	Terminal troughs
Deflated clearings	.76	.87	.75
Pig iron production	.51	.74	.85
Freight car orders	.83	.80	.79
R.R. stock prices	.87	.65	.62
Shares traded	.81	.84	.71
Call money rates	.75	.60	.84
R.R. bond yields	.69	.73	.82

There is thus a case for working with our assumptions when the problem is to make rough estimates of the average deviation of amplitudes. However, before taking any of these results too seriously, it is necessary to investigate how typical they are of other series and to track down the correlations found between standings at successive turning points. Preliminary investigation indicates that these correlations cannot be dismissed as technical byproducts of our method of manipulating time series.

I am indebted to Millard Hastay for giving this argument its mathematical dress.

Part III

THE CONSENSUS OF CYCLICAL BEHAVIOR

CHAPTER 9

The Aim of Part III

Doubtless readers of Part II have remarked to themselves more than once that the charts and summary tables designed to exhibit varieties of cyclical behavior reveal also heavy concentrations at or about certain dominant types. Thus Chart 2 shows a dense concentration of our timing measures in the variety that fits our reference dates most closely. Chart 3 shows an only less striking concentration of conformity indexes at 100—a concentration we later had to pronounce exaggerated. Our basic definition alleges no tendency toward uniformity in reference-cycle amplitudes and there is no marked piling up of these measures in any one column of Chart 5; yet two-thirds of the entries are packed into one-eighth of the range. Even cycle-by-cycle deviations from average behavior are dominated by common features: Tables 21 and 22 show that they differ from stage to stage within series in ways that are predetermined by the characteristics of secular, cyclical, and irregular movements on the one side and on the other by certain features of our analytic technique, while we found that among series average deviations from reference-cycle patterns follow rather closely average amplitudes and conformity in combination.

The text, as well as the charts and tables of Part II, anticipates results that it is the task of Part III to demonstrate. For even while I was stressing the varieties of cyclical behavior, I could not avoid mentioning the consensus the varieties themselves reveal when taken as a whole. As with descriptive, so with explanatory passages. Many of the problems raised for discussion concern departures from a prevailing type of behavior that is taken for granted, and the solutions suggested often invoke 'the cyclical tides'. In Section IVB of Chapter 7, for example, I asserted explicitly that the specific cycles of every activity in a national economy "are partially shaped by those congeries of specific cycles in other activities which we call business cycles". Thus I have not only exhibited part of the factual evidence of covariation among our series, but I have also assumed the full validation of the fundamental concept I profess to be examining.

These whirlpools in the onward flow of the investigation will not, I hope, give rise to confusion or misgivings. Nothing comes logically first and nothing comes logically last in a universe of discourse where all the elements are interdependent. At the outset we must assume relations that we cannot demonstrate until the end.

What may trouble the reader more is the implication that, at this late day, the concept of business cycles still needs to be tested. But impatience on that score would be a mark of scientific immaturity. A rather rough notion of some phenomenon may prove sufficient to guide early efforts to understand it. At a later stage, when rival explanations have accumulated, and competent judges differ as to which explanation best fits the facts, it becomes necessary to define concepts more rigorously and test them more systematically. What is put to the test in Part III is not merely the notion that business undergoes cyclical fluctuations of some sort, but the hypothesis that the cycles in question have the characteristics set down in the several clauses of our definition, that historical instances of these phenomena occurred within the intervals marked off by our reference dates, that the time series we have collected can be made to reveal the cyclical movements in different sectors and aspects of a national economy, and that the analytic methods we have devised are fit tools to that end. Surely, no one should take all this for granted unless adequate factual evidence is submitted to his scrutiny.

However, Part III is not limited to this general authentication of our definition, dates, sample of series, and statistical methods. It offers a summary of what happens during a typical

American business cycle—a summary derived from records of actual experience. In large part, this summary repeats what has been known to careful observers, merely putting familiar impressions into definite form, shoving under them a more solid foundation, and expressing them in the National Bureau's quantitative form. But, generalized though it be, the summary also brings out certain features of business cycles that have not been hitherto observed, and that could hardly be discovered until investigators had at their disposal some such array of measures as the National Bureau's long and costly labors have provided. If the aim of economic theory is to attain under- standing of economic experience, any valid summary of the cyclical consensus is a basic contribution to the theory of busi- ness cycles. For such a summary presents the broad facts a theory should explain. On the one hand, it affords a better guide than has hitherto been available to the detailed investi- gations that should be made. On the other hand, it offers criteria by which to judge the validity and adequacy of explanations. A summary of actual experience is an empirical construction that can be improved upon, as what it helps to learn suggests clearer concepts, more efficient methods of analysis, and addi- tional data that should be incorporated.

Concerning the consensus of cyclical behavior, our sample can be made to give two types of evidence. The most convinc- ing type, and the type that tells us most about the nature of the consensus, is elicited by examining our full sample in detail. It is especially interesting to cross-examine series that at first seem to contradict the notion of a consensus in cyclical movements, but often turn out on more skillful questioning to be offering confirmation. However, using the full sample is a cumbersome process, especially when we have to go back of statistical lists and counts to economic weighings. So we had best begin with the less complete evidence offered by a relatively few com- prehensive series that are widely known by name at least, and have the specious advantage of commanding more confidence than they merit.

"Obviously, no single time series can reveal business cycles as we have defined them." [1] The most that a single series can accomplish is to show the net resultant of movements in many activities. To find out whether these net resultants arise from the covariation of many components or from fluctuations peculiar to a dominant few, one must examine the many components themselves. But if a man finds that the best accredited index numbers of physical production and commodity prices, the broadest samples of employment, the biggest totals of bank clearings, the most trustworthy estimates of gross national product and national income, the volume of freight hauled by all railroads, and retail sales have all expanded and then contracted in concert, he may be excused for jumping to the conclusion that covariation has prevailed among economic activities. His confidence in this conclusion may be a bit shaken, but it will not be destroyed, by reading what the several compilers of these series have to say about the limitations of their own figures. In any case, few consumers of statistics have the troublesome habit of going behind the titles of series that behave plausibly. Even the National Bureau's admission that it has used these comprehensive series whenever they were available as aids in fixing its own reference dates will not arouse grave suspicion of a trick, because it can be argued that the consensus of all these master indicators regarding the locations of peaks and troughs must be about right.

Taking full, and rather unfair, advantage of this happy confidence, let us begin our tests of the consensus alleged by our definition in the cyclical fluctuations of many economic activities, by examining the reference-cycle patterns of the most comprehensive American series we have analyzed.

[1] *Measuring Business Cycles*, p. 11.

CHAPTER 10

The Evidence of Comprehensive Series

I A STATISTICAL SUMMARY

Table 31 shows how the most comprehensive series in our American sample have typically behaved during business cycles. Concerning each series the table tells (1) the period and (2) number of reference cycles covered by our analysis, (3) the timing variety, (4) the indexes of conformity, (5) the mean reference-cycle amplitudes, (6) the reference-cycle pattern, (7) the average deviation from the average pattern, (8) the average rates of change per month from segment to segment of reference cycles, and (9) the average deviation of these rates of change. As far as possible we have used monthly or quarterly data; but 3 annual series are so important for present purposes that we add them in a final section of the table. Chart 7, which follows the table, exhibits graphically the reference-cycle patterns of all series in the table. No specific-cycle measures are included, which means that the full amplitudes of the fluctuations characteristic of the individual series are understated in varying degrees; also that the information concerning leads and lags is limited to the broad inferences that can be drawn from the variety of timing and the direction of average patterns from one stage to the next.

Since this is our first attempt to see how several of the National Bureau's measures of cyclical behavior in various parts of the economy fit together, and what composite picture they give of business cycles, we should examine Table 31 with critical care before forming any opinion about the trustworthiness and adequacy of the evidence it gives.

II SCOPE AND ADEQUACY OF COMPREHENSIVE SERIES

In its small and technical fashion, Table 31 is an epitome of the nation's cultural progress toward knowing itself. Most of

Table 31

Typical Behavior of Comprehensive American Series with Respect to Business Cycles

A CONFORMITY AND AMPLITUDE

Series[a]	Period Covered[f]	No. of Cycles	Expansion Stages	Index of Conformity to			Av. Reference-Cycle Amplitude		
				Reference exp.	Reference contr.	Business cycles	Expansion	Contraction	Full cycle
PHYSICAL VOLUME OF PRODUCTION									
1 Industrial production (FRB index)	1919-1938	5	I-V	+100	+100	+100	+35	−32	+68
2 Fuel and electricity (NBER index)	1919-1938	5	I-V	+100	+100	+100	+26	−15	+40
3 Pig iron	1879-1938	16	I-V	+100	+100	+100	+54	−45	+99
TRANSPORTATION									
4 Railroad freight ton miles	1904-1938	9	I-V	+100	+78	+100	+28	−23	+51
PRICES									
5 'All' commodities, wholesale (BLS index)	1891-1938[b]	11	I-V	+64	+82	+100	+9	−9	+18
TRADE									
6 Wholesale trade sales, 9 lines, value (FRB index)	1919-1927	3	I-V	+100	+100	+100	+18	−19	+37
7 Department store sales (FRB index), deflated	1921-1938	4	I-V	+100	+50	+100	+16	−10	+26
8 Agricultural marketings, phys. vol. (DC index)	1919-1938	5	Irreg.	+60	−20	+33	+1.4	−0.8	+2.2
9 Exports, value	1867-1938[b]	16	Irreg.[d]	+62	0	+27	+15	−1	+16
10 Imports, value	1867-1938[b]	16	VIII-V	+88	+50	+77	+26	−19	+45
EMPLOYMENT AND INCOMES									
11 Factory employment (BLS index)	1914-1938	6	I-V	+100	+100	+100	+22	−23	+45
12 Factory payrolls (BLS index)	1919-1938	5	I-V	+100	+100	+100	+36	−40	+76
13 Income payments, total (Barger, Commerce)	1921-1938	4	I-V	+100	0	+100	+23	−18	+40
INVESTMENTS									
14 Construction contracts, value (Dodge)	1912-1938	7	VIII-IV	+71	+50	+86	+43	−30	+74

Table 31 (cont.)

15	Security issues, corporate, value (*Jour. of Com.*)	1908-1938	8	VIII-IV	+100	+50	+60	+47	-46	+93
16	Cash from security issues on N.Y. Stock Exchange (Ayres)	1868-1921	14	VIII-V	+87	+73	+93	+58	-39	+97
17	Incorporations, no. (Evans)	1861-1938	19	VIII-V	+68	+60	+84	+27	-10	+37
	DEALINGS IN SECURITIES									
18	Shares sold on N.Y. Stock Exchange, no.	1879-1938	16	VIII-IV	+88	+75	+94	+41	-36	+77
19	Bonds sold on N.Y. Stock Exchange, par value	1891-1938	13	VII-II	-57	-71	-70	-15	+35	-50
20	Common stock prices, 'all' (Cowles index)	1879-1938	16	VIII-IV	+88	+65	+88	+27	-20	+47
21	R.R. bond prices (Macaulay index)ᵃ	1858-1933	19	VI-III	-42	-45	-66	-3.5	+6.4	-9.9
	BUSINESS PROFITS AND FAILURES									
22	Net profits, all corporations (Barger)	1921-1938	4	I-V	+100	+100	+100	+169	-175	+343
23	Business failures, no. (Dun's)	1879-1938	16	V-IX	-50	-75	-84	-22	+26	-48
24	Business failures, liabilities (Dun's)	1879-1938ᵇ	14	IV-VII	-71	-100	-100	-67	+59	-125
	BANK CLEARINGS OR DEBITS									
25	Total	1879-1938ᵇ	14	VIII-V	+100	+86	+92	+30	-21	+51
26	New York City	1854-1938ᶜ	18	VIII-IV	+100	+78	+94	+32	-28	+60
27	Outside New York City	1879-1938ᵇ	14	VIII-V	+100	+57	+85	+26	-11	+37
	INDEXES OF BUSINESS ACTIVITY									
	Adjusted for trend									
28	Ayres	1854-1938	21	I-V	+100	+100	+100	+17	-19	+36
29	American Tel. and Tel. Co.	1879-1938	16	I-V	+100	+100	+100	+23	-25	+48
30	Persons	1879-1938	16	I-V	+100	+100	+100	+22	-23	+45
31	Deposits activity (Snyder)	1879-1938	16	VIII-IV	+88	+75	+94	+14	-17	+31
	Not adjusted for trend									
32	Axe-Houghton	1879-1938	16	I-V	+100	+88	+100	+29	-21	+50
33	American Tel. and Tel. Co.	1900-1938	10	VIII-V	+100	+100	+100	+32	-23	+55
34	Babson	1908-1938	8	I-V	+100	+100	+100	+29	-23	+52

Table 31 (cont.)

B REFERENCE-CYCLE PATTERNS

Series[a]	I	II	III	IV	V	VI	VII	VIII	IX	Mean Av. Deviation, All Stages[b]
					Average Standing at Stage					
PHYSICAL VOLUME OF PRODUCTION										
1 Industrial production	85.1	94.4	102.5	113.3	120.3	115.9	101.2	89.4	87.8	9.4
2 Fuel and electricity	87.3	93.0	93.8	104.8	112.8	112.3	107.8	99.7	98.3	5.8
3 Pig iron	70.5	88.9	101.9	114.0	124.7	121.6	101.0	83.7	79.8	13.6
TRANSPORTATION										
4 Railroad freight ton miles	87.3	93.4	99.1	109.0	115.0	111.7	102.9	92.6	91.6	6.2
PRICES										
5 'All' commodities, wholesale	96.4	98.8	100.9	103.1	105.1	104.6	100.1	97.2	96.3	4.3
TRADE										
6 Wholesale trade sales, 9 lines, value	92.9	98.5	100.6	109.0	110.6	106.8	96.9	93.5	91.5	6.6
7 Department store sales, deflated	90.8	94.4	99.4	104.8	106.7	105.6	103.8	99.6	97.0	3.5
8 Agricultural marketings, phys. vol.	100.2	102.3	99.6	102.2	101.6	100.8	101.8	102.3	100.8	4.3
9 Exports, value	89.4	95.5	99.2	102.1	104.4	106.0	107.2	103.0	103.1	10.7
10 Imports, value	87.9	93.4	101.3	109.9	114.7	109.8	99.7	95.8	95.9	10.8
EMPLOYMENT AND INCOMES										
11 Factory employment	90.9	96.4	103.4	109.2	112.7	110.2	101.1	92.1	89.9	6.8
12 Factory payrolls	86.9	93.1	102.9	113.1	123.1	120.3	104.3	88.0	83.2	12.5
13 Income payments, total	90.0	94.6	100.3	108.9	112.7	111.5	105.3	97.8	95.1	9.1
INVESTMENTS										
14 Construction contracts, value	78.3	95.3	110.1	123.5	127.1	114.8	96.3	93.2	98.7	17.6
15 Security issues, corporate, value	85.5	99.3	119.2	125.9	113.8	99.5	90.8	79.8	94.1	25.8
16 Cash from security issues on N.Y. Stock Exchange	80.7	94.9	108.6	109.1	120.4	110.2	92.8	81.1	94.2	26.3
17 Incorporations, no.	85.6	90.6	97.9	107.5	109.6	107.3	100.3	99.4	104.2	12.0

Table 31 (cont.)

DEALINGS IN SECURITIES											
18	Shares sold on N.Y. Stock Exchange, no.	83.3	113.3	108.7	113.8	108.6	95.0	89.6	77.7	95.6	18.2
19	Bonds sold on N.Y. Stock Exchange, par value	98.9	111.8	108.6	102.3	100.4	89.6	95.0	100.5	115.4	19.7
20	Common stock prices, 'all'	86.6	96.1	103.7	111.7	110.3	106.3	95.5	91.5	92.9	9.3
21	R.R. bond prices	98.2	99.6	101.7	101.1	98.9	97.9	98.5	98.9	99.9	3.4
BUSINESS PROFITS AND FAILURES											
22	Net profits, all corporations	30.4	97.0	134.8	182.4	199.2	151.3	78.4	35.2	24.6	58.1
23	Business failures, no.	107.8	101.7	93.3	87.1	86.1	89.1	105.7	110.2	112.2	13.4
24	Business failures, liabilities	109.1	89.0	86.4	76.6	85.3	120.0	135.4	118.5	107.2	22.0
BANK CLEARINGS OR DEBITS											
25	Total	85.0	95.0	101.4	111.4	112.3	108.0	98.1	91.7	95.8	8.5
26	New York City	86.2	97.3	105.4	114.9	114.9	105.5	92.4	87.0	91.9	10.4
27	Outside New York City	84.9	91.8	97.7	107.4	110.1	109.4	102.9	98.8	99.7	6.6
INDEXES OF BUSINESS ACTIVITY											
	Adjusted for trend										
28	Ayres	91.7	99.2	103.5	107.2	108.7	104.6	96.9	90.9	89.8	5.6
29	American Tel. and Tel. Co.	88.4	97.3	102.7	107.8	111.6	108.1	97.0	88.9	87.1	5.8
30	Persons	89.2	97.6	103.1	108.4	111.0	107.8	98.1	89.9	88.0	5.8
31	Deposits activity	94.2	102.1	103.7	107.1	107.1	103.5	96.0	90.4	91.6	6.4
	Not adjusted for trend										
32	Axe-Houghton	84.2	93.0	100.0	108.3	113.4	111.1	101.1	93.1	92.6	6.7
33	American Tel. and Tel. Co.	82.8	92.3	100.9	108.7	114.5	110.9	99.7	91.4	90.8	6.7
34	Babson	85.5	93.6	101.2	109.8	114.9	109.6	100.6	92.9	92.2	6.7

Table 31 (cont.)

C RATES OF CHANGE IN SUCCESSIVE REFERENCE-CYCLE SEGMENTS

Series[a]	Weighted Av. Rate of Change per Month[b] in Segment								Mean Av. Deviation, All Segments[c]
	I-II	II-III	III-IV	IV-V	V-VI	VI-VII	VII-VIII	VIII-IX	
PHYSICAL VOLUME OF PRODUCTION									
1 Industrial production	+2.0	+1.0	+1.4	+1.6	−1.2	−2.2	−1.8	−0.4	0.92
2 Fuel and electricity	+1.3	+0.1	+1.4	+1.8	−0.1	−0.7	−1.2	−0.4	0.85
3 Pig iron	+4.0	+1.6	+1.5	+2.3	−0.9	−3.3	−2.8	−1.1	2.46
TRANSPORTATION									
4 Railroad freight ton miles	+1.3	+0.7	+1.2	+1.3	−0.9	−1.4	−1.7	−0.3	0.98
PRICES									
5 'All' commodities, wholesale	+0.5	+0.3	+0.3	+0.5	−0.2	−0.7	−0.5	−0.3	0.49
TRADE									
6 Wholesale trade sales, 9 lines, value	+1.6	+0.4	+1.4	+0.4	−1.3	−1.9	−0.7	−0.7	1.46
7 Department store sales, deflated	+0.7	+0.5	+0.6	+0.4	−0.3	−0.3	−0.6	−0.7	1.26
8 Agricultural marketings, phys. vol.	+0.5	−0.3	+0.3	−0.1	−0.2	+0.2	+0.1	−0.4	0.39
9 Exports, value	+1.3	+0.5	+0.4	+0.5	+0.4	+0.2	−0.6	+0.02	0.94
10 Imports, value	+1.2	+1.0	+1.1	+1.0	−1.2	−1.4	−0.5	+0.04	1.42
EMPLOYMENT AND INCOMES									
11 Factory employment	+1.1	+0.8	+0.6	+0.7	−0.7	−1.5	−1.5	−0.7	0.64
12 Factory payrolls	+1.4	+1.2	+1.3	+2.2	−0.7	−2.4	−2.4	−1.3	1.15
13 Income payments, total	+0.8	+0.7	+1.0	+0.7	−0.3	−1.0	−1.2	−0.6	0.48
INVESTMENTS									
14 Construction contracts, value	+3.7	+1.8	+1.6	+0.8	−3.5	−3.0	−0.5	+1.6	3.14
15 Security issues, corporate, value	+3.1	+2.5	+0.8	−2.7	−3.9	−1.4	−1.7	+3.9	5.52
16 Cash from security issues on N.Y. Stock Exchange	+2.8	+1.8	+0.1	+2.2	−2.3	−3.0	−2.0	+2.9	8.31
17 Incorporations, no.	+1.1	+0.9	+1.1	+0.4	−0.6	−1.0	−0.1	+1.2	1.78

260

Table 31 (cont.)

DEALINGS IN SECURITIES									
18	Shares sold on N.Y. Stock Exchange, no.	+6.6	−0.6	+0.7	−1.1	−3.9	−0.9	−1.9	+5.1	4.76
19	Bonds sold on N.Y. Stock Exchange, par value	+2.9	−0.4	−0.8	−0.4	−3.1	+0.9	+0.9	+4.2	4.14
20	Common stock prices, 'all'	+2.1	+1.0	+1.0	−0.3	−1.1	−1.8	−0.6	+0.4	1.18
21	R.R. bond prices	+0.3	+0.3	−0.1	−0.5	−0.3	+0.1	+0.1	+0.3	0.48
BUSINESS PROFITS AND FAILURES									
22	Net profits, all corporations	+11.8	+4.4	+5.5	+3.0	−10.7	−11.4	−6.8	−2.3	3.89
23	Business failures, no.	−1.3	−1.1	−0.8	−0.2	+0.8	+2.9	+0.8	+0.6	1.79
24	Business failures, liabilities	−4.1	−0.3	−1.3	+1.8	+9.0	+2.6	−2.8	−2.9	6.48
BANK CLEARINGS OR DEBITS									
25	Total	+2.2	+0.8	+1.3	+0.2	−1.2	−1.5	−1.0	+1.1	1.14
26	New York City	+2.4	+1.0	+1.2	−0.1	−2.4	−1.9	−0.8	+1.2	1.84
27	Outside New York City	+1.5	+0.8	+1.2	+0.6	−0.2	−1.0	−0.6	+0.2	0.69
INDEXES OF BUSINESS ACTIVITY									
	Adjusted for trend									
28	Ayres	+1.6	+0.5	+0.5	+0.3	−1.1	−1.1	−0.9	−0.3	0.84
29	American Tel. and Tel. Co.	+2.0	+0.7	+0.6	+0.8	−1.0	−1.8	−1.3	−0.5	0.81
30	Persons	+1.8	+0.7	+0.7	+0.6	−0.9	−1.6	−1.3	−0.5	0.79
31	Deposits activity	+1.7	+0.2	+0.4	0.0	−1.0	−1.2	−0.9	+0.3	0.89
	Not adjusted for trend									
32	Axe-Houghton	+1.9	+0.9	+1.0	+1.1	−0.7	−1.6	−1.3	−0.1	0.84
33	American Tel. and Tel. Co.	+2.1	+1.1	+1.0	+1.3	−1.0	−1.8	−1.3	−0.2	0.89
34	Babson	+1.8	+1.0	+1.1	+1.1	−1.5	−1.4	−1.2	−0.2	0.80

Table 31 (concl.)

D CYCLICAL MEASURES OF KUZNETS' ANNUAL SERIES

Series [a] (in current prices)	Period Covered	No. of Cycles	Expansion Stages	Index of Conformity to			Av. Reference-Cycle Amplitude [j]		
				Reference exp.	Reference contr.	Business cycles	Expansion	Contraction	Full cycle
Gross national product	1921-38	4	I-V	+100	+50	+100	+21	-16	+38
National income	1921-38	4	I-V	+100	+50	+100	+22	-18	+40
Personal incomes	1921-38	4	I-V	+100	0	+100	+16	-12	+28

Series	Av. Reference-Cycle Standing at Stage					Mean Av. Deviation, All Stages [g]	Weighted Av. Change per Month [h] in Reference-Cycle Segment				Mean Av. Deviation, All Segments [i]
	I	III	V	VII	IX		I-III	III-V	V-VII	VII-IX	
Gross national product	92.6	98.3	113.9	107.0	97.5	8.6	+0.3	+0.9	-0.8	-1.0	0.38
National income	92.2	98.5	114.6	107.0	97.0	9.2	+0.4	+1.0	-0.8	-1.1	0.40
Personal incomes	94.0	98.3	110.4	105.9	98.9	6.3	+0.3	+0.7	-0.5	-0.8	0.34

a For full identification of series, see Appendix B.

b Omits 1914-21.

c Omits 1861-67 and 1914-21.

d I-V after 1914.

e The series fits VI-III and VII-III timing equally well. The conformity and amplitude entries are averages of measures made on both timing plans.

f Identifies the complete reference cycles covered by the series. This period, however, differs somewhat from that covered by some of the conformity and amplitude measures; see Measuring Business Cycles, Ch. 5, Sec. X. The conformity indexes include an additional contraction at the beginning in series 12, 14, 16, 17, 20, 21 (VI-III version), and 33; they include an additional expansion at the end in series 6, 16, and 21 (VII-III version); and both the conformity indexes and the amplitude measures include an additional cycle at the beginning in series 19.

g In deriving the mean of the average deviations at all stages, the average deviations at stages I and IX receive a weight of one-half each. The average deviations at individual stages are given in Table 43.

h See Measuring Business Cycles, pp. 150-1, 167.

i The average deviations for the individual segments are given in Table 43.

j See the supplementary measures in Table 15.

the records upon which economic series rest have been started to meet administrative needs, public or private. Only of late have Americans begun to grasp the social value of systematic knowledge of how their economy is working. Hence, when a student tries to summarize what has happened in past decades, he finds the data at his disposal extremely uneven in scope and quality. What he wants most to know is frequently reported least adequately, if at all, while matters of secondary interest can sometimes be traced back by months for a century.

The most comprehensive daily record of economic activities kept in the United States represents payments made through banks. Not all, but most transactions are 'settled' by a payment in coin, paper money, or check.[1] If we could total all payments, we would come nearer to including all economic dealings than in any other way. Though no one really knows how large is the share of payments by check, all authorities agree that it makes some four-fifths or more of the total.[2] According to Federal Reserve reports, supplemented in minor degree by estimates for nonreporting institutions, debits charged by banks to deposit accounts averaged $723 billion a year in 1919–38.[3] This imposing figure excludes not only the substantial volume of payments in paper money and coin, but also payments of one bank to another. Even so, it is almost ten times as large as Simon Kuznets' estimate of average gross national product at current prices in these years. The chief reasons why the volume of payments by check so vastly exceeds the total value of goods produced annually are (1) that most costs of producing a good are paid out before it is ready for its first sale, (2) that these partially or wholly finished products then commonly change hands several times on their

[1] Among the exceptions are agricultural rents paid by sharing the actual produce, and settlements effected mainly by offsetting sums payable against sums receivable in books of account (a method largely used in interbank transactions). Formal organizations for clearing claims are operated by stock exchanges, railroads, and banks.

[2] Cf. *Business Cycles: The Problem and Its Setting*, pp. 117–8.

[3] Computed from Table 55 in *Banking and Monetary Statistics* (Board of Governors of the Federal Reserve System, 1943), p. 254.

Chart 7

Average Reference-Cycle Patterns of American Comprehensive Series

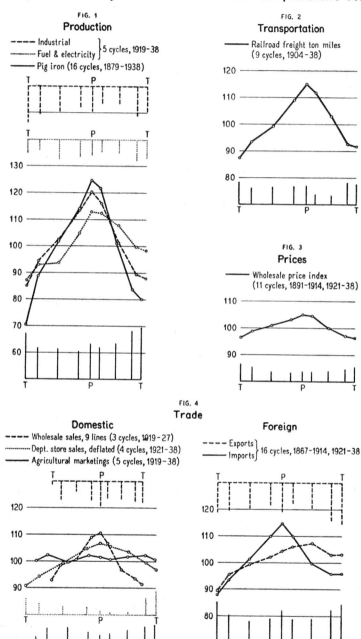

FIG. 1
Production

- - - - Industrial
.... Fuel & electricity } 5 cycles, 1919-38
———— Pig iron (16 cycles, 1879-1938)

FIG. 2
Transportation

———— Railroad freight ton miles
(9 cycles, 1904-38)

FIG. 3
Prices

———— Wholesale price index
(11 cycles, 1891-1914, 1921-38)

FIG. 4
Trade

Domestic

- - - - Wholesale sales, 9 lines (3 cycles, 1919-27)
.... Dept. store sales, deflated (4 cycles, 1921-38)
———— Agricultural marketings (5 cycles, 1919-38)

Foreign

- - - - Exports ⎫
———— Imports ⎬ 16 cycles, 1867-1914, 1921-38

See Tables 31 and 43 for data on which chart is based and Appendix B for sources.

264

Chart 7 (cont.)

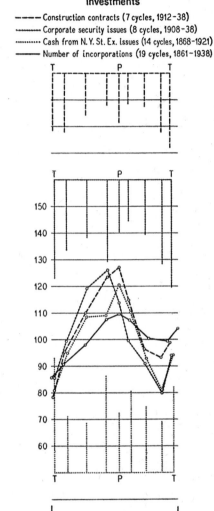

FIG. 6

Investments

— — — Construction contracts (7 cycles, 1912–38)
········· Corporate security issues (8 cycles, 1908–38)
·········· Cash from N.Y. St. Ex. Issues (14 cycles, 1868–1921)
————— Number of incorporations (19 cycles, 1861–1938)

FIG. 5

Employment and Incomes

— — — Factory employment (6 cycles, 1914–38)
········· Factory payrolls (5 cycles, 1919–38)
————— Income payments (4 cycles, 1921–38)

Horizontal scale, in months

0   12   24   36   48   60

265

Chart 7 (cont.)

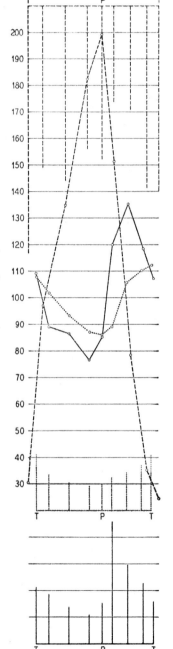

FIG. 8
Business Profits and Failures

–––– Net profits, all corporations (4 cycles, 1921-38)
········· Business failures, number (16 cycles, 1879-1938)
——— Business failures, liabilities (14 cycles, 1879-1914, 1921-38)

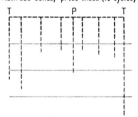

FIG. 7
Dealings in Securities

–––– Shares sold, number (16 cycles, 1879-1938)
········ Bonds sold, par value (13 cycles, 1891-1938)
········ Common stocks, price index (16 cycles, 1879-1938)
——— Railroad bonds, price index (19 cycles, 1858-1933)

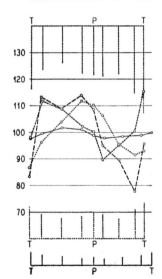

Chart 7 (concl.)

FIG. 9

Bank Clearings or Debits

- - - - New York City (18 cycles, 1854-61, '67-1914, '21-38)
.... Outside New York City ⎱ 14 cycles,
———— Total ⎰ 1879-1914, 1921-38

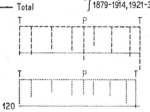

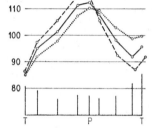

FIG. 10

Indexes of Business Activity Trend-Adjusted

- - - - Ayres (21 cycles, 1854-1938)
.... A.T.&T.
.... Persons ⎱ 16 cycles,
———— Deposits activity, Snyder ⎰ 1879-1938

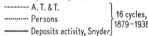

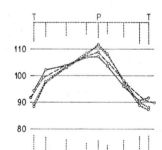

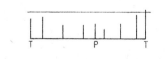

FIG. 11

Indexes of Business Activity Unadjusted for Trend

- - - - A.T.&T. (10 cycles, 1900-38)
.... Axe-Houghton (16 cycles, 1879-1938)
———— Babson (8 cycles, 1908-38)

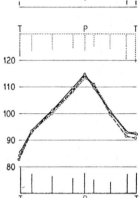

FIG. 12

National Product and Income

- - - - Gross national product ⎱
.... National income ⎰ 4 cycles, 1921-38
———— Personal incomes

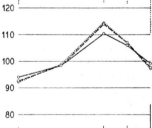

Horizontal scale, in months |⊢—⊥—┼—⊥—┼—⊥—┼—⊥—┼—⊥—┼—⊥—|
0   12   24   36   48   60

way to final consumers, (3) that there is a vast volume of trading in durable property, especially securities and real estate, (4) that these dealings are usually conducted through brokers and thus swell the volume of payments, and (5) that another large volume of payments arises from the making and repaying of loans. So comprehensive, indeed, are the grand totals of debits to deposit accounts, and so vague has been knowledge about the relative magnitudes of its components, that not much analytic use has been made of the figures.[4] Economists have usually preferred to take debits in New York City and outside of it separately, holding that the New York figures are dominated by fluctuations in financial transactions, especially dealings on the Stock Exchange, and that the 'outside' figures are dominated by fluctuations in the production and distribution of current income.

What we do here with these intriguing data is to present our reference-cycle measures of total, New York, and outside debits, spliced upon their somewhat less inclusive predecessors—the reports of bank clearings. For we believe that the time-honored distinction drawn between the meaning of New York and 'outside' clearings or debits is justified. But no more than our predecessors can we say how much financial transactions influence outside debits, or how much the production and distribution of current income influence debits in New York. And even if we could separate these components we should still regard the record of payments as too comprehen-

---

[4] Morris A. Copeland has recently made a material addition to our knowledge of the magnitude and composition of money payments. See his "Study of Money Flows in the United States", a forthcoming publication of the National Bureau. By dividing the economy into sectors and estimating the volume of each sector's transactions with the others, he obtains the total amount and the major components of transactions in the 'main money circuit'. Subtracting these totals from debits, he derives estimates of the volume of 'technical transactions', which include money changing (as in transferring deposits from one bank to another), duplicate payments made through a third party, and the large volume of payments on account of trading in assets, making loans, and repaying loans. These 'technical transactions' apparently amounted to between 300 and 400 billion dollars a year in 1936–42, or roughly half of total debits in those years. The transactions in the 'main money circuit', nevertheless, are more than three times as large as gross national product in the same years.

sive for most of our purposes. Certainly we should wish to separate financial operations into new investments and trading in existing property. Not less we should wish to find out how far the changes in payments connected with current production and distribution of income represent fluctuations in the physical volume of goods flowing to final users, fluctuations in the number of times these goods change hands, and fluctuations in their unit prices. In short, as soon as we try to use comprehensive series, our thoughts run beyond what the stately totals tell us, and we demand other series that are more meaningful because more homogeneous, yet broad enough to cover some analytic concept that will seem to be a satisfactory stopping point for whatever we have in mind—until we begin to think carefully about it.[5]

In following this lead, we are handicapped by the fragmentary character of the record of physical production. No comprehensive index by months can be carried far back of World War I.[6] Thereafter we have the Federal Reserve Board index of industrial production, which makes use of the wealth of

[5] George Garvy of the Research Department, Federal Reserve Bank of New York, has provided a valuable analysis of what clearings and debits include. See his *Debits and Clearings Statistics: Their Background and Interpretation* (Board of Governors of the Federal Reserve System, Oct. 1947), and "Development of Bank Debits and Clearings and Their Use in Economic Analysis" (Columbia dissertation, 1950, unpublished). See also Copeland, *op. cit.*, Ch. 2 and 10. Similar scholarly critiques of other statistical records are much to be desired. As economics advances beyond the stage of speculation, it will require ever more exact knowledge of what its observational data actually represent.

It is significant that Copeland does not base his "Study of Money Flows in the United States" upon the record of debits. Instead Copeland's "underlying idea is that money flows register themselves in the accounts of business enterprises, governments, and various other transactors in the economy, and that consequently we should be able to construct a picture of money flows from *accounting reports*" (italics mine). See the National Bureau's *Twenty-Seventh Annual Report*, March 1947, p. 33.

[6] The best approximations are to be found among the 'business indexes'. For example, the 1944 revision of the American Telephone and Telegraph Company's series, which was carried back to 1899, was called an 'index of *industrial* activity'; and the Babson series, our analysis of which begins in 1904, is properly named 'index of the *physical volume* of business activity'. But the sample of monthly production data available before 1919 is meager at best.

detailed data on mining and manufactures that have become available. The difficulty of measuring the output of highly fabricated products that undergo frequent qualitative changes has been met after a fashion by using data on manhours adjusted for changes in productivity. But despite its broad coverage the index has notable gaps: it omits farming, construction work, and the vast volume of services that are not incorporated in commodities.[7]

To supplement this official index we use the National Bureau's own index of the production of coal, petroleum, and electricity, because all industries, including farming in recent years, have become dependent upon mechanical power, while all families use these goods (indirectly if not directly) for heating, cooking, lighting, and transportation. So, also, we may regard the ton miles of freight hauled by railroad as a general index of physical output, because virtually all products must be moved once or several times from their place of origin to their final destination, and the nation's railroads are still incomparably greatest among its common carriers.[8] Finally, I include pig iron among the comprehensive series, partly because the other indexes and records of production are so short, partly because it typifies the heavy industries that play so large a role in business cycles.

To represent commodity prices in the United States, the Bureau of Labor Statistics index has no serious rival. The indexes of wholesale prices that have been carried back into years before 1890 are almost inevitably overweighted with farm products. We might have included also the official index of the cost of living; but it has no such industrial range as the wholesale index, and we are not ready for detailed comparisons between prices at wholesale and retail.

Concerning the number of times commodities change ownership on their way from the producers of raw materials to final users, there seem to be few if any systematic data. But in recent years attempts have been made to extend statistical

[7] See *Measuring Business Cycles*, pp. 73–5.

[8] See Thor Hultgren, *op. cit.*, Ch. 1.

recording into the field of mercantile distribution. The index of sales at wholesale in 9 lines formerly used by the Federal Reserve Board has been supplanted by improved measures, though it still stands as perhaps the best indicator in its field before 1939. Department store sales cover a wider range of merchandise and of customers than any other retail series in the years that concern us. Agricultural marketing as estimated by the Department of Commerce is the best record of farmers' sales before the middle 'thirties. Since then the Bureau of Agricultural Economics has prepared improved estimates. The grievous gap in this section of the table is the lack of comprehensive series on orders from manufacturers—a gap that has been partially filled since 1929 by the National Industrial Conference Board and since 1939 by the Department of Commerce indexes of the value of orders. The historical dominance of political or administrative over economic considerations in shaping statistical records is illustrated by the contrast between our recent and still fragmentary data on domestic trade upon the one hand, and upon the other the relatively long and complete records of commodity imports and exports. To the American businessman and worker, the ill reported domestic trade must have represented markets and sources of supply running to perhaps ten times the dollar volume of foreign trade.

Use of resources is implied, of course, by all records of current output. Direct monthly records of employment are recent and as imperfect as similar records of production. The Bureau of Labor Statistics indexes in the table represent only the number of workers whose names are on factory payrolls from month to month, and the total wages paid to them—a sum that is influenced by the number of hours worked, wage rates, and the industrial composition of the working forces. Fortunately, the third series in this group—the estimates of income based on Barger's quarterly data[9] in 1921–28, and the Department of Commerce's monthly figures for 1929–38—is supposed to cover personal incomes of all types.

[9] See Harold Barger, *Outlay and Income in the United States, 1921–1938* (National Bureau, 1942), Ch. V; see also Appendix B, series 13 of Table 31.

Comprehensive data on investment expenditure prior to 1939 are available only by years. Monthly data are largely limited to records of early stages in the business planning of investments soon to be made. That is probably a fair interpretation to put upon most, though by no means all, charters of incorporation taken out by business enterprises, a sample of which running back by months to 1860 we owe to the enterprise of G. Heberton Evans.[10] The letting of contracts for construction work is fairly conclusive evidence that certain parties will presently be 'putting money into' buildings, railroads, dams, and other structures a modern nation wants. And the two series on the issuing of corporate securities, one fairly long but confined to cash raised by issues upon the New York Stock Exchange, the other shorter but wider in scope, show one of the early stages through which large-scale investment operations pass when the capital to be invested is raised from the public.

Of course, the New York Stock Exchange is one of the chief agencies for obtaining 'capital' to put into new investments. In even larger measure, however, it is the country's chief market for dealing in outstanding securities. Here more than in any other place are determined the prices of stocks and bonds that have so many direct and indirect, obvious and subtle, influences upon cyclical movements, and here more than anywhere else are centered the speculative booms and collapses upon which earlier economists laid such stress. Would that we had similar comprehensive series recording real estate transactions and prices; but this phase of economic activities is by its nature so dispersed that summaries would be exceedingly difficult to make or interpret.

According to our basic definition, business cycles occur in nations where most economic activities are organized in business enterprises conducted for profit. If so, profits and losses should play critical roles in generating and propagating cyclical movements. It has long been known that the net incomes of

[10] For details, see his *Business Incorporations in the United States, 1800–1943* (National Bureau, 1948).

most enterprises are subject to wide oscillations; but our definite information on this crucially important item was long confined to a relatively brief and doubtfully representative list of corporations whose accounts were published for special reasons either by their own officials or by some public agency. The relatively comprehensive information available for recent years in the United States is a byproduct of federal taxes upon the income of business corporations. By using, as his chief guide, the quarterly income statements of the corporations that publish such figures, Harold Barger put the official annual data of the Internal Revenue Bureau upon a quarterly basis from 1921 to 1938.[11] Along with this series we use the much longer record of commercial failures compiled by one of the country's leading agencies that has made a business of reporting upon the credit worthiness of other enterprises. Bank failures are not included.

The monthly and quarterly section of the table closes with cyclical measures of several of the best known indexes specifically designed to represent changing business conditions. A critique of these constructions, as they stood in the middle 1920's, was given in *Business Cycles: The Problem and Its Setting* (pp. 290–357). Though the indexes designed by Ayres, Axe and Houghton, and Babson are of later date, and though some of the older series have been revised since 1927, I shall not elaborate further the limitations imposed upon all general indexes of business conditions by the paucity of data, especially before World War I, or the logical limitations inherent in an effort to summarize what happens during business cycles by a single figure for each month in a stretch of years. Rather must I stress again the considerable extent to which different compilers perforce use the same data, and the general similarity among their technical methods, despite countless differences of detail. So prominent are these common features of the business indexes in the table, barring Snyder's index of deposits activity, that the likeness among our measures of the different indexes may be supposed to be mathematically foreordained. That

---

[11] See Barger, *op. cit.*, Appendix B.

conclusion, however, would be an exaggeration. Granted the similarity in statistical procedures, there remain sufficient differences among the data and weighting schemes used by the compilers of these indexes to prevent close agreement among their results, unless there were a marked consensus in the cyclical behavior of series that various compilers think fit for admission to an index of business activity.

So much for the present concerning the matters represented in our table. It is scarcely less important to notice what sectors of the economy are omitted. I have mentioned the lack of comprehensive series on orders from manufacturers and real estate transactions; also I have explained why no index of retail prices is used. Among other matters conspicuous by their absence are inventories, wage rates, hours of work per week, the output per manhour, interest rates, the external operations and internal conditions of the banks, the volume of the circulating medium and its velocity of circulation, taxes, and savings. On some of these subjects systematic data can be had, but we have not yet analyzed them—taxes, for example. On others we have numerous series that we hope to present later. Few if any of them are of comprehensive scope.[12]

A further defect of the table is the diversity of periods covered. The extremes are 3 reference cycles in wholesale trade sales and 21 in Ayres' index of business activity. Of course we might have established strict uniformity in this respect by cutting the longest series down to match the shortest. We deem it more important to give each series the best possible chance to show what cyclical behavior is typical of the factor it represents. The more cycles we can include the better this chance is, except when so marked a change has occurred in typical behavior that the series should be divided into segments, or when potent irregular factors have produced exceptionally violent movements in a few cycles. There is no example of the

12 Of course, 'comprehensiveness' is a matter of degree and purpose, and perhaps some of the series singled out here as 'comprehensive' are no more so than a few that are omitted. See in this connection, Table 13 above.

first type of exception in the present table,[18] and the second
type is limited to the exclusion from price and value series of
cycles accompanying the Civil War and World War I. While
uniformity of the periods covered is highly desirable in close
comparisons between matched series, it is of minor moment
here. Indeed, the demonstration of a consensus among our
comprehensive series may be regarded as all the more striking
when some of the series cover less than 20 and others more
than 70 years.

Another technical blemish is that, despite the defects for
our purposes of so coarse a time unit as a year, we have had to
take Kuznets' estimates of gross national product and national
income in annual form, or go without these most significant of
all comprehensive series. But this cloud also has its silver lining:
cyclical movements in different parts of the economy must
be much alike in timing and direction to shine through the
obscuring veil of annual reporting during so disturbed and
confused a period as that between the two world wars.

Finally, I may point out in very general terms that doubts
can be raised concerning the evidence regarding cyclical behavior given by every series in our sample. (1) Seldom can the
consumer of statistics suppose that the compilers of comprehensive series had accurate information at their disposal. For
example, the actual value of every lot of merchandise ex-
ported, or every contract let for construction, or the liabilities
of every commercial enterprise that fails, can hardly be ascertained by any clerk or field agent, however faithful. (2) In
a few instances, precision is probably approximated very
closely. I know no reason to question the arithmetical cor-

18 However, we confine railroad ton miles to the period since 1904 because of the great secular changes in the cyclical behavior of railroading. See
above, Chart 1, Figures 13–14; and *Measuring Business Cycles*, Ch. 10, Sec.
VIII. Also, in the interests of simplicity, our table blinks a notable shift in
the cyclical behavior of exports. Prior to 1914 exports bore a decidedly irregular relation to business cycles; since then they have conformed well. The
conformity indexes for 1867–1914 are +50, −33, +4; for 1921–38, +100,
+100, +100. The average full-cycle amplitude for the first period is 0.5; for
the second, 63.6.

rectness of the long series on bank clearings in New York City, apart from possible errors of transcription and printing. But doubts of another sort come in. What revisions have been made since the 1850's in the rules concerning items admissible to exchange through the clearing house; how has the volume of clearings been affected by the admission of new banks to membership and by amalgamations among old members; what effects were produced by the creation of the New York Stock Clearing House in 1892 and its reorganization in 1920; what part of the transactions represent financial activities and what part represent industry and trade?[14] (3) When some aggregate or index is built up by combining numerous components, as in making a comprehensive price index or estimating gross national product, problems of weighting arise and introduce new uncertainties. (4) Closely related are the problems of sampling encountered whenever an effort is made to approximate some 'universe' by measuring individual items that are accessible to observation.

To give an adequate account of how all the comprehensive series in Table 31 have been made, of what they cover and of the varying margins of uncertainty surrounding them, would constitute a large and tedious contribution to economic knowledge.[15] How much there is to be known about some of the more significant series may be judged by examining the second volume of Simon Kuznets' *National Income and Its Composition*. Gaining fuller knowledge of the observations of economic processes is one of the sure ways to improve the trustworthiness of our conclusions. But we cannot now extemporize the results of investigations that must be made, if at all, by many men with special access to records and special familiarity with numerous branches of business and government. Only in the fields it is cultivating intensively can the National Bureau go much further than other consumers of statistics toward

---

[14] See the discussion of these matters in Garvy's dissertation, *op. cit.*, Ch. 2.
[15] Many of the series in Table 31 are briefly described in *Historical Statistics of the United States, 1789–1945* (Bureau of the Census, 1949), especially Appendix I which was prepared by Geoffrey H. Moore.

testing the data it draws from reputable sources, public and private. In the present case, we have to take many of the comprehensive series on trust, knowing that they have respectable antecedents and supposing that they represent more or less faithfully what their titles suggest. If we find a large measure of agreement in these fallible efforts to summarize what has typically happened during business cycles in various sectors of the economy over periods that differ considerably, we can argue that the consensus would probably be more notable if the observations were less subject to errors and omissions, and if the periods were more uniform.

III   TYPICAL BEHAVIOR OF COMPREHENSIVE SERIES DURING BUSINESS CYCLES

A   CYCLICAL TIMING

Most basic of all our measures are those concerned with the reference-cycle stages during which a series has typically expanded and the other stages during which it has typically contracted. For the crucial question concerning business cycles, as we define them, is whether there actually have been general tides of expansion and of contraction in the economic activities of nations within which private enterprise prevails during the periods marked off by our reference dates. Unless our timing measures indicate a decided preponderance of expansion in stages I–V, and of contraction in stages V–IX, it is scarcely worth while to examine the reference-cycle patterns or any of their derivatives.

But before we can take seriously our judgments concerning the varieties of timing typical of comprehensive series, we should face the element of circuitous reasoning implicit in our statistical operations. In fixing our reference dates for the United States, we attached considerable importance to the specific-cycle turning dates of certain among the comprehensive series in Table 31. So far as the troughs and peaks in any group of series determined our choice of reference dates, it is a foregone conclusion that the reference-cycle timing of

series in this group will show a regular relation of some sort
to our business-cycle chronology. But we see nothing vicious
in this relation. A series that influences our choice of reference
dates appreciably because it is comprehensive is a series that
represents an appreciable fraction of aggregate activity; its
peaks and troughs therefore contribute appreciably to what
we are seeking to find—the peaks and troughs in aggregate
activity itself. Suppose that we could divide aggregate activity
into 100 components, that we had an excellent time series to
represent each component, that we knew precisely what
weight to assign each series, and that their specific-cycle turns
followed one another in an immutable order. Then we could
fix a superlative set of reference dates, to which each of the
hundred series would bear a predetermined relation. The
degree of intercorrelation between the reference dates and
the specific-cycle turning dates of the series would be at a
maximum, and doubts about the significance of the results at
a minimum.

In Table 4, we found that 43.5 percent of the 794 monthly
or quarterly series of our full American sample typically have
their troughs in stage I and their peaks in stage V, while another
4.8 percent typically have their peaks in I and their troughs in
V. Among the comprehensive series in Table 31, the concentration of cyclical turns on the reference dates is only a little
greater than in the whole sample: 50 instead of 48 percent have
I–V or V–IX timing. But 35 percent of the comprehensive
series as against 15 percent of all series have VIII–IV or VIII–V
timing, and the proportion of series scattered among the other
timing types is smaller in the comprehensive group than in the
full sample.

Thus there is a striking consensus in the direction of movements typical of comprehensive series during the phases of
expansion and contraction, if our judgments of typical timing
are not grievously in error. But this consensus differs significantly from stage to stage, as the schedule in Table 32 shows.

This schedule gives a summary view of a typical business
cycle in the United States as reflected by comprehensive series

Table 32

From Stage I to II
30 of the 34 comprehensive series typically rise.
 2 typically fall: the number and liabilities of failures. Of course, a decline
   in these series means an improvement in business conditions.
 2 series with irregular timing, agricultural marketings and total exports,
   sometimes rise and sometimes fall.

From Stage II to III
29 of the comprehensive series rise.
 3 fall: the two series on failures, and bond sales on the New York Stock
   Exchange.
 2 series with irregular timing sometimes rise and sometimes fall.

From Stage III to IV
28 of the comprehensive series rise.
 4 fall: the two series on failures, bond sales, and bond prices.
 2 series with irregular timing sometimes rise and sometimes fall.

From Stage IV to V
23 series rise, including the liabilities of firms failing—a bad sign.
 9 series fall: the number of failures, bond sales, bond prices, shares sold on
   the New York Stock Exchange, prices of common stocks, bank clearings
   or debits in New York City, Snyder's index of deposits activity, construction contracts let, and corporate security issues as compiled by the *Journal
   of Commerce.*
 2 series with irregular timing sometimes rise and sometimes fall.

From Stage V to VI
 2 series rise: the number and liabilities of failures.
30 series fall.
 2 series with irregular timing sometimes rise and sometimes fall.

From Stage VI to VII
 2½ series rise: the two series on failures, and bond prices in one of the
   timing varieties that seem equally appropriate.
29½ series fall, including bond prices in its alternative timing variety.
 2 series with irregular timing sometimes rise and sometimes fall.

From Stage VII to VIII
 3 series rise: the number of failures, bond prices, and bond sales.
29 series fall, including the liabilities of firms failing.
 2 series with irregular timing sometimes rise and sometimes fall.

From Stage VIII to IX
15 series rise: the number of failures, bond prices, bond sales, shares sold,
   stock prices, 3 series on bank clearings or debits, Snyder's index of
   deposits activity, the A T & T index of business before adjustment for
   trend, total imports, construction contracts let, both our series on security
   issues, and Evans' series on the number of incorporations.
17 series fall, including the liabilities of firms failing.
 2 series with irregular timing sometimes rise and sometimes fall.

[a] Based upon 'expansion stages' in Sec. A of Table 31.

on production, prices, trade, employment, incomes, investments, dealings in securities, business profits and losses, bank
clearings or debits, and finally several indexes of business activity. Fallible as these series may be, they embody a large part of
the most careful and prolonged observations that have been
made by public and private agencies upon economic activities
of numerous sorts over variable periods that stretch back in
one or two instances to the 1850's.

Two of these series have no regular relation in time to the
cyclical tides. For reasons stated in Chapter 5, Section II, farm
crops, and hence a major part of what farmers have to sell, have
irregular cyclical timing. So also do total exports from the
United States before World War I, when exports were dominated largely by agricultural products. Let us put these two
series aside.

Of the 32 remaining monthly or quarterly series, *all* indicate
a bettering of business conditions from stage I to stage II; the
two records of business failures, by declining. Thereafter, the
consensus becomes less complete stage by stage to the culmination of expansion. In stages II–III bond sales begin to drop;
in III–IV bond prices begin to fall; in IV–V the declines are
swelled by prices and sales of stocks, clearings in New York,
two series representing plans for investments, and a business
index especially sensitive to financial operations. Also, the liabilities of failures begin to rise. Thus the tide that had been
rising so generally, becomes confused by crosscurrents in the
last stage of expansion. In the transition from IV–V to V–VI
the mixed condition of affairs gives way to a new unanimity of
movement: except for the two irregulars we have set aside, all
the comprehensive series denote a worsening of business conditions. As contraction continues, countercurrents begin to
develop much as they did in expansion. Now it is bond prices
that give the first signs of recovery, in VI–VII; then in VII–
VIII bond sales, and the liabilities of failures (which begin to
decline); finally in VIII–IX no less than 15 of the 32 series move
upward, including the number of failures, while liabilities fall
further. On this evidence the last stage of contraction is even

more marked by crosscurrents than the last stage of expansion. But this confusion, like that of IV–V, gives place to near unanimity after the tide has turned.[16]

These statements, the reader should bear in mind, are based upon our judgments concerning the 3, 4, or 5 consecutive reference-cycle stages during which a series tends to rise, and the remaining 5, 4, or 3 consecutive stages during which it tends to fall—provided, indeed, that the series exhibits any variety of regular cyclical timing.[17] Average reference-cycle patterns do not always rise in fact during each of the stages that we put down as characteristic of expansion in a series, or fall invariably during each stage put down as characteristic of contraction. Still less do series always behave during individual cycles as their timing varieties suggest. Both sorts of departures from what we deem typical will be examined in the sequel. We are merely putting first our broadest and simplest sketch of business cycles, with the intent of filling in details after the reader has seen where these details belong.

B CONFORMITY TO BUSINESS CYCLES

We noted in Chapter 6 that the wider the range of activities covered by a series, the higher tend to be its indexes of conformity to the cyclical tides, because the broader the coverage of a series the more mutual offsetting will occur among the irregular movements of less than economy-wide incidence that impinge upon it. But we noted also that the relatively long series in our sample have lower conformity indexes on the average than the short series. "Granted the tendency of a series to conform, it is more likely to have a perfect record for 3 or 4 cycles than it is to continue conforming perfectly throughout a run twice or thrice as long." [18] Our comprehensive series, it

16 For further analysis, see the essay "New Facts on Business Cycles", in the *Thirtieth Annual Report* of the National Bureau, May 1950; also Geoffrey H. Moore, "Statistical Indicators of Cyclical Revivals and Recessions", *op. cit.*, Sec. 3 and 6.

17 Perhaps the reader should refresh his memory of how the timing varieties are determined. See Ch. 5, Sec. I.

18 See Ch. 6, Sec. II.

so happens, are decidedly longer on the average than the other series in the full sample. Series covering 10 or more cycles form only 23 percent of the full sample and 62 percent of the comprehensive group.

Perhaps more important than the influence of broad coverage in raising the conformity indexes of the comprehensive group, or the influence of long duration in lowering these indexes, are the more or less accidental differences between the full sample and the comprehensive group in the economic character of the activities represented. For example: the comprehensive group has a relatively larger number of business indexes, which are practically designed to conform perfectly, and no series on inventories, which conform only moderately well on the whole. It has only one series on commodity prices, and that one a close conformer, whereas the full sample has 147 series on commodity prices, with a rather modest record of conformity. Some of the differences in makeup count in the opposite way; for example, the lack of a comprehensive series on new orders from manufacturers—a 17-series group of excellent conformers in the full sample. But on the whole, the differences in economic composition seem to favor higher conformity indexes in the smaller sample.[19]

About the net resultant of the various factors bearing upon the two sets of conformity measures, there can be no doubt. Table 33 makes it clear that, despite their greater average length, the comprehensive series conform better to cyclical expansions, to cyclical contractions, and to business cycles as wholes than do the other series of our sample. If we relied merely upon the evidence of comprehensive series, we would find a more striking consensus in their cyclical movements than we find in our larger and far more detailed sample of series.

C REFERENCE-CYCLE AMPLITUDES

Our basic definition hypothesizes a consensus of cyclical movements in timing and direction only; it says nothing about a

[19] A reader who wishes to make more detailed comparisons between the two samples can cover most of the materials by using Tables 8 and 31.

Table 33

SUMMARIES OF NUMERICAL VALUES OF CONFORMITY INDEXES
OF 34 COMPREHENSIVE SERIES AND OF FULL SAMPLE
OF MONTHLY OR QUARTERLY SERIES[a]

MEDIAN AND QUARTILES OF CONFORMITY INDEXES

	Expansion		Contraction		Business Cycles	
	Comprehensive series	Full sample	Comprehensive series	Full sample	Comprehensive series	Full sample
Upper quartile	100	100	100	100	100	100
Median	100	67	78	60	100	78
Lower quartile	71	45	57	33	85	50

DISTRIBUTION OF INDEXES OF BUSINESS-CYCLE CONFORMITY

	Number of Series		% of Total Number[b]	
Business-Cycle Index	Comprehensive series	Full sample	Comprehensive series	Full sample
100	18	291	52.9	36.7
90-99	5	19	14.7	2.4
80-89	5	70	14.7	8.8
70-79	2	95	5.9	12.0
60-69	2	64	5.9	8.1
50-59	..	73	...	9.2
40-49	..	40	...	5.0
30-39	1	43	2.9	5.4
20-29	1	34	2.9	4.3
10-19	..	36	...	4.5
1- 9	..	12	...	1.5
0	..	17	...	2.1
Total	34	794	100.0	100.0

[a] Based upon Table 6 and Sec. A of Table 31. The conformity indexes are taken without regard to sign.
[b] Failure of detail to total 100 percent is due to rounding.

consensus in amplitudes. What theoretical expectations we entertain regarding the relations among the degrees of expansion or contraction in different parts of a national economy are based upon our conviction that all these parts are interdependent, and that therefore some proportion must be maintained among their changes if the system is to continue functioning. Indeed, this matter of the interrelations among

Table 34

AVERAGES AND QUARTILES OF AMPLITUDES

	Reference-Cycle Amplitude	
	Comprehensive series	*Full sample*
Lower quartile	37	18
Median	48	34
Upper quartile	68	60
Arithmetic mean	59.7	50.7

DISTRIBUTION OF AMPLITUDES

	% of Series[b]	
Reference-Cycle Amplitude	*Comprehensive series*	*Full sample*
0- 9.9	5.9	12.2
10- 19.9	5.9	16.0
20- 29.9	2.9	15.4
30- 39.9	14.7	13.1
40- 49.9	23.5	10.8
50- 59.9	20.6	7.6
60- 69.9	17.6	4.3
70- 79.9	5.9	3.3
80- 89.9	. . .	3.4
90- 99.9	8.8	1.1
100-149.9	2.9	7.3
150-199.9	. . .	2.1
200-249.9	. . .	2.0
250-299.9	. . .	1.3
300-349.9	2.9	0.1
350-399.9	. . .	0.1
400 & over	. . .	0.1
Total	100.0	100.0

[a] The unit of observation is the average full-cycle amplitude of a series, taken without regard to sign. Based upon Tables 10 and 35.
[b] Failure of detail to total 100 percent is due to rounding.

reference-cycle amplitudes may well be a promising clue to follow in searching for explanations of cyclical recessions, and also of revivals.

The last section of Chapter 7 demonstrated that the reference-cycle amplitude of a comprehensive series tends to be lower than the mean amplitude of its component series. Each component has its individual amplitude measured from standings in the peak and trough stages that are characteristic of its own behavior. When these stages differ from one component to another, the peaks of the comprehensive series will not be so high as the correspondingly weighted mean of the individual peaks; nor will the troughs in the comprehensive series be so low as the mean troughs of the components. And our amplitudes are merely differences between average standings at peaks and troughs, when these standings are expressed in percentages of reference-cycle bases.

Yet the amplitudes of our comprehensive series, taken without regard to sign, run on a higher level than those of our full sample. Table 34 shows that the quartiles, medians, and arithmetic means of the small sample of series with wide coverage are all substantially higher than the corresponding measures of the full sample. The explanation appears when we compare the makeup of the two samples as presented in Tables 11 and 31, or better Table 35. The groups with mean amplitudes below 25 points in Table 11 (bond yields, production of foodstuffs, employment in factories making perishable goods, hours of work per week, rates of pay, prices of semidurable goods, and prices of farm products and foods) are represented sketchily if at all in the sample of comprehensive series. On the other hand, this sample is relatively strong in series that represent financial operations concerned with investments, dealings in stocks, business failures, and profits. Not our choice so much as the availability of data is responsible for these differences between the two samples.

A second comparison between the two samples in Table 34 concerns the range covered by the reference-cycle amplitudes from lowest to highest, and the degree of concentration

Table 35

ARRAY OF AVERAGE REFERENCE-CYCLE AMPLITUDES OF COMPREHENSIVE SERIES[a]

Series	Average Amplitude Expansion	Contraction	Full cycle
Agricultural marketings	+1.4	−0.8	+2.2
Bond prices	−3.5	+6.4	−9.9
Exports	+15	−1	+16
Prices, wholesale	+9	−9	+18
Department store sales	+16	−10	+26
Deposits activity	+14	−17	+31
Business index, Ayres	+17	−19	+36
Wholesale trade sales	+18	−19	+37
Bank clearings outside N.Y. City	+26	−11	+37
Incorporations	+27	−10	+37
Production of fuels	+26	−15	+40
Income payments	+23	−18	+40
Imports	+26	−19	+45
Factory employment	+22	−23	+45
Business index, Persons	+22	−23	+45
Common stock prices	+27	−20	+47
Failures, no.	−22	+26	−48
Business index, A T & T, adj.	+23	−25	+48
Bond sales	−15	+35	−50
Business index, Axe-Houghton	+29	−21	+50
R.R. freight ton miles	+28	−23	+51
Bank clearings, total	+30	−21	+51
Business index, Babson	+29	−23	+52
Business index, A T & T	+32	−23	+55
Bank clearings, N.Y. City	+32	−28	+60
Industrial production	+35	−32	+68
Construction contracts	+43	−30	+74
Factory payrolls	+36	−40	+76
Shares traded	+41	−36	+77
Security issues	+47	−46	+93
Cash from issues on N.Y. Stock Exchange	+58	−39	+97
Pig iron production	+54	−45	+99
Failures, liabilities	−67	+59	−125
Net corporate profits	+169	−175	+343

[a] Based upon Table 31, Sec. A. For fuller titles, see that table.

around the central tendencies of the two arrays. One of the comprehensive series has an amplitude close to zero while another runs above 300, so that in range covered the smaller sample virtually matches the larger. But there is a considerable contrast in the distribution of the two arrays, arising mainly from the above-mentioned paucity of comprehensive series with low amplitudes.

Finally, Table 35 lists the comprehensive series in the order of their mean amplitudes. Low amplitude measures may be due primarily to irregular timing, as in agricultural marketings and exports, or to inherent steadiness. Thus the prices of the railroad bonds collected by Frederick R. Macaulay, and adjusted for gradual improvement in quality, have been notably more stable than common stocks or even commodity prices at wholesale. The comprehensive indexes support our previous conclusion based upon more carefully matched evidence that these commodity prices in turn are subject to less violent cyclical fluctuations than industrial output.[20] At the higher end of the range we find the most volatile form of income—net profits of business enterprises—and various indicators of plans for investing capital, producing investment goods, and trading in securities. In the middle range, say reference-cycle amplitudes of 25 to 75, come the indicators of mass production and mercantile distribution of commodities, employment, and the payment of incomes to persons, together with some financial operations closely connected with the mass flow of goods through the economy, and all the indexes specifically designed by statisticians to measure business or industrial activity.

Simple and reasonable as this summary sounds, the table presents puzzles aplenty. For example: how comes it that our index of retail purchases has an amplitude of only 26, while income payments rise and fall by 40 percent? If industrial production has a typical amplitude of 68, wholesale prices have one of 18, and the two sets of movements are positively correlated, why do not outside clearings rise and fall by more than 37 percent? Why does the number of incorporations rise and fall less than the number of business failures fall and rise? The time has not yet come to attempt answers to these questions and others like them that may arise in the reader's mind; but it is well to realize now that our statistical findings are piling up,

[20] See Ch. 7, Sec. IVF.

not merely a bulky mass of factual evidence, but also a host of problems that we must eventually face.

D REFERENCE-CYCLE PATTERNS

What we have learned about the cyclical timing, conformity, and amplitude of the comprehensive series tells us much about their reference-cycle patterns. The dominance of I–V timing and of close conformity assures us that most of these patterns will rise from reference-cycle troughs to peaks, then decline to the terminal troughs. The considerable divergences among amplitudes suggest that the standings of the 34 series at stages I, V, and IX will cover a rather wide range. At the intermediate stages the scatter will presumably be less, though still appreciable. These differences among the standings at successive stages will be augmented by the presence in our comprehensive sample of two series with irregular timing, three that are inverted, and larger numbers that have leads of one or two stages at one or both turns. They will be augmented also by divergences among the intracycle trends. Thus, when the reference-cycle patterns of our comprehensive series are assembled in a single table, we should get the impression of tidal movements that sweep over the economy as a whole but that are no more uniform in its various parts than the oceanic tides are uniform in all ports.

How well Table 36 confirms these expectations, the reader can see for himself. No one will doubt the dominance of a common pattern in the stage-by-stage arrays. Unless the comprehensive series grossly misrepresent the activities suggested by their titles, we can say in the language of our basic definition that expansions occur "at about the same time in many economic activities, followed by similarly general recessions, contractions, and revivals". But at no stage of the cycle are the movements wholly unanimous in direction; still less do different activities expand or contract in the same degree. These minority divergences in direction of change and the pervasive differences in amplitude are no less characteristic traits of business cycles than the common features stressed by our definition,

Table 36

STAGE-BY-STAGE DISTRIBUTION OF AVERAGE REFERENCE-CYCLE STANDINGS OF 34 MONTHLY OR QUARTERLY COMPREHENSIVE SERIES[a]

Reference-Cycle Standing	Percentage of Series Having Indicated Standing in Stage								
	I	II	III	IV	V	VI	VII	VIII	IX
190-199.9	....	....	....	....	2.9	....	....	....	....
180-189.9	....	....	....	2.9	....	....	....	....	....
170-179.9	....	....	....	....	....	....	....	....	....
160-169.9	....	....	....	....	....	....	....	....	....
150-159.9	....	....	....	....	....	2.9	....	....	....
140-149.9	....	....	....	....	....	....	....	....	....
130-139.9	....	....	2.9	....	....	....	2.9	....	....
120-129.9	....	....	....	5.9	14.7	8.8	....	....	....
110-119.9	....	5.9	5.9	20.6	47.1	26.5	....	5.9	5.9
100-109.9	8.8	8.8	64.7	64.7	26.5	47.1	47.1	8.8	11.8
90- 99.9	26.5	79.4	23.5	....	2.9	8.8	44.1	55.9	58.8
80- 89.9	55.9	5.9	2.9	2.9	5.9	5.9	2.9	20.6	17.6
70- 79.9	5.9	....	....	2.9	....	....	2.9	5.9	2.9
60- 69.9	....	....	....	....	....	....	....	....	....
50- 59.9	....	....	....	....	....	....	....	....	....
40- 49.9	....	....	....	....	....	....	....	....	....
30- 39.9	2.9	....	....	....	....	....	....	2.9	....
20- 29.9	....	....	....	....	....	....	....	....	2.9
Total[b]	100.0	100.0	100.0	100.0	100.0	100.0	100.0	100.0	100.0

SUMMARIES OF DISTRIBUTIONS

	I	II	III	IV	V	VI	VII	VIII	IX
Highest standing	109.1	113.3	134.8	182.4	199.2	151.3	135.4	118.5	115.4
Next to highest standing	107.8	111.8	119.2	125.9	127.1	121.6	107.8	110.2	112.2
Upper quartile	91.7	98.8	103.7	111.7	114.9	111.5	102.9	98.9	98.7
Median	87.3	95.4	101.6	108.8	112.0	108.0	99.9	92.8	94.2
Lower quartile	85.0	93.4	99.6	104.8	107.1	104.6	96.3	89.4	90.8
Next to lowest standing	70.5	89.0	93.3	87.1	86.1	89.6	89.6	77.7	79.8
Lowest standing	30.4	88.9	86.4	76.6	85.3	89.1	78.4	35.2	24.6
Range									
Full	78.7	24.4	48.4	105.8	113.9	62.2	57.0	83.3	90.8
Excl. both extreme items	37.3	22.8	25.9	38.8	41.0	32.0	18.2	32.5	32.4
Interquartile	6.7	5.4	4.1	6.9	7.8	6.9	6.6	9.5	7.9
No. of series with standings of									
100 or higher	3	5	25	32	31	29	17	5	6
Under 100	31	29	9	2	3	5	17	29	28

[a] Based upon Table 31, Sec. B.
[b] Failure of detail to total 100 percent is due to rounding.

and illustrated by the present table among many others. Indeed, the rather wide ranges covered by the arrays of reference-cycle standings and their shifts from stage to stage are among the most significant features of the exhibit.

Nor are these differences in standings, or the stage-by-stage shifts in the ranges they cover, inscrutable results of chance. We know in advance much about the types of activity that will hold very low or very high rankings in the arrays for stages I, V, and IX; we can foretell something about the rankings of these series at stages intermediate between troughs and peaks; we can even formulate certain expectations concerning the nature of the series that will occupy middle positions in the arrays.

The series that have very low standings at stage I tend to have very high rankings at stage V; for these series are predominantly characterized by large reference-cycle amplitudes, I–V timing, and close conformity. Rapidly rising intracycle trends also tend to produce low standings at I and high standings at V; but this influence is usually of secondary moment. However, rising trends often suffice to prevent series that stand high at V from standing as low at IX as they stood at I.

Similarly, the series that stand very high at stage I tend to rank low at V. Their characteristics are like those which produce low standings at I and high at V, except that V–IX takes the place of I–V timing, and falling take the place of rising intracycle trends. But inversion is not very common— less than 10 percent of all our series are inverted, and only 3 of the 34 comprehensive series. As many or more of the high rankings at I and low rankings at V are due to irregular timing, or to very low amplitudes combined with trends that decline or approach the horizontal. For the reference-cycle patterns of irregular series tend to approximate straight lines, that is, a set of values that differ from 100 only as the intracycle trend makes the later stages somewhat higher (or lower) than the earlier ones. Any series that stands close to 100 at stage I will have a high rank in the array for that stage, and any that stands close to 100 at stage V will then rank low. Similar remarks apply to series with very narrow cyclical amplitudes: whatever their timing, their standings at the reference-cycle peaks and troughs will not differ much from 100, and so will rank high at the troughs, low at the peaks.

It is harder to specify what types of series will occupy middle positions in the array at stage I or, for that matter, at any of the later stages; for the central parts of these arrays are much more densely populated than their outer parts, and small, accidental differences in standing may produce considerable differences in ranking. However, we can lay down three or four rules. (1) Series that have some claim to represent changes in business or industrial activity at large are likely to have I–V timing or a nearly related variant, close conformity, and medium amplitudes. Hence their reference-cycle standings should hover in and about the central portions of the range covered by the full arrays of reference-cycle standings in successive stages. This rule covers not only business indexes specifically designed by competent statisticians to represent (as best may be) the cyclical fluctuations of the whole economy, but also such series as total movements of freight, total volume of payments effected through banks, total number of factory employees, total income payments to individuals, and even total imports. (2) The series we have already noticed that tend to stand very low at stage I, very high at stage V, and low again at IX have to work their way up through the economy during the successive stages of expansion, and slide down again during the stages of contraction. Hence some of these series belonging to the 'prince or pauper' class are likely to find themselves temporarily in a middling position at stage II, III, IV, VI, VII, or VIII. (3) Similarly, the series that stand very high at the troughs and low at the peaks of business cycles sometimes approximate the median position at an intermediate stage, as they recede in relative position during expansion or climb upward again during contraction. (4) The effects of these dominant factors upon the ranking of series at successive stages are more or less tangled by leads or lags (which create most con-

Table 37

COMPREHENSIVE SERIES HAVING VERY LOW, MIDDLE, AND
VERY HIGH AVERAGE STANDINGS AT THE
NINE STAGES OF REFERENCE CYCLES[a]

Stage I

	Standing
VERY LOW STANDING	
Net corporate profits	30.4
Pig iron production	70.5
Construction contracts	78.3
Cash from issues on N.Y. Stock Exchange	80.7
MIDDLE STANDING	
Factory payrolls	86.9
Production of fuels	87.3
R.R. freight ton miles	87.3
Imports	87.9
Business index, A T & T, adj.	88.4
VERY HIGH STANDING	
Bond sales	98.9
Agricultural marketings	100.2
Failures, no.	107.8
Failures, liabilities	109.1

Stage II

	Standing
VERY LOW STANDING	
Pig iron production	88.9
Failures, liabilities	89.0
Incorporations	90.6
Bank clearings outside N.Y. City	91.8
MIDDLE STANDING	
Bank clearings, total	95.0
Construction contracts	95.3
Exports	95.5
Common stock prices	96.1
Factory employment	96.4
VERY HIGH STANDING	
Deposits activity	102.1
Agricultural marketings	102.3
Bond sales	111.8
Shares traded	113.3

Stage III

	Standing
VERY LOW STANDING	
Failures, liabilities	86.4
Failures, no.	93.3
Production of fuels	93.8
Bank clearings outside N.Y. City	97.7
MIDDLE STANDING	
Imports	101.3
Bank clearings, total	101.4
Bond prices	101.7
Pig iron production	101.9
Industrial production	102.5
VERY HIGH STANDING	
Shares traded	108.7
Construction contracts	110.1
Security issues	119.2
Net corporate profits	134.8

Stage IV

	Standing
VERY LOW STANDING	
Failures, liabilities	76.6
Failures, no.	87.1
Bond prices	101.1
Exports	102.1
MIDDLE STANDING	
Business index, Persons	108.4
Business index, A T & T	108.7
Income payments	108.9
Wholesale trade sales	109.0
R.R. freight ton miles	109.0
VERY HIGH STANDING	
Bank clearings, N.Y. City	114.9
Construction contracts	123.5
Security issues	125.9
Net corporate profits	182.4

Stage V

	Standing
VERY LOW STANDING	
Failures, liabilities	85.3
Failures, no.	86.1
Bond prices	98.9
Bond sales	100.4
MIDDLE STANDING	
Business index, Persons	111.0
Business index, A T & T, adj.	111.6
Bank clearings, total	112.3
Factory employment	112.7
Income payments	112.7
VERY HIGH STANDING	
Factory payrolls	123.1
Pig iron production	124.7
Construction contracts	127.1
Net corporate profits	199.2

Table 37 (concl.)

Stage VI	Standing	Stage VIII	Standing
VERY LOW STANDING		**VERY LOW STANDING**	
Failures, no.	89.1	Net corporate profits	35.2
Bond sales	89.6	Shares traded	77.7
Shares traded	95.0	Security issues	79.8
Bond prices	97.9	Cash from issues on N.Y.	
		Stock Exchange	81.1
MIDDLE STANDING			
Business index, Persons	107.8	**MIDDLE STANDING**	
Bank clearings, total	108.0	Factory employment	92.1
Business index, A T & T, adj.	108.1	R.R. freight ton miles	92.6
Bank clearings outside		Business index, Babson	92.9
N.Y. City	109.4	Business index, Axe-Houghton	93.1
Business index, Babson	109.6	Construction contracts	93.2
VERY HIGH STANDING		**VERY HIGH STANDING**	
Failures, liabilities	120.0	Agricultural marketings	102.3
Factory payrolls	120.3	Exports	103.0
Pig iron production	121.6	Failures, no.	110.2
Net corporate profits	151.3	Failures, liabilities	118.5

Stage VII	Standing	Stage IX	Standing
		VERY LOW STANDING	
VERY LOW STANDING		Net corporate profits	24.6
Net corporate profits	78.4	Pig iron production	79.8
Shares traded	89.6	Factory payrolls	83.2
Security issues	90.8	Business index, A T & T, adj.	87.1
Bank clearings, N.Y. City	92.4		
		MIDDLE STANDING	
MIDDLE STANDING		Common stock prices	92.9
Imports	99.7	Security issues	94.1
Business index, A T & T	99.7	Cash from issues on N.Y.	
Prices, wholesale	100.1	Stock Exchange	94.2
Incorporations	100.3	Income payments	95.1
Business index, Babson	100.6	Shares traded	95.6
VERY HIGH STANDING		**VERY HIGH STANDING**	
Failures, no.	105.7	Incorporations	104.2
Exports	107.2	Failures, liabilities	107.2
Production of fuels	107.8	Failures, no.	112.2
Failures, liabilities	135.4	Bond sales	115.4

* Based upon Sec. B of Table 31. See that table for fuller titles of series.

fusion around the cyclical turns), by differences among intra-cycle trends, and by random movements, that we may or may not be able to explain.

Indications of the net outcome of these various influences that determine the relative standings of our comprehensive

Table 38

STAGES IN WHICH COMPREHENSIVE SERIES
HAVE EXTREME AND MIDDLE STANDINGS[a]

Series	Very Low in Stages	Middling in Stages	Very High in Stages
Failures, liabilities	II,III,IV,V	...	I,VI,VII,VIII,IX
Net corporate profits	I,VII,VIII,IX	...	III,IV,V,VI
Failures, no.	III,IV,V,VI	...	I,VII,VIII,IX
Pig iron production	I,II,IX	III	V,VI
Shares traded	VI,VII,VIII	IX	II,III
Bond sales	V,VI	...	I,II,IX
Construction contracts	I	II,VIII	III,IV,V
Security issues	VII,VIII	IX	III,IV
Agricultural marketings	...	...	I,II,VIII
Exports	IV	II	VII,VIII
Factory payrolls	IX	I	V,VI
Bond prices	IV,V,VI	III	...
Production of fuels	III	I	VII
Cash from issues on N.Y. Stock Exchange	I,VIII	IX	...
Incorporations	II	VII	IX
Bank clearings, N.Y. City	VII	...	IV
Bank clearings outside N.Y. City	II,III	VI	...
Business index, A T & T, adj.	IX	I,V,VI	...
Deposits activity	...	...	II
Bank clearings, total	...	II,III,V,VI	...
R.R. freight ton miles	...	I,IV,VIII	...
Imports	...	I,III,VII	...
Factory employment	...	II,V,VIII	...
Income payments	...	IV,V,IX	...
Business index, Persons	...	IV,V,VI	...
Business index, Babson	...	VI,VII,VIII	...
Common stock prices	...	II,IX	...
Business index, A T & T	...	IV,VII	...
Industrial production	...	III	...
Prices, wholesale	...	VII	...
Wholesale trade sales	...	IV	...
Business index, Axe-Houghton	...	VIII	...

[a] Based upon Table 37.

series are supplied by Tables 37 and 38. The full array of 34
series might be presented for each of the nine stages, but that
would make the tables very bulky. Our skeleton arrays enable
the reader to trace for himself the most striking migrations of
series that start at the bottom, work their way to the top, then

fall back to the lowest rank, and the opposite migrations from top rank to lowest, and back to the top. Table 38 makes it especially easy to follow the cyclical fortunes of individual series.

It is interesting to note that all but 2 of our comprehensive series appear at some stage in one of the 4 very low, the 5 middle, or the 4 very high positions. The exceptions are depart-ment store sales and Ayres' index of business activity. One series (the liabilities of firms that fail) ranks among the lowest or the highest 4 in each of the 9 stages. Two more series, corpo-rate profits and the number of firms failing, appear in the top or bottom groups of 8 stages. Fifteen times series that are moving out of or into one of the extreme positions find them-selves in one of the middle positions; but 30 times these middle positions are occupied by series that have at no time ranked very high or very low.

Thus our comprehensive series picture the American econ-omy as expanding rather vigorously on the average between the months we have selected to mark the troughs of business cycles and the months selected to mark the next peaks; then contracting somewhat less than they had expanded between the peak dates and the next later months selected to mark cyclical troughs. But these movements differ so widely in amplitude from one series to another that the course of business cycles cannot well be represented by a single line, however many factors have been considered in drawing it. The very essence of the phenomenon is omitted unless the chart of busi-ness cycles contains numerous lines that indicate the wide differences among the rates at which, and also some of the differences in the times at which, various elements in the economy expand and contract. For, unless these divergencies in cyclical behavior are pictured by fit symbols, we have no suggestion of the basic business-cycle problem: how an eco-nomic system of interrelated parts develops internal stresses during expansions, stresses that bring on recessions, and how the uneven contractions of its varied parts pave the way for revivals.

The tables of this section go far beyond assuring us that a large majority of economic activities fluctuate in unison; they tell us also some of the systematic changes these activities undergo in relation to one another as the cycle progresses from stage to stage and phase to phase. Table 37 makes these cyclical alterations in the proportions of the economic system concrete by naming in each of the nine stages some of the factors that are relatively most shrunken, relatively most bloated, and relatively nearest to the median condition of the other comprehensive series. On the basis of what these series can be made to tell, we could go some distance toward describing what happens during business cycles. And we could attempt to explain these cycles by the interlocking developments that the present evidence reveals. But, significant as this evidence is, the full sample, which includes the few comprehensive series used here and much besides, provides a far better basis for description and analysis. Also, the measures most effective for describing and analyzing a continuous process are not average standings during certain months, but rather the average rates of change per month from stage to stage of reference cycles. To avoid confusion with the intervals we have been calling stages and yet be concise, the second set of intervals (from the middle of stage I to the middle of stage II, from the middle of II to the middle of III, and so on) will be called reference-cycle 'segments'.

E   RATES OF CHANGE DURING SUCCESSIVE SEGMENTS OF REFERENCE CYCLES

The average rates of change from stage to stage of the reference cycles are closely related to the average standings with which we have been dealing; they are made by subtracting the average standing of a series during one reference-cycle stage from its average standing in the following stage, and dividing the difference by the average number of months between the middle of the earlier and the middle of the later stage. Both the average standings and the average rates of change per month are expressed in percentages of reference-cycle bases; but of course the standings run on a much higher level than the rates of change. In each cycle the monthly standings must average 100; there is no 'must' about the rates of change per month. Empirically we find that, among our comprehensive series, these rates range from −11.4 to +11.8; disregarding signs they equal or exceed 1 percent of the reference-cycle bases per month more often than they fall short of 1 percent per month.[21] Running on so low a level, these measures are subject to average deviations much smaller absolutely than the deviations of the standings, but the deviations of the rates of change are large in relation to their own mean values.[22] Other characteristics are brought out in Table 39, which corresponds in general to Table 36 for the reference-cycle standings.

As summarized here, the average rates of change per month merely exhibit the consensus among the characteristic cyclical movements of our comprehensive series in a fresh fashion. A large majority of the series rise in segments I–II to IV–V; a slightly smaller but still large majority fall in segments V–VI to VII–VIII; only when the tide is turning in VIII–IX is the majority narrow (19 series fall, 15 rise). If we reversed the signs of the two series on commercial failures, as we well might, the consensus would be still more emphatic. The rates as well as the directions of change seem rather orderly for the most part, decidedly so if we exclude the most volatile pair of series —net profits of corporations and the liabilities of commercial failures, which provide 6 of the 8 entries exceeding ±5.0 percent per month and 12 of the 32 entries exceeding ±2.5 percent. Half or more of the entries in each segment fall within a range that is never more and usually less than 1.3 percent. If we take the band across Table 39 between +1.9 and −1.9 percent per month we include more than four-fifths of the

[21] According to Table 39, the 34 comprehensive series equal or exceed a change of 1 percent monthly 149 times and fall short of that level 123 times. The arithmetic mean rate computed without regard to sign is 1.39 percent of reference-cycle bases.

[22] The reader who wishes to experiment with the two sets of average deviations of the comprehensive series will find convenient data in Sections B and C of Table 31.

Table 39

SEGMENT-BY-SEGMENT DISTRIBUTION OF AVERAGE RATES OF CHANGE
IN 34 MONTHLY OR QUARTERLY COMPREHENSIVE SERIES[a]

AVERAGE CHANGE PER MONTH	I-II	II-III	III-IV	IV-V	V-VI	VI-VII	VII-VIII	VIII-IX
	% OF SERIES MOVING AT INDICATED RATE DURING SEGMENT							
+11.9 to +11.0	2.9	....	....	....	....	....	....	....
+10.9 to +10.0	....	....	....	....	....	....	....	....
+9.9 to +9.0	....	....	....	....	2.9	....	....	....
+8.9 to +8.0	....	....	....	....	....	....	....	....
+7.9 to +7.0	....	....	....	....	....	....	....	....
+6.9 to +6.0	2.9	....	....	....	....	....	....	....
+5.9 to +5.0	....	....	2.9	....	....	....	....	2.9
+4.9 to +4.0	2.9	2.9	....	....	....	....	....	2.9
+3.9 to +3.0	5.9	....	....	2.9	....	....	....	2.9
+2.9 to +2.0	23.5	2.9	....	8.8	....	5.9	....	2.9
+1.9 to +1.0	41.2	29.4	50.0	23.5	....	....	....	11.8
+0.9 to 0.0	14.7	50.0	35.3	41.2	5.9	11.8	11.8	20.6
−0.1 to −0.9	....	11.8	8.8	17.6	41.2	11.8	35.3	44.1
−1.0 to −1.9	2.9	2.9	2.9	2.9	29.4	52.9	38.2	5.9
−2.0 to −2.9	....	....	....	2.9	5.9	5.9	11.8	5.9
−3.0 to −3.9	....	....	....	....	11.8	8.8	....	....
−4.0 to −4.9	2.9	....	....	....	....	....	....	....
−5.0 to −5.9	....	....	....	....	....	....	....	....
−6.0 to −6.9	....	....	....	....	....	....	2.9	....
−7.0 to −7.9	....	....	....	....	....	....	....	....
−8.0 to −8.9	....	....	....	....	....	....	....	....
−9.0 to −9.9	....	....	....	....	....	....	....	....
−10.0 to −10.9	....	....	....	....	2.9	....	....	....
−11.0 to −11.9	....	....	....	....	....	2.9	....	....
Total[b]	100.0	100.0	100.0	100.0	100.0	100.0	100.0	100.0

SUMMARIES OF DISTRIBUTIONS

Fastest rise	+11.8	+4.4	+5.5	+3.0	+9.0	+2.9	+0.9	+5.1
Next to fastest rise	+6.6	+2.5	+1.6	+2.3	+0.8	+2.6	+0.8	+4.2
Upper quartile	+2.2	+1.0	+1.2	+1.3	−0.3	−0.7	−0.6	+0.6
Median	+1.65	+0.75	+1.00	+0.60	−0.95	−1.40	−1.10	−0.20
Lower quartile	+1.1	+0.3	+0.4	0.0	−1.3	−1.8	−1.7	−0.5
Next to fastest fall	−1.3	−0.6	−0.8	−1.1	−3.9	−3.3	−2.8	−2.3
Fastest fall	−4.1	−1.1	−1.3	−2.7	−10.7	−11.4	−6.8	−2.9
Range								
Full	15.9	5.5	6.8	5.7	19.7	14.3	7.7	8.0
Excl. both extreme items	7.9	3.1	2.4	3.4	4.7	5.9	3.6	6.5
Interquartile	1.1	0.7	0.8	1.3	1.0	1.1	1.1	1.1

Table 39 (concl.)

	I- II	II- III	III- IV	IV- V	V- VI	VI- VII	VII- VIII	VIII- IX
Arithmetic mean								
With regard to sign	+1.93	+0.78	+0.86	+0.65	−1.12	−1.39	−1.19	+0.27
Without regard to sign	2.25	0.94	1.04	0.97	1.72	1.80	1.31	1.09
No. of series that								
Rise	32	29	30	25°	3	6	4	15
Fall	2	5	4	8°	31	28	30	19
No. of series in which change								
Equals or exceeds 1% per month	29	13	19	14	18	26	18	12
Is less than 1% per month	5	21	15	20	16	8	16	22

ᵃ Based upon Table 31, Sec. C. The rates of change are expressed in reference-cycle relatives.

ᵇ Failure of detail to total 100 percent is due to rounding.

ᶜ One series remains constant.

entries. But all this is merely saying again what has already been said once or twice in other terms about the general dominance of a common cyclical pattern in the movements of our comprehensive series.

What Table 39 adds to our knowledge concerns a feature of business cycles that is revealed by our reference-cycle patterns but may not have caught the reader's attention. In Chart 7 it is easy to see that most of the reference-cycle patterns rise less steeply in segment II–III than in I–II. In segments III–IV or IV–V a goodly proportion of the series show a partial recovery from this retardation; in general, however, the pace of expansion slackens before recession sets in. During contraction a somewhat different pattern prevails. Declines dominate the economy from the peak to the trough; but the fall accelerates somewhat in the second segment of contraction, whereas the rise is much retarded in the second segment of expansion. Then VII–VIII brings a moderate retardation, whereas III–IV brought a moderate reacceleration. Finally VIII–IX is like IV–V in that the rate of change becomes slower; but this retardation is much more marked at the end of contraction than at the end of expansion.

Thus the notions often suggested by the picturesque phrasing beloved of writers upon 'booms and busts'—that prosperity grows at a dizzier pace the longer it lasts, and that slumps gather momentum as they proceed—are wrong if our measures are right. Scarcely less misleading are the implications of the mathematical constructions often used to represent business cycles. A set of straight lines sloping upward to represent expansion, connected at a sharp peak with downward sloping straight lines to represent contraction, misrepresents the facts in that the pace of change is pictured as uniform between trough and peak, and likewise between peak and trough, whereas in fact the pace changes from segment to segment in ways that recur in cycle after cycle, as will be shown more clearly below (Sec. F). Sine curves are not less objectionable; they place the fastest rate of change in the middle of expansion and of contraction. What our observations suggest is that the shapes of business cycles are phenomena *sui generis*.

While the quartiles, medians, and arithmetic means of Table 39 give us a clearer view of these changes in pace as well as in direction of movement than any of our earlier exhibits, Table 40 leads to a more intimate view. In this table the characteristic cyclical movement of each of our 34 comprehensive series during each segment of business cycles is compared with its behavior during the subsequent segment. The entries are to be read as follows: During reference-cycle segment I–II, 32 of our comprehensive series rise and 2 fall. In segment II–III, 1 of the 32 series that had risen in the preceding segment continues to rise at the same rate; 28 series continue to rise, but more slowly, while 3 of the series that had risen in I–II now fall. Finally, the 2 series that had fallen in segment I–II (the number and liabilities of commercial failures) fall further in segment II–III but more slowly. Thus, while business conditions con-

Table 40

CHANGE FROM SEGMENT TO SEGMENT OF REFERENCE CYCLES IN THE TYPICAL DIRECTION AND RATE OF MOVEMENT OF 34 MONTHLY OR QUARTERLY COMPREHENSIVE SERIES[a]

NO. OF SERIES THAT CHANGE DURING GIVEN AND FOLLOWING SEGMENTS IN THE WAY INDICATED

Behavior during Given Segment	Following Segment	Segments I-II	Segments II-III	Segments III-IV	Segments IV-V	Segments V-VI	Segments VI-VII	Segments VII-VIII	Segments VIII-IX
Rise	*(no. of series)*	*32*	*29*	*30*	*25*	*3*	*6*	*4*	*15*
	Rise faster	0	16	12	1	1	0	2	9
	Rise same rate	1	4	1	0	0	2	0	1
	Rise slower	28	8	11	1	2	2	1	4
	No change	0	0	1	0	0	0	0	0
	Fall	3	1	5	23	0	2	1	1
No change	*(no. of series)*	*0*	*0*	*0*	*1*	*0*	*0*	*0*	*0*
	Rise	0	0	0	0	0	0	0	0
	No change	0	0	0	0	0	0	0	0
	Fall	0	0	0	1	0	0	0	0
Fall	*(no. of series)*	*2*	*5*	*4*	*8*	*31*	*28*	*30*	*19*
	Rise	0	2	1	1	3	0	12	18
	No change	0	0	0	0	0	0	0	0
	Fall slower	2	1	2	1	5	20	15	0
	Fall same rate	0	0	0	0	2	2	1	0
	Fall faster	0	2	1	6	21	6	2	1

[a] Based upon Table 31, Sec. C.

tinue to improve during the second segment of reference cycles, according to our comprehensive series the rate of improvement becomes slower. For none of these series rise faster in II–III than in I–II: 1 rises at the same rate, 28 rise more slowly, while in 3 series the retardation goes to the length of producing a fall; even the two series on bankruptcies are retarded in their decline.

What happens during business cycles, as represented by comprehensive series, is summed up by the following schedule of the developments shown by Tables 31, 39, and 40.

Segment I–II

All 34 of the comprehensive series indicate that business conditions are improving. The 2 series on failures give this indication by falling. The average rate of improvement, as shown by the median, quartiles, and arithmetic means, is more rapid than at any other stage of the cycle.

Segment II–III

Business continues to expand, but the rate of improvement suffers a sharp and general retardation. The only comprehensive series that escapes this setback is bond prices, which continue to rise at the same rate as in I–II. The 2 series on failures fall more slowly; 28 series rise more slowly; 3 series that rose in I–II now fall—the number of bonds and of shares sold on the New York Stock Exchange, both of which led the revival, and agricultural marketings, a series with irregular timing.

Segment III–IV

Reacceleration is the rule as expansion continues; but the pace of advance, while faster than in II–III, does not regain the speed of I–II. Of the 29 comprehensive series that rose in II–III, 16 now rise faster; 4 rise at the same rate (wholesale prices, stock prices, and 2 indexes of business conditions); 8 are further retarded (iron production, exports, factory employment, total contracts for construction, both our series on security issues, and a pair of business indexes), while 1 series begins to

fall (bond prices). It will be noted that these further retarda-
tions are largely in series that represent investments. Finally,
the 5 series that fell in II–III show an even more mixed state of
affairs in III–IV: agricultural marketings and shares sold on the
Stock Exchange rise again; the number of failures goes on
falling but more slowly; bond sales and the liabilities of failures
go on falling but at a faster rate.

Segment IV–V

While the business tide continues to rise during IV–V, it becomes fuller of eddies. More series fall than in any earlier
segment of expansion: the list includes the *Journal of Commerce* series on corporate issues, sales on the Stock Exchange
of both bonds and stocks, also their prices, bank clearings in
New York which are much influenced by security transactions, and the number of failures. Quite as ominous as any of
the declines is the rise in the liabilities of failures. All these
declines, be it noted, and also the threatening rise, occur in
financial activities rather than in those concerned immediately
with the production and distribution of goods. True, agricultural marketings decline slightly, but our averages for this
irregular series do not express typical behavior. Further, of the
24 series that rise in both III–IV and IV–V, almost half rise at
slower rates in the later segment. The retarded series include
wholesale and retail sales, imports, income payments, construction contracts, incorporations, profits, total clearings, clearings outside New York (as noted above, New York clearings
fall), and a couple of business indexes. Snyder's index of deposits activity ceases to rise. The series that rise at higher rates
include our indexes of production, transportation, prices, factory employment, payrolls, Ayres' series on issues of securities,
3 business indexes, and exports—the last an irregular series.
There is a suggestion here that the accumulating financial
difficulties are accompanied (perhaps in part produced) by
a slower growth of distribution to consumers at the same
time that physical output is growing faster. But there are
conflicts of evidence (for example, between Ayres and the

Journal of Commerce regarding issues of securities) and the evidence is far from complete.

Segment V–VI

In comparison with segment IV–V the situation becomes clearer immediately after recession. Apart from exports (an irregular series as already noted), the pair on failures are the only comprehensive series that rise. Of those that had begun to fall before the peak, most now fall at a faster rate.

Segment VI–VII

Whereas the second segment of expansion was dominated by retardation of the rise then in progress, the second segment of contraction is dominated by acceleration of the fall. Aside from failures, the only series to rise are the irregularly timed agricultural marketings and exports, bond sales on the Stock Exchange, and bond prices. This recuperating interest in bonds may be called the first sign of reviving investments; it may also be called a sign that investors are trying to minimize risks rather than to maximize incomes.

Segment VII–VIII

One notable improvement comes in the realm of finance: the liabilities, though not the number, of failing firms fall rather sharply, which may mean that the process of 'liquidation' has passed its most explosive stage and may presently begin working its drastic cures. Bond sales and prices continue to rise at the same rates as in VI–VII, but one of our irregulars (exports) at last begins to fall. In short, the business situation continues to get worse, but it gets worse at a slower rate. That is the story of the various averages presented in Table 39, while Table 40 shows that 20 of the 28 series that fell in VI–VII fall more slowly in VII–VIII.

Segment VIII–IX

If our comprehensive series can be trusted, and that is not a foregone conclusion, revival is a more gradual change than recession. In the last segment of expansion only 8 series fall;

in the last segment of contraction fully 15 rise. Of the 30 series that fell in VII–VIII, 12 now rise, 15 decline more slowly, 1 sags at the same rate, and only 2 fall faster (the liabilities of failures and department store sales). True, the net resultant of the many mixed movements is a further decline in aggregate activity, if we have dated cyclical troughs aright. But among the series that now turn upward are all of our comprehensive series representing preparations for investments soon to be made and readiness to incur business risks. The near future certainly looks more promising for the employment of economic resources, above all labor, than the present.

Segment I–II again

In coming back to the point in the cycle at which we broke into it, we may note how abundantly these promises of improvement are kept in the segment with which we began. Every series expands, except the two that indicate improvement by falling. We found one exception to the general downturn of activities in V–VI; now we find no genuine exception to the upturn.

However, let us recall once again that we are dealing not only with a limited body of evidence, but also with what we have ventured to call 'characteristic' cyclical behavior. Before we go on to exploit our full sample of time series, we should see how gravely the conclusions we have drawn from the evidence of comprehensive series concerning the consensus of cyclical behavior would be undermined if, instead of dealing with what happens in a typical cycle, we dealt with what happens in each individual cycle covered by our data.

F   CYCLE-BY-CYCLE DIFFERENCES

Our standard measures cover two closely related but not identical concepts of the segment-by-segment changes that are characteristic of a series. One is the set of changes implied by the variety of timing under which we classify a series. Assignment to any variety of regular timing is tantamount to a statement of the reference-cycle segments during which the series has typically risen, and of the remaining segments during which it has typically fallen. The second concept and set of measures comes from the average reference-cycle pattern of a series, or the rates of change per month that we derive from the average pattern. We expect and find close agreement between the first and second set of measures; for observation of the direction of change of the average pattern from segment to segment is one, though not the sole, factor in forming our judgment concerning the variety of timing.[23]

There is still a third plan of ascertaining the direction of movements of our series in successive segments of the reference cycles. In each segment of each reference cycle covered by each of our series, we can observe whether the series rises, remains unchanged, or falls. That is, we can drop our judgments of characteristic timing and the average standings during all cycles covered by a series, and inspect what actually happens in each segment of each cycle.

In Table 41 observations of this simple sort upon our 34 comprehensive series are compared with observations based upon average reference-cycle patterns, and with the implications of our judgments concerning the timing varieties to which the series in question severally belong. According to Table 31 the analyses of our comprehensive series cover in the aggregate 400 reference cycles. In the first segment of these cycles, I find 339 advances, 6 cases of no change, and 55 declines. Reduced to a percentage basis to facilitate comparison, these figures mean that in almost 85 percent of the instances we are considering there was a rise in segment I–II, although our sample includes 30 observations upon business failures in I–II and 21 more observations upon series with irregular timing.

Now the consensus in cyclical behavior determined by observing individual cycles is less striking than the consensus determined by observing the stage-by-stage movements in

---

[23] The average standings of a series do not always rise during all the stages selected as characteristic of its expansion, or fall during all the stages assigned to contraction by its timing variety. See *Measuring Business Cycles*, Ch. 5, Sec. X.

Table 41

THREE SETS OF OBSERVATIONS UPON CONSENSUS IN THE MOVEMENTS
OF 34 MONTHLY OR QUARTERLY COMPREHENSIVE SERIES DURING
SUCCESSIVE SEGMENTS OF REFERENCE CYCLES

DIRECTION OF MOVEMENT	REFERENCE-CYCLE SEGMENT							
	I-II	II-III	III-IV	IV-V	V-VI	VI-VII	VII-VIII	VIII-IX
% of 34 Comprehensive Series That Typically Rise or Fall According to Their Variety of Cyclical Timing[a]								
Rise	91.2	88.2	85.3	70.6	8.8	11.8	11.8	47.1
Fall	8.8	11.8	14.7	29.4	91.2	88.2	88.2	52.9
% of Same Series in Which the Average Reference-Cycle Standings Rise or Fall[b]								
Rise	94.1	85.3	88.2	73.5	8.8	17.6	11.8	44.1
Do not change	...	...	...	2.9	...	...	...	...
Fall	5.9	14.7	11.8	23.5	91.2	82.4	88.2	55.9
% of 400 Reference Cycles Covered by Same Series in Which the Reference-Cycle Standings Rise or Fall[b]								
Rise	84.8	77.8	72.2	66.0	28.8	27.8	28.0	45.8
Do not change	1.5	2.2	3.0	2.2	2.8	1.8	2.0	2.5
Fall	13.8	20.0	24.8	31.8	68.5	70.5	70.0	51.8

[a] It is assumed that one of the two series with irregular timing (exports and agricultural marketings) rises in each segment and that the other falls. The 'expansion stages' of Macaulay's series of bond prices are taken as VI-III; see Table 31, note e.

[b] Failure of detail to total 100 percent is due to rounding.

average reference-cycle patterns, or by drawing inferences from judgments concerning typical timing. Table 41 indicates that the latter two methods yield similar results: the largest difference is 5.9 percent between the percentages of series that fall in IV–V. In general, observations of average reference-cycle standings show a slightly more marked consensus than do inferences from timing varieties. But in every segment these changes in average reference-cycle standings show an appreciably greater concentration of movements in the upward or the downward direction than do the observations of individual cycles. This is least (4.1 percent) in segment VIII–IX when the economy is fullest of crosscurrents; it is greatest (22.7 percent) in segment V–VI; it averages 12.2 percent.

Of course, a difference of this sort is to be expected, though we have no *a priori* basis for saying how large it should be. The random movements that influence the direction of change in every series, during every segment of every cycle, push now in the same direction as the cyclical movements that characteristically impinge upon a series, now in the opposite direction. The net resultant of all random forces acting during a given segment of a given cycle upon a given series may be feeble or strong in comparison with the corresponding cyclical influences. But what we have learned concerning the behavior of time series by analyzing hundreds of them from several countries over various periods, and then trying to account for what we find, leaves with us a healthy respect for the potency of irregular movements. That every now and then a relatively strong irregular impulse counter to the current cyclical movements will bring about a rise in some segment when a decline is expected, or force a decline when a rise occurs in most cycles, is no reason for distrusting the representative value of our timing judgments or of the average reference-cycle patterns. For the cycle-by-cycle indications of direction of change and the indications of direction we get by observing average behavior over all cycles covered by a series represent different concepts; they should not produce numerically equal results.

All three ways of summing up the consensus in the direction of movement of our comprehensive series agree, however, upon certain fundamental features of American business cycles during the period covered by our investigation to date: (1) A substantial majority of economic activities rise in stages I–V and a substantial majority fall in V–IX. (2) These majorities are greater if we seek to eliminate irregular cycle-by-cycle movements by averaging of some sort; but they remain significantly large if we take each segment of each cycle as a unit to be counted by itself. (3) The majorities of series that rise during the segments dominated by cyclical expansion are on the whole larger than the majorities that fall during the segments dominated by contraction, presumably because our sample includes many more rising than declining intracycle trends. Of course, the rising trends tend to reinforce compliance with cyclical expansions and to oppose compliance with cyclical contractions. (4) Crosscurrents in the business situation are most prominent in the last segment of cyclical expansion and the last segment of cyclical contraction.

APPENDIX A

Supplement of Reference-Cycle Measures

Table 42

REFERENCE-CYCLE MEASURES OF SERIES IN CHART 1*

Series No. in App. B (1)	Fig. No. in Chart 1 (2)	Series, Period Covered, and No. of Reference Cycles (3)	I (4)	II (5)	III (6)	IV (7)	V (8)	VI (9)	VII (10)	VIII (11)	IX (12)	Expansion Stages (13)	Ex-pansion (14)	Con-trac-tion (15)	Full cycle (16)	Ex-pan-sion (17)	Con-trac-tion (18)	Busi-ness cycles (19)
			Average and Average Deviation of Ref.-Cycle Relatives at Stage										Average Reference-Cycle Amplitude			Index of Conformity to Business cycles		
1	1	Index of industrial production (1919-38; 5)	85.1 14.0	94.4 10.8	102.5 9.7	113.3 7.8	120.3 9.8	115.9 6.6	101.2 6.7	89.4 11.6	87.8 9.7	I-V	+35.2	−32.5	+67.7	+100	+100	+100
2	1	Index of agricultural marketings (1919-38; 5)	100.2 1.8	102.3 5.1	99.6 5.4	102.2 3.8	101.6 2.6	100.8 3.2	101.8 4.5	102.3 5.8	100.8 6.5	Irreg.	+1.4	−0.8	+2.2	+60	−20	+33
3	2	Index of production, producer goods (1919-38; 5)	83.7 18.9	96.5 13.4	106.7 13.3	117.9 10.6	124.3 13.5	117.0 7.9	97.2 7.6	80.4 14.3	78.6 11.8	I-V	+40.6	−45.7	+86.3	+100	+100	+100
4	2	Index of production, consumer goods (1919-38; 5)	88.9 6.8	95.2 6.4	100.9 4.6	111.0 4.4	111.9 4.8	105.2 2.7	101.2 5.7	94.7 5.6	94.3 7.5	I-V	+23.0	−17.6	+40.6	+100	+100	+100
5	3	Index of production, durable manufactures (1919-38; 5)	79.1 23.6	92.1 17.8	106.7 14.8	120.3 15.0	130.7 18.0	124.7 12.1	102.3 9.1	78.9 19.2	75.3 17.6	I-V	+51.5	−55.3	+106.8	+100	+100	+100
6	3	Index of production, nondurable manufactures (1919-38; 5)	88.9 7.5	95.9 6.0	101.0 5.1	108.9 4.0	113.3 5.2	108.9 3.5	98.3 5.7	96.7 5.3	96.9 5.1	I-V	+24.4	−16.5	+40.9	+100	+60	+100
7	4	Automobile production, trucks (1914-38; 6ª)	59.3 22.9	76.2 15.4	101.0 18.0	127.0 15.4	153.0 23.1	132.9 13.8	113.9 23.6	92.8 36.0	88.3 35.3	I-V	+93.7	−64.8	+158.5	+100	+71	+100
8	4	Automobile production, passenger cars (1914-38; 6)	63.2 19.7	83.2 18.5	113.4 19.1	129.6 14.8	123.4 25.4	104.8 28.6	94.2 21.6	80.5 19.1	78.8 22.0	I-V	+60.2	−44.6	+104.8	+100	+67	+82
9	5	Cattle slaughtered under fed. insp. (1908-38; 8ª)	93.4 11.3	97.5 9.0	101.2 5.3	106.5 5.1	106.7 7.1	105.1 5.7	102.0 8.3	96.0 3.9	96.7 4.6	I-V	+13.3	−10.0	+23.3	+50	+89	+62

Table 42 (cont.)

10	5	Hogs slaughtered, commercial (1879-1938; 16)	98.8 / 10.5	102.9 / 11.2	100.1 / 7.2	97.7 / 4.8	99.0 / 10.7	97.5 / 11.0	101.0 / 8.3	104.6 / 5.7	102.9 / 7.5	V-IX	+0.3	+3.8	-3.5	-12	-38	-35
11	6	Butter production in factories (1919-38; 5ᵃ)	97.4 / 4.1	98.3 / 3.1	95.5 / 3.0	96.9 / 2.9	98.7 / 3.3	99.3 / 3.2	102.3 / 2.4	105.7 / 3.3	109.9 / 5.8	V-IX	+1.3	+11.3	-10.0	+20	-67	-40
12	6	Ice cream production in factories (1919-38; 5ᵃ)	85.3 / 11.1	90.4 / 7.9	98.2 / 6.2	106.1 / 7.6	110.0 / 10.5	111.6 / 11.5	107.4 / 7.2	104.0 / 12.7	98.5 / 16.7	I-VI	+26.3	-13.1	+39.4	+100	+33	+60
13	7	Cotton consumption by mills (1924-38; 3ᵃ)	90.4 / 18.2	99.9 / 7.4	98.0 / 9.5	112.9 / 9.5	120.3 / 12.3	111.1 / 9.6	98.7 / 10.6	93.2 / 13.2	92.2 / 7.5	VIII-V	+25.6	-27.1	+52.7	+67	+71	+67
14	7	Index of rayon deliveries (1924-38; 3ᵃ)	65.3 / 6.1	77.6 / 4.7	85.5 / 5.6	98.7 / 17.0	115.4 / 23.0	112.6 / 12.2	113.2 / 26.7	111.7 / 22.5	122.3 / 16.1	I-V	+50.0	+6.9	+43.1	+100	-50	+33
15	8	Beehive coke production (1897-1919; 6)	74.8 / 13.4	92.5 / 6.7	98.9 / 8.1	110.5 / 6.7	118.4 / 10.3	113.8 / 7.0	98.9 / 10.8	78.5 / 12.8	80.2 / 21.3	I-V	+43.6	-38.3	+81.9	+100	+67	+100
15	8	Beehive coke production (1919-38; 5)	79.2 / 32.2	92.9 / 29.7	103.9 / 36.3	141.8 / 20.5	203.0 / 72.6	164.8 / 47.6	93.4 / 23.5	51.5 / 22.6	42.0 / 12.2	I-V	+123.8	-161.0	+284.8	+100	+100	+100
16	9	Construction contracts, total, value (1912-38; 7ᵃ)	78.3 / 21.8	95.3 / 22.3	110.1 / 15.8	123.5 / 12.3	127.1 / 18.6	114.8 / 11.6	96.3 / 12.7	93.2 / 22.3	98.7 / 28.1	VIII-IV	+43.2	-30.4	+73.6	+71	+50	+86
17	9	Building permits, value, 20-120 cities (1908-38; 8ᵃ)	86.0 / 29.1	101.4 / 28.2	115.8 / 19.3	121.0 / 26.0	115.4 / 22.7	98.8 / 13.6	95.0 / 26.2	96.4 / 26.0	92.2 / 25.3	VIII-IV	+33.6	-24.7	+58.3	+75	+33	+88
18	10	Contracts, private construction, value (1919-38; 5)	83.1 / 35.0	104.9 / 38.9	117.0 / 29.1	133.0 / 22.1	139.5 / 26.8	122.4 / 21.7	96.5 / 22.9	84.0 / 29.8	88.3 / 29.2	VIII-V	+58.5	-55.6	+114.1	+60	+60	+100
19	10	Contracts, public construction, value (1919-38; 5)	79.7 / 20.4	96.1 / 10.6	102.6 / 10.5	104.9 / 7.5	111.0 / 15.5	107.9 / 12.9	101.8 / 10.4	102.6 / 19.2	102.8 / 31.2	Irreg.	+31.4	-8.3	+39.7	+60	-60	-11
20	11	Contracts, public & institutional buildings, value (1919-38; 5)	79.1 / 30.2	90.2 / 17.3	105.2 / 11.3	109.2 / 13.5	112.0 / 17.9	112.0 / 21.5	108.5 / 10.6	103.3 / 23.4	108.8 / 38.4	VIII-V	+29.8	-8.7	+38.5	+60	-20	+11

Table 42 (cont.)

Series No. in App. B (1)	Fig. No. in Chart 1 (2)	Series, Period Covered, and No. of Reference Cycles (3)	Average and Average Deviation of Ref.-Cycle Relatives at Stage									Expansion Stages (13)	Average Reference-Cycle Amplitude			Index of Conformity to Business cycles		
			I (4)	II (5)	III (6)	IV (7)	V (8)	VI (9)	VII (10)	VIII (11)	IX (12)		Expansion (14)	Contraction (15)	Full cycle (16)	Expansion (17)	Contraction (18)	Business cycles (19)
21	11	Contracts, commercial buildings, value (1919-38; 5)	87.1 / 31.7	99.9 / 27.2	111.9 / 18.1	131.9 / 24.6	136.4 / 23.6	121.4 / 18.8	95.5 / 22.7	81.7 / 28.2	87.3 / 28.5	VIII-V	+57.8	-54.7	+112.5	+100	+60	+100
22	11	Contracts, industrial buildings, value (1919-38; 5)	67.2 / 20.7	95.1 / 24.6	116.3 / 31.2	150.5 / 26.8	175.0 / 40.5	134.6 / 33.2	88.6 / 23.7	60.6 / 30.0	60.9 / 27.8	VIII-V	+115.7	-114.4	+230.1	+100	+100	+100
23	12	Contracts, residential buildings, value (1919-38; 5a)	96.1 / 48.3	112.4 / 53.2	121.3 / 33.9	133.0 / 23.4	129.4 / 27.0	106.6 / 18.0	95.7 / 25.6	97.0 / 30.2	106.0 / 36.9	VII-IV	+36.7	-37.3	+74.0	+60	+67	+80
24	12	Contracts, residential buildings, floor space (1919-38; 5)	100.0 / 44.5	116.4 / 55.5	123.6 / 32.6	134.8 / 24.1	125.7 / 25.0	102.0 / 16.9	92.6 / 22.7	92.9 / 26.4	101.1 / 35.9	VII-IV	+41.4	-42.1	+83.5	+60	+60	+78
25	13	Railroad freight ton miles (1867-1904; 9)	82.0 / 6.5	85.7 / 6.1	92.1 / 4.4	99.3 / 3.1	102.9 / 3.2	105.1 / 3.4	107.3 / 3.4	111.6 / 7.3	115.2 / 10.0	VIII-V	+23.6	+8.7	+14.9	+100	-56	+76
26	13	Railroad gross earnings (1867-1904; 9a)	84.1 / 5.7	87.8 / 6.1	93.1 / 3.6	101.3 / 3.5	105.3 / 2.9	106.7 / 2.0	106.9 / 5.1	106.0 / 5.1	106.7 / 6.3	I-VI	+22.6	0	+22.6	+100	-40	+78
27	14	Railroad freight ton miles (1904-38; 9)	87.3 / 8.3	93.4 / 6.2	99.1 / 6.6	109.0 / 6.7	115.0 / 7.0	111.7 / 3.9	102.9 / 3.4	92.6 / 8.2	91.6 / 7.7	I-V	+27.8	-23.4	+51.2	+100	+78	+100
28	14	Railroad revenue passenger miles (1919-38; 5)	100.6 / 13.6	102.1 / 10.4	104.4 / 8.7	109.3 / 7.4	110.1 / 9.7	108.9 / 6.4	102.5 / 7.7	91.6 / 12.8	87.2 / 14.9	II-V	+8.0	-21.6	+29.6	+20	+100	+100
29	14	Railroad gross earnings (1904-14, 1921-38; 7)	91.6 / 9.5	96.2 / 7.8	100.1 / 7.5	108.8 / 7.1	113.6 / 8.0	109.9 / 5.0	101.4 / 4.1	93.1 / 8.6	90.9 / 10.0	I-V	+21.9	-22.7	+44.6	+100	+71	+100
30	15	Index of factory employment, total (1921-38; 4c)	89.6 / 12.7	95.7 / 8.4	101.8 / 6.8	109.4 / 5.4	113.8 / 7.6	111.1 / 5.6	102.5 / 6.4	94.1 / 9.0	90.4 / 8.9	I-V	+24.2	-23.3	+47.5	+100	+100	+100

Table 42 (cont.)

31	15	Average hours worked per week, manufacturing, wage earners (1921-38; 4)	98.4 6.4	101.8 4.8	103.0 4.9	106.0 4.4	106.8 4.8	103.6 2.8	97.3 2.3	91.6 6.4	90.4 6.6	I-V	+8.4	−16.4	+24.8	+100	+100 +100
32	15	Index of factory payrolls, total (1921-38; 4*)	85.9 20.4	93.2 15.8	102.8 12.9	115.3 10.7	125.0 15.1	120.2 11.0	104.9 11.0	91.1 16.9	85.9 19.0	I-V	+39.2	−39.1	+78.3	+100	+100 +100
33	16	Index of factory employment, food products (1919-38; 5)	94.8 7.5	98.3 4.6	101.6 2.9	104.7 3.4	106.3 3.7	106.2 3.2	101.1 4.1	96.5 6.8	96.3 4.9	I-V	+11.5	−10.0	+21.5	+100	+100 +100
34	16	Index of factory employment, textiles (1919-38; 5)	94.5 9.3	100.1 5.2	102.3 5.1	107.0 3.5	109.5 4.3	107.0 2.4	96.7 5.0	94.6 5.0	94.1 7.1	I-V	+15.0	−15.5	+30.5	+100	+60 +78
35	16	Index of factory employment, iron & steel products excluding machinery (1919-38; 5)	86.7 18.7	94.7 12.7	103.2 9.5	111.7 6.1	118.3 7.6	116.5 6.5	104.3 8.5	88.1 15.3	83.2 13.5	I-VI	+29.7	−33.3	+63.0	+100	+100 +100
36	16	Index of factory employment, machinery (1919-38; 5)	84.7 17.3	89.9 11.3	100.4 8.1	114.8 6.3	123.7 11.3	121.5 8.8	107.3 11.0	88.5 18.3	81.2 19.4	I-VI	+36.8	−40.3	+77.1	+100	+100 +100
37	17	Index of wholesale prices, 'all' commodities (1891-1914, 1921-38; 11)	96.4 6.5	98.8 5.4	100.9 3.7	103.1 3.3	105.1 3.8	104.6 3.7	100.1 4.0	97.2 4.7	96.3 5.6	I-V	+8.7	−8.9	+17.6	+64	+82 +100
37	17	Index of wholesale prices, 'all' commodities (1861-67; 1)	55.9	62.0	85.2	129.3	120.9	115.0	112.9	106.5	102.2	I-V	+65.0	−18.7	+83.7	+100	+100
37	17	Index of wholesale prices, 'all' commodities (1914-19; 1)	65.9	68.8	92.2	122.0	131.1	133.4	132.2	127.2	129.8	I-V	+65.2	−1.3	+66.5	+100	+100
38	18	Index of wholesale prices, raw materials (1921-38; 4*)	94.1 16.1	101.2 12.6	108.3 8.1	109.7 7.1	110.1 9.8	106.5 8.4	96.4 6.6	91.1 11.1	89.0 13.4	I-V	+16.0	−21.1	+37.1	+50	+60 +71
39	18	Index of wholesale prices, semi-manufactured goods (1921-38; 4*)	95.9 15.2	101.3 12.1	103.0 8.3	108.3 6.3	112.3 6.8	107.5 5.8	99.3 8.0	92.7 8.8	90.4 9.2	I-V	+16.4	−22.0	+38.4	0	+100 +100

Table 42 (cont.)

Series No. in App. B (1)	Fig. No. in Chart 1 (2)	Series, Period Covered, and No. of Reference Cycles (3)	Average and Average Deviation of Ref.-Cycle Relatives at Stage									Expansion Stages (13)	Average Reference-Cycle Amplitude			Index of Conformity to Business cycles		
			I (4)	II (5)	III (6)	IV (7)	V (8)	VI (9)	VII (10)	VIII (11)	IX (12)		Expansion (14)	Contraction (15)	Full cycle (16)	Expansion (17)	Contraction (18)	Business cycles (19)
40	18	Index of wholesale prices, finished products (1921-38; 4ᵃ)	97.7 / 9.0	100.4 / 6.1	104.5 / 5.2	105.1 / 3.5	106.3 / 4.1	104.4 / 4.5	99.2 / 4.4	95.2 / 6.2	93.4 / 7.8	I-V	+8.6	-13.0	+21.6	+50	+100	+100
41	18	Index of wholesale prices, foods (1891-1914, 1921-38; 11ᵃ)	97.4 / 7.7	100.0 / 6.1	101.8 / 4.6	103.1 / 3.5	104.5 / 5.4	103.8 / 4.3	99.5 / 3.5	96.9 / 5.8	97.1 / 7.5	I-V	+7.2	-7.4	+14.6	+64	-17	+43
42	18	Index of wholesale prices, textiles (1891-1914, 1921-38; 11ᵃ)	96.7 / 9.4	99.9 / 6.6	100.9 / 5.2	103.2 / 4.1	105.1 / 4.7	104.0 / 3.6	101.2 / 5.5	95.6 / 5.8	92.8 / 6.4	I-V	+8.4	-12.3	+20.7	+45	+67	+62
43	18	Index of wholesale prices, metals & metal products (1891-1914, 1921-38; 11ᵃ)	96.6 / 9.0	97.8 / 7.3	98.5 / 5.6	104.7 / 5.2	109.1 / 5.6	107.3 / 6.2	100.9 / 6.7	95.2 / 6.3	93.7 / 6.8	I-V	+12.5	-15.4	+27.9	+64	+83	+100
44	19	Wholesale prices, 12 foods' (1921-38; 4)	97.6 / 14.6	103.8 / 10.1	106.5 / 4.6	106.3 / 4.5	107.4 / 6.6	105.8 / 6.7	94.8 / 3.7	88.2 / 8.6	88.2 / 9.3	I-V	+9.9	-19.3	+29.2	+50	+100	+100
45	19	Retail prices, 12 foods' (1921-38; 4)	98.6 / 12.6	101.5 / 8.2	104.6 / 4.8	105.1 / 3.9	105.7 / 5.1	106.4 / 4.7	99.1 / 3.7	91.4 / 8.5	90.1 / 10.1	I-V	+7.2	-15.6	+22.8	0	+100	+100
46	20	Index of farm prices, 58 foods (1921-38; 4ᵃ)	94.4 / 15.4	.... /	103.8 / 7.0	....	112.7 / 10.1	....	101.0 / 6.8	....	88.2 / 17.1	I-V	+18.2	-24.4	+42.6	+50	+60	+100
47	20	Index of retail prices, 58 foods (1921-38; 4ᵃ)	98.6 / 8.5	.... /	101.5 / 3.4	....	106.4 / 4.8	....	101.0 / 3.4	....	93.6 / 10.5	I-V	+7.8	-12.8	+20.6	+50	+60	+71
48	21	Pig iron production (1879-1938; 16)	70.5 / 17.1	88.9 / 11.8	101.9 / 11.5	114.0 / 10.6	124.7 / 13.3	121.6 / 12.0	101.0 / 13.5	83.7 / 18.2	79.8 / 19.5	I-V	+54.2	-44.9	+99.1	+100	+100	+100
49	21	Wholesale price, pig iron (1879-1914, 1921-38; 14ᵉ)	90.6 / 12.8	95.0 / 10.2	96.2 / 7.1	106.7 / 6.7	113.8 / 8.7	111.8 / 10.7	102.7 / 10.4	93.8 / 8.4	89.9 / 8.0	I-V	+23.1	-23.8	+46.9	+44	+100	+91

Table 42 (cont.)

No.	Ref.	Series	I	II	III	IV	V	VI	VII	VIII	IX	Phase						
50	22	Cotton crop (1870-1938; 17[h])	100.0 *12.3*	.... *....*	96.2 *6.1*	.... *....*	103.0 *10.6*	.... *....*	103.7 *7.1*	.... *....*	107.0 *14.3*	Irreg.	+2.9	+4.1	-1.2	+28	-36	-12
51	22	Wholesale price, cotton, N.Y. City (1870-1914, 1921-38; 15)	100.1 *16.2*	98.2 *14.6*	101.7 *15.0*	105.9 *11.0*	107.4 *11.2*	102.9 *8.7*	100.2 *15.0*	97.2 *15.7*	91.1 *17.7*	I-V	+7.3	-16.3	+23.6	+33	+47	+43
52	23	Wheat crop (1867-1938; 18)	96.9 *9.8*	.... *....*	100.3 *7.2*	.... *....*	101.7 *7.3*	.... *....*	101.9 *8.0*	.... *....*	104.0 *14.0*	Irreg.	+4.8	+2.3	+2.5	+39	+11	-3
53	23	Wholesale price, wheat, Chicago (1867-1914, 1921-38; 16[g])	102.4 *18.6*	111.2 *14.3*	106.1 *10.0*	101.3 *9.3*	101.9 *9.9*	100.0 *8.4*	92.3 *8.6*	93.8 *12.0*	96.3 *17.0*	VII-II	-18.8	+14.2	-33.0	-67	-44	-82
54	24	Corn crop (1867-1938; 18)	100.2 *11.4*	.... *....*	100.1 *6.5*	.... *....*	98.1 *8.8*	.... *....*	102.3 *6.5*	.... *....*	106.7 *11.4*	Irreg.	-2.2	+8.6	-10.8	-44	-33	-26
55	24	Wholesale price, corn, Chicago (1867-1914, 1921-38; 16[i])	99.8 *22.2*	105.1 *18.9*	102.0 *13.7*	99.6 *14.2*	103.1 *17.4*	105.7 *15.6*	98.1 *13.3*	99.8 *18.8*	99.8 *24.7*	Irreg.	+3.3	-3.2	+6.5	-25	+6	-20
56	25	Potato crop (1891-1938; 13[j])	98.9 *11.8*	.... *....*	101.9 *8.7*	.... *....*	100.8 *5.9*	.... *....*	101.3 *4.8*	.... *....*	100.6 *7.4*	Irreg.	+1.9	-0.1	+2.0	+17	-6	+14
57	25	Wholesale price, potatoes, Chicago (1891-1914, 1921-38; 11[a])	112.2 *44.4*	109.2 *38.3*	108.1 *25.3*	95.2 *21.6*	89.1 *21.1*	97.5 *24.3*	91.2 *12.3*	99.8 *26.3*	95.1 *31.4*	V-IX	-23.1	+6.0	-29.1	-9	0	-24
58	26	Hogs slaughtered, commercial (1879-1938; 16)	98.8 *10.5*	102.9 *11.2*	100.1 *7.2*	97.7 *4.8*	99.0 *10.7*	97.5 *11.0*	101.0 *8.3*	104.6 *5.7*	102.9 *7.5*	V-IX	+0.3	+3.8	-3.5	-12	-38	-35
59	26	Wholesale price, hogs, Chicago (1879-1914, 1921-38; 14[k])	88.7 *16.0*	94.3 *15.0*	100.9 *10.2*	107.9 *10.1*	111.1 *15.4*	111.8 *14.8*	97.9 *10.6*	92.0 *11.0*	93.4 *14.0*	I-V	+22.4	-17.7	+40.1	+53	+53	+48
60	27	Department store sales (1921-38; 4[l])	93.0 *10.0*	96.4 *7.8*	100.9 *6.7*	106.9 *5.8*	110.0 *5.2*	109.0 *4.0*	105.2 *4.9*	97.2 *12.2*	93.2 *14.4*	I-VI	+16.1	-15.9	+32.0	+60	+60	+78
61	27	Department store sales, deflated (1921-38; 4[l])	90.8 *5.9*	94.4 *4.2*	99.4 *3.1*	104.8 *2.9*	106.7 *1.5*	105.6 *1.0*	103.8 *1.2*	99.6 *6.4*	97.0 *8.9*	I-V	+15.9	-9.7	+25.6	+60	+20	+78
62	27	Sales by grocery chain stores, adj. for trend and prices (1921-38; 4[l])	101.9 *3.2*	103.0 *4.3*	99.7 *3.4*	102.9 *1.9*	99.9 *2.1*	98.6 *1.9*	99.6 *3.3*	99.1 *4.7*	98.3 *4.8*	Irreg.	-2.0	-1.6	-0.4	-60	+20	+11

Table 42 (cont.)

Series No. in App. B (1)	Fig. No. in Chart 1 (2)	Series, Period Covered, and No. of Reference Cycles (3)	Average and Average Deviation of Ref.-Cycle Relatives at Stage									Expansion Stages (13)	Average Reference-Cycle Amplitude			Index of Conformity to Business cycles		
			I (4)	II (5)	III (6)	IV (7)	V (8)	VI (9)	VII (10)	VIII (11)	IX (12)		Expansion (14)	Contraction (15)	Full cycle (16)	Expansion (17)	Contraction (18)	Business cycles (19)
63	28	Butter consumption (1919-38; 5[a])	94.0 _3.5_	95.5 _3.1_	96.5 _2.2_	97.8 _2.4_	98.8 _4.7_	99.7 _3.4_	102.5 _1.9_	105.4 _4.3_	106.9 _5.3_	V-IX	+4.8	+8.1	−3.3	+20	−67	−40
64	28	Newsprint paper consumption (1919-38; 5)	87.9 _6.8_	93.5 _5.9_	100.8 _3.3_	106.2 _3.4_	108.0 _4.7_	105.8 _5.2_	103.6 _4.5_	99.7 _6.5_	97.1 _9.3_	I-V	+20.2	−10.9	+31.1	+100	+20	+100
65	28	Vacuum cleaners, floor, shipments (1919-38; 5)	81.2 _20.7_	95.5 _20.4_	101.2 _13.2_	116.1 _12.4_	135.5 _10.0_	124.6 _13.4_	94.2 _15.6_	89.7 _24.1_	85.7 _20.3_	VIII-V	+57.1	−45.8	+102.9	+60	+60	+78
66	29	New orders, locomotives (1870-1938; 17)	57.5 _31.8_	82.1 _27.3_	123.0 _46.9_	149.2 _32.4_	121.1 _58.8_	101.4 _36.4_	69.6 _20.2_	57.2 _25.5_	63.9 _41.9_	VIII-IV	+92.7	−92.0	+184.7	+100	+100	+100
67	29	New orders, freight cars (1870-1938; 17)	71.5 _53.5_	81.1 _28.4_	108.7 _31.3_	142.9 _37.1_	126.3 _54.7_	91.0 _39.5_	59.8 _24.9_	60.9 _34.2_	89.3 _58.1_	VIII-IV	+90.0	−82.0	+172.0	+100	+65	+100
68	29	New orders, railroad passenger cars (1870-1938; 17)	72.2 _40.6_	105.6 _38.4_	126.7 _58.0_	119.9 _30.1_	119.6 _52.8_	95.6 _48.1_	64.5 _34.8_	60.9 _33.9_	88.9 _59.5_	VIII-IV	+60.4	−59.1	+119.5	+76	+88	+94
69	29	New orders, oak flooring (1912-38; 7[w])	96.6 _33.9_	105.9 _37.2_	116.9 _24.7_	117.8 _24.4_	104.0 _25.4_	87.1 _20.4_	82.4 _24.0_	106.3 _27.5_	130.6 _38.3_	VII-III	+44.6	−37.9	+82.5	+67	+43	+83
70	29	New orders, steel sheets (1919-33; 4[n])	98.3 _49.0_	111.0 _32.5_	132.1 _21.9_	128.2 _21.6_	130.8 _24.6_	102.2 _21.7_	84.6 _18.1_	71.6 _23.6_	94.0 _30.4_	VIII-III	+60.2	−60.5	+120.7	+100	+100	+100
71	29	Index of orders, machine tools & forging machinery (1919-38; 5)	64.1 _41.3_	88.1 _44.7_	121.0 _34.3_	163.7 _35.4_	180.4 _37.4_	137.7 _20.6_	91.6 _34.5_	68.0 _36.1_	59.4 _36.7_	I-V	+116.3	−121.0	+237.3	+100	+100	+100
72	30	Total exports, value (1867-1914, 1921-38; 16)	89.4 _11.3_	95.5 _10.6_	99.2 _9.9_	102.1 _8.4_	104.4 _11.0_	106.0 _7.8_	107.2 _9.9_	103.0 _14.2_	103.1 _15.6_	I-V	+15.0	−1.2	+16.2	+62	0	+27

Table 42 (cont.)

		Item											Phase						
73	30	Total imports, value (1867-1914, 1921-38; 16)	87.9	93.4	101.3	109.9	114.7	109.8	99.7	95.8	95.9		VIII-V	+26.1	−18.9	+45.0	+88	+50	+77
			15.5	*10.5*	*8.2*	*9.2*	*12.3*	*9.0*	*9.2*	*12.6*	*14.7*								
74	31	Cotton stocks in public storage & at compresses (1914-38; 6ᵃ)	104.1	98.5	88.1	87.0	82.4	88.8	108.9	125.3	123.9		V-IX	−21.7	+41.5	−63.2	−33	−43	−50
			29.9	*19.8*	*14.5*	*13.9*	*16.9*	*15.6*	*14.1*	*21.2*	*25.7*								
75	31	Cotton stocks at mills (1914-38; 6ᵃ)	89.4	95.6	99.3	104.9	112.9	109.3	99.1	97.7	94.8		I-V	+23.5	−18.0	+41.5	+67	+100	+100
			11.7	*6.0*	*8.2*	*5.5*	*9.9*	*7.4*	*8.9*	*12.8*	*13.6*								
76	31	Cotton consumption by mills (1914-38; 6ᵃ)	91.3	99.6	100.6	111.1	115.2	106.9	95.8	89.0	90.0		VIII-V	+25.0	−26.2	+51.2	+67	+71	+67
			11.7	*4.7*	*7.8*	*6.6*	*9.7*	*8.6*	*7.8*	*8.7*	*9.6*								
77	32	Commercial paper rates, N.Y. City (1858-1914; 14ᵃ)	90.8	89.2	93.5	103.0	120.1	120.6	110.9	94.2	90.6		II-VI	+31.4	−33.9	+65.3	+86	+73	+93
			11.2	*6.8*	*8.6*	*11.8*	*15.5*	*12.0*	*15.0*	*10.8*	*13.4*								
78	32	90-day time-money rates on Stock Exchange loans, N.Y. City (1891-1914; 7ᵃ)	82.3	81.5	94.3	96.8	116.7	127.3	120.9	85.8	76.7		I-VI	+45.0	−50.6	+95.6	+100	+75	+86
			17.2	*13.5*	*5.9*	*11.8*	*9.5*	*7.0*	*23.2*	*14.1*	*16.0*								
79	32	Call money rates, N.Y. City (1858-1914; 14ᵃ)	73.3	79.4	95.8	125.0	163.5	130.2	105.6	77.3	72.8		I-V	+90.1	−90.7	+180.8	+71	+100	+100
			21.2	*23.7*	*15.5*	*25.8*	*64.8*	*31.7*	*31.5*	*21.2*	*23.6*								
77	32	Commercial paper rates, N.Y. City (1914-33; 5ᵉ)	98.0	92.9	99.8	112.4	121.3	115.4	104.5	95.9	88.4		II-VI	+22.5	−32.7	+55.2	+67	+67	+100
			11.9	*14.2*	*18.1*	*18.8*	*22.3*	*11.3*	*15.7*	*12.1*	*15.9*								
78	32	90-day time-money rates on Stock Exchange loans, N.Y. City (1914-33; 5ᵉ)	91.1	91.1	106.1	126.1	138.0	120.2	100.7	90.1	83.0		I-VI	+29.1	−37.3	+66.4	+33	+83	+82
			14.1	*17.5*	*23.1*	*30.3*	*32.8*	*9.8*	*20.1*	*19.2*	*25.4*								
79	32	Call money rates, N.Y. City (1914-33; 5ᵉ)	89.2	90.9	105.8	137.2	148.4	123.8	99.1	91.8	85.9		I-V	+59.2	−62.6	+121.8	+33	+83	+82
			20.1	*21.8*	*25.7*	*29.6*	*37.4*	*14.4*	*22.1*	*23.8*	*34.3*								
80	32	Discount rates, Fed. Res. Bank of N.Y. (1914-33; 5ᵉ)	105.0	96.3	101.0	104.9	111.9	110.1	101.0	98.8	92.8		II-V	+15.6	−25.2	+40.8	+33	+50	+100
			17.0	*11.6*	*16.4*	*15.3*	*12.9*	*4.1*	*16.5*	*9.0*	*9.8*								

Table 42 (cont.)

Series No. in App. B (1)	Fig. No. in Chart 1 (2)	Series, Period Covered, and No. of Reference Cycles (3)	Average and Average Deviation of Ref.-Cycle Relatives at Stage									Expansion Stages (13)	Average Reference-Cycle Amplitude			Index of Conformity to Business cycles		
			I (4)	II (5)	III (6)	IV (7)	V (8)	VI (9)	VII (10)	VIII (11)	IX (12)		Expansion (14)	Contraction (15)	Full cycle (16)	Expansion (17)	Contraction (18)	Business cycles (19)
81	33	Weighted av. of interest rates charged customers by banks, N.Y. City (1919-33; 4¹)	98.8 *9.6*	97.8 *5.8*	100.0 *7.2*	102.1 *8.5*	106.4 *7.6*	103.5 *2.9*	99.3 *6.6*	97.6 *4.4*	93.4 *6.0*	II-V	+8.6	−17.3	+25.9	+20	+100	+56
82	33	Weighted av. of interest rates charged customers by banks, 8 northern & eastern cities (1919-33; 4¹)	99.7 *10.4*	97.7 *6.6*	99.0 *6.8*	100.7 *7.2*	102.6 *7.0*	102.6 *2.1*	98.5 *5.0*	98.6 *3.8*	96.6 *3.4*	II-VI	+5.0	−10.1	+15.1	+20	+100	+33
83	33	Weighted av. of interest rates charged customers by banks, 27 southern & western cities (1919-33; 4ⁿ)	100.8 *6.7*	98.9 *5.2*	97.9 *4.1*	98.3 *4.4*	99.8 *4.4*	101.0 *2.2*	99.8 *3.5*	100.1 *3.4*	99.0 *3.3*	III-VI	+3.2	−8.2	+11.4	+20	+50	+75
84	34	Yields of American railroad bonds (1858-1933; 19ᵃ)	102.0 *5.1*	100.5 *4.0*	98.3 *3.3*	98.9 *2.6*	101.0 *3.1*	102.0 *2.5*	101.5 *3.2*	101.1 *3.8*	100.2 *4.7*	III-VIᵇ	+3.7	−6.2	+9.9	+47	+30	+68
85	34	Yields of high grade corporate & municipal bonds (1900-33; 9ᵉ)	99.9 *5.1*	98.0 *3.6*	97.0 *1.9*	98.9 *1.8*	100.6 *2.6*	102.1 *2.8*	102.0 *3.6*	101.3 *3.5*	100.4 *3.2*	III-VII	+5.0	−5.7	+10.7	+40	+40	+68
86	35	Yields of American railroad bonds (1867-1900; 8)	105.4 *4.0*	103.7 *3.4*	100.9 *3.0*	99.7 *2.5*	100.6 *3.0*	100.2 *1.7*	100.1 *2.9*	97.9 *2.8*	96.7 *4.4*	III-VIᵉ	−0.7	−7.1	+6.4	0	+50	+60
86	35	Yields of American railroad bonds (1900-19; 5)	97.0 *1.4*	96.3 *0.9*	96.1 *1.0*	99.7 *2.6*	102.0 *3.9*	103.9 *3.0*	104.3 *2.4*	104.2 *2.1*	104.7 *1.3*	III-VIᵃᵃ	+7.8	+2.6	+7.2	+100	−40	+100
87	36	Lawful money holdings, all national banks (1879-1914; 10ᵉ)	95.2 *9.0*	96.5 *6.8*	98.1 *2.3*	98.6 *2.2*	97.8 *2.8*	97.9 *3.7*	100.4 *4.2*	111.8 *6.8*	117.7 *9.6*	V-IX	+2.6	+18.1	−15.5	+20	−80	−84

Table 42 (cont.)

36	88	Loans and discounts, all national banks (1879-1914; 10)	88.0 / 5.4	91.4 / 4.2	95.8 / 3.0	100.7 / 2.2	104.7 / 2.5	106.0 / 3.0	105.6 / 4.9	106.2 / 4.8	108.0 / 5.4	VIII-V	+17.9	+1.5	+16.4	+100	−40	+100
36	89	Investments, all national banks (1879-1914; 10)	84.8 / 8.6	88.0 / 8.4	93.8 / 5.6	100.1 / 1.9	103.5 / 3.1	105.2 / 4.0	106.8 / 5.8	112.7 / 7.1	117.8 / 8.4	VII-IV	+24.3	+6.7	+17.6	+100	−40	+58
36	90	Individual deposits, all national banks (1879-1914; 10)	86.3 / 7.1	91.8 / 4.5	96.4 / 2.7	102.1 / 2.5	106.2 / 2.9	105.3 / 3.4	103.6 / 4.1	105.0 / 3.4	108.0 / 4.6	VIII-V	+22.3	−1.2	+23.5	+100	+10	+100
37	91	Loans and discounts, national banks, N.Y. City (1885-1914; 9ᵉ)	92.2 / 7.4	97.3 / 5.9	99.9 / 3.5	101.8 / 3.5	102.4 / 5.4	99.1 / 3.5	100.2 / 4.9	104.9 / 3.9	110.4 / 6.3	VII-IV	+15.8	−1.6	+17.4	+100	+17	+52
37	92	Loans and discounts, national banks, reserve cities other than central (1885-1914; 9)	88.9 / 5.4	92.2 / 4.1	95.8 / 2.2	100.7 / 2.5	105.8 / 3.3	106.4 / 4.0	104.7 / 4.9	106.3 / 5.0	108.2 / 5.6	VIII-V	+17.9	+0.6	+17.3	+100	−11	+88
37	93	Loans and discounts, national banks, country districts (1885-1914; 9ᵉ)	90.1 / 4.4	91.7 / 4.1	95.1 / 2.6	100.2 / 3.1	104.8 / 3.3	107.1 / 3.0	106.1 / 4.1	105.4 / 6.1	107.1 / 7.9	I-VI	+17.0	0	+17.0	+100	−20	+89
38	94	Lawful money holdings, national banks, N.Y. City (1885-1914; 9ᵉ·ᵉ)	104.9 / 15.7	106.2 / 12.0	99.7 / 2.8	96.3 / 5.0	94.7 / 4.7	91.9 / 6.3	91.6 / 7.4	111.7 / 12.1	117.1 / 16.6	VI-II	−14.3	+24.9	−39.2	−30	−80	−58
38	95	Lawful money holdings, national banks, reserve cities other than central (1885-1914; 9ᵉ)	94.4 / 6.0	96.3 / 3.4	98.6 / 3.2	99.9 / 3.4	99.0 / 3.8	99.8 / 5.5	100.2 / 3.7	110.4 / 4.2	112.2 / 6.6	VII-IV	+17.2	+0.3	+16.9	+100	−22	+65
38	96	Lawful money holdings, national banks, country districts (1885-1914; 9ᵉ·ᵉ)	92.4 / 2.6	93.6 / 2.3	96.6 / 2.2	99.0 / 1.1	100.9 / 2.6	103.3 / 2.7	108.8 / 5.9	107.6 / 4.1	107.6 / 4.3	II-VII	+15.2	−0.4	+15.6	+100	+30	+84
39	97	Investments, national banks, N.Y. City (1885-1914; 9ᵉ)	89.9 / 10.1	92.9 / 9.2	97.9 / 4.3	99.6 / 4.0	99.4 / 5.7	101.8 / 7.1	105.7 / 7.9	111.9 / 10.8	118.2 / 10.7	VII-III	+17.3	+7.8	+9.5	+100	−30	+37

Table 42 (cont.)

Series No. in App. B (1)	Fig. No. in Chart 1 (2)	Series, Period Covered, and No. of Reference Cycles (3)	I (4)	II (5)	III (6)	IV (7)	V (8)	VI (9)	VII (10)	VIII (11)	IX (12)	Expansion Stages (13)	Expansion (14)	Contraction (15)	Full cycle (16)	Expansion (17)	Contraction (18)	Business cycles (19)
			Average and *Average Deviation* of Ref.-Cycle Relatives at Stage										Average Reference-Cycle Amplitude			Index of Conformity to Business cycles		
98	39	Investments, national banks, reserve cities other than central (1885-1914; 9)	87.9 *8.3*	91.7 *8.8*	94.0 *6.4*	99.3 *2.5*	106.6 *6.8*	105.9 *6.7*	104.6 *7.4*	114.1 *11.3*	122.1 *11.1*	VII-IV	+24.6	+5.2	+19.4	+100	−11	+59
99	39	Investments, national banks, country districts (1885-1914; 9*)	86.3 *4.8*	89.8 *4.7*	95.0 *3.6*	100.4 *2.0*	103.2 *2.7*	104.8 *4.0*	105.8 *3.9*	110.8 *5.1*	115.4 *8.0*	VII-IV	+21.6	+5.3	+16.3	+100	−70	+63
100	40	Individual deposits, national banks, N.Y. City (1885-1914; 9*)	93.8 *6.7*	101.8 *6.7*	103.1 *3.2*	100.7 *3.5*	105.0 *8.4*	96.9 *4.6*	96.2 *5.4*	100.0 *2.9*	108.3 *5.0*	VII-III	+18.2	−6.9	+25.1	+100	+80	+100
101	40	Individual deposits, national banks, reserve cities other than central (1885-1914; 9)	88.7 *5.6*	93.6 *3.5*	96.3 *2.5*	101.7 *2.7*	105.8 *4.2*	104.7 *5.2*	102.6 *4.7*	106.2 *3.6*	108.8 *3.1*	VIII-V	+19.7	+0.4	+19.3	+100	−11	+88
102	40	Individual deposits, national banks, country districts (1885-1914; 9*)	87.8 *4.9*	90.9 *4.3*	95.2 *2.7*	101.4 *3.2*	105.7 *3.0*	107.0 *4.7*	105.3 *4.5*	105.9 *5.7*	108.1 *7.9*	VIII-V	+20.2	+0.2	+20.0	+100	−20	+100
103	41	Ratio of reserves to net deposits, national banks, N.Y. City (1885-1914; 9*)	108.4 *9.2*	104.6 *6.2*	99.1 *3.0*	95.6 *2.4*	94.7 *3.5*	96.6 *5.8*	97.0 *4.9*	104.6 *8.2*	102.9 *6.6*	V-VIII	−13.8	+9.9	−23.7	−100	−67	−100
104	41	Ratio of reserves to net deposits, national banks, reserve cities other than central (1885-1914; 9*)	106.0 *5.1*	104.2 *3.1*	102.0 *2.7*	99.2 *2.2*	95.1 *2.4*	94.1 *2.8*	97.1 *2.4*	101.4 *6.5*	103.1 *5.9*	VI-IX	−11.9	+7.7	−19.6	−100	−56	−88

Table 42 (cont.)

105	41	Ratio of reserves to net deposits, national banks, country districts (1885-1914; 9f,a)	104.4 *4.6*	104.0 *3.1*	102.9 *1.9*	100.6 *1.8*	96.8 *2.5*	95.2 *2.2*	96.0 *2.2*	99.6 *5.0*	100.6 *5.5*	VI-II	−8.8	+4.4	−13.2	−100	−20	−95
106	42	Total loans, reporting Fed. Res. member banks (1919-38; 5)	95.6 *9.0*	96.3 *6.0*	96.5 *4.7*	101.5 *3.4*	105.8 *4.0*	108.2 *4.7*	105.4 *2.8*	97.9 *8.6*	93.9 *12.9*	I-VI	+12.6	−14.2	+26.8	+100	+20	+33
107	42	Investments, reporting Fed. Res. member banks (1919-38; 5)	91.3 *16.1*	94.3 *12.4*	100.9 *6.4*	104.8 *8.5*	101.5 *7.6*	99.0 *6.1*	102.6 *4.8*	104.4 *6.2*	108.0 *8.4*	VII-III	+15.9	+1.6	+14.3	+60	−60	+78
108	43	Ratio of reserves held to reserves required, Fed. Res. member banks in N.Y. City (1919-33; 4a)	100.6 *3.0*	99.3 *1.8*	99.4 *1.6*	99.6 *2.0*	98.6 *1.5*	98.7 *1.3*	99.2 *0.5*	103.0 *3.8*	101.8 *2.7*	V-IX	−2.1	+3.2	−5.3	−50	−20	−75
109	43	Ratio of reserves held to reserves required, Fed. Res. member banks outside N.Y. City (1919-33; 4a)	99.5 *1.4*	99.5 *1.4*	99.2 *1.3*	99.3 *1.2*	99.2 *1.2*	99.2 *1.2*	99.7 *0.6*	102.1 *2.7*	105.8 *8.2*	V-IX	−0.3	+6.6	−6.9	0	−20	−50
110	44	Cash obtained through new security issues on N.Y. Stock Exchange (1868-1921; 14f)	80.7 *43.0*	94.9 *21.1*	108.6 *18.8*	109.1 *36.3*	120.4 *22.2*	110.2 *30.6*	92.8 *24.8*	81.1 *19.0*	94.2 *32.4*	VIII-V	+57.7	−39.3	+97.0	+87	+73	+93
111	44	Total corporate security issues (1908-38; 8)	85.5 *37.1*	99.3 *26.5*	119.2 *21.9*	125.9 *30.8*	113.8 *19.8*	99.5 *15.6*	90.8 *20.8*	79.8 *31.9*	94.1 *40.7*	VIII-IV	+46.9	−46.1	+93.0	+100	+50	+60
112	45	New corporate issues (1919-38; 5)	63.0 *33.1*	86.2 *27.0*	110.6 *34.9*	147.6 *49.4*	140.6 *61.2*	138.6 *41.0*	93.6 *21.6*	79.8 *38.8*	88.1 *47.0*	I-V	+77.6	−52.5	+130.1	+100	+20	+33
113	45	Corporate issues for refunding (1919-38; 5)	102.4 *81.6*	118.8 *66.5*	101.5 *30.4*	140.3 *38.0*	121.5 *32.9*	90.6 *42.6*	72.6 *21.5*	98.6 *64.3*	114.6 *72.4*	VII-IV	+61.3	−67.7	+129.0	+100	+60	+56
114	46	New corporate issues, long-term bonds and notes (1919-38; 5)	77.9 *45.6*	79.3 *28.2*	86.9 *36.6*	118.1 *46.2*	116.7 *40.8*	129.0 *29.2*	107.8 *15.8*	98.4 *32.9*	102.7 *40.9*	I-VI	+51.2	−26.3	+77.5	+60	−20	+33

Table 42 (cont.)

Series No. in App. B (1)	Fig. No. in Chart 1 (2)	Series, Period Covered, and No. of Reference Cycles (3)	I (4)	II (5)	III (6)	IV (7)	V (8)	VI (9)	VII (10)	VIII (11)	IX (12)	Expansion Stages (13)	Expansion (14)	Contraction (15)	Full cycle (16)	Expansion (17)	Contraction (18)	Business cycles (19)
			Average and Average Deviation of Ref.-Cycle Relatives at Stage										*Average Reference-Cycle Amplitude*			*Index of Conformity to Business cycles*		
115	46	New corporate issues, stocks (1919-38; 5)	39.1 / *24.7*	89.4 / *35.4*	122.1 / *49.6*	185.0 / *59.1*	174.1 / *82.1*	146.5 / *59.3*	75.7 / *38.3*	64.8 / *59.9*	61.1 / *49.9*	I-V	+135.0	−113.0	+248.0	+100	+60	+78
116	47	Index of 'all' common stock prices (1879-1933; 15ᵃ)	88.9 / *10.6*	97.1 / *8.5*	104.9 / *7.0*	110.5 / *6.8*	108.7 / *7.8*	104.8 / *7.8*	95.4 / *7.8*	91.7 / *11.5*	93.6 / *13.6*	VIII-IV	+23.6	−18.7	+42.3	+88	+65	+88
117	47	Index of American railroad stock prices (1858-1933; 19ᵃ)	91.0 / *13.8*	96.9 / *10.7*	104.0 / *7.7*	109.4 / *7.0*	106.9 / *7.0*	104.3 / *7.4*	97.7 / *7.9*	92.5 / *11.5*	94.7 / *12.2*	VIII-IV	+19.8	−16.9	+36.7	+79	+60	+74
118	47	Index of American railroad bond prices (1858-1933; 19ᵃ)	98.2 / *5.0*	99.6 / *4.0*	101.7 / *3.4*	101.1 / *2.6*	98.9 / *3.1*	97.9 / *2.5*	98.5 / *3.1*	98.9 / *3.8*	99.9 / *4.8*	VI-IIIᵇᵇ	−3.8	+7.4	−11.2	−47	−30	−68
119	48	Stocks, no. of shares sold on N.Y. Stock Exchange (1891-1938; 13ᵉ)	84.6 / *23.1*	116.9 / *30.0*	109.3 / *15.4*	114.9 / *14.4*	109.4 / *22.1*	94.1 / *13.3*	86.6 / *13.4*	78.1 / *15.7*	98.8 / *42.2*	VIII-IV	+41.3	−36.7	+78.0	+88	+75	+94
120	48	Bond sales, par value, N.Y. Stock Exchange (1891-1938; 13ᵃ)	98.9 / *23.6*	111.8 / *16.5*	108.6 / *14.0*	102.3 / *17.8*	100.4 / *18.5*	89.6 / *19.0*	95.0 / *18.1*	100.5 / *25.2*	115.4 / *32.7*	VII-II	−16.8	+37.3	−54.1	−57	−71	−70
121	49	Net profits, all corporations (1921-38; 4)	30.4 / *93.3*	97.0 / *61.2*	134.8 / *66.0*	182.4 / *54.0*	199.2 / *57.9*	151.3 / *36.2*	78.4 / *39.2*	35.2 / *68.7*	24.6 / *70.0*	I-V	+168.8	−174.6	+343.4	+100	+100	+100
122	49	Net profits, manufacturing corporations (1921-38; 4)	43.0 / *115.3*	114.8 / *91.0*	161.5 / *100.2*	207.0 / *88.1*	224.3 / *93.4*	161.4 / *41.9*	56.5 / *66.6*	10.6 / *97.2*	5.2 / *91.8*	I-V	+181.3	−219.0	+400.3	+100	+100	+100
123	50	Net incomes of all corporations reporting incomes (1921-38; 4ᵃ)	76.4 / *24.0*	....	109.6 / *15.2*	....	129.4 / *17.9*	....	99.7 / *16.5*	....	82.2 / *26.9*	I-V	+52.9	−47.2	+100.1	+100	+100	+100
124	50	Net deficits of all corporations reporting no incomes (1921-38; 4)	129.5 / *50.3*	....	83.2 / *14.8*	....	78.2 / *13.6*	....	99.8 / *20.4*	....	114.9 / *30.0*	V-IX	−51.2	+36.6	−87.8	−50	−100	−100

Table 42 (concl.)

(1)	(2)	(3)	I	II	III	IV	V	VI	VII	VIII	IX	(13)	(14)	(15)	(16)	(17)	(18)	(19)
125	51	Number of business failures (1879-1938; 16)	107.8	101.7	93.3	87.1	86.1	89.1	105.7	110.2	112.2	V-IX	-21.7	+26.1	-47.8	-50	-75	-84
			21.1	*13.3*	*10.3*	*9.2*	*9.8*	*12.4*	*14.2*	*17.0*	*21.0*							
126	51	Liabilities of business failures (1879-1938; 16)	109.7	88.9	82.9	74.2	81.1	115.5	131.9	119.1	109.8	IV-VII	-62.1	+57.7	-119.8	-75	-88	-87
			27.6	*22.9*	*16.2*	*13.3*	*18.2*	*42.5*	*31.0*	*26.9*	*21.2*							
127	52	Gross farm income (1870-1914, 1921-38; 15ᵃ)	93.2	....	99.9	....	106.3	....	103.9	....	99.9	I-V	+13.1	-6.3	+19.4	+60	+12	+24
			9.4	....	*4.0*	....	*6.7*	....	*4.7*	....	*10.4*							
127	52	Gross farm income (1911-14, 1921-38; 5ᵃ)	92.1	....	103.3	....	111.3	....	102.6	....	95.2	I-V	+19.2	-16.1	+35.3	+100	+33	+56
			12.2	....	*7.3*	....	*10.6*	....	*8.5*	....	*17.3*							
128	52	Net income of farm operators from farming (1911-14, 1921-38; 5ᵃ)	82.7	....	106.1	....	116.8	....	103.8	....	93.1	I-V	+34.1	-23.6	+57.7	+100	+67	+100
			18.6	....	*9.6*	....	*13.5*	....	*11.3*	....	*20.7*							

*See Appendix B for sources of the data. The average deviations at the nine stages are shown in italics. In annual series averages and average deviations are confined to five stages.

a Conformity indexes include an additional contraction at the beginning.
b Conformity indexes cover 1913-38.
c Conformity indexes cover 1914-38.
d Conformity indexes cover 1918-38.
e Conformity indexes cover 1913-14, 1921-38.
f The measures in col. (4)-(19) are based on the four patterns computed by taking unweighted averages of the reference-cycle patterns for twelve food prices (wheat flour, Minneapolis; bread, N. Y.; bacon, Chicago; lard, N. Y.; butter, Chicago; granulated sugar, N. Y.; potatoes, Chicago; coffee, N. Y.; bananas, N. Y.; oranges, Chicago; prunes, N. Y.; canned tomatoes, N. Y.) for each of the four cycles in 1921-38.
g Conformity indexes cover 1854-61, 1867-1914, 1921-38.
h Conformity indexes cover 1834-61, 1867-1938.
i Conformity indexes cover 1860-61, 1867-1914, 1921-38.
j Conformity indexes cover 1867-1938.
k Conformity indexes cover 1858-61, 1867-1914, 1921-38.
l Conformity indexes cover 1919-38.
m Col. (14)-(16) cover 1914-38; conformity indexes cover 1913-38.

n Conformity indexes cover 1919-37.
o Col. (11) and (12) cover 1900-27, with average standings adjusted to level of col. (10); conformity indexes cover 1899-1937.
p Col. (12) covers 1879-1912.
q Conformity indexes cover 1868-1914.
r Conformity indexes cover 1879-1914.
s Col. (12) covers 1885-1912.
t Conformity indexes cover 1865-1923.
u Conformity indexes cover 1873-1938.
v Conformity indexes cover 1879-1938.
w Conformity indexes cover 1888-1938.
x Conformity indexes cover 1910-14, 1921-38.
y On a III-VII basis, which could have been taken equally well, the successive entries for col. (14)-(19) are: +3.1, -5.7, +8.8, +37, +60, +58.
z On a III-VII basis, which could have been taken equally well, the successive entries for col. (14)-(19) are: -0.8, -7.0, +6.2, +25, +75, +60.
aa On a III-VII basis, which could have been taken equally well, the successive entries for col. (14)-(19) are: +8.2, +0.1, +8.1, +100, +20, +78.
bb On a VII-III basis, which could have been taken equally well, the successive entries for col. (14)-(19) are: +5.5, -3.2, +8.7, +60, +37, +63.
Note, moreover, that the conformity indexes then cover 1858-1937.

Table 43

SUPPLEMENT TO TABLE 31 AND CHART 7*

Series No. in App. B (1)	Fig. No. in Chart 7 (2)	Series (3)	Average Deviation of Standings at Stage									Average Deviation of Rates of Change per Month in Segment							
			I (4)	II (5)	III (6)	IV (7)	V (8)	VI (9)	VII (10)	VIII (11)	IX (12)	I-II (13)	II-III (14)	III-IV (15)	IV-V (16)	V-VI (17)	VI-VII (18)	VII-VIII (19)	VIII-IX (20)
1	1	Industrial production (FRB index)	14.0	10.8	9.7	7.8	9.8	6.6	6.7	11.6	9.7	0.7	0.7	1.0	0.7	0.5	1.9	0.9	1.0
2	1	Production of fuel & electricity (NBER index)	5.0	4.1	7.3	6.2	5.6	4.5	4.9	7.8	6.9	0.7	0.9	1.6	1.4	0.7	0.4	0.6	0.5
3	1	Pig iron production	17.1	11.8	11.5	10.6	13.3	12.0	13.5	18.2	19.5	2.2	1.3	2.0	1.9	2.6	3.9	3.2	2.6
4	2	Railroad freight ton miles	8.3	6.2	6.6	6.7	7.0	3.9	3.4	8.2	7.7	0.3	0.6	0.8	1.5	1.3	1.0	1.4	0.9
5	3	Wholesale prices, 'all' commodities (BLS index)	6.5	5.4	3.7	3.3	3.8	3.7	4.0	4.7	5.6	0.6	0.3	0.3	0.6	0.7	0.6	0.5	0.3
6	4	Wholesale trade sales, 9 lines, value (FRB index)	1.4	7.0	4.0	7.2	9.3	6.3	6.6	7.4	7.8	2.8	0.5	2.4	1.0	0.9	1.8	0.6	0.1
7	4	Department store sales (FRB index), deflated	5.9	4.2	3.1	2.9	1.5	1.0	1.2	6.4	8.9	0.4	0.4	0.2	0.4	0.2	0.3	0.6	0.6
8	4	Agricultural marketings (DC index)	1.8	5.1	5.4	3.8	2.6	3.2	4.5	5.8	6.5	1.3	0.8	0.6	0.6	1.7	0.4	0.9	1.2
9	4	Exports, value	11.3	10.6	9.9	8.4	11.0	7.8	9.9	14.2	15.6	1.6	1.0	1.0	1.9	1.7	1.3	1.0	1.9
10	4	Imports, value	15.5	10.5	8.2	9.2	12.3	9.0	9.2	12.6	14.7	1.6	0.7	0.8	1.2	1.7	2.1	1.8	1.8
11	5	Factory employment (BLS index)	11.3	8.0	6.0	4.7	6.6	5.1	5.7	8.8	8.5	0.6	0.3	0.4	0.5	0.4	0.9	1.1	0.9
12	5	Factory payrolls (BLS index)	17.1	12.7	10.5	10.3	13.6	9.0	9.3	17.2	18.4	0.9	1.0	0.7	1.6	0.9	1.7	1.6	0.8
13	5	Income payments, total (Barger, Commerce)	11.6	9.8	7.4	7.5	8.3	6.4	6.5	12.9	16.1	0.4	0.2	0.3	0.4	0.3	0.8	0.8	0.6

Table 43 (cont.)

14	6	Construction contracts, value (Dodge)	21.8	22.3	15.8	12.3	18.6	11.6	12.7	22.3	28.1	3.1	1.3	3.0	1.9	2.9	4.1	2.6	6.2
15	6	Security issues, corporate, value (Jour. of Com.)	37.1	26.5	21.9	30.8	19.8	15.6	20.8	31.9	40.7	7.0	4.9	4.4	6.1	5.8	5.8	3.0	7.2
16	6	Cash from security issues on N.Y. Stock Exchange (Ayres)	43.0	21.1	18.8	36.3	22.2	30.6	24.8	19.0	32.4	9.6	3.2	8.4	9.6	11.2	9.1	6.4	9.0
17	6	Incorporation, no. (Evans)	17.9	13.2	12.1	7.2	10.3	11.9	13.7	10.4	17.3	1.9	1.0	1.4	2.1	1.7	1.7	2.1	2.3
18	7	Shares sold on N.Y. Stock Exchange, no.	23.6	27.2	13.1	12.4	21.0	12.4	14.1	15.1	37.0	5.5	5.7	2.3	4.1	3.8	2.7	4.3	9.7
19	7	Bonds sold on N.Y. Stock Exchange, par value	23.6	16.5	14.0	17.8	18.5	19.0	18.1	25.2	32.7	3.6	3.1	3.4	4.4	4.4	3.6	3.5	7.1
20	7	Common stock prices, 'all' (Cowles index)	12.0	9.1	7.6	8.2	9.5	9.1	7.4	11.0	13.5	0.8	0.7	0.9	1.2	1.2	1.9	1.1	1.6
21	7	R.R. bond prices (Macaulay index)	5.0	4.0	3.4	2.6	3.1	2.5	3.1	3.8	4.8	0.4	0.5	0.4	0.4	0.6	0.6	0.4	0.5
22	8	Net profits, all corporations (Barger)	93.3	61.2	66.0	54.0	57.9	36.2	39.2	68.7	70.0	4.5	4.7	3.0	0.4	3.8	9.0	3.9	1.8
23	8	Business failures, no. (Dun's)	21.1	13.3	10.3	9.2	9.8	12.4	14.2	17.0	21.0	2.3	0.8	1.0	1.0	2.2	2.6	2.0	2.4
24	8	Business failures, liabilities (Dun's)	21.4	18.7	13.8	10.9	15.3	46.0	29.8	22.9	15.8	4.1	1.7	1.3	3.0	16.3	9.9	10.2	5.3
25	9	Bank clearings or debits, total	10.5	9.1	6.0	7.3	7.2	6.4	7.2	11.8	15.4	1.2	0.7	0.8	1.1	1.1	1.5	0.9	1.8
26	9	Bank clearings or debits, N.Y. City	10.9	10.7	8.6	9.2	12.8	7.4	9.8	11.4	16.4	1.6	1.1	1.1	2.2	2.9	2.0	1.4	2.4
27	9	Bank clearings or debits, outside N.Y. City	9.3	6.8	4.9	5.8	5.5	5.7	6.0	8.7	10.3	0.5	0.3	0.4	0.7	0.8	1.3	0.8	0.7
28	10	Business activity, adj. for trend (Ayres index)	7.2	5.4	5.4	4.7	6.2	4.9	5.2	6.3	6.7	0.7	0.5	0.7	0.7	0.9	1.5	1.0	0.7

Table 43 (concl.)

Series No. in App.B (1)	Fig. No. in Chart 7 (2)	Series (3)	Average Deviation of Standings at Stage									Average Deviation of Rates of Change per Month in Segment							
			I (4)	II (5)	III (6)	IV (7)	V (8)	VI (9)	VII (10)	VIII (11)	IX (12)	I-II (13)	II-III (14)	III-IV (15)	IV-V (16)	V-VI (17)	VI-VII (18)	VII-VIII (19)	VIII-IX (20)
29	10	Business or industrial activity, adj. for trend (A T & T Co. index)	7.3	5.5	5.0	4.6	5.8	4.4	5.6	8.0	8.2	0.5	0.5	0.6	0.6	0.8	1.8	0.9	0.8
30	10	Industrial production & trade (Persons index)	7.5	6.7	5.7	4.6	5.4	3.8	5.6	7.0	7.3	0.8	0.6	0.6	0.4	0.8	1.4	1.0	0.7
31	10	Deposits activity (Snyder)	7.5	8.0	5.0	5.2	5.6	3.6	5.6	8.8	10.8	1.2	0.9	0.6	1.0	0.8	1.0	0.7	0.9
32	11	Trade & industrial activity (Axe-Houghton index)	8.5	6.4	5.9	5.3	6.2	4.8	5.6	9.6	10.7	0.4	0.6	0.6	0.7	0.8	1.6	1.1	0.9
33	11	Industrial activity, unadj. for trend (A T & T Co. index)	9.3	6.0	5.2	6.0	7.5	6.0	4.5	9.0	9.1	0.4	0.5	0.6	0.7	0.6	2.2	1.0	1.1
34	11	Physical volume of business (Babson index)	9.9	7.5	6.6	5.8	7.8	5.2	4.4	7.3	7.8	0.5	0.4	0.6	1.0	0.8	1.2	0.7	1.2
35	12	Gross national product, current prices (Kuznets)b	7.8	..	5.8	..	7.4	..	8.0	..	18.3	..	0.2	..	0.3	..	0.4	..	0.6
36	12	National income, current prices (Kuznets)b	8.6	..	6.3	..	8.0	..	8.4	..	19.4	..	0.1	..	0.3	..	0.5	..	0.7
37	12	Personal incomes, current prices (Kuznets)b	5.2	..	4.1	..	5.8	..	5.9	..	13.9	..	0.05	..	0.2	..	0.5	..	0.6

a See Appendix B for sources of the data.

b Annual data. Hence entries in col. (4)-(12) are confined to five stages. The entries in col. (14), (16), (18), and (20) refer successively to I-III, III-V, V-VII, and VII-IX.

APPENDIX B

Sources of Data

This Appendix lists sources of individual time series cited in various charts and tables throughout the book. Some of the notes include explanatory details to help the reader identify the series. To economize space, titles of series are generally not listed, but each note bears the number (or numbers) of the corresponding series in the table to which it refers. All monthly and quarterly series are adjusted for seasonal variations unless otherwise stated. Where no contrary indication is given, the seasonal adjustment has been made by the Business Cycles Unit of the National Bureau.

CHART 1 AND TABLE 42

Series No.	Fig. in Chart 1	Source
1	1	Monthly, av. 1935-39 = 100. *Federal Reserve Bulletin*, Aug. 1940, pp. 764-5. Seasonal adjustment by compiler.
2	1	Monthly. 1919: Federal Reserve Board index, av. 1919 = 100. *Ibid.*, Oct. 1925, p. 739. 1920-38: Department of Commerce index, av. 1923-25 = 100. *Survey of Current Business*, March 1933, pp. 19-20, 23, and later issues.
3-4	2	Monthly, av. 1923-25 = 100. 1919-33: Y. S. Leong's index. *Journal of the American Statistical Association*, June 1935, pp. 370-1. 1934-38: Furnished by G. W. Hervey, Consumers' Counsel Division, Agricultural Adjustment Administration. Seasonal adjustment by compilers.
5-6	3	Same as series 1.
7-8	4	Monthly, number. 1913-June 1921: *Survey of Current Business*, June 1927, p. 22. Compiled by National Automobile Chamber of Commerce. July 1921-1938: Bureau of the Census, *Automobiles*, Dec. 1931 and later issues. Data are for domestic factory sales including units assembled in foreign countries from parts made in the United States.

CHART 1 AND TABLE 42 (cont.)

Series No.	Fig. in Chart 1	Source

9   5   Monthly, number. U. S. Department of Agriculture, Production and Marketing Administration, *Livestock Market News Statistics and Related Data*, 1947, p. 34.

10   5   Monthly, number. Slaughter under federal inspection since 1907. U. S. Department of Agriculture, Agricultural Marketing Service, *Livestock, Meats, and Wool Market Statistics and Related Data*, 1940, p. 34.

11   6   Monthly, in pounds. 1918: U. S. Department of Agriculture, "Summary of Dairy Situation," Supplement to *The Dairy Situation*, April 1934, p. 30. Monthly figures in this source are incomplete, and were raised in the ratio of the annual total for 1918 shown in the following source to the incomplete annual total. 1919-37: USDA, "Production and Consumption of Manufactured Dairy Products," *Technical Bulletin* No. 722, April 1940, p. 63. 1938: *Survey of Current Business*, 1942 Supplement, p. 115. Compiled by USDA.

12   6   Monthly, in gallons. 1918-36: See p. 71 of second source in preceding note. 1937: Furnished by Bureau of Agricultural Economics. 1938: U. S. Department of Agriculture, Agricultural Marketing Service, *Production of Manufactured Dairy Products, 1938*, March 1940.

13   7   Monthly, in running bales. Bureau of the Census, "Cotton Production and Distribution," *Bulletin* No. 135, and later numbers.

14   7   Monthly, av. 1935-39 = 100. *Federal Reserve Bulletin*, Aug. 1940, p. 842. Seasonal adjustment by compiler.

15   8   Monthly, in short tons. Bureau of Mines, *Mineral Resources*, 1925, Pt. II, p. 543, and later issues (*Minerals Yearbook* since 1932).

16   9   Monthly. Furnished by F. W. Dodge Corp. Data are for 27 states 1910-24, 36 states 1924-27, and 37 states 1927-38.

17   9   Monthly. 1907-12: Data for 20 cities, furnished by Babson's Statistical Organization, Inc. (now Business Statistics Organization, Inc.). 1912-38: Data for 120 cities, from *Dun and Bradstreet Monthly Review*, Sept. 1935, p. 31; *Dun's Statistical Review*, Jan. 1939, p. 5.

CHART 1 AND TABLE 42 (cont.)

Series No.	Fig. in Chart 1	Source
18	10	Monthly. Sum of data for residential, commercial, industrial, and utilities construction, including theaters and (in 1938) terminals but excluding water supply systems. For source and states covered see series 16.
19	10	Monthly. Sum of data for public and institutional buildings (series 20) and public works, including water supply systems. For source and states covered see series 16.
20	11	Monthly. Sum of data for educational, hospital and institutional, public, religious, and social and recreational buildings, excluding theaters. For source and states covered see series 16.
21	11	Same as series 16. Airports excluded 1931-33.
22	11	Same as series 16. Includes pipe lines and excludes industrial power plants throughout.
23	12	Same as series 16.
24	12	Monthly, in square feet. Same source and coverage as series 16.
25	13	Monthly. Furnished by Babson's Statistical Organization, Inc. (now Business Statistics Organization, Inc.). Purports to represent revenue freight only. Seasonal adjustment by compiler.
26	13	Monthly. Furnished by A. H. Cole. For description of data see *Review of Economic Statistics*, Feb. 1936, pp. 31 ff. Seasonal adjustment by compiler.
27	14	Monthly. 1904-19: Same as series 25. 1919-21: Interstate Commerce Commission, *Statistics of Railways*, 1922, p. XCV. Includes nonrevenue freight. 1921-38: ICC, *Revenue Traffic Statistics of Class 1 Steam Railways*. Revenue freight only.
28	14	Monthly. See sources of series 27.
29	14	Gross earnings (1904-08), Operating revenues (1908-14, 1921-38). Monthly. 1904-08: Same as series 26. 1908-09: Interstate Commerce Commission, *Bulletin of Revenues and Expenses of Steam Roads*. 1910-14, 1921: ICC, *Statistics of Railways*, 1921, p. XCIX. 1922-38: ICC, *Operating Revenues and Operating Expenses of Class 1 Steam Rail-*

CHART 1 AND TABLE 42 (cont.)

Series No.	Fig. in Chart 1	Source

ways. Switching and terminal companies included Nov. 1910-1914, 1921-31; excluded 1908-Oct. 1910, 1932-38.

30   **15**   Monthly. 1914-19: Av. 1923 = 100. Bureau of Labor Statistics, *Monthly Labor Review*, Dec. 1925, p. 121. Seasonal adjustment by National Bureau. 1919-38: Av. 1923-25 = 100. BLS, *Employment and Pay Rolls*, Dec. 1940, p. 28. Seasonal adjustment by Board of Governors of the Federal Reserve System (*Federal Reserve Bulletin*, Oct. 1938, p. 838, and later issues).

31   **15**   Monthly. Through 1933: National Industrial Conference Board, *Wages, Hours, and Employment in the United States, 1914-36*, pp. 44-7. 1934-38: *The Conference Board Economic Record*, March 28, 1940, pp. 115-6.

32   **15**   Same as series 30, except that seasonal adjustment is by National Bureau throughout.

33   **16**   Monthly, av. 1923-25 = 100. Bureau of Labor Statistics data, seasonally adjusted by Board of Governors of the Federal Reserve System. *Federal Reserve Bulletin*, Oct. 1938, pp. 842-5; Oct. 1939, p. 880.

34   **16**   Monthly, av. 1923-25 = 100. Bureau of Labor Statistics data, seasonally adjusted by Board of Governors of the Federal Reserve System. 1919-32: *Ibid.* 1933-38: Furnished by Board of Governors.

35-6   **16**   Same as series 33.

37   **17**   Monthly. Not adjusted for seasonal variations. 1861-67: Av. 1910-14 = 100. G. F. Warren and F. A. Pearson, *Prices* (Wiley, 1933), p. 12. 1891-1938: Av. 1926 = 100. Bureau of Labor Statistics, *Bulletin* Nos. 543 and 572 and (since 1932) *Wholesale Prices.*

38-43   **18**   Monthly, av. 1926 = 100. Same source as series 37, second segment. All except foods not adjusted for seasonal variations.

44   **19**   Monthly. See note *f* to Table 42 for composition. Individual series from Bureau of Labor Statistics, *Bulletin* No. 320 and later numbers and (since 1932) *Wholesale Prices*, except coffee and prunes, which were furnished by BLS. Wheat flour, bread, prunes, bananas, tomatoes, sugar, and coffee not adjusted for seasonal variations.

CHART 1 AND TABLE 42 (cont.)

Series No.	Fig. in Chart 1	Source

45   19   Monthly. See note *f* to Table 42 for composition. 1921-Nov. 1931, 1933-34: Bureau of Labor Statistics, *Bulletin No. 315* and later numbers and *Retail Prices*. Data for Dec. 1931-Dec. 1932 from BLS monthly mimeographed reports. 1935-38: BLS, *Retail Food Prices by Cities*. Wheat flour, bread, prunes, tomatoes, sugar, and coffee not adjusted for seasonal variations.

46   20   Annual, av. 1926 = 100. 1913-14, 1921-36: Richard O. Been and F. V. Waugh, *Price Spreads between the Farmer and the Consumer* (Bureau of Agricultural Economics, 1936) and supplement thereto (1941). 1937-38: Derived from Table 505, *Agricultural Statistics*, 1943.

47   20   Same as series 46.

48   21   Monthly, daily averages, in long tons. 1879-1921: Frederick R. Macaulay, *The Movements of Interest Rates, Bond Yields and Stock Prices in the United States since 1856* (National Bureau, 1938), App. A, Table 27, Pt. II, col. 4, pp. A255-69. 1922-38: *Iron Age*, Jan. 4, 1934, p. 164, and later issues. Seasonal adjustment by Macaulay through 1921, thereafter by Business Cycles Unit.

49   21   Monthly, in dollars per long ton. Not adjusted for seasonal variations. 1854-61, 1867-91: American Iron and Steel Association, *Annual Statistical Report*, 1881, p. 57, and later issues. Price of No. 1 anthracite foundry pig iron, Philadelphia. 1890-1914, 1921-38: Computed from data in Bureau of Labor Statistics, *Bulletin*, through 1931; *Wholesale Prices*, March 1932 and later issues, thereafter. Weighted average of prices of four leading grades: (1) Bessemer, Pittsburgh, (2) Foundry No. 1, Philadelphia (1890-1914), Basic f.o.b. Mahoning or Shenango Valley furnace (1921-38), (3) Foundry No. 2, northern, f.o.b. Pittsburgh, (4) Grayforge, southern, coke, f.o.b. Cincinnati (1890-1914), Foundry No. 2, southern, f.o.b. Birmingham (1921-38). The weights are quantities marketed in 1909 (for 1890-1914) and in 1923-25 (for 1921-38).

50   22   Annual, in bales of 500 lbs. gross weight. 1834-61, 1867-98: U. S. Department of Agriculture, Bureau of Statistics, "Cotton Crop of the United States, 1790-1911," *Circular*

CHART 1 AND TABLE 42 (cont.)

Series No.	Fig. in Chart 1	Source

No. 32, Aug. 1912. 1899-1938: *Agricultural Statistics*, 1939, pp. 102-3.

51   22   Monthly, in cents per pound. 1870-89: Shepperson's *Cotton Facts*, 1882-83, pp. 40-1, and later issues. 1890-1914, 1921-28: Furnished by U. S. Department of Agriculture, Division of Statistical and Historical Research. 1929-38: Bureau of Labor Statistics, *Bulletin* Nos. 521, 543, and 572 and (since 1932) *Wholesale Prices.*

52   23   Annual, in bushels. 1867-1910: Food Research Institute, *Wheat Studies*, Vol. II, No. 7, June 1926, pp. 260-1. 1911-38: *Agricultural Statistics*, 1939, pp. 9-10.

53   23   Monthly, in cents per bushel. 1854-61, 1867-82: James E. Boyle, *Chicago Wheat Prices for Eighty-One Years* (1922), pp. 69-70. 1883-1914, 1921-38: *Wheat Studies*, Vol. XI, No. 3, Nov. 1934, p. 118, and later December issues.

54   24   Annual, in bushels. *Agricultural Statistics*, 1939, pp. 44-5.

55   24   Monthly, in cents per bushel. 1860-61, 1867-70: H. A. Wallace and E. N. Bressman, *Corn and Corn Growing* (Wiley, 1928), 3rd ed., pp. 341-3. 1871-1914, 1921-38: Chicago Board of Trade, *Annual Reports.*

56   25   Annual, in bushels. *Agricultural Statistics*, 1939, p. 230; 1944, p. 225.

57   25   Quarterly, 1890-1908, monthly, 1908-38; in dollars per 100 lbs. Bureau of Labor Statistics, *Bulletin* No. 39 and later numbers and (since 1932) *Wholesale Prices.*

58   26   Same as series 10.

59   26   Monthly, in dollars per 100 lbs. 1858-59 and 1921-38: Chicago Board of Trade, *Annual Reports*. 1860-61, 1867-1914: H. A. Wallace, *Agricultural Prices* (Des Moines, Wallace Publishing Co., 1920), pp. 116-7.

60   27   Monthly, av. 1923-25 = 100. *Federal Reserve Bulletin*, Aug. 1936, p. 631, and later issues. Seasonal adjustment by compiler.

61   27   Monthly, av. 1923-25 = 100. Dollar sales (series 60) ad-

CHART 1 AND TABLE 42 (cont.)

Series No.	Fig. in Chart 1	Source

justed for price changes. Deflating index supplied by Federal Reserve Bank of New York.

62   27   Monthly, in per cent of trend. Furnished by Federal Reserve Bank of New York. Seasonal adjustment by compiler.

63   28   Monthly, in pounds. 1918: Computed from monthly production and cold-storage holdings data in Bureau of Agricultural Economics, "Summary of Dairy Situation Statistics," Supplement to *The Dairy Situation*, April 1934, pp. 30, 87; annual production data (to which the monthly data were raised) in U. S. Department of Agriculture, "Production and Consumption of Manufactured Dairy Products," *Technical Bulletin* No. 722, April 1940, p. 29; and import and export data in *Monthly Summary of Foreign Commerce*. 1919-38: *The Dairy Situation*, Aug. 1940, p. 11.

64   28   Monthly, in short tons. 1919-May 1923: *Newsprint Paper Review*, Jan. 1922 and later issues. Data from Federal Trade Commission. June 1923-1938: *Survey of Current Business*, Sept. 1938, pp. 20, 52, and later issues. Data collected by American Newspaper Publishers' Association. First segment adjusted by deducting farm magazine newsprint, which the second segment omits, and by lowering to the level of the second segment. Second segment adjusted for changes in firms reporting.

65   28   Quarterly, number. 1919-22: Furnished by Vacuum Cleaner Manufacturers Association. 1923-38: *Ibid.*, 1932 Supplement, pp. 230-1, and later supplements.

66   29   Quarterly, number. 1870-1924: John E. Partington, *Railroad Purchasing and the Business Cycle* (Brookings, 1929), pp. 219-26. 1924: Furnished by *Railway Age*. 1925-38: *Survey of Current Business*, 1932 Supplement and later issues. Data since 1924 are compilations by *Railway Age*.

67   29   Quarterly, number. 1870-1924: Partington, *loc. cit.* Orders by domestic railroads. 1924-38: *Iron Trade Review* (*Steel* after June 1930), Jan. 5, 1928, p. 123, and later January issues. Orders by domestic and foreign railroads and by noncarriers.

CHART 1 AND TABLE 42 (cont.)

Series No.	Fig. in Chart 1	Source
68	29	Same as series 66.
69	29	Monthly, in board feet. *Survey of Current Business*, May 1924, pp. 36-7, and later issues. Compiled by National Oak Flooring Manufacturers Association (before 1934 by Oak Flooring Manufacturing Association of the U. S. and Southern Oak Flooring Industries).
70	29	Monthly, in short tons. 1919-22: Bureau of the Census, *Record Book of Business Statistics*, Pt. II, p. 23. 1923-36: *Survey of Current Business*, 1932 Supplement, pp. 216-7, and later issues. Compiled by National Association of Sheet and Tin Plate Manufacturers and National Association of Flat Rolled Steel Manufacturers. No seasonal adjustment after 1931.
71	29	Monthly, average monthly value of shipments in 1926 = 100. *Ibid.*, July 1934, p. 20, and later issues. Compiled by National Machine Tool Builders' Association. Not adjusted for seasonal variations.
72-3	30	Monthly. Bureau of Foreign and Domestic Commerce (or its predecessors), *Monthly Summary of Commerce and Finance*, Dec. 1910, pp. 1120-6, and later issues (*Monthly Summary of Foreign Commerce* since July 1914). Exports include reexports of foreign merchandise; imports represent 'general imports'.
74-6	31	Same as series 13.
77	32	Monthly. 1857-Jan. 1937: F. R. Macaulay, *The Movements of Interest Rates, Bond Yields and Stock Prices in the United States since 1856* (National Bureau, 1938), App. A, Table 10, col. 3, pp. A142-61. Feb. 1937-1938: Computed from weekly data in *Bank and Quotation Record* of the *Commercial and Financial Chronicle*. Seasonal adjustment by Macaulay through 1933; no seasonal adjustment thereafter.
78	32	Monthly. 1890-Jan. 1937: Macaulay, *op. cit.*, App. A, Table 10, col. 2, pp. A150-61. Feb. 1937-1938: *Federal Reserve Bulletin*. Seasonal adjustment by Macaulay through 1933; no seasonal adjustment thereafter.
79	32	Monthly. 1857-Jan. 1937: Macaulay, *op. cit.*, App. A,

CHART 1 AND TABLE 42 (cont.)

Series No.	Fig. in Chart 1	Source

		Table 10, col. 1, pp. A142-61. Feb. 1937-1938: Board of Governors of Federal Reserve System, *Banking and Monetary Statistics*, p. 451. Seasonal adjustment by Macaulay through May 1931; no seasonal adjustment thereafter.
80	32	Monthly. 1914-21: Simple average of rates for commercial, agricultural, and livestock paper, computed from data in Federal Reserve Board, *Discount Rates of the Federal Reserve Banks, 1914-1921* (1922). 1922-38: *Banking and Monetary Statistics*, pp. 440-2. Not adjusted for seasonal variations.
81-3	33	Monthly. Federal Reserve Board, *Annual Report*, 1931, p. 82, and *Federal Reserve Bulletin*, Oct. 1939, p. 908. Not adjusted for seasonal variations.
84	34	Monthly. Macaulay, *op. cit.*, App. A, Table 10, col. 5, pp. A142-61. Adjusted for 'economic drift'. Not adjusted for seasonal variations.
85	34	Monthly. Through 1928: Standard Statistics Co., *Standard Trade and Securities: Base Book, Standard Statistical Bulletin*, Jan. 1932, p. 125. 1929-37: Average of yields of municipal, railroad, public utilities, and industrial bonds, computed from data in Standard and Poor's Corp., *Trade and Securities Statistics: Long Term Security Price Index Record*, 1941, pp. 127-8, 137-8. Not adjusted for seasonal variations.
86	35	Same as series 84.
87	36	Call dates. *Annual Report of the Comptroller of the Currency*, 1916, Vol. II, pp. 336-61. Includes: (1) specie, (2) legal tender notes, (3) 1879-1900: U. S. certificates of deposit for legal tender notes, (4) April-Dec. 1901: U. S. certificates for gold deposited (after 1901 included in specie).
88	36	Call dates. Same source as series 87. 'Overdrafts' included when given separately.
89	36	Call dates. Same source as series 87. Includes entries under 'other stocks, bonds, securities, etc.' Not adjusted for seasonal variations.

CHART 1 AND TABLE 42 (cont.)

Series No.	Fig. in Chart 1	Source
90	36	Call dates. Same source as series 87. Includes individual deposits and dividends unpaid. No deduction of float.
91-3	37	Call dates. *Annual Report of the Comptroller of the Currency*. 'Overdrafts' included when given separately. 'Reserve cities other than central' include all reserve cities except New York, Chicago, and St. Louis. For New York City data, see also *Review of Economic Statistics*, Oct. 1924, pp. 291-6.
94-6	38	Call dates. *Annual Report of the Comptroller of the Currency*. For coverage see series 87. For an alternative source of New York City data, see series 91-3.
97-9	39	Call dates. *Annual Report of the Comptroller of the Currency*. For coverage see series 89. Country districts not adjusted for seasonal variations.
100-2	40	Call dates. *Ibid.* For coverage see series 90.
103-5	41	Call dates. *Ibid.* For reserve cities other than central, and for country districts, reserves include nonreserve balances with reserve agents. Deposits are net of amounts due from other banks and clearing house exchanges. Prior to April 1902, series called 'Ratio of reserve held' or 'Ratio of reserve' in source; thereafter called 'Cash on hand, due from reserve agents, and in the redemption fund, per cent'. 'Reserve cities other than central' include all reserve cities except New York until March 1887; thereafter Chicago and St. Louis are also excluded.
106-7	42	Monthly average of weekly figures for 101 cities. Board of Governors of the Federal Reserve System, *Banking and Monetary Statistics*, pp. 132-56. Investments not adjusted for seasonal variations.
108	43	1918-28: Ratio of monthly averages of weekly figures, derived from *Federal Reserve Bulletin* and *Banking and Monetary Statistics*, pp. 164 ff. Reserves held are shown directly; reserves required were computed as the weighted sum of net demand deposits and time deposits, the weights being the respective reserve percentages. 1929-33: Ratio of monthly averages of daily figures, *ibid.*, p. 397.
109	43	Ratio of monthly averages of all-bank data less New York

CHART 1 AND TABLE 42 (cont.)

Series No.	Fig. in Chart 1	Source

City data. Data for all member banks obtained as follows: 1918-28: Monthly averages of weekly figures. Reserves held from Federal Reserve Board, *Annual Reports*, and *Banking and Monetary Statistics*, pp. 378 ff. Reserves required computed from estimated net demand deposits and time deposits weighted by their respective reserve percentages. Sources include FRB, *Member Bank Call Reports* and *Federal Reserve Bulletin*, and *Commercial and Financial Chronicle*. 1929-33: Monthly averages of daily figures, *Banking and Monetary Statistics*, p. 396. For sources of New York data see series 108.

110 44 Quarterly. Domestic corporate bonds and stocks sold for cash, including issues for refunding. Sum of 'bonds listed' and 'stocks listed', in L. P. Ayres, *Turning Points in Business Cycles* (Macmillan, 1939), pp. 182-97.

111 44 Monthly, in dollars. Bonds, notes, and stocks; domestic, Canadian, and foreign issues included; refunding issues included. *Journal of Commerce*, Jan. issues, 1908 and later years. No seasonal adjustment after 1930.

112 45 Monthly, in dollars. Bonds, notes, and stocks; domestic, Canadian, and foreign issues included; refunding issues excluded. *Commercial and Financial Chronicle.*

113 45 Monthly, in dollars. Bonds, notes, and stocks; domestic, Canadian, and foreign issues included. Same source as series 112. See also *Survey of Current Business*, 1932 Supplement, pp. 94-5, and later supplements.

114 46 Monthly, in dollars. Domestic and Canadian issues only; refunding issues excluded. Same source as series 112.

115 46 Monthly, in dollars. Preferred and common stocks; domestic and Canadian issues only; refunding issues excluded. Same source as series 112.

116 47 Monthly, av. 1926 = 100. Alfred Cowles, 3rd, and Associates, *Common-Stock Indexes, 1871-1937* (Bloomington, Principia Press, 1938), pp. 66-7. Not adjusted for seasonal variations.

117 47 Monthly, in dollars per share. F. R. Macaulay, *The Movements of Interest Rates, Bond Yields and Stock Prices in*

CHART 1 AND TABLE 42 (concl.)

Series No.	Chart 1	Source

the United States since 1856 (National Bureau, 1938), App. A, Table 10, col. 6, pp. A142-61. Not adjusted for seasonal variations.

118   47   Monthly prices obtained by dividing average monthly yields (series 84) into $4.00.

119   48   Monthly. Excludes 'odd lots' and 'stopped' sales. 1879-97: *Commercial and Financial Chronicle.* 1898-1938: *New York Stock Exchange Bulletin,* Aug. 1934, pp. 10A-B, and later issues.

120   48   Monthly. 1888-97: *New York Times,* 1905, *passim.* 1898-1938: Same source as series 119.

121-2   49   Quarterly. Harold Barger, *Outlay and Income in the United States, 1921-38* (National Bureau, 1942), App. B, Table 28, pp. 297-9. Seasonal adjustment by compiler.

123-4   50   Annual. *Statistics of Income,* 1932, p. 47; 1940, Pt. 2, p. 282. For 1936-38 dividends on the stock of domestic corporations and interest on government obligations subject to excess profits tax were subtracted, and gifts were added, to make data for these years comparable to earlier data.

125-6   51   Quarterly, 1879-97, monthly, 1897-1938. 1879-Feb. 1933: *Dun's Review.* March 1933-Jan. 1937: *Dun and Bradstreet Monthly Review.* Feb. 1937-1938: *Dun's Statistical Review.* Includes manufacturing and mining concerns, builders, employers of labor in mechanic arts; also trading concerns, agents and brokers; but not professional men, banks (after 1892), or railroads. See *Dun's Review,* Dec. 30, 1893, pp. 2-3, and Feb. 1936, p. 21.

127   52   Annual. 1869-1911: Gross income — the value of farm output less the value of farm products (feedstuffs and seed) used in farm production. U. S. Department of Agriculture, "Gross Farm Income and Indices of Farm Production and Prices in the United States, 1869-1937," *Technical Bulletin* No. 703, Dec. 1940, p. 24. 1910-14, 1921-38: Cash income from farm marketings, plus government payments. Bureau of Agricultural Economics, *Crops and Markets,* July 1943, p. 136.

128   52   Annual. Gross farm income adjusted for changes in livestock and crop inventories, minus total expenses of agricultural production. *Agricultural Statistics,* 1942, p. 662.

CHART 7 AND TABLES 31 AND 43

Series No.	Fig. in Chart 7	Source
1	1	See note on series 1 of Table 42.
2	1	Monthly, av. 1923-25 = 100. Weighted aggregate of seasonally adjusted production data for anthracite coal, bituminous coal, crude petroleum, and electric power. The weight for each is the average value of a unit of output during 1922-31. For electric power the unit value was computed net of the cost of fuel consumed and of current purchased.
3	1	See note on series 48 of Table 42.
4	2	See note on series 27 of Table 42.
5	3	See note on series 37 of Table 42.
6	4	Monthly, av. 1923-25 = 100. *Federal Reserve Bulletin,* Dec. 1927, pp. 826-7, and later issues. Seasonal adjustment by compiler.
7	4	See note on series 61 of Table 42.
8	4	See note on series 2 of Table 42.
9-10	4	See note on series 72-3 of Table 42.
11	5	See note on series 30 of Table 42.
12	5	See note on series 32 of Table 42.
13	5	1921-28: Sum of quarterly series on (1) 'short-term income', (2) 'long-term income', (3) income distributed by government, together with quarterly interpolations of annual series on (4) entrepreneurial net income (except in agriculture, service, and miscellaneous industries), (5) dividend payments, and (6) dividend and interest payments from abroad. Based on data from Harold Barger, *Outlay and Income in the United States, 1921-38* (National Bureau, 1942) and Simon Kuznets, *National Income and Its Composition, 1919-1938* (National Bureau, 1941), Vol. I. For fuller description see Bureau of the Census, *Historical Statistics of the United States, 1789-1945* (1949), p. 321. 1929-38: Monthly. Furnished, with seasonal adjustment, by Department of Commerce.
14	6	See note on series 16 of Table 42.
15	6	See note on series 111 of Table 42.
16	6	See note on series 110 of Table 42.

CHART 7 AND TABLES 31 AND 43 (cont.)

Series No.	Fig. in Chart 7	Source
17	6	Monthly. G. Heberton Evans, Jr., *Business Incorporations in the United States, 1800-1943* (National Bureau, 1948), pp. 80-1.
18	7	See note on series 119 of Table 42.
19	7	See note on series 120 of Table 42.
20	7	See note on series 116 of Table 42.
21	7	See note on series 118 of Table 42.
22	8	See note on series 121-2 of Table 42.
23-4	8	See note on series 125-6 of Table 42.
25	9	Clearings (1879-1914), Debits (1921-38). Monthly, in dollars. 1879-1914: Daily averages for a varying (generally increasing) number of cities. 1879-83, *The Public* (formerly *The Financier*); 1884-1914, *Commercial and Financial Chronicle*. 1921-38: Board of Governors of the Federal Reserve System, *Banking and Monetary Statistics*, pp. 234-5.
26	9	Clearings (1854-61, 1867-1914), Debits (1921-38). Monthly, in dollars. 1854-61, 1867-1914: Daily averages. 1854-Sept. 1860 and 1867-74, New York State Chamber of Commerce, *Annual Report;* Oct. 1860-1861, *The Bankers' Magazine;* 1875-83, *The Public* (formerly *The Financier*); 1884-1914, *Commercial and Financial Chronicle.* 1921-38: Same as series 25.
27	9	Series 25 minus series 26.
28	10	Monthly, in per cent of trend. L. P. Ayres' index. Cleveland Trust Company, *American Business Activity since 1790,* 16th edition, March 1943. Seasonal adjustment by compiler.
29	10	Monthly, in per cent of trend. Seasonal adjustment by compilers. 1879-1900: M. C. Rorty's index. *Harvard Business Review,* Jan. 1923, p. 159. 1900-38: American Telephone and Telegraph Company, Chief Statistician's Division, *Industrial Activity as Related to Long-Term Growth* (a confidential release, Sept. 6, 1944).
30	10	Monthly, in per cent of trend. Seasonal adjustment by compilers. 1879-1918: W. M. Persons, *Forecasting Busi-*

CHART 7 AND TABLES 31 AND 43 (concl.)

Series No.	Fig. in Chart 7	Source

ness Cycles (Wiley, 1931), pp. 93-147. 1919: *Review of Economic Statistics*, April 1923, p. 76. 1919-38: Edwin Frickey, *Barron's Index of Business since 1899* (Barron's, 1943).

31   10   Monthly. Seasonal adjustment by compilers; smoothed throughout by a three-month moving average. 1879-1918: In per cent of seven-year moving average. Carl Snyder's index, *Review of Economic Statistics*, Oct. 1924, p. 258. 1919-38: Av. 1935-39 = 100. Furnished by the Federal Reserve Bank of New York.

32   11   Monthly, av. 1910 = 100. Not adjusted for trend. Furnished by E. W. Axe and Co., Inc., New York. Seasonal adjustment by compiler.

33   11   Monthly, av. 1939 = 100. Not adjusted for trend. American Telephone and Telegraph Co., Chief Statistician's Division, *The Growth of Industrial Activity in the United States* (a confidential release, Sept. 6, 1944). Seasonal adjustment by compiler.

34   11   Monthly, av. 1923-27 = 100. Not adjusted for trend. Furnished by Babson's Statistical Organization, Inc. (now Business Statistics Organization, Inc.). Seasonal adjustment by compiler.

35   12   Annual. Simon Kuznets, *National Product since 1869* (National Bureau, 1946), worksheet for Table I 14, p. 51.

36-7   12   Annual. Simon Kuznets, *National Income and its Composition, 1919-1938* (National Bureau, 1941), Vol. I, Table 58, pp. 322-3.

TABLE 2

*Series
No.*   *Source*

1   See note on series 1 of Table 42.

2   Monthly, in dollars. 1854-61, 1867-1914: See note on series 26
     of Table 31. 1921-38: *Commercial and Financial Chronicle.*

3   See note on series 77 of Table 42.

4   See note on series 21 of Table 42.

5   See note on series 85 of Table 42.

6   Monthly, in dollars. Plans filed. Includes Bronx through 1904.
     1869-79: *The City Record* (New York), Jan. 19, 1880, p. 104.
     1880-1909, 1917-19: *Real Estate Record and Builders' Guide;*
     monthly data derived from weekly data for 1880, Oct. 1899-
     1902, 1917-19. 1910-16, 1920-27: *Annual Report of the Build-
     ing Department* (New York, Borough of Manhattan).

7   Monthly, in barrels. *Savannah Weekly Naval Stores Review
     and Journal of Trade.* Covers stocks in Jacksonville, Savannah,
     and Pensacola. For 1920-38, see also *Survey of Current Busi-
     ness,* June 1922, p. 49, and later issues.

8   Monthly, in bushels. 1879-85: New York Produce Exchange,
     Annual Statistical Reports. Includes Canada but excludes
     Pacific Coast; also includes wheat in transit by rail. 1885-88:
     Chicago Board of Trade, *Annual Reports;* coverage approxi-
     mately as for 1879-85. Quantity in transit by rail not included
     in July 1885 and in 1886. 1888-1927: *Bradstreet's.* Includes
     Pacific Coast (except July 1888) and excludes Canada; also
     excludes wheat in transit by rail. San Francisco data excluded
     1904-27. 1927-38: *Agricultural Statistics,* 1938, p. 22; 1939,
     p. 22. Domestic wheat, excluding wheat in transit by rail.

TABLE 9

Series and Source

Index of wholesale prices, 'all' commodities (1891-1914, 1921-38).
See note on series 37 of Table 42.

Construction contracts, total, value (1910-38).
See note on series 16 of Table 42.

Index of industrial production (1919-38).
See note on series 1 of Table 42.

Index of factory payrolls (1918-38).
See note on series 32 of Table 42.

Index of factory employment (1914-38).
See note on series 30 of Table 42.

TABLE 12

Series No.	Source
1	Monthly. Retail sales of shoes (series 7) divided by average retail price of shoes. The latter series was obtained by adjusting an index of the price of several staple sorts of shoes furnished by the National Industrial Conference Board. The adjustment, based on data from *Biennial Census of Manufactures*, allows for changes in the volume of shoes sold in various price ranges.
2	Monthly, av. 1923-25 = 100. Wholesale sales of shoes (series 8) divided by an index of factory prices of shoes, furnished by the Tanners' Council of America.
3	Monthly, in pairs. Bureau of the Census, *Production of Boots, Shoes, and Slippers Other than Rubber in the United States* (monthly releases).
4	Monthly, av. 1923-25 = 100. Seasonal adjustment by Board of Governors of the Federal Reserve System. Through 1930: Bureau of Labor Statistics, "Revised Indexes of Factory Employment and Pay Rolls, 1919 to 1933," *Bulletin* No. 610, pp. 69-70, 104. 1931-38: BLS, mimeographed releases, *Revised Index Numbers of Factory Employment and Pay Rolls*, Sept. 1938, and *Indexes of Factory Employment and Pay Rolls, January 1935 to February 1940*, May 1940.
5	Monthly, in equivalent hides. 1921-34: Furnished by the Tanners' Council of America. 1935-38: *Survey of Current Business*, 1938 Supplement, p. 124, and later issues.

TABLE 12 (concl.)

Series No.	Source

6   Monthly, number. 1921-34: Furnished by the Tanners' Council of America. 1935-38: Commodity Exchange, Inc., *Daily Market Report, Monthly Statistical Supplement: Hides,* July 11, 1941.

7   Monthly, in dollars. Computed from data for shoe departments of department stores furnished by Federal Reserve Banks in seven Districts, from data on sales of shoe chains from several sources including the Department of Commerce (1935 on), and, after 1935, from information on independent shoe stores collected by the Department of Commerce.

8   Monthly, av. 1923-25 = 100. 1919-35: Computed from data on sales of shoe wholesalers in ten Federal Reserve Districts (1919-29) and six to nine Districts (1930-35), furnished by the Federal Reserve Board. The data for each District were weighted by sales of shoe wholesalers as given in the 1929 Census of Distribution. 1936-38: Computed from data in Bureau of Foreign and Domestic Commerce, *Wholesalers' Sales and Collections on Accounts Receivable* (monthly mimeographed releases).

9   Monthly. Total shoe production (series 3) multiplied by average factory price of shoes, for which data were furnished by the Tanners' Council of America.

10   Monthly, av. 1923-25 = 100. Same source as series 4, but seasonal adjustment by National Bureau.

11   Monthly. Cattle hide and kip leather production (series 5) multiplied by average price per hide of cattle hide leather. The price series is a weighted average of two Bureau of Labor Statistics series: (1) wholesale price of leather, sole, oak, scoured backs; (2) wholesale price of side leather, Boston. The weights are production figures, furnished by the Tanners' Council of America.

12   Monthly. Number of hides moving into sight (series 6) multiplied by the Tanners' Council index of hide prices converted to dollars.

TABLE 13

Series No.	Source
1	See note on series 30 of Table 42.
2	See note on series 31 of Table 42.
3	See *supra*, p. 134.
4	See note on series 1 of Table 42.
5	Monthly, av. 1926 = 100. Furnished by Federal Reserve Bank of New York. Includes wage rates or earnings per employee in manufacturing, railways, clerical occupations, teaching, building, farming, road building, retail trade, bituminous coal mining, telephone and telegraph concerns, power and light utilities, hotels, and laundries. Seasonal adjustment by compiler.
6	See note on series 31 of Table 42. No seasonal adjustment after 1930.
7	Monthly. New York State Department of Labor, *The Industrial Bulletin*, Jan. 1935 and Jan. 1942. Covers office and shop employees.
8	See note on series 32 of Table 42.
9	Monthly, in per cent of trend. Furnished by Federal Reserve Bank of New York. Seasonal adjustment by compiler.
10	Monthly, av. 1935-39 = 100. Furnished by Department of Commerce, which compiled the index from Bureau of Labor Statistics data.

TABLE 16

Series No.	Source
1	Annual, in short tons. 1890-1930: E. G. Nourse and others, *America's Capacity to Produce* (Brookings, 1934), pp. 550-1. 1931-38: Bureau of Mines, *Minerals Yearbook*, 1937, p. 876; 1940, p. 838.
2	Annual, in short tons. *Ibid.*, 1945, p. 853.
3	Annual (by fiscal years). U. S. Geological Survey (1924 and later years by Bureau of Mines), *Mineral Resources*, 1923, Pt. II, p. 582, and later issues (*Minerals Yearbook* since 1932).
4-6	Annual (by fiscal years). *Ibid.*, 1945, pp. 968-9.

TABLE 16 (cont.)

Series No.	Source
7	Annual (by fiscal years), in short tons. *Ibid.*, 1918, Pt. II, p. 1486, and later issues.
8-9	Annual (by fiscal years), in short tons. American Iron and Steel Institute, *Annual Statistical Reports.*
10	Annual (by fiscal years), in short tons. 1907-30: E. G. Nourse and others, *op. cit.*, p. 557. 1931-39: American Bureau of Metal Statistics, *Yearbook*, 1937, p. 24, and later issues.
11	Annual. Bureau of the Census, "Cotton Production and Distribution," *Bulletin* No. 179.
12-3	Annual. 1913-21: E. G. Nourse and others, *op. cit.*, pp. 576-8. 1922-38: Derived from Bureau of the Census, "Cotton Production and Distribution," *Bulletin* Nos. 170, 176.
14-5	Annual (by calendar years, 1890-1914, by fiscal years, 1915-39); tractive power in pounds. Interstate Commerce Commission, *Statistics of Railways*, 1889, p. 14, and later issues.
16	Annual (by fiscal years). Locomotives, including steam, diesel, and electric, assigned to road freight and road passenger service. Locomotives assigned to yard switching service are not included in this series, but they are included in series 14-5 (steam only). Freight locomotives for 1921-34 from Interstate Commerce Commission, *Freight and Passenger Service Operating Statistics of Class I Steam Railways;* 1935-39 from ICC, *Motive Power and Car Equipment of Class I Steam Railways.* Passenger locomotives for 1921-33 furnished by ICC; 1934-39 from same sources as freight locomotives.
17-9	Annual (by fiscal years). Same as locomotives assigned to freight service; see series 16.
20	Annual (by calendar years, 1890-1914, by fiscal years, 1915-39). Interstate Commerce Commission, *Statistics of Railways*, 1942, p. 152. Covers mileage operated in first track, other main tracks, and yard tracks and sidings.
21-2	Annual (by fiscal years). Automobile Manufacturers Association, *Automobile Facts and Figures, 1946-47*, p. 22.
23	Annual, in long tons. U. S. Department of Commerce, Bureau of Navigation and Steamboat Inspection, *Merchant Marine Statistics*, 1935, pp. 24-6, and later issues.

Table 16 (cont.)

Series No.	Source

24   Annual (by calendar years, 1867-1914, by fiscal years, 1919-39). *Statistical Abstract of the United States*, 1910, p. 257, and later issues.

25   Monthly. Same source as series 16.

26-8   Monthly. Same source as series 17-9.

29-30   See note on series 16 of Table 42.

31   See note on series 21 of Table 42.

32   See notes on series 22 of Table 42.

33   See note on series 20 of Table 42.

34   Monthly. Sum of data, furnished by F. W. Dodge Corp., for utilities (including pipe lines), petroleum refineries, industrial power plants, airports (1931-38) and terminals (1938), but excluding water supply systems. For states covered see note on series 16 of Table 42.

35   Monthly. Sum of data, furnished by F. W. Dodge Corp., for public works and water supply systems. For states covered see note on series 16 of Table 42.

36   See note on series 71 of Table 42.

37   See note on series 66 of Table 42.

38   See note on series 67 of Table 42.

39   See note on series 68 of Table 42.

40   Quarterly, in long tons. John E. Partington, *Railroad Purchasing and the Business Cycle* (Brookings, 1929), pp. 219-26.

41   Monthly, in long tons. Bureau of the Census, *Record Book of Business Statistics*, Pt. II, p. 18. Collected by American Pig Iron Association. Not adjusted for seasonal variations.

42   Monthly, in short tons. American Institute of Steel Construction, Inc., *Annual Report*, 1941, pp. 88-9.

43   See note on series 70 of Table 42.

44   Monthly, in board feet. 1919-29: Data for 192 mills. Furnished by Southern Pine Association through April 1929; remainder of 1929 from *Survey of Current Business*, 1931 Supplement, p. 63. 1929-38: Total industry estimates. Furnished by Southern

TABLE 16 (cont.)

Pine Assn. through 1933; balance of the period, *ibid.,* 1938 Supplement. The second segment was lowered to the level of the first on the basis of the overlapping data in 1929.

45   See note on series 69 of Table 42.

46   Quarterly, 1902-11, monthly, 1912-33; in tons. 1902-08: Standard Statistics Co., *Standard Trade and Securities: Base Book, Standard Statistics Bulletin,* 1932, p. 263. 1909-22: Bureau of the Census, *Record Book of Business Statistics,* Pt. II, p. 22. 1923-33: *Survey of Current Business,* 1932 Supplement, pp. 212-3, and later issues.

47-50   Monthly, in per cent of trend. Compilations by Federal Reserve Bank of New York. Seasonal adjustment by compiler.

51   Monthly, av. 1922-24 = 100. *Ibid.,* pp. 220-1, and later issues. Compiled by National Machine Tool Builders' Association.

52   Monthly. 1919-22: Bureau of the Census, *Record Book of Business Statistics,* Pt. II, p. 41. 1923-38: *Survey of Current Business,* 1932 Supplement, pp. 222-3, and later issues. Compiled by Association of Manufacturers of Woodworking Machinery.

53   Monthly. *Ibid.,* Feb. 1927, p. 24, and later issues. Compiled by Hydraulic Society.

54   Monthly, number. 1918-19: *Federal Reserve Bulletin,* Feb. 1919, p. 162; Feb. 1920, p. 183. 1920-37: Bureau of the Census, *Railroad Locomotives,* Dec. 1931 and later issues. For Aug. 1918-1919 steam locomotives only are included; thereafter, both steam and electric.

55-6   Monthly, number. Compiled by American Railway Car Institute. 1918: Furnished by compiler. 1919-38: *Survey of Current Business,* March 1940, p. 16. No seasonal adjustment after June 1929 (freight cars); after 1928 (passenger cars).

57-8   See note on series 7-8 of Table 42.

59   Monthly, in long tons. *Iron Age.* Computed by deducting pig iron production at steel mills from total production.

60   Monthly, in long tons per average working day. *Ibid.,* Jan. 4, 1934 (for 1900-32), Jan. 4, 1940 (for 1933-38). Since July 1917, compiled by American Iron and Steel Institute.

TABLE 16 (cont.)

Series
No.   *Source*

61   Monthly, 1919-33, quarterly, 1933-38; in short tons. 1919-22: Bureau of the Census, *Record Book of Business Statistics*, Pt. II, p. 23. 1923-33: *Survey of Current Business*, 1932 Supplement, pp. 216-7, and later issues; compiled by National Association of Sheet and Tin Plate Manufacturers and National Association of Flat Rolled Steel Manufacturers. 1934-38: *Ibid.*, Nov. 1940, p. 14; compiled by American Iron and Steel Institute.

62   Same as series 44.

63   See note on series 69 of Table 42.

64   Monthly, in barrels of 376 lbs. net. 1912-20: W. M. Persons and others, *The Problem of Business Forecasting* (Houghton Mifflin, 1924), pp. 160-1. Compiled by U. S. Geological Survey (for 1911-19 from data collected by Portland Cement Association). 1921-38: USGS (1924 and later years by Bureau of Mines), *Mineral Resources*, 1921, Pt. II, p. 217, and later issues (*Minerals Yearbook* since 1932).

65   Monthly, in square feet. 1923-24, 1928-38: *Survey of Current Business*, 1932 Supplement, pp. 258-9, and later issues. Compiled by Plate Glass Manufacturers of America. 1925-27: Furnished by compiler.

66   See note on series 30 of Table 42.

67   Monthly, av. 1923-25 = 100. 1919-22: Computed from seasonally-adjusted indexes for six industries (iron and steel; machinery; stone, clay, and glass products; nonferrous metals; automobiles; and furniture) given in *Federal Reserve Bulletin*, Nov. 1930, pp. 666, 672, 674, and Dec. 1936, p. 957. Industry indexes in unadjusted form compiled by Bureau of Labor Statistics. 1923-38: Compiled by BLS and adjusted for seasonal variations by Board of Governors of the Federal Reserve System. *Ibid.*, Oct. 1938, pp. 842-5, and later issues.

68   Monthly, av. 1923-25 = 100. 1919-22: Computed from seasonally-adjusted indexes for 5 industries (textile products, leather manufactures, food products, tobacco manufactures, and paper and printing), *ibid.*, p. 842. Industry indexes in unadjusted form compiled by Bureau of Labor Statistics. 1923-38: Same as series 67.

TABLE 16 (cont.)

69-70   See note on series 33 of Table 42.

71   Monthly, av. 1923-25 = 100. 1919-22: Bureau of Labor Statistics
        index, furnished by Federal Reserve Board in seasonally-
        adjusted form. 1923-38: Compiled by BLS and adjusted for
        seasonal variations by Board of Governors of the Federal Re-
        serve System. *Ibid.,* pp. 842-5, 849, and Oct. 1939, p. 880.
        1919-23 cover automobile employment only.

72   Monthly, av. 1923-25 = 100. Computed from indexes of em-
        ployment for (1) cement, (2) brick, tile, and terra cotta,
        (3) millwork (lumber), (4) structural and ornamental metal
        work, (5) cast-iron pipe, (6) steam and hot water heating
        apparatus and steam fittings, (7) plumbers' supplies. These
        components are weighted by the average number employed
        in 1923-25. For 1923-30 only the first six components, and for
        1919-22 only the first three components, are included. The
        indexes are given in Bureau of Labor Statistics, "Revised In-
        dexes of Factory Employment and Pay Rolls, 1919 to 1933,"
        Bulletin No. 610, and mimeographed releases, *Revised Index
        Numbers of Factory Employment and Pay Rolls,* Sept. 1938,
        and *Indexes of Factory Employment and Pay Rolls, January
        1935 to February 1940,* May 1940.

73-4   See note on series 33 of Table 42.

75   See note on series 32 of Table 42.

76   Monthly, av. 1923-25 = 100. 1919-22: Computed from indexes
        of payrolls for (1) iron and steel, (2) machinery, (3) auto-
        mobiles, (4) furniture, (5) stone, clay, and glass, using aver-
        age payrolls in 1923-25 as weights. Sources of these indexes
        are the first two cited in note on series 72. 1923-38: BLS,
        Employment and Pay Rolls, Dec. 1940 and later issues.

77   Monthly, av. 1923-25 = 100. 1919-22: Computed from indexes
        of payrolls for textile products, leather manufactures, food
        products, tobacco manufactures, and paper and printing, using
        average payrolls in 1923-25 as weights. For sources of these
        indexes, see series 76. 1923-38: Same as series 76.

78-9   Monthly, av. 1923-25 = 100. See last two sources in note on
        series 72.

80   Monthly, av. 1923-25 = 100. 1919-30: See first source in note

TABLE 16 (cont.)

Series No.	Source
	on series 72. 1931-38: Same as series 78-9. 1919-23 cover automobile payrolls only.
81	Monthly, av. 1923-25 = 100. Computed from indexes of payrolls for seven industries, using average payrolls in 1923-25 as weights. For industries covered and sources, see series 72.
82	Same as series 78-9.
83	Same as series 80.
84	Monthly. 1914-29: Bureau of Labor Statistics, *Bulletin* No. 553. 1930-37: Ohio Department of Industrial Relations, Division of Labor Statistics, *Report No. 29*. 1938: Furnished by foregoing compiler.
85-6	See note on series 31 of Table 42. No seasonal adjustment of earnings after 1930.
87	Monthly, in long tons. 1919-22: Bureau of the Census, *Record Book of Business Statistics*, Pt. II, p. 13. 1923-38: *Survey of Current Business*, 1932 Supplement, pp. 198-9, and later issues. Compiled by Lake Superior Iron Ore Association. Covers only Lake Superior region.
88	Monthly, in long tons. *Record Book of Business Statistics*, Pt. II, p. 19. Compiled by American Pig Iron Association.
89-90	Monthly, in short tons. 1919-22: *Ibid.*, p. 24. Since 1923: *Survey of Current Business*, 1932 Supplement, pp. 216-7, and later issues. Compiled by National Association of Sheet and Tin Plate Manufacturers and National Association of Flat Rolled Steel Manufacturers. No seasonal adjustment of unsold stocks after 1933.
91	Monthly, in short tons. 1910-14, 1919-25: *Record Book of Business Statistics*, Pt. II, pp. 47, 49. Compiled by American Copper Producers' Association through June 1914, by American Metal Market for July-Dec. 1914, by Copper Export Association for 1919-23, and by American Bureau of Metal Statistics for 1924-25 (and later years). 1926: Amer. Metal Market, *Metal Statistics*, 1936, p. 248. 1927-38: Amer. Bur. of Metal Statistics, *Yearbook*, 1927, p. 10, and later issues. Covers stocks in North and South America from 1919 on. Not adjusted for seasonal variations.

TABLE 16 (cont.)

Series
No.
Source

92   Monthly, in long tons. 1893-1914, 1920-27: New York Metal Exchange, *Official Daily Market Report.* 1928-38: Commodity Exchange, Inc., *Daily Market Report, Monthly Statistical Supplement: Tin and Copper.* Includes visible supply in licensed warehouses, landing, and afloat.

93   Same as series 64.

94   Monthly, in board feet. Same source as series 44. Not adjusted for seasonal variations.

95   See note on series 69 of Table 42.

96   Monthly, in long tons. *Survey of Current Business*, 1932 Supplement, pp. 248-9, and later issues. Covers stocks in and afloat to the United States. Compiled by Rubber Manufacturers' Association and, for some years, by Bureau of Foreign and Domestic Commerce, Leather and Rubber Division. Not adjusted for seasonal variations.

97-8   Monthly, number. *Ibid.*, May 1939, pp. 17-8. Compiled by Rubber Manufacturers' Association.

99   Monthly, in equivalent hides. 1921-April 1932: Bureau of the Census, *Monthly Report on Hides, Skins and Leather.* May 1932-1938: Furnished by Tanners' Council of America.

100   Monthly, number. Furnished by Tanners' Council of America.

101   Monthly, in equivalent hides. 1921-34: Furnished by Tanners' Council of America. 1934-38: Commodity Exchange, Inc., *Daily Market Report, Monthly Statistical Supplement: Hides,* Jan. 1940. Compiled by Bureau of the Census through April 1932, and by Tanners' Council thereafter.

102   Monthly, in equivalent hides. 1921: Furnished by Tanners' Council of America. 1922-31: Computed by deducting 'in process' stocks, furnished by Tanners' Council, from total 'in process and finished' stocks, given in *Survey of Current Business,* Jan. 1935, p. 19. 1932-38: Commodity Exchange, Inc., *Daily Market Report, Monthly Statistical Supplement: Hides,* Jan. 1935 and later issues. Compiled by Bureau of the Census through April 1932, and by Tanners' Council thereafter.

103   Monthly, in equivalent hides. Furnished by Tanners' Council of America.

TABLE 16 (cont.)

Series No.	Source

104   Monthly, in running bales. *Commercial and Financial Chronicle*. Includes stocks at United States ports and at interior towns, adjusted for changes in the number of ports and towns.

105-6   See note on series 13 of Table 42.

107   Monthly, in short tons. Includes Canadian mills. United States data for 1918-19 from Federal Trade Commission, *Statistical Summary of the Paper Industry*, Jan. 1922 and later issues. All other data from Newsprint Service Bureau. Compiled by FTC for 1918-May 1923 (U. S. data) and by Newsprint Service Bureau otherwise.

108   See note on series 64 of Table 42.

109   Monthly, av. 1935-39 = 100. *Federal Reserve Bulletin*, June 1946, p. 594. Seasonal adjustment by compiler.

110   See note on series 110 of Table 42.

111   See note on series 111 of Table 42.

112   See note on series 112 of Table 42.

113   See note on series 115 of Table 42.

114   Monthly, 1919-33, quarterly, 1933-38. For source and coverage see note on series 114 of Table 42. No seasonal adjustment after 1932.

115   See note on series 114 of Table 42.

116   See note on series 113 of Table 42.

117   See note on series 17 of Table 31.

118   See note on series 119 of Table 42.

119   See note on series 120 of Table 42.

120   See note on series 116 of Table 42.

121   See note on series 118 of Table 42.

122-4   See note on series 91-3 of Table 42.

125   Call dates. Computed by dividing loans, country districts (series 124), by the number of country banks.

126   See note on series 88 of Table 42.

127   See note on series 106-7 of Table 42.

TABLE 16 (cont.)

Series
No.   *Source*

128-9   Board of Governors of the Federal Reserve System, *Banking and Monetary Statistics*, pp. 132-56. Monthly averages of weekly figures for 101 cities. For Sept. 1934-1937 loans on securities are the sum of (1) loans to brokers and dealers in securities and (2) loans to others on securities. 1938 loans on securities computed on a similar basis from weekly data in *Federal Reserve Bulletin.*

130-2   See note on series 97-9 of Table 42.

133   See note on series 89 of Table 42.

134   See note on series 106-7 of Table 42.

135   *Banking and Monetary Statistics*, pp. 134-56. Monthly averages of weekly figures for 101 cities. For Oct. 1933-Sept. 1934 fully guaranteed government obligations (estimated) were deducted from the published data, which include them for that period.

136   See note on series 79 of Table 42.

137   See note on series 77 of Table 42.

138   See note on series 78 of Table 42.

139   Monthly. 1919-20: W. W. Riefler, *Money Rates and Money Markets in the United States* (Harper, 1930), pp. 232-3. 1921-38: Computed from data in *Federal Reserve Bulletin*, Federal Reserve Board *Annual Reports*, and *Survey of Current Business*, June 1928, p. 21. Components and weights:

    Average rate on stock exchange call loan renewals   3
    Prevailing rate on prime commercial paper, 4-6 mos.   3
    Prevailing rate on prime bankers' acceptances, 90 days   2
    Prevailing rate on stock exchange time loans, 90 days   2

Same data available in Riefler, *op. cit.*, to fewer digits. Not adjusted for seasonal variations.

140-2   See note on series 81-3 of Table 42.

143   See note on series 84 of Table 42.

144   Quarterly. F. R. Macaulay, *The Movements of Interest Rates, Bond Yields and Stock Prices in the United States since 1856* (National Bureau, 1938), App. A, Table 13, pp. A174-6. Not adjusted for seasonal variations.

TABLE 16 (concl.)

Series
No.   *Source*

145   See note on series 85 of Table 42.

146   Monthly. *Survey of Current Business,* Nov. 1937, p. 19, and
        later issues. Compiled by Moody's Bond Survey. Not adjusted
        for seasonal variations.

TABLE 19 AND CHART 6

Series and Source

Clearings outside New York City, deflated.
  Monthly, daily averages, in dollars. *Unsmoothed:* F. R. Macaulay,
  op. cit., App. A, Table 27, Pt. II, col. 2, pp. A256-69. Through 1918
  the series represents clearings in a generally increasing number of
  cities, adjusted to comparable levels by overlapping; since 1919 it
  is based on bank debits in 140 centers outside New York City. The
  first segment is adjusted to the level of the second, and the entire
  series is deflated by Snyder's index of the general price level. Seasonal
  adjustment by Macaulay through 1927, by Business Cycles Unit
  thereafter. *Smoothed: ibid.,* Table 30, col. 2, pp. A290-6.

Railroad stock prices.
  Monthly, in dollars per share. *Unsmoothed:* see note on series 117
  of Table 42. *Smoothed: ibid.,* Table 17, col. 2, pp. A207-14.

Pig iron production.
  Monthly, daily averages, in long tons. *Unsmoothed:* see note on
  series 48 of Table 42. *Smoothed: ibid.,* Table 31, col. 2, pp. A298-303.

Call money rates.
  Monthly. *Unsmoothed:* see note on series 79 of Table 42. *Smoothed:
  ibid.,* Table 21, col. 2, pp. A223-30.

TABLES 24 AND 29

Series and Source

Clearings outside New York City, deflated.
See note on corresponding series (unsmoothed) of Table 19. The series was extended to 1938 by the methods used in its construction for the period to 1933.

Pig iron production.
See note on series 48 of Table 42.

Freight car orders.
See note on series 67 of Table 42.

Shares traded, N.Y. Stock Exchange.
See note on series 119 of Table 42.

Railroad stock prices.
See note on series 117 of Table 42.

Call money rates.
See note on series 79 of Table 42.

Railroad bond yields.
See note on series 84 of Table 42.

TABLE 25

Series No.	Source
1	Monthly, number. Bureau of the Census, "Cotton Production and Distribution," *Bulletin* No. 135 and later numbers.
2	Monthly. 1920-33: National Industrial Conference Board, *Wages, Hours, and Employment in the United States, 1914-36*, pp. 52-5. 1934-38: NICB, *Conference Board Economic Record*, March 28, 1940, p. 118.
3	See note on series 31 of Table 42.
4	Monthly, av. 1923-25 = 100. For source see note on series 4 of Table 12. Seasonal adjustment by National Bureau.
5	Monthly, in per cent of trend. *Review of Economic Statistics*, April 1924, pp. 90-2, and later issues. Compiled and seasonally adjusted by Elizabeth Boody, Harvard Economic Service.
6	Monthly, av. 1926 = 100. Bureau of Labor Statistics, *Bulletin* Nos. 543 and 572 and (since 1932) *Wholesale Prices*. Not adjusted for seasonal variations.

TABLE 25 (concl.)

Series No.	Source

7   Monthly, av. 1923-25 = 100. *Federal Reserve Bulletin,* Dec. 1927, pp. 826-7, and later issues.

8   Monthly, in per cent of trend. 1913-24: Same as series 5. 1924-38: *Federal Reserve Index of Industrial Production,* Oct. 1943. Includes iron ore, copper, zinc, and silver; also (1924-38) lead and gold. Seasonal adjustment by compilers.

9   Monthly. Federal Reserve Board, *Annual Report,* 1932, pp. 152-4; 1933, p. 223. Includes banks subsequently reopened, but excludes voluntary liquidations.

10   See note on series 47-50 of Table 16.

11   Monthly, 1923-33, quarterly, 1933-38; in long tons. *Survey of Current Business,* Dec. 1932, p. 20, and later issues. Compiled by American Bureau of Metal Statistics through 1933 and by American Iron and Steel Institute thereafter.

12   Monthly, in per cent of trend. Furnished by Federal Reserve Bank of New York. Seasonal adjustment by compiler.

13   See note on series 70 of Table 42.

14   Monthly, in square feet. Derived from data, furnished by F. W. Dodge Corp., for total building excluding (1) public works and public utilities, (2) industrial power plants, and (3) airports (1931-38). For states covered see note on series 16 of Table 42.

15   See note on series 48 of Table 42.

TABLE 28

Series No.	Source

1   Monthly. *Unadjusted:* see note on series 48 of Table 42. *Trend-adjusted:* in per cent of trend. Furnished by F. R. Macaulay. Seasonal adjustment by Macaulay through 1921, by Business Cycles Unit thereafter.

2   Monthly. *Unadjusted:* in kilowatt hours. 1919: University of Illinois, Bureau of Business Research, "The Nature of Cyclical Fluctuations in Electric Power Production Data," *Bulletin* No. 16 (1927). 1920-33: *Survey of Current Business,* Nov. 1927, p. 26, and later issues. Includes power production by electric railways and electrified steam railroads. *Trend-*

TABLE 28 (concl.)

adjusted: in per cent of trend. Computed as the ratio of seasonally adjusted data to a straight line trend fitted by least squares to annual averages of seasonally adjusted monthly data in 1919-32.

3   Monthly. *Unadjusted:* see note on series 61 of Table 42. *Trend-adjusted:* in per cent of trend. Furnished by the Federal Reserve Bank of New York; seasonal adjustment by compiler.

4   Monthly. *Unadjusted:* see note on first series (unsmoothed) of Table 19. *Trend-adjusted:* in per cent of trend. Furnished by F. R. Macaulay. Seasonal adjustment by Macaulay through 1927, by Business Cycles Unit thereafter.

5   Monthly; in dollars *(unadjusted)*, in per cent of trend *(trend-adjusted)*. Edwin Frickey, "Bank Clearings Outside New York City, 1875-1914," *Review of Economic Statistics,* Oct. 1925, pp. 260-1. Seasonal adjustment by compiler, except for 1903-14 (unadjusted series), which were seasonally adjusted by National Bureau.

6   Monthly; av. 1899 = 100 *(unadjusted)*, in per cent of trend *(trend-adjusted)*. 1900-July 1932: American Telephone and Telegraph Company, Chief Statistician's Division, *Index of Industrial Activity in the United States* (a confidential report, Oct. 20, 1932). Aug. 1932-1933: Adjusted data from the company's *Summary of Business Conditions in the United States;* unadjusted data furnished by Chief Statistician's Division. Seasonal adjustment by compiler.

7   See notes on series 33 and 29 of Table 31.

8   Monthly. *Unadjusted:* see note on series 32 of Table 31. *Trend-adjusted:* in per cent of trend. 1879-1918: *Annalist,* Jan. 16, 1931, p. 162. 1919-27: Furnished by E. W. Axe and Co., Inc. Seasonal adjustment by compiler.

9   Monthly. *Unadjusted:* see note on series 84 of Table 42. *Trend-adjusted:* in per cent of trend. Computed from Macaulay, *op. cit.,* App. A, Table 11, cols. 1 and 3, pp. A163-70. Not adjusted for seasonal variations.

TABLE 29
See notes on Table 24, *supra.*

TABLE 31
See notes on Chart 7, *supra.*

TABLE 42
See notes on Chart 1, *supra.*

TABLE 43
See notes on Chart 7, *supra.*

Index

When not given explicitly, references to sources of data are identifiable by a combination of page number and series number, the latter in parentheses, e.g., 329(2). To avoid duplicate entries, references to two or more time series are sometimes combined. For example, under "Banks, Federal Reserve member", the entry "loans: on securities, all other" refers to two series, "loans on securities" and "all other loans".

Abramovitz, Moses, 64n, 144, 168

Administered prices, conformity and timing, xiii, 59, 95, 172

Aggregate economic activity; *see* Business activity, general

Aggregates and their components
amplitude, 175-7, 285
conformity, 88-9, 96-8
use of, in cyclical analysis, 98

Agricultural marketings
amplitude, 173, 256, 286-7, 312
conformity, 173, 256, 312
rates of change per month, 260, 302-4, 326
reference-cycle pattern, 32, 258, 264, 292-4, 312, 326
scope and source of data, 271, 329(2)
timing, 256, 279-80, 307, 312

Agriculture; *see also* Farm products and foods
influence on business cycles, 57-8
irregular timing and conformity, xii, xiii, 56-8, 95

AT&T index of industrial activity
amplitude, 257, 286
conformity, 257
rates of change per month, 261, 302-3, 328
reference-cycle pattern, 259, 267, 291-4, 328
sources of data, 342(29), 343(33), 360(6)
timing, 257, 279
trend adjustment, effect on average deviations, 241-2

Amplitude
reference-cycle, Ch. 7; *see also* Capital; Consumer purchases; Labor; Land; Producer purchases
of aggregates and of their components, 175-7, 285
amplification due to size of inventories, 117, 121-8
average deviations of, 216-8, 246-8
bias in average, 101-4
of business cycles, 6, 182-4
of comprehensive series, 282-8
computation of, 100
of consumer purchases, 114-20
distribution of, in sample of time series, 100-3, 284-7
effect of durability of commodities on, 115-7, 168-9, 174
of fixed capital, 138-44
influence on average deviations, 219-20, 222-7, 229
of necessities and luxuries, 114-5
of paired series on prices and production, 170-5, 177-82
of producer purchases, 120-8
ranking of groups of series by average, 104-7
relation to conformity, 89, 99, 105-7
of working capital, 144-9
specific-cycle, relation to reference-cycle amplitude, 105 ff.

363

NATIONAL BUREAU PUBLICATIONS ON BUSINESS CYCLES

I Books on Business Cycles

Business Cycles and Unemployment (1923)
Committee on Unemployment and Business Cycles of the
President's Conference on Unemployment, and a Special
Staff of the National Bureau
$\qquad$ 448 pp., $4.10

Employment, Hours and Earnings in Prosperity and Depression, United States, 1920-1922 (1923)
W. I. King
$\qquad$ 150 pp., 3.10

Business Annals (1926)
W. L. Thorp, with an introductory chapter, "Business Cycles
as Revealed by Business Annals," by Wesley C. Mitchell
$\qquad$ 382 pp., 2.50

Migration and Business Cycles (1926)
Harry Jerome
$\qquad$ 258 pp., 2.50

Business Cycles: The Problem and Its Setting (1927)
Wesley C. Mitchell
$\qquad$ 514 pp., 5.00

*Planning and Control of Public Works (1930)
Leo Wolman
$\qquad$ 292 pp., 2.50

*The Smoothing of Time Series (1931)
F. R. Macaulay
$\qquad$ 174 pp., 2.00

Strategic Factors in Business Cycles (1934)
J. M. Clark
$\qquad$ 256 pp., 1.50

German Business Cycles, 1924-1933 (1934)
C. T. Schmidt
$\qquad$ 308 pp., 2.50

Public Works in Prosperity and Depression (1935)
A. D. Gayer
$\qquad$ 482 pp., 3.00

Prices in Recession and Recovery (1936)
Frederick C. Mills
$\qquad$ 602 pp., 4.00

Some Theoretical Problems Suggested by the Movements of
Interest Rates, Bond Yields and Stock Prices in the United
States since 1856 (1938)
F. R. Macaulay
$\qquad$ 612 pp., 5.00

Consumer Instalment Credit and Economic Fluctuations (1942)
Gottfried Haberler

262 pp., 2.50

Measuring Business Cycles (1946)
A. F. Burns and Wesley C. Mitchell

592 pp., 5.00

Price-Quantity Interactions in Business Cycles (1946)
Frederick C. Mills

158 pp. 1.50

Changes in Income Distribution During the Great Depression (1946)
Horst Mendershausen

192 pp., 2.50

American Transportation in Prosperity and Depression (1948)
Thor Hultgren

432 pp., 5.00

Inventories and Business Cycles, with Special Reference to Manufacturers' Inventories (1950)
Moses Abramovitz

672 pp., 6.00

II   Books Partly Concerned with Business Cycles

The Behavior of Prices (1927)
Frederick C. Mills

598 pp., 7.00

Recent Economic Changes in the United States (1929)
Committee on Recent Economic Changes of the President's Conference on Unemployment, and a Special Staff of the National Bureau

2 vol., 990 pp., 7.50

Seasonal Variations in Industry and Trade (1933)
Simon Kuznets

480 pp., 4.00

Production Trends in the United States since 1870 (1934)
A. F. Burns

396 pp., 3.50

Industrial Profits in the United States (1934)
R. C. Epstein

692 pp., 5.00

Ebb and Flow in Trade Unionism (1936)
Leo Wolman

272 pp., 2.50

The International Gold Standard Reinterpreted, 1914-1934 (1940)
William Adams Brown, Jr.

2 vol., 1474 pp., 12.00

National Income and Its Composition, 1919-1938 (1941)
Simon Kuznets

1012 pp., 5.00

Financing Small Corporations in Five Manufacturing Industries, 1926-36 (1942)
C. L. Merwin

192 pp., 1.50

The Financing of Large Corporations, 1920-39 (1943) 160 pp., 1.50
Albert R. Koch

Corporate Cash Balances, 1914-43: Manufacturing and Trade
(1945) 148 pp., 2.00
Friedrich A. Lutz

National Income: A Summary of Findings (1946) 160 pp., 1.50
Simon Kuznets

Value of Commodity Output since 1869 (1947) 320 pp., 4.00
W. H. Shaw

Business Incorporations in the United States, 1800-1943
(1948) 196 pp., 6.00
G. Heberton Evans, Jr.

III   Papers on Business Cycles

Testing Business Cycles (Bulletin 31, March 1, 1929)
Wesley C. Mitchell

The Depression as Depicted by Business Annals (Bulletin 43,
September 19, 1932)
Willard L. Thorp

Gross Capital Formation, 1919-1933 (Bulletin 52, November 15, 1934) .50
Simon Kuznets

The National Bureau's Measures of Cyclical Behavior (Bulletin 57,
July 1, 1935) .50
Wesley C. Mitchell and Arthur F. Burns

Production during the American Business Cycle of 1927-1933 (Bulletin
61, November 9, 1936) .50
Wesley C. Mitchell and Arthur F. Burns

Technical Progress and Agricultural Depression (Bulletin 67, November 29, 1937) .50
Eugen Altschul and Frederick Strauss

Statistical Indicators of Cyclical Revivals (Bulletin 69, May 28, 1938) .50
Wesley C. Mitchell and Arthur F. Burns

*Commodity Flow and Capital Formation in the Recent Recovery and
Decline, 1932-1938* (Bulletin 74, June 25, 1939) .25
Simon Kuznets

A Significance Test for Time Series and Other Ordered Observations
(Technical Paper 1, September 1941) .50
W. Allen Wallis and Geoffrey H. Moore

Railway Freight Traffic in Prosperity and Depression (Occasional
Paper 5, February 1942) .25
Thor Hultgren

* *Wartime 'Prosperity' and the Future* (Occasional Paper 9, March 1943)   .35
Wesley C. Mitchell

Railroad Travel and the State of Business (Occasional Paper 13, December 1943)   .35
Thor Hultgren

Railway Traffic Expansion and Use of Resources in World War II (Occasional Paper 15, February 1944)   .35
Thor Hultgren

**Economic Research and the Keynesian Thinking of Our Times* (Twenty-sixth Annual Report, June 1946)
Arthur F. Burns

The Role of Inventories in Business Cycles (Occasional Paper 26, May 1948)   .50
Moses Abramovitz

The Structure of Postwar Prices (Occasional Paper 27, July 1948)   .75
Frederick C. Mills

Wesley Mitchell and the National Bureau (Twenty-ninth Annual Report, May 1949)
Arthur F. Burns

Statistical Indicators of Cyclical Revivals and Recessions (Occasional Paper 31, 1950)   1.50
Geoffrey H. Moore

Cyclical Diversities in the Fortunes of Industrial Corporations (Occasional Paper 32, 1950)   .50
Thor Hultgren

Behavior of Wage Rates during Business Cycles (Occasional Paper 34, 1950)   1.00
Daniel Creamer

New Facts on Business Cycles (Thirtieth Annual Report, May 1950)
Arthur F. Burns

**Out of print.*